# The Amicus Brief:

## Answering the Ten Most Important Questions About Amicus Practice

## *4th Edition*

REAGAN W. SIMPSON AND MARY R. VASALY



TORT TRIAL INSURANCE

AMERICAN BAR ASSOCIATION
Defending Liberty
Pursuing Justice

Cover design by ABA Design.



Printed in the United States of America.

19 18 17 16 15 5 4 3 2 1

ISBN: 978-1-63425-224-9

e-ISBN: 978-1-63425-225-6

**Library of Congress Cataloguing-in-Publication data**

Simpson, Reagan Wm. (Reagan William), author.
The amicus brief : answering the ten most important questions about amicus practice / by Reagan Wm. Simpson and Mary R. Vasaly; Tort, Trial and Insurance Practice Section, American Bar Association. -- 4th edition.
pages cm
Includes bibliographical references and index.
ISBN 978-1-63425-224-9 (alk. paper)
1. United States. Supreme Court--Decision making. 2. Amici curiae--United States--Influence. 3. Public interest law--United States. I. Vasaly, Mary R., author. II. American Bar Association. Tort Trial and Insurance Practice Section, sponsoring body. III. Title.
KF8748.S536 2015
347.73'262--dc23

2015017049

# CONTENTS

# FOREWORD

At the 1997 ABA Annual Meeting in San Francisco, the TIPS Appellate Advocacy Committee presented a well-attended program on amicus practice. The panelists were the Honorable Kathryn Mickle Werdegar of the California Supreme Court, former U.S. Solicitor General and D.C. Circuit Judge Kenneth W. Starr, and these TIPS members: Pamela Beckham, Alan J. Lazarus, Karen M. Grundy, Mukesh Advani, and Mark E. Solomons. Based on that program, Reagan Simpson, who was the program chair, wrote the first edition of this book. Since then, Reagan and Judge Mary R. Vasaly have collaborated in producing three more editions. As well as being the most expansive update, this fourth edition features many new examples of amicus briefs by premier appellate lawyers and a compendium of amicus rules in U.S. jurisdictions. As shown by its revised title, this edition aims to address every key facet of the increasingly important amicus practice.

# ABOUT THE AUTHORS

Reagan W. Simpson is a partner in the Houston, Texas law firm of Yetter Coleman LLP, a litigation boutique, where he has an appellate and a trial practice. After graduating from the University of Texas School of Law, he served as a law clerk to the late Thomas Gibbs Gee, Judge of the United States Court of Appeals for the Fifth Circuit. Reagan is a Fellow of both the American Academy of Appellate Lawyers and the American College of Trial Lawyers. He is also an Advocate in the American Board of Trial Advocates and a Member of the American Law Institute.

Mary Vasaly is a state trial court judge sitting in Hennepin County, Minnesota. Before her appointment to the bench, she practiced law for more than 25 years with Maslon LLP, where she was a partner in the litigation group. Her practice focused on appeals as well as commercial litigation. She has been named to Best Lawyers in America and was selected twice by *Minnesota Lawyer* magazine as an "Attorney of the Year." Vasaly is a fellow of the American Academy of Appellate Lawyers and the American Bar Foundation. She has chaired ABA TIPS' Appellate Advocacy Committee and the Council of Appellate Lawyers in the ABA's Judicial Division. Locally, she has served as President of the Hennepin County Bar Association and Minnesota Women Lawyers and Chair of the Minnesota State Bar Association Litigation Section's Governing Council. She serves as a member of the Minnesota Supreme Court's Advisory Committee on the Rules of General Practice. She co-edits the 8th Circuit Appellate Practice Manual and contributes to a number of other publications.

Ms. Vasaly may be contacted at the Hennepin County Government Center, 300 South Sixth Street, Minneapolis, MN 55487; by telephone at (612) 348-0087; or by email at mary.vasaly@courts.state.mn.us.

# AMICUS BRIEFS: ANSWERING THE TEN MOST IMPORTANT QUESTIONS ABOUT AMICUS PRACTICE

## WHAT IS AN AMICUS BRIEF?

### *The Original Amicus Curiae*

An amicus brief is filed by an "amicus curiae," a term defined as: "A friend of the court. A term applied to a bystander who, without having interest in the cause, of his own knowledge makes a suggestion on a point of law or fact for the information of the presiding judge."[1] The submission of amicus briefs precedes even the common law, having its roots in ancient Rome. The role of the original amicus was to provide a court with legal information that was beyond its notice or expertise.[2] In England, the amicus brief first appears in the 17th century,[3] and its role was principally to assist judges in avoiding errors.[4] For example, a Member of Parliament filed an amicus brief to advise the court of the meaning of a statute based on his personal knowledge of the relevant legislative history.[5]

---

1. Samuel Krislov, *The Amicus Curiae Brief: From Friendship to Advocacy*, 72 YALE L.J. 694 (1963).
2. Allison Lucas, *Friends of the Court? The Ethics of Amicus Brief Writing in First Amendment Litigation*, 26 FORDHAM URBAN L.J. 1605, 1605 (1999); Alexander Wohl, *Friends with Agendas—Amicus Curiae Briefs May be More Popular Than Persuasive*, 46 A.B.A. J., Nov. 1996, at 46–48; Karen O'Connor & Lee Epstein, *Court Rules and Workload: A Case Study of Rules Governing Amicus Curiae Participation*, 8 JUST. SYS. J. 35, 36 (1983); Ernest Angell, *The Amicus Curiae: American Development of English Institutions*, 16 INT'L & COMP. L.Q. 1017, 1017 (1967); Fowler v. Harper & Edwin D. Etherington, *Lobbyists Before the Court*, 101 U. PA. L. REV. 1172, 1176 (1953).
3. Michael Rustad & Thomas Koenig, *The Supreme Court and Junk Social Science: Selective Distortion in Amicus Briefs*, 72 N.C.L. REV. 91, 97 (1993) (citing Protector v. Geering, Hardres 85, 145 Eng. Rep. 394 (1656)).
4. Sylvia H. Walbolt & Joseph H. Lang, Jr., *Amicus Briefs: Friend or Foe of Florida Courts*, 32 STETSON L. REV. 269, 270 (2003).
5. Nancy Bage Sorenson, *The Ethical Implications of Amicus Briefs: A Proposal for Reforming Rule 11 of the Texas Rules of Appellate Procedure*, 30 ST. MARY'S L.J. 1219, 1225 (1999).

The first amicus brief in the United States was submitted when the Supreme Court requested Henry Clay's assistance in determining the application of the commerce clause to a land agreement between Kentucky and Virginia.[6] To this day, courts may appoint amici curiae to assist them. After Clay's service to the Supreme Court, amicus briefs began to be filed by the United States, state governments, attorneys for client organizations, and lobbyists representing private and trade organizations.[7] Governmental entities filed amicus briefs even in private disputes, when public interests were implicated.[8]

The function of the amicus curiae at common law was to advise the judge of relevant opinions, to prevent any manifest error.[9] The amicus curiae had the further role of informing the judge of a relevant fact, such as a party's death or the collusive or fraudulent nature of a suit.[10] Traditionally, then, the sole objective of the amicus was to prevent an uninformed legal or factual error. Analogous was the status of the original jury—namely, members of the community who were knowledgeable about the parties and the relevant facts.[11] Example 13 is an amicus brief that provides facts relating to the case in a Counter-Statement of Facts section of the brief.

Such traditional participation by an amicus occurs even today. A law professor or an attorney in a specialized field may submit an unsolicited brief or letter to the court suggesting that the court has made a legal error in a recent decision or simply providing "neutral" data that may assist the court in making its decision without advocating whether one side is favored by the data.[12] That type of amicus submission was contemplated by the United States Supreme Court when it promulgated its first written

---

6. *Id.* (citing Green v. Biddle, 21 U.S. (8 Wheat.) I (1823)).

7. Rustad & Koenig, *supra* n.3, at 96.

8. Walbolt & Lang, *supra* n.4, at 270; *see, e.g.*, Gibbons v. Ogden, 22 U.S. I (1824); Martin v. Hunter's Lessee, 14 U.S. 304 (1816).

9. *Id.* at 694 (quoting ABBOTT'S DICTIONARY OF TERMS & PHRASES); *see also* Edmund R. Beckwith & Rudolph Sobernheim, *Amicus Curiae—Minister of Justice*, 17 FORDHAM L. REV. 38, 38 (1948).

10. Krislov, *supra* n.1, at 695.

11. B. Michael Dann, *Free the Jury*, 23 LITIG., Fall 1996, at 5.

12. EUGENE GRESSMAN, KENNETH S. GELLER, STEPHEN M. SHAPIRO, TIMOTHY S. BISHOP & EDWARD A. HARTNETT, SUPREME COURT PRACTICE 740 (9th ed. 2007) (hereinafter cited as SUPREME COURT PRACTICE). A "no-argument" amicus brief with such data was filed in No. 13-1010, *M&G Polymers USA, LLC v. Tackett*, in the United States Supreme Court.

rule on the subject of amicus briefs in 1937.[13] A variant of the traditional amicus brief is one submitted by a law professor or specialist who advocates a policy choice but does not do so because of any allegiance to a party.[14]

### *The Modern Friend*

The amicus submission has evolved into something very different from its original role. The modem-day amicus is rarely a neutral friend of the court. To the contrary, an interest in the litigation is one of the factors that courts use to decide whether to accept an amicus brief, although that interest cannot be a direct pecuniary one.[15] Thus, a more recent definition of amicus curiae is: "A person with strong interest in or views on the subject matter of an action [who] . . . petition[s] the court for permission to file a brief, ostensibly on behalf of a party but actually to suggest a rationale consistent with its own views."[16]

In the last several decades, attorneys acting as amici often represent private clients who are either interested in the case or in the manner in which the court will dispose of it.[17] Amici are sometimes disparagingly referred to as "lobbyists of the court."[18] The amicus brief has become a means of advocacy for interest groups, private individuals, and business concerns that are nothing more than extensions of the parties; they are friends of the litigants rather than of the courts.[19] That type of amicus participation began with industry trade groups and later expanded into minority

---

13. Krislov, *supra* n.1, at 694.
14. Ben Glassman, *Representing Law, Representing Truth: Legal Realism and Issues in the Ethics of Representation,* 44 HARVARD L. REV. I, 25–26 (2000);*see, e.g.,* Price v. GMAC, LLC, 562 F.3d 618, 629 (4th Cir. 2009) (discussing amicus brief filed by "Bankruptcy Professors," as well as amicus brief by National Association of Consumer Bankruptcy Attorneys.
15. Ed R. Haden & Kelly Fitzgerald Pate, *The Role of Amicus Briefs,* ALABAMA LAWYER (Mar. 2009) at 115, 117.
16. BLACK'S LAW DICTIONARY 75 (5th ed. 1979).
17. Robert L. Stern, APPELLATE PRACTICE IN THE UNITED STATES 302 (2d ed. 1989).
18. Wohl, *supra* n.2, at 46; *see also* Daniel A. Farber, *When the Court Has a Party, How Many "Friends Show Up?—A Note on the Statistical Distribution of Amicus Brief Filings*, 24 CONST'L COMMENTARY 19, 36 (Spr. 2007) (noting that lobbying by means of amicus briefs is different in two respects—it is more formal, and the lobbyist cannot offer the decision maker any benefits in return for support).
19. *Id.*; Rustad & Koenig, *supra* n.3, at 96 (observing that many amici are now lobbyists for private interests with a direct or indirect stake in the outcome of the litigation).

groups.[20] An example is an amicus brief filed by Michael Crichton, Larry David, Scot Turow, other writers, and the Authors Guild, Inc., in support of the petitioner concerning the right to use a real person's name in a work of fiction.[21] The International Trademark Association regularly files amicus briefs and publishes them in its Trademark Reporter.[22] The expanded nature of amicus briefs reflects Justice Black's observation, that "[m]ost cases before this Court involve matters that affect far more people than the immediate record parties."[23]

Private parties are by no means the only amici. The United States Government has often filed amicus briefs, dating back to 1812 in *Schooner Exchange v. McFadden.*[24] Indeed, the rules of the United States Supreme Court and Courts of Appeals do not require the government to obtain consent from the parties to file amicus briefs, as is the case with private amici.[25]

One commentator has decried the politicization of amicus practice by representatives of the federal government, citing examples of amicus briefs filed by the Solicitor General espousing views of the current presidential administration.[26] "One window into the soul of a presidential administration is the work of the Office of the Solicitor General."[27] Another commentator argues that the Solicitor General should confine its amicus practice to cases directly involving federal interests and that the Solicitor General's amicus briefs should be given deference in cases involving foreign relations and areas of government enforcement or policy that Congress has dedicated to the President.[28] The SEC is another example of a governmental amicus

20. Wohl, *supra* n.2, at 46–48; Walbolt & Lang, *supra* n.4, at 273.
21. *Amicus Brief of Michael Crichton et al. in* McFarlane v. Twist, 11 UCLA Enter. L. Rev. 1 (2004).
22. *See, e.g.,* Amicus Brief of International Trademark Association in *Special Effects, Ltd. v. L'Oreal SA et al.*, 97 Trademark Rptr. 793 (May–June 2007).
23. Quoted by Mary-Christine Sungaila, *Effective Amicus Practice before the United States Supreme Court: A Case Study,* 8 S. Cal. L. Rev. & Women's Stud. 187, 188 (1999).
24. 11 U.S. (7 Cranch) 116, 118 (1812).
25. S. Ct. R. 37.4; Fed. R. App. P. 29(a); *see* Michael K. Lowman, *The Litigating Amicus Curiae: When Does the Party Begin After the Friends Leave?*, Am. Univ. L. Rev. 1243, 1261 (1992) (noting the greater opportunity for the government to file amicus briefs).
26. Sorenson, *supra* n.5, at 1235–38.
27. Karen Swenson, *President Obama's Policy in the Supreme Court: What We Know So Far from the Office of the Solicitor General's Service as Amicus Curiae*, 34 S.I.U.L.J. 359 (2010).
28. Michael E. Solimine, *The Solicitor General Unbound: Amicus Curiae Activism and Deference in the Supreme Court*, 45 Ariz. St. L.J. 1183 (2013).

curiae. From 1981 to 1989, the Supreme Court adopted the SEC's argument as amicus in eight of nine cases.[29] Professional groups, such as the American Association for Justice (*see* Appendix Example 8) and the Defense Research Institute (DRI) (*see* Appendix Example 9), have filed amicus briefs.

Perhaps adopting a view similar to the commentators critical of agency amicus briefs, the First Circuit considered an agency amicus brief in *Lawson v. FMR LLC*,[30] but expressly stated that the court "owed no deference" to the agency's brief.[31] In *Christopher v. SmithKline Beecham Corp.*,[32] the Supreme Court discussed at some length whether and under what circumstances courts should defer to agency interpretations in briefs, noting that the Department of Labor had submitted inconsistent amicus briefs on an issue whose resolution could impose substantial compliance burdens.[33] In a Fair Labor Standards Act case, the Fifth Circuit expressed interest in an issue by asking for briefing on whether to approve a two-step process for collective actions that had been used by a number of district courts, with the first step being a fairly lenient one. The Department of Labor and the EEOC filed an amicus brief endorsing the two-step process for policy reasons, and the court of appeals then denied mandamus relief without oral argument.[34]

More generally, a commentator has identified seven groups within modern amici: (1) special interest groups and trade organizations; (2) parties in other, similar cases; (3) government; (4) non-litigants potentially affected by the case; (5) law professors and practitioners in specialized fields; (6) bar organizations; and (7) quasi-parties that have in some way participated in some phase of the case.[35]

Amicus participation is especially valuable to non-parties, allowing them to "have their say."[36] When legislatures make law, everyone has an opportunity to weigh in on the issue. Not so in courts, which open their doors

29. Lucas, *supra* n.2, at 1609 & n.35 (citing the nine cases).
30. 670 F.3d 61 (1st Cir. 2012).
31. *Id.* at 83.
32. 132 S. Ct. 2156 (2012).
33. *Id.* at 2165–67 (discussing deference under *Auer v. Robbins*, 519 U.S. 452 (1997), and concluding that the agency's position was not entitled to deference).
34. Brief filed January 3, 2013, in No. 12-20605, *In re Wells Fargo Bank*, n.A. (5th Cir.).
35. Pamela Stanton Baron, *The Civil Amicus Brief*, 13 App. Advocate 4, 5–6 (2000).
36. Antonin Scalia & Bryan Garner, Making Your Case: The Art of Persuading Judges, at 102 (Thomson/West St. Paul, MN 2008).

only to actual litigants. So the amicus process allows others to comment on issues of importance to them.[37] This modern amicus practice was noted over forty years ago by Professor Samuel Krislov, who explained the reason for the evolving role of amici. Professor Krislov discussed the holding in *Strawbridge v. Curtiss*[38] that "each distinct interest should be represented by persons, all of whom are entitled to sue or may be sued in the federal courts."[39] As Krislov noted, this rule of limiting the case to the parties at hand has the effect of excluding non-parties from direct participation in federal court litigation and continues the common law history of hostility to intervenors. The common law tradition was to decide specific disputes, but its decisions often had effects beyond the parties. The amicus evolved into the vehicle of expression for those other affected interests.[40] Amicus participation may even be allowed as an alternative to intervention.[41]

The evolution of the amicus submission was also precipitated by the development of what Krislov called "bureaucratically sophisticated groups" that are able to exercise influence in the judicial sphere. Organizations have the flexibility to respond with written material and information. Professor Krislov concludes:

> The amicus curiae brief represents a prime example of a legal institution evolving and developing while maintaining superficial identity with the past. It has been a catch-all device for living with some of the difficulties presented by the common law system of adversary proceeding. The United States, in particular, has allowed representation of governmental and other complex interests generated by the legal involutions of federalism. In addition, the United States Supreme Court has helped foster its development as a vehicle for broad representation of interests, particularly in disputes where political ramifications are wider than a narrow view of common law litigation might indicate. Groups inherently weak in the political arenas and unequally

37. *Id.*
38. 7 U.S. (3 Cranch) 267 (1806).
39. *Id.* at 267.
40. Supreme Court Practice, *supra* n.12, at 426–28.
41. *Id.* (discussing amicus briefs as alternative to intervention); Ne. Ohio Coalition for Homeless v. Husted, 696 F.3d 580 (6th Cir. 2012).

> endowed with resources of wealth or skills have quite naturally been the leaders in the use of the brief.[42]

Such sophisticated groups have only grown since Krislov's observations. Moreover, the ability to create the printed word has grown with technology. Thus, the general rule these days is that the amicus is an advocate. That was suggested in *Jaffe v. Redmond,*[43] by Justice Scalia, who noted that there is "no self-interested organization out there devoted to the pursuit of truth in the federal courts."[44] His comment echoes the First Circuit's conclusion that the amicus curiae is usually not disinterested or impartial.[45] As an illustration, the First Circuit cited a humorous anecdote:

> As an attorney of our acquaintance once told the court, when asked for his response to the argument of the amicus: "That fellow isn't any more a friend of the court than I am."[46]

In some cases, the amicus is simply another litigant. In other cases, the amicus is an interest group, which may have an agenda very different from any of the litigants in the case. Thus, a distinction can be made between true amicus briefs and adversarial amicus briefs, and it is possible to discern at least three classifications of amici:

- the true disinterested amicus;
- the endorsing amicus; and
- the interest group amicus.

In 1990, the United States Supreme Court issued a rule discouraging the filing of redundant amicus briefs. As Rule 37 unmistakably advises the bar, amicus briefs that do not add something to the case are not favored and are

42. Krislov, *supra* n.1, at 720.
43. 518 U.S. I (1996).
44. *Id.* at 35–36 (Scalia, J., dissenting).
45. Strasser v. Dooley, 432 F.2d 567, 569 (1st Cir. 1970).
46. *Id.* at 567 n.2.

simply a burden.[47] That has not, however, decreased the extent of amicus practice in that Court or elsewhere.

The "elsewhere" of amicus practice is expanding as well. A new forum for amicus briefs is the international arena. A commentator who has noted this development refers to "an evolving global administrative law norm" for amicus briefs, following the common law tradition into international arbitrations.[48] The same commentator notes the increasing use of amicus briefs in civil law countries.[49] Some developing countries complain about the advocacy of non-governmental organizations through amicus briefs.[50] But allowing greater participation of amici in international arbitrations may provide for more thorough examination of complex issues and minimize inconsistency in decision making.[51] One commentator suggests general principles for evaluating the increasing participation by non-governmental organizations in international arbitrations.[52] Other commentators urge regulation of amicus briefs in international arbitrations, after discussing the rise of amicus briefing in these international proceedings and the pros and cons of the current practice. [53]

## *The Prevalence of Amicus Filings*

Amicus practice is most prevalent at the highest court in the land. The vast majority of the cases that make it to the Court's oral argument calendar are now accompanied by at least one amicus brief.[54] Less frequent is the

---

47. S. Ct. R. 37.1.

48. Steven Kochevar, *Amicus Curiae in Civil Law Jurisdictions*, 12 Yale L.J. 1653, 1658 (2013).

49. *Id.* at 1659–63.

50. *Id.* at 1658; *see also* Dinah Shelton, *The Participation of Nongovernmental Organizations in International Judicial Proceedings*, 88 Am. J. Int'l L. 611 (1994).

51. Alberto R. Salazar, *Defragmenting International Investment Law to Protect Citizen-Consumers: The Role of* Amicus Curiae *and Public Interest Groups*, 19 Law & Bus. Rev. of Americas 183 (2013).

52. Eric. De Brabandare, *NGOs and the "Public Interest": The Legality and Rationale of Amicus Curiae Interventions in International Economic and Investment Disputes*, 12 Chi. J. Int'l Law 85 (2011).

53. Katia Fach Gomez, *Rethinking the Role of Amicus Curiae in International Investment Arbitration: How to Draw the Line Favorably for the Public Interest*, 35 Fordham Int'l L.J. 510 (2012); Eugenia Levine, *Amicus Curiae in International Investment Arbitration: The Implications of an Increase in Third-Party Participation*, 29 Berkeley J. of Int'l L. 200 (2011).

54. Wohl, *supra* n.2, at 46; Supreme Court Practice, *supra* n.12, at 740.

filing of amicus briefs at the initial stage of the petition for certiorari, often because many potential amici want to use their resources in cases that will actually be heard. Nevertheless, amicus briefs have been found to be influential at the certiorari stage.[55] Effective amicus briefs were filed by Ohio and several other states in *City of Boerne v. Flores*[56] and by the Southern Christian Leadership Conference in *Scheidler v. National Organization .for Women Inc.*,[57] resulting in the grant of review.[58] It is seldom advisable to file an amicus brief opposing a petition for certiorari, since doing so may bring attention to the case and actually increase the chance the certiorari will be granted.[59] In contrast, amicus briefs are helpful when supporting the grant of review, increasing the chance of securing review from 8.5 to 37.1 percent.[60] Whether filing an amicus brief at such an initial stage can be helpful in state courts will depend on the jurisdiction.[61]

The number of amicus briefs being routinely filed in the Supreme Court has increased dramatically over the years. Amicus briefs are now filed in the Supreme Court in approximately 90 percent of cases, and in a recent term, 399 amicus briefs were filed in 74 of 79 cases.[62] Between the 1980 and 1991 terms, by contrast, amici appeared in 71 percent of the court's cases decided by opinion, and the figure was only 35 percent during the

---

55. *Gregory* C. Caldeira & John R. Wright, *Organized Interests and Agenda Setting in the U.S. Supreme Court,* 82 AM. POL. SCI. REV. 1109 (1988); SUPREME COURT PRACTICE, *supra* n.12, at 512 (noting one study that amicus briefs can increase grant of review from 8.5 to 37.1 percent).

56. 521 U.S. 507 (1997).

57. 537 U.S. 393 (2003).

58. Dan Schweitzer, *Fundamentals of Preparing a United States Supreme Court Amicus Brief,* J. OF APPELLATE PRAC. & PROCESS 530 (Fall 2003).

59. *Id.* at 528; SUPREME COURT PRACTICE, *supra* n.12, at 513.

60. SUPREME COURT PRACTICE, *supra* n.12, at 512 (citing H.W. Perry, Jr., DECIDING TO DECIDE 137 (1991) (Table 5.4)); G. Caldeira & J. Wright, *Amicus Curiae before the Supreme Court: Who Participates, When, and How Much?,* 52 J. POL. 782 (1990); Mayer Brown LLP, FEDERAL APPELLATE PRACTICE 420–21 (2008).

61. In Florida, for example, amicus briefs are generally not helpful when the court is deciding whether to exercise its discretion to review because of the jurisdictional limitations imposed on the supreme court. *See* Joseph H. Lang, Jr. & Christopher J. Kaiser, *Amicus Briefs,* FLORIDA APPELLATE PRACTICE & § 15.2 (Florida bar 2006).

62. SUPREME COURT PRACTICE, *supra* n.12, at 740; Farber, *supra* n.18, at 37 "Appendix: Data for the 1997 Term." Farber found that the number of amicus briefs does not necessarily mirror the importance of the case in terms of later citations by courts and commentators. *Id.* at 35–36. Farber further notes that amicus briefs in the Supreme Court tend to be filed in public interest "clumps" and industry "clumps."

1965–66 term.[63] In tabulating the numbers over the century, one extensive study of amicus briefs noted that amicus briefs are now as frequent in this century as they were rare at the beginning of the century.[64] In the last fifty years, while the United States Supreme Court has not increased its output of opinions, amicus filings have increased more than 800 percent.[65] Amicus briefs are filed at a rate of 500 per year in that Court.[66]

In a 2013 affirmative action case concerning higher education, 73 amicus briefs were filed.[67] In the *Grutter* case, more than 100 amicus briefs were filed.[68] In *Webster v. Reproductive Health Services,*[69] an abortion rights case, more than 85 amicus briefs were filed. During that same term, the civil rights case of *Patterson v. McClean Credit Union,*[70] dealing with racial harassment, drew fewer than 20 amicus briefs; but the amicus briefs in *Patterson* and *Webster* combined represented more than 100 public interest groups and nearly half the members of Congress.[71] *Stoneridge Investment Partners, LLC v. Scientific-Atlanta, Inc.*,[72] a prominent securities law case, garnered 39 amicus briefs.[73] *Citizens United*[74] attracted 54 amicus briefs. A case over legal aid funding attracted 22 amicus briefs.[75] In *Decker v. Northwest Environmental Defense Center*, 22 amicus briefs were filed, two by dueling groups of professors.[76] Twenty amicus briefs were filed in *FTC v. Phoebe Putney Health System, Inc.*[77] Almost 20 amicus briefs were submitted in

63. Wohl, *supra* n.2, at 46 (citing information from Bruce Ennis of Jenner & Block, Washington D.C.).
64. Joseph D. Kearney & Thomas W. Merrill, *The Influence of Amicus Briefs on the Supreme Court,* 148 Univ. of Pa. L. Rev. 743, 744 (2000).
65. *Id.* at 749.
66. *Id.* at 828.
67. Fisher v. Univ. of Tex. at Austin, 133 S. Ct. 2411 (2013).
68. Andrew Brownstein, *High Court Affirmative Action Debate: A Referendum on King's Dream,* 39 Trial 84, 86–87 (May 2003).
69. 492 U.S. 490 (1989).
70. 491 U.S. 164 (1989).
71. *Id.*
72. 552 U.S. 148 (2008).
73. Franklin A. Gevurtz, *Law Upside Down: A Critical Essay on* Stoneridge Investment Partners, LLC v. Scientific-Atlanta, Inc., 103 Nw. Univ. L. Rev. Colloquy 488 (2009).
74. Citizens United v. Fed. Election Comm'n, 558 U.S. 310 (2010).
75. Phillips v. Washington Legal Found., 524 U.S. 156 (1998); *see* Farber, *supra* n.18, at 37 "Appendix: Data for the 1997 Term."
76. 133 S. Ct. 1326, 1338 (2013) (Roberts, C.J., concurring).
77. 133 S. Ct. 1003, 1016 (2103).

*Bray v. Alexandria Women's Health Clinic,*[78] which dealt with anti-abortion protests. An amicus brief was filed by eighteen states and one territory in *Wilson v. Seiter,*[79] which considered whether general prison conditions could amount to cruel and unusual punishment.

One of the most influential private amicus curiae in the United States Supreme Court has been the American Civil Liberties Union.[80] Since 1961, the ACLU filed amicus briefs in many of the landmark cases expanding the rights of those accused of crimes.[81] From 1961 to 1981, the ACLU filed amicus briefs in 44 percent of all criminal cases in which amicus briefs were filed.[82]

There is no doubt that the proliferation of amicus briefs is the result of their perceived impact on the Court's decisions. In *Grutter v. Bollinger,*[83] a case concerning affirmative action in higher education, an influential amicus brief was filed by retired military officers, including General Norman Schwarzkopf, arguing that diversity among military officers is important to national security.[84] Justice Ginsburg asked the Solicitor General to address that brief early in the argument.[85] A commentary on the effect of amicus briefs in *Grutter* argues that amicus briefs were valuable in providing the relevant social context,[86] which was important because the Court itself stated that "context matters" when applying strict scrutiny analysis.[87] Another commentator[88] cites the amicus brief of well-known constitutional scholar Laurence Tribe as influential in shaping the opinion in *Romer v. Evans*.[89]

78. 506 U.S. 263 (1993).
79. 501 U.S. 294 (1991).
80. Lucas, *supra* n.2, at 1608–09.
81. *Id.*
82. Gregg Ivers & Karen O'Connor, *Friends as Foes: The Amicus Curiae Participation and Effectiveness of the American Civil Liberties Union for Effective Law Enforcement in Criminal Cases,* 1969–1982, 9 L. & Pol. 161 (1987).
83. 539 U.S. 306 (2003).
84. *Id.*
85. Schweitzer, *supra* n.58, at 523–24.
86. Jonathan Alger & Marvin Krislov, *You've Got to Have Friends: Lessons Learned from the Role of Amici in the University of Michigan Cases*, 30 J.C. & U.L. 503, 526 (2004).
87. 539 U.S. at 327.
88. Lucas, *supra* n.2, at 1609.
89. 517 U.S. 620 (1996) (invalidating voter initiative barring laws protecting homosexuals from discrimination).

By no means, however, is amicus practice confined to the United States Supreme Court. The amicus brief appears with regularity in federal courts of appeals and also in state supreme courts and state intermediate appellate courts.[90] Amicus briefs are cited or quoted in many federal appellate decisions.[91] For example, in *Kitchen v. Herbert*,[92] the Tenth Circuit noted "scores of amicus briefs on sociological issues" were filed in a same-sex marriage case. A "large number" of amicus briefs received attention from the First Circuit in *Massachusetts v. U.S. Department of Health & Human Services*.[93] A case that concerned depriving whooping cranes of their habitat attracted a number of amicus briefs from governmental and environmental briefs.[94]

Likewise, amici participation in state high courts is both common and effective. The number of amicus briefs filed in state high courts tripled in the 1980s, and a recent study found that 31 percent of state supreme court cases cite to them.[95] These findings are consistent with a survey of state supreme court justices indicating that many amicus briefs influence the outcome of cases.[96] The New York Court of Appeals is known to be especially receptive to amicus briefs, and the number of motions for leave to file increased from 59 to 110 early in the new century.[97] The West Virginia Supreme Court of Appeals began to rein in amicus briefs in 1980 by adopting rules that limited their length, required disclosure of who is paying for

90. *See, e.g.*, Pamela Stanton Baron, *Amicus Briefs to the Texas Appellate Courts*, Fifth Annual Conference on Techniques for Handling Civil Appeals in State and Federal Court (Univ. of Texas School of Law, June 1995) (discussing amicus practice in Texas); Randy S. Parlee, *A Primer on Amicus Curiae Briefs*, Wis. Lawyer, Nov. 1989 (discussing amicus practice in Wisconsin).
91. Federal Appellate Practice, *supra* n.60, at 420 (in 2002, amicus briefs were cited in 37 percent of cases decided and were quoted in 11 percent of those cases).
92. 755 F.3d 1193, 1240 (10th Cir. 2014).
93. 682 F.3d 1, 7 (1st Cir. 2012).
94. *Ark. Project v. Shaw*, 756 F.3d 801, 808 n.2 (5th Cir. 2014).
95. Mary-Christine Sungaila, *The IADC Amicus Brief Program: Its Increasing Success and Influence*, 81 Defense Counsel J. 32, 32–34 (2014).
96. *Id.* (citing Victor E. Flango, et al., *Amicus Curiae Briefs: The Court's Perspective*, 27 Just. Sys. J. 180, 185 (2006)); Carrie Ann Wozniak, *Amicus Briefs: What Have They Done for Courts Lately?*, Fla. B.J., Jun. 2012 (discussing increased amicus filings in Florida courts and noting the citation of amicus briefs in 14 majority opinions by the Florida Supreme Court from 2007 to 2011).
97. Matthew Laroche, *Is the New York Court of Appeals Still "Friendless?" An Empirical Study of Amicus Curiae Participation*, 701, 710–11 Alb. L. Rev. 701 (2009).

the briefs, and declined to address issues raised only by amici.[98] There is even some amicus practice in trial courts, both federal and state. For example, Massachusetts Superior Courts have requested amicus briefs in some cases.[99] Early in this new millennium, the Appellate Body of the World Trade Organization (WTO) began accepting amicus briefs.[100] That controversial practice led one commentator to predict the effect of amicus briefs on the WTO by examining their effect in the United States Supreme Court.[101]

Nevertheless, the volume of amicus briefs in those courts does not approach the level of amici participation in the Supreme Court.[102] For example, a survey of amicus practice in the Eleventh Circuit revealed that the number of amicus briefs filed annually in that court ranged from 30 to 85 from 2003 to 2007, with the number actually decreasing over time, in part because the court often denies leave to file.[103] Another survey that reached all three levels of the federal judiciary revealed a modest amicus practice in courts of appeals and a small amicus practice in district or trial courts.[104] Example 14 in the Appendix is an amicus brief filed in district court. Forty percent of all state courts of last resort had no appreciable amicus practice in the 1990s.[105]

---

98. Amy M. Smith, *The History and Evolution of Amicus Curiae in West Virginia*, 2013 W. Va. Lawyer 42 (July–Sept. 2013).

99. *See* McGonagle v. Home Depot U.S.A., Inc., No. 011208, 2004 WL 3120556 (Mass. Super. Ct. Dec. 13, 2004) (Massachusetts Commissioner of Revenue accepted court's invitation to file amicus brief); Commonwealth v. Kamper, Civ. Action No. A 00–10580, 2000 WL 1724889 (Mass. Super. Ct. Nov. 20, 2000) (court invited briefing by any interested amici); Corcoran, Mullins & Jennison, Inc. v. Flanagan, Civ. Action A No. 97-3135E, 1999 WL 823855 (Mass. Super. Ct. Aug. 16, 1999) (Boston Police Department declined court's invitation to file an amicus brief or to intervene).

100. Josh Robbins, *False Friends: Amicus Curiae and Procedural Discretion in WTO Appeals under the Hot-Rolled Lead/Asbestos Doctrine,* 44 Harv. Int'l L.J. 317, 317 (2003).

101. Andrea Kupfer Schneider, *Unfriendly Actions: The Amicus Brief Battle at the WTO,* 7 Widener Law Symposium J. 87 (2001); *see also* C.L. Lim, *Asian WTO Members and the Amicus Brief Controversy: Arguments & Strategies,* 1 Asian J. of WTO & Int'l Health & Pol. 85 (2006).

102. *See* Federal Appellate Practice, *supra* n.60, at 419 (in 2002, amicus briefs were filed in 400 of the 27,000 cases decided on the merits by United States Courts of Appeals.).

103. P. Stephen Gidiere, III, *The Facts and Fictions of Amicus Curiae Practice in the Eleventh Circuit Court of Appeals*, 5 Seton Hall Circuit Rev. 1 (2008).

104. Linda Sandstrom Simard, *An Empirical Study of Amicus Curiae in Federal Court: A Fine Balance of Access, Efficiency, and Adversarialism*, 27 Rev. of Litig. 669 (2008).

105. Paul Brace & Kellie Sims Butler, *New Perspectives for the Comparative Study of the Judiciary: The State Supreme Court Project*, 22 Just. Sys. J. 243, 253 (2001).

### *The Influence of Amicus Briefs*

There are many examples that demonstrate that amicus briefs influence judicial decisions. These examples rebut the view of some that amicus briefs are a "waste of time, effort, and money in a useless function."[106] One commentator conducted a survey of 70 former Supreme Court clerks and noted these views about amicus briefs: (1) they are more helpful in highly technical cases, statutory cases, and cases dealing with obscure areas of the law; (2) most justices at least skim amicus briefs; (3) briefs considered more carefully come from the U.S. Solicitor General, state and local governments, and the ACLU; (4) briefs by prominent academics or reputed attorneys are considered more carefully; (5) collaboration in amicus briefs is desired.[107] The clerks' recommendations: don't repeat, keep it short, and write well.[108]

Some believe that amicus briefs are most influential when they resonate with the predilections of the Court. In the first term of the Roberts Court, the position of the U.S. Chamber of Commerce was upheld in 13 of the 15 cases in which the Chamber of Commerce filed amicus briefs.[109]

Although amicus briefs were once rarely cited by the United States Supreme Court, they are now cited more frequently, demonstrating their persuasive power. A study of Supreme Court decisions from 1969 to 1981 found that amicus briefs were specifically cited by at least one Justice in only 18 percent of the cases in which one was filed.[110] From 1985 to 1995, however, more than 35 percent of Supreme Court opinions in which amicus briefs were filed contained reference to at least one amicus brief.[111]

---

106. Philip B. Kurland, *The Business of the Supreme Court, O.T. 1982*, 50 U. Chi. L. Rev. 628, 647 (1983); *see also* Philip B. Kurland & Dennis J. Hutchison, *With Friends Like These . . . .*, ABA J., Aug., 1984 at 16.

107. Kelly J. Lynch, *Best Friends? Supreme Court Law Clerks on Effective Amicus Curiae Briefs*, 20 J.L. & Pol. 33 (2004).

108. *Id.* at 69–71.

109. Robert L. Kerr, *Considering the Meaning of Wisconsin Right to Life for the Corporate Free-Speech Movement,* 14 Comm. L. & Pol. 105, 106 (Spr. 2009 (citing Jeffrey Rosen, *Supreme Court, Inc.: How the Nation's Highest Court Has Come to Side with Big Business,* N.Y. Times Mag., Mar. 16, 2008, at 39–40)).

110. Robert E. Rains, *Fair-Weather Friend of the Court-On Writing an Amicus Brief,* Trial, August 1990 at 57–60 (citing O'Conner & Epstein, *Court Rules & Work Load: A Case Study of Rules Governing Amicus Curiae Participation,* Just. Sys. J., Spring 1983, at 35–42).

111. Robert W. Bennett, *Counter-Conversationalism and the Sense of Difficulty,* 95 Nw. U. L. REV. 845, 883–84 (2001).

Sometimes the influence of an amicus brief surfaces in the dissenting opinion. In *United States v. Castleman*,[112] Justice Scalia complained that the Court had relied on definitions of "domestic violence" contained in an amicus brief filed by the National Network to End Domestic Violence against Women rather than following the statute being considered. Similarly, Justice Sotomayor criticized the Court for relying on an FDA amicus brief in resolving an issue of preemption in a design defect case.[113] Of course, dissenters sometimes cite amicus briefs to support their outvoted views, as did Justice Breyer in a case concerning the right of prisons to conduct strip searches, when he cited examples in amicus briefs of strip searches of those accused of minor offenses.[114]

Other examples exist. Citations to an amicus brief are found in the following Supreme Court opinions:

- In *McDonald v. City of Chicago*,[115] the Court cited amicus briefs in finding a consensus for a right to bear arms for self-defense.[116]
- In *Bilski v. Kappos*,[117] the Court rejected a test of patentability as the sole test, citing criticisms of the test by amici.[118]
- In *United States v. Hayes*,[119] the Court cited amicus briefs filed by the Brady Center to Prevent Gun Violence and the National Network to End Domestic Violence in interpreting a federal firearms statute.
- Justice Breyer cited in a concurring opinion an amicus brief by law professors specializing in federal Indian law in *Carcieri v. Salazar*.[120]

---

112. 134 S. Ct. 1405, 1420 (2014) (Scalia, J., dissenting).
113. Mut. Pharm. Co. v. Bartlett, 133 S. Ct. 2466, 2493–94 (2013) (Sotomayor, J., dissenting).
114. Florence v. Bd. of Chosen Freeholders of County of Burlington, 132 S. Ct. 1510, 1528 (2012) (Breyer J., dissenting).
115. 561 U.S. 742 (2010).
116. *See id.* at 777 n.27. In fact, amicus briefs were cited numerous times in the opinions issued in this case. Justice Breyer's dissent criticized the Court's reliance on amici for the consensus, noting that amicus briefs had been filed on both sides of the incorporation issue. 130 S. Ct. at 3124 (Breyer, J., dissenting).
117. 561 U.S. 593 (2010).
118. 130 S. Ct. at 3227.
119. 555 U.S. 415, 427 (2009).
120. 555 U.S. 379, 398 (2009) (Breyer, J. concurring).

- *McConnell v. Federal Election Commission,*[121] the decision on campaign reforms against "soft-money," quoted from an amicus brief to discuss the coercive circumstances that can surround soft-money contributions.
- In *Lawrence v. Texas,*[122] the Court noted the filing of "scholarly amicus briefs" and cited those briefs in deciding to strike down an anti-sodomy law.
- *Republican Party of Minnesota v. White,*[123] contains frequent references to amicus briefs, including a brief filed by the ABA on the issue of the constitutionality of restrictions on campaign speech by candidates for judicial offices.
- The Court cited amici in its opinion in *Jaffee v. Redmond,*[124] which dealt with the patient/psychotherapist privilege.
- *U.S. Bancorp Mortgage Co. v. Bonner Mall Partnership,*[125] a case involving the propriety of vacating federal civil judgments when the parties reach a settlement during the appellate process, cited amicus submissions.
- *Winthrow v. Williams,*[126] dealing with federal habeas review of alleged *Miranda* violations, cited to amicus briefs.
- *Mapp v. Ohio,*[127] which concerned the application of the exclusionary rule to the states, contained references to amicus briefs.
- The Court also cited amicus briefs in *Teague v. Lane,*[128] which barred peremptory jury challenges for reasons related to race; *Gregg v. Georgia,*[129] a death-penalty case; and *Sullivan v. Zebley,*[130] which dealt with social security benefits for disabled children.

121. 540 U.S. 93, 125 n.13 (2003).
122. 539 U.S. 558, 567–68, 572 (2003).
123. 536 U.S. 765, 773, 776, 788 n.l5 (2002).
124. 518 U.S. 1 (1996).
125. 513 U.S. 18, 24 n.2 (1994).
126. 507 U.S. 680, 690 n.6 (1993).
127. 367 U.S. 643 (1961).
128. 489 U.S. 288 (1989).
129. 428 U.S. 153, 233–36 (Marshall, J., dissenting).
130. 493 U.S. 521, 531 n.9, 534 n.13, 536 n.l7 (1990). This amicus brief appears as Example 1 in the Appendix.

In federal courts of appeals, amicus briefs are frequently quoted or discussed. Examples include:

- In *David v. Alphin*,[131] the Fourth Circuit "received and considered amicus briefs" in a class action for breach of fiduciary duty against a financial institution.
- In *Massachusetts v. U.S. Department of Health & Human Services*,[132] the court received many amicus briefs on both sides of the issue, some of which "proved very helpful."[133]
- In *Hitachi v. Home Electronics (America) Inc. v. United States*,[134] the Federal Circuit understood the importance of the issue because of the amicus briefs.
- In *Collazo-Santiago v. Toyota Motor Corp.*,[135] the First Circuit addressed but rejected two arguments made by the amicus curiae.
- Judge Posner considered, but rejected, an amicus brief filed by HUD in *Krzalic v. Republic Title Co.*[136]
- Amici successfully argued for implied immunity in a suit over an alleged conspiracy to manipulate stock prices in *Friedman v. Salomon/Smith Barney, Inc.*[137]
- In a separate concurring and dissenting opinion in *White v. Ford Motor Co.*,[138] dealing with the excessiveness of an award of exemplary damages of almost $70 million, a Ninth Circuit judge noted the maximum statutory fine for the defendant's conduct as stated in an amicus brief.
- In *Community Health Center v. Wilson-Coker*,[139] an amicus brief filed by the United States "clarified" a party's position on interpreting the Medicaid Act, resulting in a decision to overrule the district court's interpretation in favor of the Secretary of Health & Human Services.

---

131. 704 F.3d 327, 330 n.1 (4th Cir. 2013).
132. 682 F.3d 1 (1st Cir. 2012).
133. *Id.* at 7.
134. 676 F.3d 34 (Fed. Cir. 2012).
135. 149 F.3d 23, 27 nn.4 & 5(1st Cir. 1998).
136. 314 F.3d 875, 877, 881–82 (7th Cir. 2002).
137. 313 F.3d 796, 799 (2d Cir. 2002).
138. 312 F.3d 998, 1030 (9th Cir. 2002) (Graber, J., concurring in part & dissenting in part).
139. 311 F.3d 132, 137 n.8, 139 (2d Cir. 2002).

- The Seventh Circuit extensively discussed amici's arguments in *In re Volpert.*[140]
- The Ninth Circuit quoted from the ACLU's amicus brief in *Federal Election Commission v. Christian Action Network.*[141]
- The D.C. Circuit discussed, and rejected, the argument by amicus for a more stringent standard of review in *Independent Petroleum Association v. Babbitt.*[142]
- The Fifth Circuit discussed an issue raised only by the amici in *Bridges v. City of Bossier.*[143]
- An amicus brief submitted by the United States was quoted at length in *United States v. Chevron U.S.A., Inc.*[144]

Amicus briefs are also filed in district courts,[145]and federal district courts have cited amicus briefs in their opinions, as shown by these examples:

- In *Mason v. SmithKline Beecham Corp.*,[146] the court considered amicus briefs by the FDA in holding that a claim was preempted by federal law.
- In *United States v Boeing Co.*,[147] the court detailed the amicus brief's argument about industry practices and reliance on an alleged common understanding about a particular type of provision in a defense contract.

---

140. 110 F.3d 494, 499–500 (7th Cir. 1997).
141. 110 F.3d 1049, 1061 (9th Cir. 1997).
142. 92 F.3d 1248, 1258 (D.C. Cir. 1996).
143. 110 F.3d 1049, 1061 (9th Cir. 1997).
144. 72 F.3d 740, 745 (9th Cir. 1995).
145. Courts of appeals have commented on the filing of amicus briefs in district courts. *See, e.g.*, Nautilus Ins. Co. v. Country Oaks Apartments Ltd., No. 08-50652, 2009 WL 1067587 (5th Cir. Apr. 22, 2009) (plaintiffs filed amicus brief in district court declaratory judgment action on whether insurer's policy covered their claim against the apartment owner); United States v. Custer Battles, LLC, 562 F.3d 295, 300 (4th Cir. 2009) (government did not intervene in district court qui tam action but filed numerous amicus briefs).
146. 546 F. Supp. 2d 618, 625 (C. D. Ill. 2008). The defendant actually submitted FDA amicus briefs filed in other cases as summary judgment evidence. *See* SmithKline Beecham Corp.'s Opposition to Motion to Strike at 2007 WL 4802117. The Consumer Product Safety Improvement Act, Pub. L. 110–314, 122 Stat. 3016 (2008), limited the consideration of agency amicus briefs and statements on the issue of preemption. *See* John B. O'Loughlin, *Consumer Product Safety Improvement Act: Not the Last Word on Preemption,* 23 TOXICS L. RPTR. 1104 (BNA) (Dec. 11, 2008).
147. 73 F. Supp. 2d 897, 904 (S.D. Ohio 1999).

- The court discussed at length but rejected an Indian tribe's arguments in its amicus brief supporting removal jurisdiction in a suit between casino developers and their competitors in *Sonoma Falls Developers, LLC v. Nevada Gold & Casinos, Inc.*[148]
- The court agreed with an argument "aptly" made by an amicus curiae in *California v. Mendonca.*[149]
- In *Milk Industry Foundation v. Glickman,*[150] the court considered the citations to evidence in the record that were contained in amicus briefs, although the court rejected amici's position.

Amici are also often mentioned in state courts. In a decision by the Texas Supreme Court, amici were applauded for their efforts with this statement: "(S]everal excellent amicus briefs in this case have offered pertinent and helpful observations and suggestions."[151] In another case, dozens of amicus briefs, including one by state legislators, caused the Texas Supreme Court to withdraw its opinion, set new oral arguments, and issue a new opinion, albeit with the judgment unchanged.[152] A number of California courts have likewise referred to amici as "helpful."[153] Further, the California Supreme Court has, on occasion, discussed arguments of amici at some length in its opinions.[154] In another example, the Supreme Court of Massachusetts

148. 272 F. Supp. 2d 919, 925–27 (N.D. Cal. 2003).
149. 957 F. Supp. 1072, 1124–25 n.6 (N.D. Cal. 1997).
150. 949 F. Supp. 882, 895 (D.D.C. 1996).
151. Reed v. Wylie, 597 S.W.2d 743, 750 (Tex. 1980) (Spears, J., concurring).
152. Entergy Gulf States, Inc. v. Summers, 282 S.W.3d 433 (Tex. 2009).
153. *See, e.g.,* Thorn v. Superior Court, I Cal. 3d 666, 674 n.8, 464 P.2d 56, 62 n.8, 83 Cal. Rptr. 600, 606 n.8 (Cal. 1970); City of Carmel-By-The-Sea v. Young, 2 Cal. 3d 259, 276, 466 P.2d 225, 238, 85 Cal. Rptr. 1, 14 (Cal. 1970) (Mosk, J., dissenting); Thrifty-Tel, Inc. v. Bezenek, 46 Cal. App. 4th 1559, 1569, 54 Cal. Rptr 2d 468, 475 (Cal. Ct. App. 1996); Williams v. Weisser, 273 Cal. App. 2d 726, 732 n.5 78 Cal. Rptr. 542, 545 n.5 (Cal. Ct. App. 1969); Faus v. Nelson, 241 Cal. App. 2d 320, 329, 50 Cal. Rptr. 483, 488 (Cal. Ct. App. 1966); Armistead v. City of Los Angeles, 152 Cal. App. 2d 319, 324, 313 P.2d 127, 130 (Cal. Ct. App. 1957); *accord* State v. Superior Court, 29 Cal. 3d 210, 216, 625 P.2d 239, 242, 172 Cal. Rptr. 696, 699 (Cal. 1981) (arguments of "extensive briefs by amici curiae" noted as being "of considerable assistance").
154. *See, e.g.,* Potter v. Firestone Tire & Rubber Co., 6 Cal. 4th 965, 863 P.2d 795, 25 Cal. Rptr. 2d 550 (Cal. 1993); People v. Wharton, 53 Cal. 3d 522, 809 P.2d 290, 280 Cal. Rptr. 631 (Cal. 1991).

has commented on the quality of amicus briefs and has addressed issues raised by amici.[155]

Even when amicus briefs are not acknowledged in opinions, "[n]ot infrequently a good amicus brief may help shape the judicial decision."[156] In some situations, amicus briefs are very influential and the court's ruling may actually rest on a ground set forth in an amicus brief that was not stressed or even raised by a party.[157] For example, in *Romer v. Evans,* a case involving a voters' initiative barring the enactment of a law protecting homosexuals from discrimination, Justice Kennedy, writing for the majority, adopted arguments of the amicus, written by Professor Laurence H. Tribe and several other constitutional scholars. Nevertheless, Justice Kennedy never cited Tribe's brief in the opinion.[158]

Another example is *United States v. Winstar Corp.*[159] The Court cited remarks by a director of the now-defunct Federal Savings & Loan Insurance Corporation and deposition testimony from an official at the Atlanta Federal Home Loan Bank—both of which had been quoted in the amicus brief filed by the Franklin Financial Group.[160]

In some instances—as with Henry Clay's initial amicus brief in this country—courts solicit amicus briefs.[161] The influence of an amicus brief is likely to increase when the court itself invites the brief.[162] The Ninth Circuit issued

155. Polaroid v. Travelers Indem. Co., 610 N.E.2d 912, 920 n.l5 (Mass. 1993); Royal-Globe Ins. Co. v. Craven, 585 N.E.2d 315, 319 (Mass. 1992).

156. Supreme Court Practice, *supra* n.12, at 741; Michael E. Tigar, Federal Appeals Jurisdiction & Practice, 564 (2d ed. (1993); Bruce J. Ennis, *Effective Amicus Briefs,* 33 Cath. U.L. Rev. 603, 603 (1984) (dispelling the notion that amicus briefs are not influential and important).

157. Supreme Court Practice, *supra* n.12, at 741 (citing Humana, Inc. v. Forsyth, 525 U.S. 299 (1999). Freytag v. Comm'r of Internal Revenue, 501 U.S. 868 (1991); Teague v. Lane, 489 U.S. 288 (1989); Mapp v. Ohio, 367 U.S. 643 (1961).

158. Romer v. Evans, 517 U.S. 620 (1996); Wohl, *supra* n.2, at 46.

159. 518 U.S. 839 (1996).

160. *Id.* at 847 n.3 & 850 n.6.

161. *See, e.g.,* Kings County v. Santa Rosa Band of Indians, 429 U.S. 812 (1976); Qantas Airways, Ltd. v. Foremost Int'l Tours, 425 U.S. 957 (1976); Younger v. Harris, 393 U.S. 813 (1968).

162. Supreme Court Practice *supra* n.12, at 516–17, 738 (noting that Supreme Court occasionally invites non-parties to file briefs); Federal Appellate Practice, *supra* n.60, at 405 (also noting that D.C. Circuit Rule 29 allows the court to appoint a non-party to file a brief); *see, e.g.,* Smart v. Local 702 Int'l Bhd. of Elec. Workers, 562 F.3d 798, 806 n.6 (7th Cir. 2009) (thanking law professor for excellent amicus brief submitted at court's request); De Mercado v. Mukasey, Nos. 06-70361 & 06-70366, 2009 WL 1382915 (9th Cir. May 19, 2009) (court-appointed amicus curiae argued this immigration case for petitioners); *cf.* Cochran v. Holder,

an order that extended a general invitation to amicus input on the meaning of federal regulations that the court had to interpret.[163] An even more general invitation to amici was expressed by Chief Judge Judith S. Kaye of the New York Court of Appeals. Judge Kaye wrote a 1988 article in the *New York Law Journal* encouraging lawyers to submit amicus briefs so that the court would not miss any legal issues.[164] Forty-three times since 1954, the United States Supreme Court has invited lawyers to brief an argument that was abandoned by the party that prevailed below. In 2008, the Court heard two such cases, when the government agreed with the petitioners in criminal cases.[165]

The trend, however, is in the opposite direction. After being inundated by amicus briefs, the Court adopted Rule 37.1, expressly discouraging amicus briefs that do not add to the case.[166] As one commentary has noted:

> Not all amicus briefs are read by all of the Justices. The number is so great that most of the Justices have their law clerks sift out the briefs or parts of briefs which they think add enough to the party's brief to be worth reading. Many "say little more than 'me too'—the amicus agrees with one side in the controversy." Such briefs may impress the members of the amicus organization, but they will not help with the Supreme Court. Merely stating one's views as to how a case should be decided is not a legitimate reason for filing an amicus brief . . . Briefs that add nothing to the substantive factual or legal presentation by the parties are not likely to survive the preliminary examination by the law clerks, or to influence favorably a Justice or clerk who reads them. On the contrary they are regarded as wasteful of valuable Court time.[167]

---

564 F.3d 318, 324 (4th Cir. 2009) (EEOC declined court's invitation to file amicus brief on proper interpretation of EEOC regulation).

163. Palomar Med. Ctr. v. Sebelius, 672 F.3d 1152 (9th Cir. 2012).

164. Daniel Wise, *Amicus Briefs Illuminate Top Court Issues,* New York L.J. (Jan. 1994).

165. Brian P. Goldman, *Should the Supreme Court Stop Inviting Amici Curiae to Defend Abandoned Lower Court Decisions?*, 63 Stan. L. Rev. 907, 907 (2011). This author notes that prior to 1954, the Court had never appointed an amicus curiae to "support an orphaned argument" and argues that the current Court should more narrowly limit the occasions where it does so. *Id.*

166. *See* Supreme Court Practice, *supra* n.12, at 512 (discussing Rule 37.1).

167. *Id.* at 665.

The incidence of so-called "me too" amicus briefs has been investigated with somewhat surprising results. An analysis of the language and topics of amicus briefs filed from 2002 to 2004 in the Supreme Court reveals that amicus briefs "overwhelmingly contain original information," in part because they primarily argue outside the record.[168] That is echoed by a comment made by former Justice Sandra Day O'Connor, who remarked that amicus briefs address "points of law, policy considerations, or other points of view" not raised by the parties.[169]

As amicus briefs have proliferated, and as they have evolved from neutral submissions to opportunities for partisan advocacy, their overall effectiveness may have decreased. Certainly, the sheer number of amicus briefs tends to discourage judges from reading them. Thus, it is hardly surprising that a statistical study of amicus briefs in the United States Supreme Court failed to support the hypothesis that amicus briefs filed by state governments influenced proponents of federalism on the Court.[170] The authors surmised that amicus briefs may have become so "commonplace" that they have been "rendered meaningless."[171]

On the other hand, another statistical study indicates that "amicus briefs appear to affect success rates in a variety of contexts."[172] Sheer numbers of amicus briefs do not correlate with success, although small disparities in amicus briefs may support success rates.[173] Instead, amicus briefs by institutional litigants and experienced lawyers are the most effective.[174] The authors of one study explain that result by what they call the "Legal Model" of the amicus brief, which posits that amicus briefs are successful when they impart valuable new information.[175] Competing models are the "Attitudinal Model" (positing that judges decide cases based on their attitudes) and the

168. Paul M. Collins, Jr., Pamela C. Corley & Jesse Hammer, *Me Too? An Investigation of Repetition in U.S. Supreme Court Amicus Curiae Briefs*, 97 JUDICATURE 228, 234 (Mar.–Apr. 2014).
169. *Id.* at 229 (quoting a speech by Justice O'Connor to the Henry Clay Memorial Foundation).
170. Ruth Colker & Kevin M. Scott, *Dissing States, Invalidation of State Action During the Rehnquist Era,* 88 VA. L. REV. 1301, 1333–38.
171. *Id.* at 1338.
172. Kearney & Merrill, *supra* n.64, at 750.
173. *Id.* at 750, 796–97.
174. *Id.* at 750.
175. *Id.* at 750, 775–89.

"Interest Group Model" (positing that judges decide cases in accord with positions taken by interest groups).[176] The Attitudinal Model has the least support in statistical findings, and the Interest Group Model only equivocal support.[177] The Legal Model emerges as the best explanation because "legal doctrine matters."[178] A later survey of the effect of amicus briefs in New York state courts showed no support for the Attitudinal Model and support for the Information and Interest Group Models.[179]

A survey of the entire federal judiciary, which yielded a 23– 30 percent response rate, led to interesting conclusions.[180] First, a reputable brief writer is more likely to get the court's attention. The mere number of amicus briefs is not that significant, but the views of groups that may be affected by the decision is of importance to the court. Amicus briefs are viewed as helpful when they add legal arguments missing from the parties' briefs or when the named parties do not have strong representation. Supreme Court justices are interested in facts outside the record that amici can provide, but lower court judges, especially district judges, are not as interested in extra-judicial information.

A study of amicus briefs in the specialized area of patent law reveals that most amicus briefs are filed by the so-called patent insiders—the government, companies, lawyers, and industry groups.[181] Amicus briefs help in persuading the Supreme Court to grant review and appellate courts to grant rehearing.[182] Amicus briefs on the merits, however, seem to have much less success, unless filed by the government.[183]

176. *Id.* at 779–87.
177. *Id.* at 830.
178. *Id.*
179. Laroche, *supra* n.97, at 751.
180. Simard, *supra* n.104, at 688–96.
181. Colleen V. Chien, *Patent Amicus Briefs: What the Court's Friends Can Teach Us About the Patent System*, 1 U.C. Irvine L. Rev. 397, 432 (2011); *see also* Joy Lynn Bala, *Amicus Briefs: Sounding Off on Reforming Inequitable Conduct*, 45 Loy. L.A. L. Rev. 125, 143 (2011).
182. *Id.* at 424–27.
183. *Id.* at 427–431.

## WHAT ARE THE FUNCTIONS OF AMICUS BRIEFS?

The amicus brief serves a number of functions. Generally speaking, amicus briefs can be useful to expose novel facts or legal arguments as well as signal to the court the importance of the case.[184] Other functions include:

- examining policy issues;
- providing a more attractive advocate;
- supporting the grant of discretionary review;
- supplementing a party's brief;
- endorsing a particular position;
- providing a historical perspective;
- providing technical assistance;
- showing potential unintended consequences;
- muting or minimizing expected precedent or paving the way for future precedent;
- defining the nature and scope of a problem;
- correcting, limiting, publishing or "de-publishing" a decision; and
- applying political pressure.[185]

One or more of these purposes will usually guide the decision whether to spend resources on the filing of an amicus brief. Some organizations make ad hoc decisions on whether to file amicus briefs, and others develop specific policy statements on amicus participation. An Internet search of "amicus brief policy" will reveal numerous such policy statements by professional associations.

---

184. David Orozco & James G. Conley, *Friends of the Court: Using Amicus Briefs to Identify Corporate Advocacy Positions in Supreme Court Patent Litigation*, 2011 U. Il. J.L. Tech. & Pol'y 107 (2011). These authors also believe that by promoting perceptions of responsiveness and inclusiveness, accepting "amicus briefs enhance[s] the court's own institutional legitimacy and standing in the eyes of others." *Id.* at 122–23.

185. Baron, *supra* n.35, at 4–8; Charles E. Carpenter, Jr., *The Role of Amicus Briefing*, in Appellate Practice in Federal and State Courts, at 9–15 to 9–21(2013, David M. Axelrad, ed.).

### *Examining Policy Issues*

When larger policy or social issues are implicated by a decision, the amicus has a role that the parties often cannot play because, for example, the facts may be outside the record. Further, the parties are confined by the procedures in the case as well as the extent to which error has been preserved below. The amicus, however, can weigh in on any number of issues, even those that are not technically before the court, and emphasize the policies and values at stake.

The facts an amicus presents may not be contained in the record of the case, and may extend beyond the facts of the particular case at issue.[186] Such facts should be common-knowledge facts or resemble legislative facts rather than facts about the particular case.[187] Nevertheless, the amicus should not lose sight of the case actually before the court and should not stray too far from core legal issues. After all, the court is limited to deciding the dispute at hand. If an amicus emphasizes policy issues that are not implicated by the case, then the amicus can actually hurt the litigant it supports.

Problems can arise, of course, concerning the validity of information outside the record. One commentator has discussed the reliance of the National Labor Relations Board (NLRB) on social science statistics filed by parties and amici, given that the NLRB has no economists on staff.[188] The commentator questions whether the Board can effectively evaluate such data. At a higher level, a commentator critiques the reliance of the United States Supreme Court on economic evidence submitted in amicus briefs in antitrust cases, likening the Court's action in antitrust law as akin to rulemaking under the Administrative Procedure Act.[189] The commentator notes that the members of the Court have no particular training in industrial organization and none has an economics degree.[190]

---

186. SUPREME COURT PRACTICE, *supra* n.12, at 741–42.
187. *Id.*
188. Xenia Tashlitsky, *A Critique of Supplying the NLRB with Social Science Expertise Through Party/Amicus Briefs*, 1 U.C. IRVINE L. REV. 1257 (2011).
189. Rebecca Haw, *Amicus Briefs and the Sherman Act: Why Antitrust Needs a New Deal*, 89 TEX. L. REV. 1247 (2011).
190. *Id.* at 1263.

### *Providing a More Attractive Advocate*

In some situations, a party to the litigation may not be the strongest advocate for a position because it is not an attractive litigant. One may recall Justice Clark's observation in *Mapp v. Ohio* that legal rules in the area of criminal justice are often for the "'benefit of a guilty person.'"[191] An amicus may be a much more attractive voice in articulating an argument.

An example is an amicus brief solicited by billboard owners attacking a city ordinance banning billboards in *Metromedia, Inc. v. City of San Diego*.[192] The owners solicited amicus support from the American Civil Liberties Union, which then argued that a ban on billboards would chill an effective form of political speech. The billboard owners were not in a position to advance the argument because they rented the billboards to others and did not themselves engage in first amendment activities.[193] Another example is, once again, the ACLU in the Supreme Court case dealing with a Nazi parade in Skokie, Illinois.[194] In that case, the ACLU was a much more attractive voice arguing to preserve the first amendment rights at issue than the party who was involved.

### *Supporting a Grant of Discretionary Review*

Another role for the amicus is to increase the chance that a court will grant discretionary review. Supreme Court Rule 10 states the considerations governing review on writ of certiorari. Rule 10 states that a petition for writ of certiorari will be granted "only for compelling reasons."[195] The rule then lists examples of the "character" of the reasons the Court will consider, although the rule states that the listed considerations are "neither controlling nor fully measuring the Court's discretion." The listed considerations are:

(a) a United States court of appeals has entered a decision in conflict with the decision of another United States court of appeals on the same "important" matter; has decided an "important" federal question in

191. 367 U.S. 643, 658 (1961) (quoting Miller v. United States, 357 U.S. 301, 313 (1958)).
192. 453 U.S. 490 (1981).
193. *See* Ennis, *supra* n.156, at 606–07.
194. Nat'l Socialist Party of Am. v. Village of Skokie, 432 U.S. 43 (1997).
195. S. Ct. R. 10.

a way that conflicts with a decision by a state court of last resort; or has so far departed from the accepted and usual course of judicial proceedings, or sanctioned such a departure by a lower court, as to call for an exercise of this Court's supervisory power.

(b) a state court of last resort has decided an important federal question in a way that conflicts with the decision of another state court of last resort or the decision of a United States court of appeals; and

(c) a state court or a United States court of appeals has decided an important question of federal law that has not been, but should be, settled by this Court, or has decided an important federal question in a way that conflicts with relevant decisions of this Court.[196]

Obviously, the United States Supreme Court hears very few cases, and the same is true of many state supreme courts. The amicus that files its brief prior to consideration of the petition for certiorari may help a party overcome the initial hurdle of obtaining a grant of discretionary review.[197] Indeed, the mere fact that many amicus briefs have been filed may convince the court that the case is significant and review should be granted.[198] Justice Roberts has stated that having amicus support on a petition makes a big difference because it helps convince the court that the issue is important to more people than just the parties. Amicus support may influence a jaded court that suspects that most petitioners exaggerate the importance of their cases in an effort to obtain review. For these same reasons, an amicus who is satisfied with the lower court's decision should postpone filing an amicus brief until after review is granted—an earlier filing may serve only to emphasize the importance of the case and encourage review.[199]

196. S. Ct. R. 10.

197. *See* Supreme Court Practice, *supra* n.12, at 513 (noting that, in the United States Supreme Court, amicus briefs "add force to a petitioner's contention that the case has public importance extending beyond the interests of the parties").

198. John F. Duffy, *The* Festo *Decision and the Return of the Supreme Court to the Bar of Patents,* 2002 Supreme Court Rev. 273, 300 (2002).

199. Supreme Court Practice, *supra* n.12, at 513.

### *Supplementing a Party's Brief*

The fourth function of an amicus brief—supplementing a party's brief—may be the most frequent. Sometimes significant issues arise in cases in which the parties are represented by inexperienced or unskilled lawyers. In these cases, the quality of briefing can be poor, creating the risk that the issues and the parties' positions will not be presented clearly to the court.[200] The amicus can shore up a party's weak brief.

Even a good brief may omit, owing to page limitations, case law developments in other states or other relevant material.[201] This is particularly true in complex cases, where parties simply may not have the space to say all that needs to be said. Amicus support can provide the additional arguments that simply do not fit into, or otherwise do not appear in, the main briefs. They can also "defend" arguments made by opposing amici.[202]

Finally, in some cases, the amicus may make arguments that a party omits because it prefers not to make them. For example, the party may believe that it is less risky to distinguish a prior case rather than argue that it should be overruled. An amicus brief may be more suited to advance the riskier position.

A form of supplementation that is usually not advisable is restating or adding to the issues as framed by the parties. While flexibility is a hallmark of amicus briefs, restating issues may create inconsistencies, and trying to

200. Stephen M. Shapiro, *Amicus Briefs in the Supreme Court,* ABA SEC. LITIG., APPELLATE PRACTICE MANUAL 341 (Priscilla Anne Schros ed., ABA 1992); MAKING YOUR CASE, *supra* n.36, at 104, 106 (noting, however, that it is unethical to allow the party to dictate what points the amicus brief should cover).

201. Brief writers have sometimes attempted to avoid page limitations by reducing font size and making arguments in the small print of footnotes. *See* Voices for Choices v. Ill. Bell Tel. Co., 339 F.3d 322, 544 (7th Cir. 2003) (Posner, J. in chambers) (noting that amicus briefs "may be used to make an end run around court-imposed limitations on the length of the parties' briefs"); *cf.* United States v. Boeing Co., 73 F. Supp. 2d 897, 900 (S.D. Ohio 1999) (rejecting argument that amicus brief was in reality an impermissible surreply). Appellate courts have curbed this conduct by declining to accept briefs when they violate rules governing font size and footnotes. Federal Rule of Appellate Procedure 32 sets the maximum length of briefs and specifies permissible font size, typeface, margins, spacing, and paper size. Local rules of courts of appeals may have additional rules and limitations. Supreme Court Rule 33 imposes detailed printing specifications.

202. MAKING YOUR CASE, *supra* n.36, at 106.

reframe issues is not a justification for an amicus brief, unless the parties have truly been unable to articulate the issues in a meaningful way.[203]

### *Providing a Historical Perspective*

The record on appeal often concentrates on the facts at hand, not the larger historical perspective. Sometimes, historians testify at trial, as Stephen Ambrose did in a suit against cigarette manufacturers.[204] When that has not happened, however, amicus briefs can provide a historical background. The contribution of historical background was a crucial feature of the amicus briefs submitted in *Brown v. Board of Education,*[205] according to one commentator.[206]

### *Providing Technical Expertise*

As lawsuits have become more complex and technical, particularly with respect to scientific issues, there is an increasing need for amicus briefs to provide technical assistance.[207] The Third Circuit has expressly noted that "'[s]ome friends of the court are entities with particular expertise not possessed by any party to the case.'"[208] Such expert amicus briefs mark perhaps a return to one of the early purposes of amicus briefs—preventing courts from basing their decisions on erroneous scientific or technical concepts.

### *Endorsing a Party*

An amicus brief may be filed to show support for a party or a position, including a risky position that a party may not have addressed out of concern for its effect on the overall appeal.

A typical endorsing amicus brief filed by a national association may support a single litigant's claims that an adverse decision will have far-reaching

---

203. Lawrence S. Ebner, *Representing Amicus Curiae*, Aspatore (Mar. 2013).
204. Jonathan D. Martin, *Historians at the Gate: Accommodating Expert Historical Testimony in Federal Courts,* 78 N.Y.U.L. Rev. 1518, 1518–19 (2003).
205. 347 U.S. 483 (1954).
206. Martin, *supra* n.204, at 1527–28.
207. *See* Stephanie Tai, *Friendly Science: Medical, Scientific, and Technical Amici, Before the Supreme Court,* 78 Wash. U.L.Q. 789 (2000).
208. Neonatology Assocs., P.A. v. Comm'r of Internal Revenue, 293 F.3d 128, 132 (3d Cir. 2002) (quoting Luther T. Montford, *When Does the Curiae Need an Amicus?,* I J. App. Prac. & Process 279 (1999)).

ramifications. An example is *Gideon v. Wainwright.*[209] In that case, the State of Florida was defending against a challenge to the right of a state to try an indigent felony defendant without providing him counsel. The Attorney General of Florida wrote to his fellow state attorneys general asking them to file amicus briefs supporting Florida in the case. The Attorney General of Minnesota, Walter Mondale, was so enraged with Florida's position that he participated in the filing of an amicus brief *opposing* it. The brief was endorsed by 22 other states.[210] Thus, the lesson is two-fold:

- indiscriminate canvassing for amicus support can be a risky venture; and
- in the proper case, it may be a good idea to search for an unexpected friend.

Sometimes a "me too" amicus brief is effective. They may be influential because of raw political pressure. Indeed, Justice Scalia has observed that the cover of briefs by national trade associations and the like often are sufficient to accomplish the purpose of showing the broad national impact of a decision.[211] Usually, however, a "me-too" amicus brief is simply redundant and not appreciated by the reviewing court.[212]

### *Seeking to Correct, Limit, Publish, or "De-Publish" an Opinion*

The remaining functions of amicus briefs are narrower. An amicus brief may supplement a party's brief by noting the need to correct a decision that is not yet final. Often this happens after a decision has been rendered, but before the time for rehearing has passed. Further, an amicus brief may do nothing other than attempt to limit a feared unfavorable decision so that it does not go beyond the particular dispute at hand. In seeking to limit a decision, an amicus should expressly explain the unwanted ramifications or consequences of the expected opinion if it is not so limited.

---

209. 372 U.S. 335 (1963).
210. *See* Anthony Lewis, Gideon's Trumpet, chapter 10, 152–56 (1964); Rains, *supra* n.110, at 42.
211. Making Your Case, *supra* n.36, at 103.
212. Supreme Court Practice, *supra* n.12, at 742–43.

Finally, in some jurisdictions, an amicus aware of an unpublished or non-precedential decision may suggest the decision is worthy of publication or citation.[213] In California, an amicus may seek to have an opinion that it considers unwise or troublesome "de-published" and thus purged from the official reporter.[214]

### *Other Purposes*

An amicus brief may serve many other functions. It may define the nature and scope of an issue. It may explain to the court potential consequences of a particular decision that the court would not desire. It may attempt to affect other litigation. A less ambitious amicus brief may attempt to persuade the court to narrow its holding in the case before it or to begin to develop a legal doctrine that can later blossom with the appropriate set of facts or the proper parties.[215]

## WHO FILES AN AMICUS BRIEF AND WHY?

An amicus brief may come from almost anywhere. Someone may be monitoring your appeal and seek leave to file a brief on their own initiative. In some instances, the court may invite participation by an amicus, although the United States Supreme Court is more prone to do so than an intermediate court of appeals.[216] Usually, however, an amicus appears because a party has solicited amicus support. The Supreme Court will not entertain amicus briefs filed by non-lawyers or by lawyers who are not members of the Supreme Court Bar.[217]

---

213. *See, e.g.*, California Rule of Court 987.

214. California Rule of Court 979.

215. *See* Carpenter, *supra* n.185, at 9–17 to 9–21.

216. John Turron, *The U.S. Supreme Court Asks White House to File Amicus Brief in Barclays Case as Britain Publicly Threatens Retaliation*, TAX NOTES INT'L. May 24, 1993, at 1246–47. *See, e.g.*, Thrifty-Tel, Inc. v. Bezenek, 46 Cal. App. 4th 1559, 1569, 54 Cal Rptr 2d 468, 475 (Cal. Ct. App. 1996) (court notes that it had solicited amicus briefs); Beverly Hills Multispeciality Group, Inc. v. Workers' Comp. Appeals Bd., 26 Cal. App. 4th 789, 32 Cal. Rptr. 293 (Ca. Ct. App. 1994) (court had invited several organizations to submit amicus briefs).

217. SUPREME COURT PRACTICE, *supra* n.12, at 516.

The most influential amicus is still the United States Solicitor General.[218] The Solicitor General is the chief advocate before the Court for the executive branch of the federal government and an informal advisor to the Court. Some refer to the Solicitor General as "the tenth Justice."[219] The Solicitor General appears in approximately 70 to 80 percent of the Supreme Court's cases each term.[220]

The Solicitor General is in the unique position of being asked periodically by the Supreme Court to provide its view as to whether the Court should grant certiorari. The Supreme Court issues such requests ("Calls for the View of the Solicitor General," or "CVSG") because many cases request the Court to interpret or apply a federal statutory, or regulatory scheme that a federal agency administers. The parties' views on the issue are usually diametrically opposed. The objective view of the Solicitor General can help the Court gauge more accurately whether in fact the question has wide ranging consequences.[221] The Solicitor General can also advise the Court whether planned statutory or regulatory amendments may render the question moot.[222]

When a petition for certiorari is pending and the Court issues a CVSG, the advocate should "greet, meet, and engage the invitee in conversation."[223] Since the Solicitor General's opinion is given extraordinary weight,[224] it is helpful to arrange to meet with him or her to present the client's position on the matter and to offer to provide background or record materials. One commentator wisely suggests that the advocate should address at the meeting

218. *Id.* at 797 (citing LEE EPSTEIN ET AL., THE SUPREME COURT COMPENDIUM: DATA, DECISIONS & DEVELOPMENTS 632 (2d ed. 1996); Kevin T. McGuire, *Explaining Executive Success in the U.S. Supreme Court,* 51 POL. RES. Q. 505, 507, 522 (1998); Reginald Sheehan et al., *Ideology, Status, and the Differential Success of Direct Parties Before the Supreme Court,* 86 AM. POL. SCI. REV. 464, 466 (1992)).

219. Wohl, *supra* n.2, at 48.

220. Patricia A. Millett, *We're Your Government and We're Here to Help: Obtaining Amicus Support from the Federal Government in Supreme Court Cases,* 10 J. OF APPELLATE PRACTICE & PROCESS 209, 210 (Spring 2009).

221. *Id.* at 213.

222. *Id.* at 214.

223. *Id.* at 216.

224. Because of the importance of the Solicitor General's opinion, Millett advises parties to write their petitions for certiorari in a way that will generate a CVSG by highlighting the government's expertise with the statutory scheme at issue, its role in administering the relevant statute, and the likely impact of the decision on governmental interests and operations. *Id.* at 217.

the policy and interests of the government, not the particular injustice done to the client, and provide a comprehensive checklist of topics: how the ruling will affect the day-to-day administration of the regulatory program, how the decision will affect legal positions and rules of law that the government has sought to establish or resist, whether the ruling is consistent with the policy interests of the government, the prospects of obtaining a decision that is consonant with the government's interests, and whether the case is appropriate for Supreme Court review at this particular time.[225] The meeting will be attended by a number of well-prepared lawyers representing the affected government agencies and the questioning can be as rigorous as a Supreme Court argument. The advocate should be well prepared. The advocate can provide a short memorandum to the Solicitor General's office within two weeks following the meeting.

If no CVSG is issued, it is unlikely that a party can independently enlist the Solicitor General as a supporter of a grant of certiorari. However, once the petition is granted, the Solicitor General may be willing to participate even if the office did not participate at an earlier stage. The advocate should request a meeting and try to persuade the Solicitor General to participate based on the government's institutional interests, the need for consistency with prior positions, and the potential implications for federal legislation or programs.[226]

Even when not asked, the Solicitor General may submit an amicus brief without consent of the parties or leave of the Court. If the Solicitor General plans to appear in support of the opponent, a meeting may also be worthwhile to try to persuade the Solicitor General to adopt a narrow view or a less damaging position. The Solicitor General often obtains permission from the Court to participate in oral argument. (The appendix to this book contains, as Example 11, excerpts from an amicus brief filed by the U.S. Solicitor General.)[227]

Amicus briefs are sometimes filed by former or existing government officials. Justice Breyer cited an amicus brief from former FCC Commissioners

225. *Id.* at 219–20.

226. *Id.* at 225.

227. *See* Ricci v. DeStefano, 556 U.S. 1162 (2009) (granting motion filed by Solicitor General to participate in oral argument as amicus curiae and for divided argument).

when dissenting from the Court's opinion in the fleeting expletives case, *Federal Communications Commission v. Fox Television Stations, Inc.*[228] Members of Congress are filing amicus briefs with increasing frequency.[229] Former judges have also participated in filing amicus briefs, as in the West Virginia campaign contribution case.[230]

As discussed earlier, amicus briefs are filed with increasing frequency in the United States Supreme Court, in state supreme courts, and in intermediate appellate courts in both the federal and state systems. The reason for their increase is an increasing recognition that judicial decisions may have profound implications beyond the particular case.[231] Another reason is the proliferation of advocacy groups.[232] Amicus briefs are a cost-effective way to make a legal pitch to the United States Supreme Court. Filing an amicus brief is sometimes seen as a simple way for the public interest group to increase its visibility. As a result, "cosmetic" amicus briefs are filed, which add nothing to the legal arguments.[233]

The amicus may not care who wins the particular lawsuit but is very interested in how the case will affect the law. Amicus briefs are particularly appropriate when private disputes have major implications for the public. To expand upon the earlier classification, amici can more specifically be divided into these groups:

- special interest organizations and trade groups;
- parties in other, similar cases;
- the government, or some agency or official of the government;
- persons affected by, but not parties to, the litigation;
- law professors and attorneys practicing in a specialized field; and
- national, state, and local bar associations.

---

228. 556 U.S. 502, 558 (2009) (Breyer, J., dissenting).
229. Carpenter, *supra* n.185, at 9–15.
230. *Id.* (discussing Caperton v. A.T. Massey Coal Co., 556 U.S. 868 (2009) in which many former state judges submitted an amicus brief).
231. Wohl, *supra* n.2, at 46 (quoting Bruce Ennis of Jenner & Block, Washington, D.C.).
232. *Id.* (quoting Dean William L. Robinson of the District of Columbia School of Law, then chair of the ABA Standing Committee on Amicus Curiae Briefs).
233. *Id.*

Some organizations and interest groups have established specific amicus programs. Examples include: the American Bar Association, American Association of Trial Lawyers and its individual state affiliates, the Product Liability Advisory Counsel, the Defense Research Institute, various state associations of defense counsel, the Christian Legal Society, and many others.

For some organizations, the amicus program is the organization's largest single activity. In such organizations, there is usually a committee or group that reviews cases and decides what cases are deserving of the submission of an amicus brief. Some organizations participate at only the appellate level, but some are willing to submit briefs at the trial court level in support of important motions. If a party intends to solicit the help of such organizations, it is important to make the request as early as possible.

Some organizations have a questionnaire or desired format for submitting requests for amicus support. In many situations, those organizations are looking for law firms or lawyers who are willing to donate their time to prepare an amicus brief. In other situations, the organizations are willing to pay for amicus briefs. The submission of an amicus brief in an important case can, in effect, be a marketing tool. Obviously, an excellent amicus brief that is widely circulated among clients and counsel is likely to increase the author's visibility and increase his or her chances of being hired in an appeal.

A comprehensive, though by no means exclusive, listing of organizations that regularly file amicus briefs is set forth below:

- **Bar Associations/Trial Lawyers/Law Associations**—Association of American Railroads; American Bar Association; American Bar Association Section on Tort and Insurance Practice; Appellate Advocacy Committee; American Association for Justice; American College of Trial Lawyers; American Academy of Appellate Lawyers; American Board of Trial Advocates; International Association of Defense Counsel;[234] American Intellectual Property Law Association; Association of Trial Lawyers of America; Attorneys Information Exchange Group; Defense Research Institute; Product Liability Advisory Counsel,

234. *See* Mary-Christine Sungaila, *The IADC Amicus Brief Program: Its Increasing Success and Influence*, 81 Defense Counsel J. 32 (2014).

Inc.; International Trademark Association; National Bar Association; Public Defenders; State and Local Bar Associations; Trial Lawyers for Public Justice.

- **Business Groups and Trade Associations**—American Bankers Association; American Farm Bureau Federation; American Hospital Association; American Institute of Architects; American Insurance Association; American Tort Reform Association; American Trucking Associations; Association of American Railroads; Association of International Automobile Manufacturers, Inc.; Association of National Advertisers, Inc.; Biotechnology Industry Organization; Aviation Insurance Association; The Business Roundtable; Chemical Manufacturers Association; Medical Device Manufacturers Association; National Association of Manufacturers; National Cable Television Association; National Paint and Coatings Association; Newspaper Association of America; Northwest Hydroelectric Association; Pharmaceutical Research & Manufacturers Association; Reinsurance Association of America; Software & Information Industry Association (formerly Software Publishers Association); United States Telephone Association; U.S. Chamber of Commerce (National Chamber Litigation Center).
- **Civil Rights Organizations**—ACLU; Asian American Legal Defense and Education Fund; Brennan Center for Justice (NYU); Center for Constitutional Rights; Equal Rights Advocates; Japanese American Citizens League; Lambda Legal Defense and Education Fund; Lawyers' Committee for Civil Rights Under Law; Mexican American Legal Defense and Educational Fund; NAACP; National Congress of American Indians; NOW Legal Defense Fund; National Women's Law Center; The Thomas Jefferson Center.
- **Consumer/Public Interest Associations**—Alliance for Justice; Common Cause; Consumer Federation of America; Public Citizen Litigation Group.
- **Criminal Justice Associations**—Americans for Effective Law Enforcement; Criminal Justice Legal Foundation; Families Against Mandatory Minimums; National Association of Criminal Defense Lawyers; Human Rights Groups; Center for Constitutional Rights; Human Rights Watch;

International Human Rights Law Group; Rights International; Southern Center for Human Rights.

- **Labor and Employment**—AFL-CIO; The ERISA Industry Committee; Equal Employment Advisory Council; AFL-CIO affiliates; National Right to Work Legal Defense Foundation; Department of Labor.[235]
- **Legal Foundations**—Atlantic Legal Foundation; Center for Individual Rights; Institute for Justice; Mountain States Legal Foundation; Pacific Legal Foundation; Southeastern Legal Foundation; Texas Justice Foundation; Washington Legal Foundation.
- **Medical and Dental Professionals**—American Dental Association; American Geriatrics Society; American Hospital Association; American Medical Association; American Nurses Association; American Psychiatric Association; American Psychological Association; National Association of Social Workers.
- **Property Rights/Environmental**—American Farm Bureau Federation; American Sheep Industry Association; Defenders of Property Rights; Defenders of Wildlife; Earthjustice Legal Defense Fund; Environmental Policy Project; Forfeiture Endangers American Rights Foundation; Intellectual Property Owners' Association; National Association of Home Builders; National Cattlemen's Beef Association; National Trust for Historic Preservation.
- **Religious Liberties Groups**[236]—Agudath Israel of America; Alliance Defending Freedom; American Catholic Lawyers Association; American Jewish Congress; Americans United for Separation of Church and State; American Center for Law and Justice; Anti-Defamation League; Catholic League for Religious and Civil Rights; Family Research Council; Institute for Public Affairs, Union of Orthodox Jewish Congregations of America (UOJCA); Liberty Counsel; National Jewish Commission on

235. *See* Deborah Thompson Eisenberg, *Regulation by Amicus: The Department of Labor's Policy Making in the Courts*, 65 Fla. L. Rev. 1223 (2013) (positing that the Department of Labor is attempting to "mold statutory interpretation," especially in wage and hour litigation, by filing amicus briefs).

236. One student commentator has raised Establishment Clause concerns about the Supreme Court's citation of amicus briefs filed by religious organizations. Tiffany Marie Westfall Ferris, *Justices Hawking Jesus: Endorsement Through Citation to Religious Amici in Supreme Court Opinions*, 21 Wm. & Mary Bill Rights J. 1259 (2013).

Law and Public Affairs; People for the American Way; national church organizations, particularly in church property disputes.

- **Governments**—The United States of America; an agency of the United States; any of the States, Commonwealths, Territories, Possessions of the United States; a city, county, town, or similar entity of the United States;[237] Conference of Chief Justices; Council of State Governments; National Association of Attorneys General; National Conference of State Legislatures; National League of Cities; National School Boards Association; State Attorneys General (National Association of Attorneys General).
- **Others**—American Association of Retired Persons; American Association of University Professors; Animal Legal Defense Fund; Center for Education Reform; Children's Defense Fund; Community Defense Counsel; Electronic Freedom Foundation; Home School Legal Defense Association; Independent Women's Forum; International Anti-Euthanasia Task Force; The Media Institute; National Alliance for the Mentally Ill; National Education Association; National Rifle Association; National Voting Rights Institute; Reporters Committee for Freedom of the Press; Welfare Law Center; and Whitman-Walker Clinic.[238]

One commentator has provided a six-page list of organizations that have filed amicus briefs in state and federal courts in Massachusetts. Identified organizations not listed above include:

- Academy of Matrimonial Lawyers
- Alliance of American Insurers
- Alliance of Automotive Manufacturers
- American Heart Association
- Associated Press
- Domestic Violence Council

237. A commentator has noted that, largely owing to historical circumstances, Supreme Court Rule 37.4 does not include foreign sovereigns or Indian Tribes in its list of amici. The commentator argues for their inclusion. Stephen R. McAllister, *The Supreme Court's Treatment of Sovereigns as Amici Curiae*, 13 Green Bag 289 (2010).
238. This list includes amici found at the MegaLaw.com website.

- Federation for Children with Special Needs
- Free Market Foundation
- International Mass Retail Association
- Numerous state and local agencies
- National Consumer Law Center
- Professional Liability Foundation, Ltd.
- Securities Industry Association
- Student Press Law Center
- Surety & Fidelity Association of America
- United Policyholders, Inc.
- Urban League[239]

Why these organizations file amicus briefs varies, of course. Questions to ask in determining whether to file an amicus brief include: whether the parties will raise the "correct" issue or the issue that concerns the potential amicus curiae; whether the parties can be expected to brief the case well; and whether the facts of the case are appropriate for raising the issue that interests the potential amicus curiae.[240] There are also practical considerations, such as whether the parties may settle prior to submission, so that the amicus effort will be wasted; whether jurisdictional problems exist; and whether there is time to file a well-written amicus brief under the court's briefing schedule.[241]

## WHEN AND HOW DO YOU SEEK AMICUS SUPPORT?

The lawyer should not seek amicus support in a routine appellate matter. In such cases, courts are likely to resent any proliferation of the briefing. The case that is appropriate for amicus support is the policy-laden case that raises novel issues or challenges the validity of a long-standing but

---

239. Joanne D'Alcomo & Hon Susan Garsh, *Role of the Amicus Brief*, II Appellate Practice In Massachusetts ch. 17 (2008) (Mass. Continuing Legal Education, Inc.).
240. Carrie Ann Wozniak, *Amicus Briefs: What Have They Done for Courts Lately*, Fla. B.J., Jun. 2012.
241. *Id.*

controversial rule of law. Amicus support is also appropriate when it is best for someone other than a party to address the broader policy issues, or when there are larger issues at stake than those the parties desire to argue. A countervailing consideration is whether the filing of an amicus brief may result in attracting powerful amicus support for the opposing party. In such a situation, the lawyer should conduct a risk-benefit analysis before seeking amicus support.

If amicus support is desired, the lawyer must locate a suitable amicus, convince it to participate, and assure that the amicus brief will in fact support the lawyer's position. The lawyer seeking amicus support should, of course, explain why the case is important to the potential amicus. Sometimes, it is helpful to present empirical data or analysis to convince the prospective amicus to participate. If the lawyer's presentation is not successful, the lawyer may have little chance to persuade a disinterested appellate court.

Clients often can help by identifying potential amici in the industry.[242] Trade associations and public-interest groups are possible amicus candidates. Indeed, because such groups are so vitally interested in legal matters—particularly those before the United States Supreme Court—they often volunteer amicus support. If the case deals with legislation, a trade association may have participated in drafting the legislation and, therefore, may give amicus support concerning the legislators' original intent. Finally, when practicing before the United States Supreme Court, the lawyer may also consider discussing possible amicus support from the Solicitor General of the United States.

An amicus brief can be helpful in showing the effects of a decision on non-parties, or on persons situated differently from the parties.[243] Thus, in deciding whether to seek amicus support, the party should consider how the case may potentially affect other persons and why the amicus is in a position to perceive the case in a broader or different context.[244]

It is wise to seek amicus support early. Many jurisdictions require an amicus brief to be filed with or soon after the principal brief of the

---

242. David G. Knibb, FEDERAL COURT OF APPEALS MANUAL § 31.14 (4th ed. 2000).
243. *See* Robert L. Stern, *Tips for Appellate Advocates,* 15 LITIG., Spring 1989, at 67.
244. *Cf.* SUPREME COURT PRACTICE, *supra* n.12, at 515, 741–42 (discussing potential benefits of amicus briefs).

party it supports. Moreover, time is needed for the amicus to discuss the issues with the supported party. Duplication of issues by an amicus is not recommended.[245]

Amici may have divergent viewpoints. Even allies can disagree over certain issues, and a bevy of conflicting briefs is not likely to be persuasive. Thus, according to one commentator, the lead counsel has several critical liaison functions in the context of an amicus brief: contacting potential amici; giving amici drafts of the primary brief; reviewing drafts of amicus briefs; and circulating updated lists of the names, addresses, and telephone numbers of potential amici.[246] These liaison functions can be onerous for someone in charge of preparing a lead brief.[247]

## HOW DO YOU WRITE AN EFFECTIVE AMICUS BRIEF?

Before beginning to write, the author of an amicus brief should obtain a copy of all other briefs that have been filed. After reading the briefs filed by other parties, it is advisable to meet, or at least speak, with counsel for the party being supported. The party's counsel may elaborate on the issues in the case, identify gaps in the briefing, suggest policy issues, and so forth. The supported party can also provide the amicus with record materials to aid the amicus in avoiding factual errors. If, however, there are timing, cost, or other practical problems associated with obtaining the record, the amicus may proceed without it. Since the amicus focuses on broad policy issues, and can avoid factual references, the record is often not critical to the writing of the brief.

Before starting to write, it can also be beneficial for the amicus to contact other potential amici in the same industry to determine whether a joint brief might be possible, at shared cost.[248] Even if more than one brief is filed, the various amici can agree to cover specific topics. Appellate practitioner

245. *Id.* at 378 (restating admonitions contained in Rule 37.1).
246. Rains, *supra* n.110, at 57–60.
247. *Id.*
248. A helpful checklist for a party who is considering enlisting amicus help is found in Herr, David & McCarthy, Michael, *Amici Curiae: Not Just Friends of the Court Anymore*, 9 Prac. Litigator 11, 16 (May 1998).

Kathleen Sullivan orchestrated amicus support in one case that challenged bans of direct wine shipments to out-of-state consumers: "We urged our friends to cover specific topics that add value to the merits . . . One laid out the history, and another laid out alternative regulations for wine shipment, showing how to protect minors and collect taxes."[249] You should be aware that judges often have clerks screen amicus briefs. For example, in the United States Supreme Court, the justices will have their clerks screen the briefs using "cues" to flag for the justices which briefs they believe should be read. Nevertheless, the justices usually will read briefs submitted by the Solicitor General, those written by advocates in whose integrity and ability the justices have special confidence, or those submitted by organizations that have a reputation for excellence, such as those filed by the ACLU.[250] Similarly, the justices can be depended upon to read briefs authored by prominent academics, well-known law firms with recognized Supreme Court practices, and organizations with particular expertise (e.g., the American Medical Association). Clerks say that they particularly like getting briefs from academics in complex cases that do not urge an outcome but provide useful background and context.

### General Contents

Ideally, an amicus brief serves to bring to the court's attention a perspective that is unique to the filing party. For example, the amicus might provide the court with background research or a thorough discussion of the relevant cases, an explanation of how the case fits into the appellate court's jurisprudence, a review of an organization's experience with the statute or rule at issue, a discussion of the background of an industry or relevant regulations, or an explanation of how the case impacts the amicus differently from the parties before the court.[251] Rule 37.1 of the U.S. Supreme Court Rules warns that an amicus brief that does not bring new and relevant material to the Court is a burden and its filing is not favored.[252] This advice should

249. *Quoted in* ABA Journal, November 2007, *Friends of the Court Are Friends of Mine.*
250. Making Your Case, *supra* n.36, at 103.
251. Shapiro, *supra* n.200 at 342, 345–46.
252. But conversely, amicus briefs cannot raise issues that are truly unique. Courts frequently reject arguments made by an amicus party on the grounds that an amicus may not introduce a new argument into a case. *See, e.g.*, United States v. Sturm. Ruger & Co., 84 F.3d 1, 6 (1st

be taken seriously by a party considering filing an amicus brief in any court. If an amicus can offer no unique arguments or viewpoint and simply wishes to support a particular group or industry, then the party should simply file a one-page brief that contains a statement of general support for a party or a position. The brief should not repeat arguments already made by the other parties.

The Federal Rules of Appellate Procedure and the Rules of the United States Supreme Court provide guidelines for the contents and form of the amicus brief. Rule 37.5 of the Supreme Court Rules states that the rules applicable to other briefs also apply to amicus briefs, except that the amicus brief need only contain: (1) the interest of the amicus; (2) the summary of the argument; (3) the argument; and (4) the conclusion. A summary of the argument is not required, however, if the brief is submitted in support of a petition for certiorari. Supreme Court Rule 37.3 requires that the cover and beginning text of an amicus brief "identify the party supported or indicate whether it suggests affirmance or reversal."[253] Because the United States, states, and local government units are not required to obtain consent to file amicus briefs, this rule does not apply to briefs submitted on their behalf. An electronic version of the brief must be filed in addition to the booklet-format brief. No reply brief is permitted.

Federal Rule of Appellate Procedure 29(c) requires that an amicus brief contain the following sections: (1) if the amicus brief is a corporation, the brief must include a disclosure statement like that required of parties by Rule 26.1; (2) a table of contents, with page references; (3) a table of authorities, including cases (alphabetically arranged), statutes and other authorities with references to the pages of the brief where they are cited; (4) a concise statement of the identity of the amicus curiae, its interest in the case, and the source of its authority to file; (5) with the exception of the United States or any agency thereof, a disclosure of whether counsel for a party authored the brief in whole or in part, whether a party or its counsel made a monetary contribution intended to fund the preparation or submission

---

Cir. 1996); Puerto Rico Telephone Co. v. Telecommunications Regulatory Bd. of Puerto Rico, 189 F.3d 1, 16, n.13 (1st Cir. 1999); Universal City Studios v. Corley, 273 F.3d 429, 444 (2d Cir. 2001).

253. Supreme Court Practice, *supra* n.12, at 738.

of the amicus brief, and whether any other party (other than the amicus curiae, its counsel, or its members) made a monetary contribution intended to fund the preparation or submission of the brief; (6) an argument, which may be preceded by a summary and which need not include a statement of the applicable standard of review; and (7) a certificate of compliance, if required by Federal Rule of Appellate Procedure 32(a)(7).

The disclosure of participation or monetary contribution by a party to the case or a third party is modeled on Supreme Court Rule 37.6, which was enacted in 1997 and revised in 2007. A main purpose of the requirement in Rule 32(c)(5) is to deter parties from using an amicus brief to circumvent the page limits on party briefs.[254] Furthermore, the disclosure will help judges assess whether the amicus thinks the issue important enough to shoulder the burden of the cost and effort of filing an amicus brief. In determining whether the brief was authored by a party "in part" it will be useful to refer to interpretations of Supreme Court Rule 37.6.

Rule 29(c) does not make clear where the corporate disclosure statement should appear, unlike Supreme Court Rule 37.6, which requires the disclosure to be in the first footnote of the first page of text, but the Committee Note for Rule 29(c) suggests it should be placed before the table of contents.[255] The brief must also comply with the form requirements of Rule 32, which governs requirements such as the cover style, binding, line spacing, and typeface.

Expect to meet filing deadlines. An amicus may not obtain extensions of time for filing. However, if a party obtains an extension of time, the extension may change the due date for the amicus brief. As one commentator, Dan Schweitzer, has suggested, you can take advantage of the extra time to polish the brief or solicit others to support the submission.[256] He also advises amici that support a petition for certiorari, to find out from the petitioner whether the respondent has waived his right to file an opposition brief because this will require you to submit the brief much sooner.[257]

254. Fed. R. App. P. 29(c)(5), Advisory Comm. Note—2010 Amendment.
255. *Id.*
256. Schweitzer, *supra* n.58, at 526.
257. *Id.* at 527 (in these circumstances, "the cert petition will be circulated to the Justices far sooner than expected.").

Most of the examples in the Appendix show fairly traditional formats and contents of amicus briefs. They are in contrast with Examples 2 and 3, which are much shorter letter briefs that do not follow the usual format of briefs. You can also find examples of a wide variety of styles by linking to briefs found on http://www.lawsource.com/also/usa.cgi?usb or http://www.abanet.org/amicus.

Related to the contents of the amicus brief is its cover. In the United States Supreme Court, Rule 33.1 (g) specifies three different colors for the covers of different types of amicus briefs: (1) cream for an amicus brief filed at the petition stage; (2) light green for an amicus brief filed on behalf of the plaintiff, petitioner, appellant, or neither side at the merits stage or in an original action at the exceptions stage; and (3) dark green for an amicus brief filed on behalf of the defendant, respondent, or appellee at the merits stage or in an original action at the exceptions stage. In the federal circuit courts, FRAP 32(a)(2) requires the cover of an amicus brief to be green. The lawyer should always check the local court rules to see if there is a particular color required for the cover of the amicus brief.

### *The Statement of Interest*

There is often a tendency to regard the statement of interest as unimportant. To the contrary, it can be the most important section of the amicus brief. Justice Roberts has commented that he wants to know immediately what interest the amicus has and how that interest differs from the parties' interests. Another justice has observed that he decides whether to read the rest of the brief based on the contents of the statement of interest.[258] One commentator offers these excellent suggestions about the content of the statement of interest of the amicus:

> Identify the amicus. Concisely identify the person or organization seeking to file the brief. If it is an organization, state when it was formed and for what purpose. Briefly identify its members and describe its

258. Of course, judges approach briefs differently. Some judges have been known to skip over the statement of interest entirely. For this reason, it is a good idea to reiterate in the body of the brief the expertise of the amicus.

activities. Mention previous amicus filings if it would strengthen the statement of interest.

Identify the interests of the amicus. The role of amicus curiae has changed over time; typically, the modern amicus is more readily identified with the interests of a particular party. If that interest is not self-evident from the description of the amicus, state the interest briefly.

Describe how the amicus can assist the court. This is important. Identify the special perspective the amicus can bring to the issues in the case. Explain why the resolution of those issues will have an impact beyond the parties to the litigation. Discuss how the amicus will assist the court in analyzing the issues and deciding the case.[259]

The statement of the interest of the amicus may be extensive. A lengthy statement appears in Example 7 in the Appendix. Sometimes, the statement of interest may extend to several pages, if it is important to identify how the court's ruling may affect the amicus or to explain to the court the special expertise or experience of the amicus. Whether the statement of interest is long or short, it is an opportunity to draw the court's attention to the broader ramifications of its decision and enhance the credibility of the amicus curiae.

### *Issues on Appeal*

One limitation on an amicus brief is that it usually cannot raise issues that the parties could have raised but did not.[260] The Supreme Court has said that it will not decide issues raised by amici that were not decided by the court of appeals or raised by the interested party.[261] As an example, in *Gilmer v. Interstate/Johnson Lane Corp.*,[262] the Supreme Court refused to tackle an issue raised by amici but not properly presented to the Court by the parties.

259. Parlee, *supra* n.90, at 15 (footnotes omitted).
260. *See* Preservation Coalition, Inc. v. Pierce, 667 F.2d 851 (9th Cir. 1982).
261. *See. e.g.*, PPL Corp. v. Comm'r of Internal Revenue, 133 S. Ct. 1897, 1907 n.6 (2013); United Parcel Serv., Inc. v. Mitchell, 451 U.S. 56, 60 n.2 (1981); Bell v. Wolfish, 441 U.S. 520, 531 n.13 (1979).
262. 500 U.S. 2 0, 25 n.2 (1991).

Similarly, in *Davis v. United States,*[263] the Supreme Court declined to consider a question raised by amici about interpretation of a federal statute on which the Department of Justice expressly declined to take a position. In *Reno v. Koray,*[264] the Court also refused to consider an issue raised by an amicus after respondent had waived it in the court of appeals and declined to renew it before the Supreme Court. Nevertheless, the Supreme Court has acknowledged its power to consider issues raised only by an amicus on "rare occasions,"[265] with notable examples being *Teague v. Lane,*[266] *Mapp v. Ohio,*[267] and *Regents v. Bakke.*[268]

Other appellate courts are likely to follow the same policy of not entertaining issues raised only by an amicus curiae. In *Compton v. Subaru of America, Inc.,*[269] the Tenth Circuit declined to entertain an issue raised by amicus curiae over the applicability of *Daubert*[270] to all expert testimony. In *Swan v. Peterson,*[271] the court refused to consider whether a criminal defendant would be convicted on hearsay alone because the issue was raised only by the amicus. In *Tyler v. City of Manhattan,*[272] the Ninth Circuit noted that it has discretion to consider issues raised only by an amicus curiae, but confined that discretion to "exceptional" cases.[273] The Ninth Circuit again followed that rule in *United States v. Wahchumwah.*[274]

"Exceptional" circumstances may justify reviewing an issue raised only by amici when: "(1) a party attempts to raise the issue by reference to the amicus brief; or (2) the issue 'involves a jurisdictional question or touches upon an issue of federalism or comity that could be considered sua

---

263. 512 U.S. 452, 457 (1994) (comment appearing in unnumbered footnote).
264. 515 U.S. 50, 55 n.2 (1995) (citing United Parcel Serv., Inc. v. Mitchell, 451 U.S. 56, 60 n.2 (1981)).
265. Supreme Court Practice, *supra* n.12, at 741.
266. 489 U.S. 288, 300, 330 (1989) (retroactivity of new, constitutionally required rule of criminal procedure).
267. 367 U.S. 643, 646 n.3 (1961) (overruling the Supreme Court's earlier decision that the exclusionary rule did not apply in state courts).
268. 428 U.S. 265, 280 n.l4 (1978) (standing).
269. 82 F.3d 1513, 1516 n.1 (10th Cir. 1996).
270. Daubert v. Merrell Dow Pharms., Inc., 509 U.S. 579 (1993).
271. 6 F.3d 1373, 1383 (9th Cir. 1993).
272. 118 F.3d 1400 (10th Cir. 1997).
273. *Id.* at 1404.
274. 710 F.3d 862, 865 (9th Cir. 2013).

sponte.'"[275] Other courts agree with that analysis.[276] An example of "exceptional" circumstances warranting review in such cases is *Bridges v. City of Bossier*.[277] In that case, the Fifth Circuit discussed an issue first raised by the amicus curiae, although the argument by amicus was actually a variation of arguments that the parties did raise in their briefing.

Although an amicus brief should address the issues raised by the parties in the brief, the amicus can use different rationale or better legal support for the desired outcome. Similarly, the amicus can restate the facts if the parties have failed to set out the facts essential to resolve the issues.

### *Focus on the Function of the Brief*

An amicus brief may serve one or more functions. Listed above were the following functions typical of amicus briefs:

- examining policy issues;
- providing a more attractive advocate;
- supporting the grant of discretionary review;
- supplementing a party's brief;
- endorsing a particular position;
- providing a historical perspective;
- providing technical assistance;
- showing potential unintended consequences;
- mooting or minimizing precedent or paving the way for future precedent;
- defining the nature and scope of a problem;
- correcting, limiting, publishing or "de-publishing" a decision; and
- applying political pressure.

The amicus brief should be written with these purposes in mind. In addition, the tone of the amicus brief should be objective overall. The advocate

275. 118 F.3d at 1404 (citation & italics omitted) (quoting Swan v. Peterson, 6 F.3d 1373, 1383 (9th Cir. 1993)).
276. *See, e.g.*, Resident Council v. HUD, 980 F.2d 1043, 1049 (5th Cir. 1993); Richardson v. Alabama State Bd. of Educ., 935 F.2d 1240, 1247 (11th Cir. 1991) (citing cases); Christopher M. v. Corpus Christi Indep. Sch. Dist., 933 F.2d 1285, 1292 (5th Cir. 1991); Wiggins Bros., Inc. v. Department of Energy, 667 F.2d 77, 83 (Temp. Emer. Ct. App. 1981).
277. 92 F.3d 329, 334 n.8 (5th Cir. 1996).

should give the court the impression that the amicus is not a partisan but, instead, wishes to aid the court in developing general legal principles. An amicus can foster the appearance of impartiality by providing the court with an analysis of both sides of the issue. Finally, the amicus brief can help the court understand why a rule urged by the parties may be unworkable in other factual situations. Some commentators have suggested that this function is often the most welcome contribution by amici from the standpoints of both the court and the parties.[278]

### *Don't Forget the Case Before the Court*

An often important purpose of the amicus brief is to explain how the court's resolution of a private dispute will affect other parties in other contexts. Nevertheless, the amicus should not completely disregard the controversy before the court. If it does, the amicus brief may be detached and appear to be irrelevant to the issues the court must decide.

It is also important to remember the level of the court that will review the amicus brief and cite only decisions persuasive to that court. For example, in the Supreme Court, rely on Supreme Court decisions. If there is no Supreme Court precedent, incorporate a persuasive lower court decision, elaborating all of the reasons that the Court should adopt its rationale.

### *Keep the Amicus Brief Short*

In writing the amicus brief, more than in writing any other brief, the lawyer should heed the admonition that briefs should be brief. If only one page is needed to articulate the position of the amicus, then file a one page brief; it will be greatly appreciated and much more effective than a lengthy, redundant brief.

The Supreme Court mandates that amicus briefs filed at the petition stage not contain more than 6,000 words.[279] Amicus briefs filed at the merits stage may contain no more than 9,000 words.[280] Similarly, FRAP 29(d) limits amicus briefs to one-half the length of the maximum permitted for a

278. David Herr & Michael McCarthy, *Amici Curiae: Not Just Friends of the Court Anymore,* Practical Litigator May 1998.
279. S. Ct. R. 33.1.
280. *Id.*

party's principal brief. No reply is permitted. As noted by the comment to the 1998 amendments to FRAP 29, an amicus brief is "supplemental." It should address "only matter not adequately addressed by the parties." This comment reflects the fact that the court already has had full briefing on the merits from the parties and has many other cases to decide.

The amendments to the timing requirements for filing amicus briefs greatly assist authors of amicus briefs to focus on relevant information that has not already been brought to the court's attention by the parties. The rule previously required the amicus to file at the same time as the party whom the amicus supported, making it difficult for the amicus to know exactly what the party would be saying at the time the amicus filed its brief. FRAP 29(e) now permits amici to file seven days *after* they have had an opportunity to review the brief of the party they support. This rule allows amici to avoid including repetitive material in their briefs. Although it is important for the amicus brief to be concise, the brief should address the amicus's position completely, including a full legal analysis and citations to legal authority.

Fortunately, in developing its argument, an amicus is freed from many of the usual conventions of brief writing. That—as well as the page number restrictions—encourages the amicus to address only the most material arguments, avoid redundancies, and omit irrelevancies. Further, the amicus often has the opportunity to go for the jugular, be dramatic, use effective hyperbole, and capture the court's attention. In the Appendix to this book, Examples 2 and 3 are very short letter briefs. Example 14 is also a short brief, which really addresses not the merits of the case but a potential remedy if the court were to agree with the state on the voter registration issue. The other examples are much longer. The length of the brief excerpted in Example 1 is the result of the extensive federal regulatory backdrop and the importance of the positions taken by the agency; as a result, the brief contains more block quotes than do many briefs. Example 5 provides excerpts from a lengthy amicus brief that concerns a controversial social and legal issue. In any event, a long amicus brief should be the rare exception.

### *Use Persuasive Case Law Support*

The United States supreme court and state supreme courts are not persuaded by lower court decisions. Although it can be helpful to cite to a particularly well-written lower court opinion on occasion, most of the argument should rest upon controlling precedent, logic, and policy arguments.

### *Address Judicial Concerns*

When issuing an opinion, an appellate court may have many concerns, but two of them are particularly relevant to the amicus. First, the court often is concerned with ensuring that it has considered and appropriately dealt with the controlling cases. If relevant precedents exist but the parties have not cited them, the amicus should so advise the court. Second, an appellate court is often concerned about the unrecognized ramifications of its opinion. An amicus brief can advise the court that a potential ruling would have disastrous or salutary effects. To inform a court about the ramifications of a particular decision, the amicus must often go outside the record. For example, it may be necessary to discuss industry practice—how things are done in the real world—so the court will know the impact that its decision will have on everyday business. In other cases, discussing the ramifications of a judicial opinion requires presentation of extensive economic data or other empirical evidence. As noted, below, a lawyer should use care in providing information to the court outside the record, making sure that the information is accurate and reliable.

## DO YOU NEED PERMISSION TO FILE AN AMICUS BRIEF?

In many jurisdictions, leave of court is necessary to file an amicus brief.[281] Leave is generally obtained on motion or application to the court.[282] Counsel

281. Stern, *supra* n.17, at 303.
282. *Id.*

for amicus should always consult local rules for any special requirements. Failure to observe such rules is likely to lead to denial of leave to file.[283]

States are split on what is required in order to file an amicus brief. Texas, Georgia, and Pennsylvania do not require any grant of permission,[284] and technically in Texas the amicus brief is received instead of filed.[285] Thirty-five states require leave, with five of them exempting some agency or agencies of government. The remainder of state appellate courts will accept amicus briefs upon granting of leave or consent of the parties, with six of those states again exempting some agency or agencies of government.[286]

The Supreme Court requires leave of court to file an amicus brief unless:

- all parties have consented to the filing in writing; or
- the brief is filed by certain designated entities–such as the United States, a federal agency, a state, or the political subdivision of a state.[287]

The 2013 changes to Supreme Court Rule 37 make clear that parties may file blanket consent, and they also emphasize that the notice requirement pertains only to petition-stage amicus briefs.

Under Federal Rule of Appellate Procedure 29, leave of court is not necessary if all of the parties consent to the filing. The consent no longer need be given in writing. Oral consent is sufficient, and the amicus brief needs only to state that all parties consented. Consent is also unnecessary if the brief is filed by the United States, a federal agency, a state, territory, commonwealth, or the District of Columbia.[288]

Courts differ on the requirements for obtaining leave to file when the parties refuse consent.[289] Federal Rule of Appellate Procedure 29(b) requires that the moving party (1) identify the movant's interest, (2) the reason

---

283. *See, e.g.*, Murrelet v. Pac. Lumber Co., 83 F.3d 1060, 1062 n.1 (9th Cir. 1996) (no attempt to show good cause for late filing of motion).
284. See excerpts from state court rules on amicus briefs in the Appendix. This information also appears in the APPELLATE PRACTICE COMPENDIUM published by the ABA's Council of Appellate Lawyers (2012, Dana Livingston, editor).
285. Tex. R. App. P. 11.
286. *Id.*
287. S. CT. R. 37.3.
288. FRAP 29(a).
289. *Id.* at 305.

why an amicus brief is desirable, and (3) why the matters asserted are relevant to the disposition of the case. The brief must accompany the motion. Supreme Court Rule 37.3(b) requires that the motion (1) be consolidated in one document with the brief sought to be filed; (2) indicate the party or parties who have withheld consent; and (3) state the nature of the movant's interest. The Supreme Court rules treat motions for leave to file an amicus brief quite differently depending on whether the motion is filed before or after the Court decides certain petitions, such as a petition for a writ of certiorari. According to Rule 37.2(b), if the case is not yet pending before the Court for oral argument, the motion for leave to file "is not favored." In cases pending before the Court for oral argument, a motion for leave to file under Rule 37.3(b) will likely be granted.

Parties rarely refuse to consent to the request of an amicus to participate. This is probably because leave to file will almost always be granted by the court if consent is withheld.[290] However, as recently as 1997, it appeared that courts might reverse their former liberality in connection with amicus filings. That year, in *Ryan v. Commodity Futures Trading Commission*, Judge Richard Posner of the Seventh Circuit issued a decision in which he suggested that amicus status should be denied on a number of grounds.[291] He stated:

> The tendency of many judges of this court, including myself, has been to grant motions for leave to file amicus curiae briefs without careful consideration of "the reasons why a brief of an amicus curiae is desirable," although the rule makes this a required part of the motion. After 16 years of reading amicus curiae briefs the vast majority of which have not assisted the judges, I have decided that it would be good to scrutinize these motions in a more careful, indeed a fish-eyed, fashion.
>
> The vast majority of amicus curiae briefs are filed by allies of litigants and duplicate the arguments made in the litigants' briefs, in effect merely extending the length of the litigant's brief. Such amicus

290. *See* Neonatology Associations, P.A. v. C.I.R., 293 F.3d 128, 132 n.1 (3d Cir. 2002); Wohl, *supra* n.2, at 48; Supreme Court Practice, *supra* n.12, at 735.
291. 125 F. 3d 1062 (7th Cir. 1997).

briefs should not be allowed. They are an abuse. The term "amicus curiae" means friend of the court, not friend of a party. *United States v. Michigan,* 940 F.2d 143, 164-65 (6th Cir. 1991). We are beyond the original meaning now; an adversary role of an amicus curiae has become accepted. *Id.* at 165. But there are, or at least there should be, limits. *Cf. New England Patriots Football Club, Inc. v. University of Colorado,* 592 F.2d 1196, 1198 n. 3 (1st Cir. 1979). An amicus brief should normally be allowed when a party is not represented competently or is not represented at all, when the amicus has an interest in some other case that may be affected by the decision in the present case (though not enough affected to entitle the amicus to intervene and become a party in the present case), or when the amicus has unique information or perspective that can help the court beyond the help that the lawyers for the parties are able to provide. *See, e.g., Miller-Wahl Co. v. Commissioner of Labor & Industry,* 694 F.2d 203 (9th Cir. 1982) (per curiam). Otherwise, leave to file an amicus curiae brief should be denied. *Northern Securities Co. v. United States,* 191 U.S. 555, 556 (1903) (Chief Justice Fuller, in chambers); *American College of Obstetricians & Gynecologists v. Thornburgh,* 699 F.2d 644 (3d Cir. 1983) (per curium); *Rucker v. Great Scott Supermarkets,* 528 F.2d 393 n.2 (6th Cir. 1976); *Strasser v. Doorley,* 432 F.2d 567, 569 (1st Cir. 1970); *United States v. Gotti,* 755 F. Supp. 1157 (E.D.N.Y. 1991); *Fluor Corp. v. United States,* 35 Fed. Cl. 284 (1996). The Chicago Board of Trade's amicus brief (attached to its motion for leave to file) falls into the forbidden category. The petitioner argues that he should not have been punished by the CFTC, because he has been rehabilitated, as shown by the Board of Trade's decision to reinstate him. The amicus brief echoes this argument, saying in effect, "Yes, indeed, he's been rehabilitated, for otherwise we wouldn't have reinstated him." The petitioner argues that he poses no threat to the public so long as he is constrained to operate under the supervision of the Board of Trade, and the Board echoes this argument too: "As long as he's under our supervision, the public is safe." The petitioner's brief is 45 pages long; the Board's brief, if allowed to be submitted, would in effect bring that length up to 62 pages.

The Board claims to have an "overriding interest" in the case because one of its members is being punished unjustly in its view, and to be able to assist the court "by expressing its strongly held view that the evidence clearly and convincingly establishes" the lack of any need for the sanction meted out by the Commission. We are not helped by an amicus curiae's expression of a "strongly held view" about the weight of the evidence, *see New England Patriots Football Club, Inc. v. University of Colorado, supra,* 592 F.2d at 1198 n.3, but by being pointed to considerations germane to our decision of the appeal that the parties for one reason or another have not brought to our attention. The amicus briefs filed in this court rarely do that; and this amicus brief is not one of the rare exceptions.

Were there some doubt about the Board of Trade's position concerning the sanctioning of Mr. Ryan, an amicus curiae brief might serve to inform us of a material consideration of which we might otherwise be unaware. There is no doubt. The Board pronounced him rehabilitated and reinstated him, and the Commission, disagreeing with the Board's evaluation of Ryan's danger to the investing public, went ahead and sanctioned him anyway. The amicus brief does not tell us anything we don't know already. It adds nothing to the already amply proportioned brief of the petitioner.

The bane of lawyers is prolixity and duplication, and for obvious reasons is especially marked in commercial cases with large monetary stakes. In an era of heavy judicial caseloads and public impatience with the delays and expense of litigation, we judges should be assiduous to bar the gates to amicus curiae briefs that fail to present convincing reasons why the parties' briefs do not give us all the help we need for deciding the appeal.

The motion for clarification is granted, and the denial of the motion for leave to file a brief amicus curiae is reaffirmed.[292]

292. *Id.* at 1063–64.

Judge Posner's comments should be taken to heart by every would-be amicus curiae. The amicus brief should never simply repeat arguments made by others. As Judge Posner noted in another chambers opinion:

> [I]t is very rare for an amicus curiae brief to do more than repeat in somewhat different language the arguments in the brief of the party whom the amicus is supporting. Those who pay lawyers to prepare such briefs are not getting their money's worth.[293]

Accordingly, Judge Posner has urged strict criteria for accepting amicus briefs. He would not accept an amicus brief for filing unless the brief will assist the court "by presenting ideas, arguments, theories, insights, facts, or data that are not to be found in the parties' briefs."[294] These grounds are so broad, one commentator has observed, that they would be "sufficient to provide any overburdened judge with an excuse for denying leave to file almost any amicus brief, no matter how helpful some other judge on the court might find the brief."[295]

Fifteen years after the *Ryan* case, a commentator noted that "[c]onvincing the Seventh Circuit or the Illinois Supreme Court to grant leave to file an amicus brief is hard and getting harder.[296] As to the Seventh Circuit, which undoubtedly has influenced the Illinois state courts on their receptiveness to amicus briefs, Judge Posner issued another in-chambers opinion erecting a triad of hurdles for amicus briefs: (1) a non-represented or poorly represented party; (2) an affected and direct interest of the amicus; and (3) a fresh perspective or new information offered by the amicus.[297] Facing such hurdles, the commentator suggests that to obtain leave from the Seventh Circuit and Illinois appellate courts, an advocate should flesh out the broader

---

293. Voices for Choices v. Ill. Bell. Tel. Co., 339 F. 3d 542, 545 (7th Cir. 2003) (Posner, J. in chambers).
294. *Id.*
295. Luther T. Munford, *When Does the Curiae Need an Amicus?* 1 J. App. Prac. & Process 279, 280 (Summer 1999).
296. Bruce Braverman, *Getting Your Amicus Brief Before the Seventh Circuit and Illinois Supreme Court*, 100 Ill. Bar J. 376 (2012).
297. Voices for Choices v. Ill. Bell Tel. Co., 339 F.3d 542, 543 (7th Cir. 2003).

perspective, explain the impact of a ruling to a pertinent group or industry, illuminate the public impact, focus on policy, and offer a unique approach.[298]

Similarly, Justice Scalia had previously filed a dissent in a case in which 14 amicus briefs were filed supporting respondents and none supporting petitioner.[299] He observed that "There is no self-interested organization out there devoted to pursuit of the truth in the federal courts. The expectation is, however, that this Court will have that interest prominently—indeed, primarily—in mind."[300] Justice Scalia was apparently suggesting that amicus briefs are a form of interest group lobbying directed at the Court.[301]

Although the United States Supreme Court almost never rejects timely amicus filings, some courts have adopted Judge Posner's "fish-eyed" view of amicus briefs.[302] The Illinois Supreme Court has adopted rules that make it more difficult to file amicus briefs. That court in 2006 denied the Chamber of Commerce leave to file an amicus brief, based on concerns that echoed Judge Posner's remarks.[303]

Other courts have not followed suit and commentators have criticized Judge Posner's view as too strict.[304] Appellate court practitioner Andrew Frey has pointed out in a lengthy article on the subject, the "anti-amicus impulse seems to derive from an unduly narrow view of the nature of litigation and the effect of judicial decisions."[305] Frey points out that non-parties who may be faced with issues similar to those being litigated in a case have a legitimate interest in the outcome.[306] He explains further that appellate courts

298. Braverman, *supra* n.296, at 377–83.
299. Jaffee v. Redmond, 518 U.S. 1 (1996).
300. *Id.* at 35–36 (Scalia, J., dissenting).
301. Joseph D. Kearney & Thomas W. Merrill, *The Influence of Amicus Briefs on the Supreme Court,* 148 U. PA. L. REV. 743, 747 (Jan. 2000).
302. *See, e.g.,* Cobell v. Norton, 246 F. Supp. 2d 59, 62–63 (D.D.C. 2003) (citing *Ryan* opinion in allowing leave to one amicus and denying leave to another); Long v. Coast Resorts, Inc., 49 F. Supp. 2d 1177, 1177–78 (D. Nev. 1999) (denying "belated and duplicative" amicus participation that would delay the litigation); United Stationers, Inc. v. United States, 982 F. Supp. 1279, 1288 (E. D. Ill. 1997); *cf.* United States v. Boeing Co., 73 F. Supp. 2d 897, 900 (S.D. Ohio 1999) (citing *Ryan* as authority for allowing participation by amicus with unique information or perspective).
303. Kinkel v. Cingular Wireless, L.L.C., No. 100925 (Ill. Jan. 11, 2006).
304. Luther T. Munford, *supra* n.295, at 279 (1999); Andrew Frey, *Amicus Curiae: Friends of the Court or Nuisances?,* 33 LITIG. 5 (Fall 2006).
305. Frey, Andrew, *Amici Curiae: Friends of the Court or Nuisance*, 33 LITIG. 5 (Fall 2006).
306. *Id.* at 6.

should liberally allow amicus filings for two reasons: (i) the First Amendment grants citizens the right to "petition the government" and submitting an amicus brief in a pending case constitutes such a petition; and (ii) amicus briefs can be extremely helpful to generalist courts and their generalist clerks because amici may have relevant expertise that the parties lack (e.g., historical understanding of a legal document), they bring a perspective to a case that the parties cannot bring because of their unique situations, and they make arguments that parties may be unwilling to make.[307]

Finally, Frey points out that the arguments against allowing liberal amicus participation (that voluminous submissions overburden courts, amici should be friends of the court, not of the parties, and parties use amicus filings to avoid a court's page limits) are easily refuted.[308] Amicus filings do not represent a significant burden on the courts. They certainly should not be rejected simply because they adopt a point of view; the fundamental assumption of our adversary system is that strong advocacy of opposing positions promotes sound decision making. And it is rarely the case that amicus briefs are used to circumvent court rules. In sum, the policies favoring amicus filings outweigh any potential drawbacks. As Frey states:

> Most people and institutions affected by the legal rules announced by appellate courts are not parties to the litigation in which those rules are laid down. To prevent those affected from having their day in court deprives them of their right to petition the government and also deprives the courts of the benefit of their views on the legal question at hand. It is no wonder, then, that courts have traditionally welcomed friends of the court to file briefs arguing in favor or against a particular result. And that is how it should be.[309]

Similarly, another commentator, Luther T. Munford, has observed that the amendments to FRAP 29 solved most of the problems that troubled Judge

---

307. *Id.* at 6, 66. *See also* Neonatology Assocs., P.A. v. Comm'r of Internal Revenue, 293 F.3d 128, 133 (3d Cir. 2002).
308. *Id.* at 67.
309. *Id.* at 68.

Posner.[310] He believes that leave should be freely granted and that *Ryan* should represent the "end of an old era, not the beginning of a new one." Amicus briefs are valuable because "sometimes the most important thing a friend can do is remind you to do what is right."[311]

United States Supreme Court Justice Samuel Alito agrees. While on the Third Circuit, he relegated *Ryan* and its progeny to a "small body of judicial opinions that look with disfavor on motions for leave to file amicus briefs."[312] In *Neonatology Associates. P.A. v. Commissioner of Internal Revenue*,[313] the Third Circuit applied the principles in Federal Rule of Appellate Procedure 29, rejecting as outmoded the concept that amici must be impartial and finding no requirement in Rule 29 that an amicus brief be filed for an unrepresented or underrepresented party. The court timely rejected the idea that a party with an interest may not file an amicus brief. Judge Alito first noted that the rule implicitly requires that a motion for leave to file should be denied if the movant does not meet the requirements of (1) an adequate interest, (2) desirability, and (3) relevance. Pointing out that the suggestion that an amicus must be impartial "became outdated long ago," Alito observed that the rules require just the opposite: an amicus *must* have an interest in the case.

On the Supreme Court, Justice Alito also rejected the notion that a friend of a party cannot also be a friend of the court: "[T]his suggestion is contrary to the fundamental assumption of our adversary system that strong (but fair) advocacy on behalf of opposing views promotes sound decision making. Thus, an amicus who makes a strong but responsible presentation in support of a party can truly serve as the court's friend."[314] Finally, Judge Alito disagreed with the assertion that an amicus must show that the party supported is inadequately represented: "[e]ven when a party is well represented, an amicus may provide important assistance to the court"

---

310. Luther T. Munford, *supra* n.295, at 283.
311. *Id.* at 284.
312. Neonatology Assocs., P.A. v. C.I.R., 293 F.3d 128, 130 (3d Cir. 2002) (citing *Ryan* and the following cases: Nat'l Org. for Women, Inc. v. Scheidler, 125 F.3d 1062 (7th Cir. 1997) (in chambers opinion); Liberty Lincoln Mercury, Inc. v. Ford Marketing Corp., 149 F.R.D. 65, 82 (D.N.J. 1993); Yip v. Pagano, 606 F. Supp. 1566, 1568 (D.N.J. 1985)).
313. 293 F.3d 128, 131–33 (3d Cir. 2002).
314. 293 F.3d at 131.

by providing background or factual references that merit judicial notice, providing special expertise, explaining the impact of the decision on an industry or making arguments that are too far-reaching to be advanced by the parties. Justice Alito concluded that motions for leave to file amicus briefs should be granted "unless it is obvious that the proposed briefs do not meet Rule 29's criteria as broadly interpreted.[315]

Another advocate for amicus briefs posits a different reason for supporting them. Ruben Garcia views amicus briefs as part of the democratic process.[316] An amicus brief, he says, is part of "deliberative democracy," related to the constitutional right to petition the government.[317] Therefore, he urges that amicus briefs should be allowed unless the submission is sanctionable.[318] His "democratic theory" of amicus briefs champions informed debate and vaunts amicus briefs as increasing the transparency of the judicial process and democratic legitimacy of courts.[319] Arguably, the recurring stagnation in the executive and legislative branches at the federal level increases the importance of the judicial system, which after all does make a decision and must provide a reasoned basis for how it decides. Amicus briefs, then, may represent public participation in the most effective decision maker in the federal government, and the cost of an amicus brief pales in comparison with the cost of lobbying or campaigns. Finally, as another commentator noted, the evolution of litigation often means that a decision in a particular case may actually have an equal or greater effect on those who are not parties, making it appropriate for those potentially affected non-parties to weigh in on the court's decision.[320]

Most courts have continued liberally to allow amicus filings, and thus opposing an amicus submission may not only be a futile gesture, it may be a strategic misstep. The opposition may emphasize the importance of the case. It is usually better not to oppose the submission, but simply to respond to the amicus brief when it is filed or to recruit an opposing amicus.

---

315. *Id.* at 133.
316. Ruben J. Garcia, *A Democratic Theory of Amicus Advocacy*, 35 FLA. STATE. L. REV. 315 (2008).
317. *Id.* at 346.
318. *Id.* at 319–20.
319. *Id.* at 346–47.
320. P. Stephen Gidiere, III, *supra* n.103, at 15.

## WHEN DO YOU FILE AN AMICUS BRIEF?

Federal appeals courts all follow Rule 29, which sets the deadline for an amicus brief as seven days after the supported party brief or, if none, the opening brief.[321] The Ninth Circuit will entertain a request by a party to file a supplemental brief in response to an amicus brief.[322] The Federal Circuit will entertain a request for supplemental words or pages to respond to amicus briefs.[323] Rule 29 itself provides that the appellate court may grant leave for later filing of an amicus brief, specifying the time for the opposing party to answer.[324] If the rules do not allow a response to an amicus brief, the party wishing to respond may consider whether to seek leave to file post-argument briefing, especially if an issue raised by amici surfaces during argument.

In the Supreme Court, leave of court or consent of the parties is required for an amicus brief, with an exemption for the Solicitor General of the United States, agencies of the federal government, and states, territories, counties, cities, or towns when filed by their appropriate law officer.[325] In connection with a petition for certiorari, an amicus brief supporting the motion must be filed within 30 days of the docketing of the case or the request for a response, whichever is later.[326] That time period will not be extended and is accompanied by a requirement of a 10-day notice of intent to file.[327] When a case is set for argument, the amicus brief is due within 7 days after the supported party brief or, if none, the brief of the petitioner or appellant, and no extension of time will be entertained.[328]

The time for filing in state appellate courts varies considerably. Eighteen states follow the practice of requiring amicus briefs to be filed at the time of the supported party brief or, if none, on the due date of the opening

321. *Id.*
322. *Id.*
323. *Id.*
324. Fed. R. App. P. 29(e).
325. S. Ct. R. 37.2, 37.3 & 37.4.
326. S. Ct. R. 37.2.
327. S. Ct. R. 37.2.
328. S. Ct. R. 37.3.

brief.[329] Nineteen states have no due date for amicus briefs.[330] Thirteen states impose other time periods, usually seven days after the supported brief, which follows federal practice, but some allow slightly more time.[331] New York, Kansas, and Washington impose deadlines in relation to the argument date.[332]

Since both the applicable state and federal rules are subject to change, you should review them anew each time a brief is filed.[333] There are typically no rules governing amicus briefs in trial courts.[334] Generally, district courts are viewed as having broad discretion to accept or reject amicus briefs.[335] District courts will usually grant leave when the amicus brief is expected to assist the court in making its decision.[336] In addition, if the amicus curiae obtains leave to file a brief in a district court, an amicus may also be permitted to participate in arguments before the court.[337] In some situations, a would-be amicus, either solicited or unsolicited, intends to take a position that could hurt the appeal of the party that the amicus is supposedly supporting. The only recourse in such a situation is to oppose the motion for leave to file the brief. A party should be able to file such an opposition, even if it solicited the amicus.

As indicated above, amicus briefs may be filed at various stages in support of the grant of review and on the merits. They may even be filed in

---

329. *Id.*
330. *Id.*
331. *Id.*
332. *Id.*
333. *See* Sorenson, *supra* n.5.
334. *See, e.g.*, United States v. Gotti, 755 F. Supp. 1157, 1159 (E.D.N.Y. 1991).
335. *See, e.g.*, Hoptowit v. Ray, 682 F.2d. 1237, 1260 (9th Cir. 1982); City of New York v. United States, 971 F. Supp. 789, 791 n.3 (S.D.N.Y. 1997); James Square Nursing Home, Inc. v. Wing, 897 F. Supp. 682 (N.D.N. Y. 1995), *aff'd on other grounds*, 84 F.3d 591 (2d Cir. 1996); Waste Mgmt. of Pa., Inc. v. City of New York, 162 F.R.D. 34, 36 (M.D. Pa. 1995) (collecting cases); Wyatt v. Hanan, 868 F. Supp. 1356, 1359 (M.D. Ala. 1994); Concerned Area Residents for the Environment v. Southview Farm, 834 F. Supp. 1410, 1413 (W.D.N.Y. 1993).
336. *See* United States v. El-Gabrowny, 844 F. Supp. 955, 957 n.1 (S.D.N.Y. 1994) (stating that a district court can grant leave to file amicus briefs when the briefs will aid the court); United States v. Gotti, 755 F. Supp. 1157, 1158–59 (E.D.N.Y. 1991).
337. *See, e.g.*, Rural Water Sys. #1 v. City of Sioux Ctr., 967 F. Supp. 1483, 1499 (N.D. Iowa 1997) (allowing participation of amicus counsel of "unusually high caliber"); Nat'l Black Police Ass'n v. Dist. of Columbia Bd. of Elections & Ethics, 924 F. Supp. 270, 273 (D.D.C. 1996).

connection with a petition for rehearing or en banc consideration.[338] The timing requirements at those stages are set by the governing procedural rules. In many jurisdictions, the amicus brief must be conditionally filed with a motion for leave, meaning that the amicus brief must be prepared without knowing if the court will grant leave to file.[339]

In some courts, amicus briefs must be filed at the same time as the brief of the party that the amicus supports, unless the court otherwise orders. The timing is different at the petition stage in the United States Supreme Court.[340] An amicus brief supporting the petitioner must be filed within 30 days after the case has been placed on the Court's docket or a response is called for by the Court, whichever is later.[341] A brief supporting the respondent must be filed within the time allowed for a brief in opposition to the petition.[342] Further, 10 days' notice prior to the due date is required to be given to the parties, unless the amicus brief is filed within those 10 days. These deadlines are designed to allow parties the opportunity to respond to amicus briefs, and the respondent may ask for an extension of time to file its brief in opposition so that it may respond to amicus briefs as well as the petition.[343]

When a case is before the Court for oral argument, an amicus brief must be filed within 7 days after the brief of the party being supported, or if no party is being supported, then within 7 days after the brief of the petitioner or appellant.[344] Federal Rule of Appellate Procedure 29(e) adopts the same 7-day rule: no later than 7 days after the brief of the party being supported

338. *See* Federal Appellate Practice, *supra* n.60, at 421. In three significant cases, the Texas Supreme Court granted rehearing after being presented with numerous amicus briefs. *See* Entergy Gulf States, Inc. v. Summers, 282 S.W.3d 433, 2009 WL 884906 (Tex. 2009); Excess Underwriters at Lloyds, London v. Frank's Casing Crew & Rental Tools, Inc., 246 S.W.3d 42 (Tex. 2008); F.F.P. Operating Partners, LLP v. Duenez, 237 S.W.3d 680 (Tex. 2007).

339. While in the United States Supreme Court most amicus briefs are filed with the parties' consent, in the absence of consent; a motion for leave must be filed and bound together with the amicus brief. *See* Supreme Court Practice, *supra* n.12, at 513–14 (discussing S. Cr. R. 37.2) In federal appeals court, the brief must typically be filed with the motion. *See* Federal Appellate Practice, *supra* n.60, at 409. The Texas Rules of Appellate Procedure are perhaps the most liberal, allowing a party to send to the clerk an amicus brief at any time, although, as noted above, the brief is technically received rather than filed by the clerk. *See* Tex. R. App. P. 11.

340. S. Ct. R. 37.2(a).

341. *Id.*

342. *Id.*

343. Supreme Court Practice, *supra* n.12, at 514 (noting the Clerk's comments that extensions will be freely given for that purpose).

344. S. Ct. R. 37.3(a).

by the amicus or, if not supporting any party, then 7 days after the principal brief of the appellant or petitioner.[345]

## HOW DO YOU RESPOND TO AN AMICUS BRIEF?

There are no rules in federal appellate courts or the Supreme Court about when or how to respond to an amicus brief. The requirement that an amicus brief be filed no later than 7 days after the brief it supports is intended to give the opposing party enough time to respond in its own brief to the argument and contents of the amicus brief, as well as allowing the amicus enough time to review the brief it supports in order to avoid duplicate arguments. [346]

The practice in state courts varies. At the time of this publication, these states had special provisions on responding to amicus briefs: Arizona, California, Colorado, Hawaii, Iowa, Kansas, Maine, Maryland, Mississippi, Nevada, New Mexico, Oklahoma, South Carolina, Washington, West Virginia, and Utah.[347] Most states tie the filing date for amicus briefs to the filing date for the briefs they support, or a few days after the supported brief's filing deadline, thus allowing the opposing party to respond to the amicus brief in its own responsive brief.[348] Appellate rules in Indiana and Vermont so provide, but the courts are to set a time for a response if the amicus brief is filed late.[349] In these states, the time for filing an amicus brief is not specified: Georgia, Idaho, Kentucky, Louisiana, Minnesota, Montana, Nebraska, Tennessee (where the court is specifically required to set a time for filing), and Texas.[350] Louisiana Uniform Rule 2-12.6 does have a general provision prohibiting further briefing after the reply brief, except on leave of court, and that provision could be invoked to respond to an amicus brief.

If an amicus has filed an effective brief in federal court or in a state court that has no procedure for filing a response, the party whose position has

345. FRAP 29(e); FEDERAL APPELLATE PRACTICE, *supra* n.60, at 412–13.
346. *Id.*
347. See Appendix for excerpts from state court rules pertaining to amicus briefs. This information is also available from APPELLATE PRACTICE COMPENDIUM, *supra* n.284.
348. *Id.*
349. *Id.*
350. *Id.*

been attacked by the amicus has two choices. First, the party can include a response to the points made by the amicus in its brief. Second, the party can recruit a counter-amicus. The choice will always depend on the particular circumstances. If the opposing amicus is effective because of the credibility or high profile it enjoys, or because it makes a particularly persuasive point that is not made by the opposing party, then the party must answer it.[351] If the party does not have space in its brief to cover the critical points raised by an amicus, it may be advisable to recruit an equally highly regarded amicus to file a response. If, on the other hand, the amicus brief makes factual errors or repeats arguments made by the parties, then it is usually not necessary to address these points. However, the lawyer should be prepared to answer questions at oral argument about the points raised by all of the parties even if not addressed in the party's brief.

With more and more frequency, groups of professors and legal historians are filing amicus briefs. In his book on advocacy, Justice Scalia points out a number of ways to respond to these briefs. It is worth pointing out to the Court that one or more of the signatories have authored no scholarly articles on the point in question, or have authored works taking contrary positions.[352] The party can also attempt to find other academic works that favor its position and provide those citations to the Court.

As always, the lawyer should consult the court's local rules before responding to an amicus brief. If leave of court is a prerequisite to filing, it may be better (or it may be required) to file the completed response with the motion or application for leave, so that the court can see how long the response is and what it contributes to the case.

---

351. *See* Making Your Case, *supra* n.36, at 104. If an amicus offers a new argument, Justice Scalia also advises pointing out to the Court that the issue was not raised below or does not fall within the question on which certiorari was granted. *Id.*

352. *Id.* at 105.

## CAN AN AMICUS CURIAE PARTICIPATE IN ORAL ARGUMENT?

Amicus parties are not automatically entitled to argument. In the federal courts of appeal, FRAP 29 provides that oral argument will be allowed "only with the court's permission." An earlier provision that stated that oral argument would be granted "only for extraordinary reasons" was deleted because the courts will permit an amicus to argue if a party is willing to share its argument time. Nevertheless, the comments to the rule suggest that in other circumstances, an amicus will not be permitted argument "absent extraordinary circumstances." It may be difficult to obtain the parties' consent to share argument time with an amicus because strategic considerations militate against sharing time. Splitting the argument among two or more lawyers reduces available argument time and risks scattering the focus of the argument. Divided argument poses additional problems. Even though counsel may agree on an allocation of issues for argument, there is no assurance that judges will save their questions for the lawyer familiar with a particular issue. Further, argument is meant to be a dialogue and dividing arguments tends to interfere with the dialogue. As a result of these considerations, instances where parties have agreed to yield argument time to an amicus are rare.[353]

In the Supreme Court, a non-party amicus must obtain leave to participate in the argument even if the party that it supports has granted a portion of its 30-minute argument time to the amicus.[354] An amicus would be well advised to try to persuade the court to give it additional time without diminishing the time allotted to the party or parties that the amicus supports, but such requests are rarely successful in the appellate courts. District courts may be more willing to allow additional argument time for the amicus curiae.[355]

353. *See* Weaver v. United States Information Agency, 87 F.3d 1429, 1435 n.2 (D.C. Cir. 1996) (party yielded one-half of its time to amicus.)

354. Supreme Court Practice, *supra* n.12, at 743, 765–66; S. Ct. R 28.7.

355. *See, e.g.*, Rural Water Sys. #1 v. City of Sioux Ctr., 967 F. Supp. 1483, 1499 (N.D. Iowa 1997); National Black Police Ass'n v. Dist. of Columbia Bd. of Elections & Ethics, 924 F. Supp. 270, 273 (D.D.C. 1996); Wyatt v. Hanan, 868 F. Supp. 1356, 1360 (M.D. Ala. 1994)

When the U.S. Solicitor General appears as an amicus, however, the rules change. The Solicitor General will usually request ten minutes of the oral argument time of the party the government supports. It is wise to grant that request. The Solicitor General is an experienced and skillful advocate who will highlight for the Court the importance of the case.[356]

In state courts, argument by amici is rare. New Mexico takes the most welcoming approach, allowing participation by an amicus if the supported party agrees to share its time.[357] South Dakota requires a sharing agreement and court approval.[358] Almost all other courts require court approval and often states that approval will be given only in extraordinary circumstances.[359] Appellate rules in Arkansas, Illinois, Louisiana, and Kansas flatly bar oral argument by amici.[360]

## ARE THERE ANY ETHICAL CONSIDERATIONS IN AMICUS PRACTICE?

Amicus briefs raise several ethical issues but there is little, if any, direct guidance on those issues. Some general considerations bear mentioning. ABA Model Rule of Professional Conduct 3.3 states, among other things, that a lawyer "shall not knowingly":

- make a false statement of fact or law to a tribunal or fail to correct a false statement of material fact or law previously made to the tribunal by the lawyer;

(permitting federal government as amicus to participate in many proceedings in the case, including evidentiary hearings and depositions.)

356. MAKING YOUR CASE, *supra* n.36, at 149; Millett, *supra* n.220, at 227 (Spring 2009). Many examples of participation by the Solicitor General in oral argument could be cited. Just one example is found in *Davenport v. Washington Education Association*, 127 S. Ct. 8115 (2006). The Solicitor General's amicus brief in that case is reprinted as Example 11 in the Appendix.

357. N.M.R. Ann. 12–215.

358. S.D.R. Civ. App. P. 15-26A-74.

359. See Appendix for excerpts from state court rules pertaining to amicus briefs. This information is also available from APPELLATE PRACTICE COMPENDIUM, *supra* n.284.

360. *Id.*

- fail to disclose to the tribunal legal authority in the controlling jurisdiction known to the lawyer to be directly adverse to the position of the client and not disclosed by opposing counsel; or
- offer evidence that the lawyer knows to be false. If a lawyer, the lawyer's client, or a witness called by the lawyer, has offered material evidence and the lawyer comes to know of its falsity, the lawyer shall take reasonable remedial measures, including, if necessary, disclosure to the tribunal. A lawyer may refuse to offer evidence, other than the testimony of a defendant in a criminal matter, that the lawyer reasonably believes is false.[361]

Typically, it is not the job of the amicus brief to deal with controlling authority. The situation could, of course, arise that neither party cites a controlling case. Even then, it is not clear whether the amicus—a nonparty—has a duty to disclose the controlling authority.[362] More often, questions about candor and honesty revolve around facts lying outside the record, and representations about the identity of the amicus.

### *Facts Outside the Record*

Because of the proliferation of amicus briefs and the increased availability of data and information, the most common method of introducing non-legal materials, such as social science evidence, to the court is through non-record evidence in amicus curiae briefs.[363] The idea for such a brief originated with Louis Brandeis. As a young lawyer in *Mueller v. Oregon,*[364] Brandeis assembled existing social science research on the detrimental impact of long work hours on women's health—marking one of the first instances in which an advocate emphasized the law-in-action over the formalistic pronouncements

---

361. Rule 3.3 further requires a lawyer to disclose any material fact to a tribunal when disclosure is necessary to avoid assisting a criminal or fraudulent act by the client, but that duty does not seem to be implicated in the situation of an amicus brief. ABA Model Rules of Professional Conduct (2008).
362. *See* ABA Model Rules of Professional Conduct Rule 3.3(a)(2) ("A lawyer shall not knowingly . . . fail to disclose to the tribunal legal authority in the controlling jurisdiction known to the lawyer to be adverse to the position of the client and not disclosed by opposing counsel.").
363. Rustad & Koenig, *supra* n.3, at 94.
364. 208 U.S. 412, 423 (1908).

of the law-in-the-books.[365] The term "Brandeis brief" has come to refer to any use of policy-oriented extra-legal arguments in briefs.[366]

The Supreme Court under Chief Justice Earl Warren was perhaps the first to use social science data extensively. *Brown v. Board of Education*[367] provides the best example of the Warren Court's use of empirical research to evaluate whether constitutional principles had been violated. In footnote 11 of the *Brown* decision, the Court reviewed the finding by social scientists that segregated school facilities caused psychological and social harm to schoolchildren. The Court further cited seven social science studies that repudiated the notion that "separate" was "equal." In *Brown*'s wake, the Court has received social science data in many cases, including school desegregation,[368] obscenity,[369] segregation by gender,[370] jury size,[371] the death penalty,[372] and individual rights.[373] Lower courts have likewise accepted such information beyond the record.[374] Commentators assert that such amicus briefs serve a useful purpose in providing the court with varied viewpoints and information about social science findings that might otherwise go unnoticed.[375] Extrinsic evidence in amicus briefs is by no means limited to social science or statistical data, as the following examples illustrate the wide variety of extra-record submissions:

- information about the nature of markets for foreign currency and options;[376]

---

365. *Id.* at 94; *see* Mueller v. Oregon, 208 U.S. 412, 423 (1908).
366. *Id.* at 93.
367. 347 U.S. 483 (1954).
368. Davis v. Board of Sch. Comm'rs, 402 U.S. 33, 36 (1971).
369. Paris Adult Theater I v. Slaton, 413 U.S. 49, 57 n.7 (1973).
370. Mississippi Univ. for Women v. Hogan, 458 U.S. 718 (1982).
371. Williams v. Florida, 399 U.S. 78, 101–02 n.48–49 (1970).
372. Lockhart v. McCree, 476 U.S. 162, 168–172 (1986).
373. Roe v. Wade, 410 U.S. 113 (1973).
374. *See, e.g.*, Adarand Constructors, Inc. v. Pena, 965 F. Supp. 1556 (D. Colo. 1997) (list of congressional hearings and reports on discrimination against minority-owned businesses; disparity studies; and academic finding of disparate treatment).
375. Supreme Court Practice, *supra* n.12, at 741; Stern, *supra* n.17, at 306–07; Rustad & Koenig, *supra* n.3, at 99.
376. Dunn v. Commodity Futures Trading Comm'n, 519 U.S. 465 (1997).

- information on state prevailing wages and wage requirements;[377]
- the number and location of endangered or threatened species;[378]
- reference to the suicide of a Nobel Prize winner in an assisted-suicide case;[379]
- a written declaration by an expert witness, which the court found "unusual" and which the court expressly did not consider, given that the expert had not been subject to cross-examination by any party;[380]
- data concerning sales of *Playboy* magazines at military exchanges;[381]
- affidavits from state legislators in a congressional redistricting case;[382]
- reference to expert studies and reports that demonstrate that diversity promotes better learning outcomes;[383] and
- reference to the experience of retired military personnel.[384]

When amicus briefs present facts beyond the record that have not withstood the rigors of examination and cross-examination at trial, it is important for those facts or data to be well documented and scrutinized. Obviously, if something is so well-known that the court can take judicial notice of the facts, then there is no problem. Often, however, the extrinsic facts offered by an amicus brief are not so well-known that they fall within the scope of the judicial notice doctrine.[385]

When an amicus brief recites facts and empirical data that fall outside the judicial notice doctrine and lie outside the record, special problems arise because judges have a limited ability to evaluate such evidence and they may approach it with skepticism. Professors Rustad and Koenig, especially, voice concern over the lack of any "appropriate mechanisms to permit the court to evaluate the findings adequately."[386] They acknowledge that by providing

---

377. California Div. of Labor Standards Enforcement v. Dillingham Constr., N.A., Inc., 519 U.S. 316 nn. 9–11 (1997).
378. Nat'l Ass'n of Home Builders v. Babbitt, 130 F.3d 1041, 1052 (D.C. Cir. 1997).
379. Compassion in Dying v. Washington, 79 F.3d 790, 824–25 n.98 (9th Cir. 1996).
380. FTC v. Staples, 970 F. Supp. 1066, 1070 n.1 (D.D.C. 1997).
381. Gen. Media Commc'ns, Inc. v. Perry, 952 F. Supp. 1072, 1075 (S.D.N.Y. 1997).
382. Vera v. Bush, 933 F. Supp. 1341 (S.D. Tex. 1996).
383. 539 U.S. 306 (2003).
384. *Id.*
385. Stern, *supra* n.17, at 306.
386. Rustad & Koenig, *supra* n.3, at 99.

social science data, third-party amici can hold in check the governmental abuse of power, but recognize that all social science is not necessarily valid. They argue that an independent mechanism is necessary to allow the court to evaluate competing claims. For example, the court could enlist "social science special masters" to assist them in evaluating social science data.[387] A similar argument supports the use of scientists to assist the trial court in ruling on the admissibility of expert testimony under *Daubert v. Merrell Dow Pharmaceuticals, Inc.*[388] As Professors Rustad and Koenig note:

> If the Court is to use empirical studies to accurately reflect social reality, it needs additional safeguards. Lobbyists serve a useful purpose. Nevertheless, they should not have unrestricted power to shape the Justices' perception of the social science literature.[389]

A contrary view was persuasively asserted by Professor Ellie Margolis in an article in the University of *San Francisco Law Review*.[390] In her article, Professor Margolis expresses the view that appellate lawyers should view non-legal materials as one of the tools at their disposal and that failing to make use of this tool may violate the ethical obligation of zealous advocacy. Recent studies, she notes, show that courts have markedly increased citation to non-legal opinions. In particular, such material is the best, and sometimes the only support for policy arguments. They "serve a unique function in supporting policy arguments that is different from other uses of legislative facts."[391] Margolis urges appellate lawyers to use such materials in cases of first impression, statutory interpretation cases, and constitutional cases. Use of such materials by amici can offer the court important assistance in rendering a decision in these cases.

All of this suggests that if it is important to include facts outside the record that are not subject to judicial notice, the amicus should cite the most reputable sources available, such as authoritative academic works. It is even

387. *See id.* at 159–60.
388. 509 U.S. 579 (1993).
389. Rustad & Koenig, *supra* n.3, at 162.
390. Ellis Margolis, *Beyond Brandeis: Exploring the Uses of Non-Legal Materials in Appellate Briefs*, 34 U.S.F.L Rev. 197 (Winter 2000).
391. *Id.* at 211.

possible to cite as yet unpublished articles and to provide facts gathered by an amicus, so long as the amicus provides the material to the court and the other parties with an explanation of the circumstances.[392] The amicus should not rely on disputed facts, and opposing parties or other amici should have the opportunity to call such facts to the court's attention.[393]

Aside from the more sophisticated problems presented by social science data, ethical considerations are raised when an amicus attempts to mislead the court about the facts or the law. The assertion of erroneous factual or legal points in an amicus brief may discredit not only the amicus but also the party that the amicus supports.

Examples 7 and 8 in the Appendix contain citations to facts extrinsic to the record. They both involve medical and scientific issues, and Example 7 contains facts relevant to persons not parties to the case. In Example 6, the state of West Virginia refers to the variety of licenses it grants in discussing the ramifications of the holding that the state is opposing as amicus. Social science data has been presented in a number of other cases, including a brief filed by the U.S. Solicitor General in a death-penalty case.

### *Participation by Others in the Amicus Brief*

Ethical issues arise when the amicus brief is paid for by a party to the appeal or when the identity of the sponsor of the brief is someone other than the sponsor listed on the brief itself. Ethical questions include the following:

- May a party pay for the cost of preparing an amicus brief?
- May a lawyer sign an amicus brief that has been written by a party's counsel?
- Is it proper to allow a party's counsel to review and comment on an amicus brief prior to its submission?
- Must a lawyer disclose his or her own interests in the case, as well as those of the client?

---

392. Shapiro, *supra* n.200, at 342, 345–46.
393. Supreme Court Practice, *supra* n.12, at 741–42.

- May a party indirectly pay for an amicus brief or otherwise provide some monetary assistance to a group or association that is filing a supporting amicus brief?
- What disclosures should be made to the court concerning financial support for the amicus brief or the interests of the lawyer?

In 1997, the Supreme Court amended Rule 37.6 to require the identification in the first footnote on the first page of text "whether counsel for a party authored the brief in whole or in part."[394] In addition, Rule 37.6 required the amicus to identify every person or entity, other than the amicus party, its members, and its counsel, "who made a monetary contribution to the preparation or submission of the brief."[395] The rule was amended in 2007, so that it now requires identification of anyone who made a contribution "intended to fund" the preparation or submission of the brief and specifically poses that question as to any party and counsel for any party.[396]

Although the Court did not explain its rationale for adopting this rule, it appears to reflect several concerns. The Court may have been concerned that parties were financing amicus briefs and that some amicus briefs may have been written by a lawyer or party that had already submitted another brief in the case.[397] Another likely concern is that parties may recruit lawyers

---

394. Rule 37.6 provided:
Except for briefs presented on behalf of *amicus curiae* listed in Rule 37.4 [that is, the United States or an agency thereof], a brief filed under this Rule shall indicate whether counsel for a party authored the brief in whole or in part and shall identify every person other than the *amicus curiae,* its members, or its counsel, who made a monetary contribution to the preparation or submission of the brief. The disclosure shall be made in the first footnote on the first page of the text.

395. Marcia Coyle, *Amicus Disclosure Worries Some Amici,* National L.J., April 1, 1996, at A14.

396. S. Ct. R. 37.6. The Rule now provides as follows with the language added in 2007 appearing in bold:
Except for briefs presented on behalf of *amicus curiae* listed in Rule 37.4 [that is, the United States or an agency thereof], a brief filed under this Rule shall indicate whether counsel for a party authored the brief in whole or in part **and whether such counsel or a party made a monetary contribution intended to fund the preparation or submission of the brief,** and shall identify every person or entity, other than the *amicus curiae*, its members, or its counsel, who made **such** a monetary contribution to the preparation or submission of the brief. The disclosure shall be made in the first footnote on the first page of the text.

397. *Id.* at 738–39.

to write amicus briefs as a method of circumventing the page limit.[398] Yet another concern is that the parties may attempt to manufacture the appearance of widespread public support for their positions.[399] Ultimately, the rule was adopted in accord with the "increasingly passionate" desire for disclosure.[400] The disclosure of who participated or paid for the brief not only assists the Court in deciding on recusal matters, but it also assists the justices in "assessing the credibility to be attached to the views submitted" by the amicus.[401] Finally, the rule discourages counsel who try to circumvent the Court's page limits by "smuggling" additional arguments into amicus briefs.[402]

Candor is advised in complying with this rule, as when a non-party pays lawyers to assist in writing the amicus brief.[403] The Federal Rule of Appellate Procedure 29(c) imposes the same requirements. State courts may also do so. Examples include California, Connecticut, Maryland, New Mexico, North Dakota, Texas, and West Virginia.[404]

As to a financial contribution, Rule 37.6 is not concerned with the amount contributed but just whether a contribution has been made.[405] Whether a counsel for a party has authored an amicus brief in part may involve a judgment call. A leading treatise on practice before the Supreme Court has suggested that disclosure is required when "counsel takes an active role writing or in rewriting a substantial or important 'part' of the amicus brief, . . . something more substantial than editing a few sentences."[406]

The Texas Supreme Court adopted a similar rule in 1997. Rule 11 of the Texas Rules of Appellate Procedure requires disclosure of any fee paid or to be paid for preparation of the brief: The rule applies to all amicus briefs filed in Texas appellate courts. Counsel should always consult local

---

398. *Id.*
399. Kearney & Merrill, *supra* n.64, at 766.
400. Bennett Boskey & Eugene Gressman, THE 1997 RESTATEMENT & REVISIONS OF THE SUPREME COURT'S 1995 RULES, 170 F.R.D. 30, 32 (1977).
401. *Id.*
402. *Id.* at 32–33. *See also supra* n.254.
403. SUPREME COURT PRACTICE, *supra* n.12, at 739–40 & n.58
404. See the Appendix to this book for a compilation of excerpts from state court rules on amicus briefs.
405. *Id.* at 740.
406. *Id.* at 739.

rules in advance to determine if any such disclosure is required or to avoid conduct that would require disclosure.

Nevertheless, rules requiring such disclosure do not preclude discussions among counsel for the amicus curiae and counsel for the supported party, as such discussions are expected, if not necessary.[407] Likewise, it is expected that counsel for a party may review and make suggestions or give advice concerning the contents of an amicus brief.[408]

### *Conflicts of Interest*

Lawyers in private practice who submit an amicus brief motivated only by their interest in the law should ensure that their existing clients do not have an interest in the final decision of the case. In such situations, the lawyer should carefully consider whether a disclosure must be made of those interests.

## CONCLUSION

An amicus brief is indeed a "friend" to the court when it is brief and avoids repeating arguments made by the parties. If the parties have overlooked controlling opinions, the amicus should supply them to the court. If the amicus has particular experience and expertise on an issue, it may supply its wisdom to the court. The amicus is also an excellent vehicle for addressing broad policy issues. In particular, the amicus can discuss ramifications of the case that may not be apparent to the court. Thus, the highest goal of an amicus brief is to provide insight that will be of considerable help to the court. The next highest goal is to provide amplification or a fresh perspective.

The time and effort devoted to submitting an amicus brief can be worthwhile. Effective amicus briefs can, and have, shaped significant decisions on important legal points or can significantly enhance the chance for a grant of discretionary appellate review. The amicus can bring to the argument policy perspectives that present the "big picture" in a way that a party's

407. *Id.* at 736–37, 739 (Rule 37.6 does not require disclosure of collaboration between counsel for party and counsel for amicus curiae.).

408. *Id.*

brief may not, and sometimes, cannot. To return to and paraphrase Justice Hugo Black, "Many cases involve matters that affect far more people than the immediate record parties."[409] For that reason, amicus participation—even as an advocate or "lobbyist"—may enable courts to reach wiser decisions in cases that require or merit information beyond the litigants' grasp or interests.

409. Shapiro, *supra* n.200, at 340.

# INDEX TO APPENDIX

# NOTES ON THE EXAMPLES IN THE APPENDIX

This publication provides practical suggestions on all aspects of amicus practice, but it does more than that. In the Appendix are reprints of excerpts from 16 outstanding amicus briefs. These briefs are offered to the reader on the theory that there is no better way to teach than by example. Because of space considerations, the briefs have not been reprinted in full, and footnotes have been eliminated. Formatting has also been modified. The reprinting of these briefs has required conversion of the documents. Every attempt has been made to correct any typographical errors that resulted from the conversion process. Thus, any such errors should be attributed to this publication, not the authors of any of the amicus briefs.

Example 1 is an amicus brief by Robert E. Rains and Nancy G. Shor that influenced the U.S. Supreme Court in writing its opinion in an important case. No higher praise can be given to amici.

Examples 2 and 3 are three letter briefs filed in the Texas Supreme Court in *Boerjan v. Rodriguez* by amici that have divergent private property interests that they ask the Court to consider when deciding the case before it. The briefs demonstrate how an amicus can, in a few paragraphs, alert the Court to the impact its decision will have on parties who are not before the Court. As this book emphasizes, brevity is a high virtue in amicus practice.

Example 4 is an example of an amicus brief that urges the Court to grant certiorari in two underlying cases. The brief in *R.J. Reynolds Tobacco Company v. Brown* is a good example of how an amicus can help explain to the Court how a lower court's decision, if allowed to stand, may have far-reaching effects on litigants and the legal system. The amicus argues that thousands of cases will be "infected by the same due process error," which the brief characterizes as "obvious and elementary," that the petitioner seeks to remedy.

Example 5 is an excerpt from a lengthy amicus brief submitted in *Hollingsworth v. Perry*. Not all amicus briefs are short, although most should be. This amicus brief is an interesting example of an amicus submission for an individual, Walter Dellinger, by lawyers at his firm, arguing that the proponents of a law have standing to represent the state's interest in upholding the constitutionality of a statute where the state refuses to defend the law. Mr. Dellinger, a former acting Solicitor General of the United States and now a law professor and practicing attorney, provides the Court with input on the fundamental legal issue of standing. The case involved California's Proposition 8 that would have amended the California Constitution to provide that only marriages between a man and a woman are valid in California. The Proposition was held to be unconstitutional in the lower courts and the state refused to appeal. The proponents appealed and sought to represent the state's interest. In its opinion, the Court quoted from this brief.

Example 6 is an amicus submission in *Christie v. NCAA* by a combination of states seeking to support the petition for certiorari by a sister state on a question of federal preemption. It is in effect a "me too" brief as it provides the Court with additional legal analysis related to the question at issue. However, participation by amicus in support of a grant of certiorari can be an effective strategy to demonstrate to the Court that a decision in the case will have a broad public impact and will clarify the law in an important legal area.

Examples 7 and 8 are briefs that not only demonstrate effective advocacy but also show how amici can cite and rely upon materials outside the record. Example 7 from *CTS Corp. v. Waldburger* involved a state statute of repose that barred the plaintiffs from recovering alleged damages caused by contaminated water at a military base. The amici are a number of individuals whose claims would be barred. They presented the Court with a number of studies and other materials supporting their position. Example 8 from *Mutual Pharmaceutical Co. v. Bartlett* concerned federal preemption regarding alleged damages caused by "dangerous prescription drugs." The brief was submitted, not by injured persons, but by a trial-lawyer association.

Example 9, filed in *Spokeo Inc. v. Robins*, was submitted by DRI, a defense bar association. It presents the Court with the point of view of experienced litigators on a procedural matter. Although the amicus arguably has a "point of view," given the litigation defense orientation of its members, it effectively uses a neutral tone to address the real world effect of the decision of the lower courts on standing. A similar excellent example, submitted in the Fifth Circuit Court of Appeals case *Dupre v. CBS Corp.*, is Example 10, which was submitted by other litigation defense interests.

Example 11 is a brief written on behalf of the Solicitor General for the United States in *Davenport v. Washington Education Association.* The U.S. Solicitor General is probably the most prolific author of amicus briefs in our justice system. The brief concerns the validity of a state-enacted opt-in requirement restricting use of funds by labor unions for contributions to candidates for public office. That case raises issues under the First Amendment and federal election laws. The brief reflects a high-level of appellate advocacy suitable to an amicus curiae. The Court granted the Solicitor General the opportunity to participate in the oral argument. *See* 127 S. Ct. 845 (2006).

Also included here are Examples 12 and 13, which are amicus briefs submitted to state supreme courts. The brief in *Aguilar v. ExxonMobil Corp.*, part of the "*Lockheed Litigation Cases*," was submitted by Matrixx Initiatives, Inc., a corporation that sells cough and cold remedies. The case deals with the court's role as a gatekeeper for admissibility of expert testimony. The brief effectively describes the impact on small companies of a rule that weakens the court's gatekeeper function. Similarly, Example 13, submitted in *Lake Adventure Community Association v. Dingman Township Zoning Hearing Board*, also describes the impact of a legal rule on parties who are not before the Court. It was submitted by two industry trade organizations.

Example 14 is a short amicus brief, submitted in the Minnesota Supreme Court in *Voters Alliance v. Minnesota*. It is an example of how an amicus curiae who is not necessarily advocating for either party's position may ask the Court to shape its ruling in a manner that avoids injury to a party not before the Court.

Example 15 is an amicus brief filed in in the Supreme Court of the United States case, *Kiobel v. Royal Dutch Petroleum Co.*, regarding the Alien Tort Statute filed by Bancroft and Arnold & Porter.

Example 16 is a brief submitted on behalf of a number of Ivy League universities by Laurence H. Tribe and Jonathan Massey in the affirmative action case of *Grutter v. Bollinger.*

# APPENDIX: EXCERPTS FROM EXAMPLES OF AMICUS BRIEFS

## EXAMPLE 1

**Authors** Robert E. Rains and Nancy G. Shor
**Case** *Sullivan v. Zebley*, 493 U.S. 521 (1990)

### BRIEF OF THE NATIONAL ORGANIZATION OF SOCIAL SECURITY CLAIMANTS' REPRESENTATIVES AS AMICUS CURIAE IN SUPPORT OF THE RESPONDENTS

### INTEREST OF AMICUS CURIAE NOSSCR

The National Organization of Social Security Claimants' Representatives (NOSSCR) is a non-profit corporation. While most of our members are attorneys in private practice, others work in programs which provide free legal services to the poor. Our members regularly represent people claiming disability benefits in administrative proceedings before the Social Security Administration of the U.S. Department of Health and Human Services (DHHS). Our members also file actions in federal court against the Secretary of DHHS ("the Secretary") appealing the final administrative denial of clients' claims for such benefits. These disability benefits have been provided by the Congress through two separate but interrelated programs: Social Security Disability Insurance Benefits under Title II of the Social Security Act and Supplemental Security Income (SSI) under Title XVI of the Social Security Act. This case involves a special sub-group of claimants for SSI: indigent, disabled children.

Unfortunately the complexities of the qualifications for SSI, the labyrinthine nature of the administrative proceedings, and the frequent intransigence of DHHS—all of which are vividly demonstrated in this case—virtually require legal representation for these children. Moreover, the parents of these claimants, themselves indigent, are often ill-equipped from many standpoints to pursue their children's claims even to aid their legal representatives in a meaningful way.

This brief is filed in a representational capacity on behalf of these special clients who, by virtue of their minority, indigency and disability, cannot speak for themselves. Our purpose is to draw to this Court's attention our nationwide experience that, notwithstanding its protestations, DHHS does not grant SSI benefits to indigent children suffering from impairments of "comparable severity" to those of adults who are granted benefits, despite the clear statutory mandate that SSI benefits be granted to such children. Further, this result is compelled by the regulations before the Court which, on their face, violate the Social Security Act.

## SUMMARY OF ARGUMENT

Although the Congress has mandated that the Department of Health and Human Services grant Supplemental Security Income to impoverished children with impairments of comparable severity to those of adults granted benefits, the Secretary of DHHS has adopted regulations which compel a contrary result in many instances. The child who is denied SSI often suffers the further adverse consequence of ineligibility for Medical Assistance even if such assistance would ameliorate the disabling condition.

At issue before the Court are the Secretary's SSI regulations which require that a child's impairment meet or equal one in the "Listing of Impairments," although adults need not meet such a requirement to be eligible. By comparison, an adult whose impairments do not meet or equal a Listing may be eligible for SSI if that adult's residual functional capacity is so limited that the individual is disabled. Indeed, some twenty-five percent (25%) of all adults initially determined to be disabled by the Secretary are granted benefits on this basis without meeting or equaling a Listing.

Contrary to the Secretary's representations to this Court, the more stringent standards applied to children necessarily result in denial of benefits in comparable cases. Although some specific children's Listings do take functional consequences into account, unless a child's impairments meet or equal a Listing, the Secretary mandates that residual functional capacity be ignored and benefits be denied. Truncating the analysis of claims for [a] child's SSI at the stage of meeting or equaling a Listing also denies to children the application of beneficial doctrines applied in adult cases such as the evaluation of disabling effects of pain and the "treating physician rule."

Disabled children are not treated comparably to adults with comparable impairments. This is best illustrated by those cases in which the Secretary denies SSI to disabled individuals when they are children and then grants them SSI as of their eighteenth (18th) birthday with no change whatsoever in the severity of their impairments. Because the Secretary's administrative procedures often drag out over the course of years, it is not unusual for NOSSCR members to represent children who become adults while their SSI claims are pending. In many of these cases the Secretary grants SSI benefits effective the day of the claimant's eighteenth (18th) birthday. NOSSCR sets forth to this Court three examples of this arbitrary result of the challenged regulatory scheme. Younger children likewise suffer from the Secretary's illegally stricter treatment of them.

There is no justification for the Secretary's disparate treatment of children. Ignoring overall functional limitations of children who do not meet or equal a Listing necessarily results in the denial of claims which would be granted if the disabled individual were an adult. The Listings are not, and cannot be, comprehensive. They cannot determine the functional impact on all children of all disabling impairments. The Secretary argues that because children do not normally work, he cannot measure their functional capacity against any benchmark. Yet he acknowledges elsewhere that for children, disability is the impact of impairments on physical, mental and emotional growth and development. He is not, as he suggests, unable to make this determination for children on an individual basis. Indeed in one of the cases NOSSCR cites to this Court, that of Leon Gable, the Secretary determined a child to be functionally disabled at age thirteen (13), but because he found that child not to meet or equal a Listing, he refused to pay the child SSI.

It is no answer to suggest, as the Secretary does, that the courts should fill in any gaps in the Listings on an ad hoc basis on judicial review, by judicially constructing new and better Listings. To effectuate the statutory mandate that children be treated in a manner comparable to adults, the Secretary must be ordered to use comparable methodology in children's cases as in adults' cases. Otherwise indigent and disabled children will continue to be denied the SSI benefits created and intended for them by Congress.

## ARGUMENT

### *I. THE SECRETARY'S SSI REGULATIONS RESULT IN THE DENIAL OF SSI TO MANY DISABLED CHILDREN WITH IMPAIRMENTS OF COMPARABLE SEVERITY TO THOSE OF ADULTS GRANTED SSI.*

The nationwide experience of NOSSCR's membership demonstrates that the Secretary's regulatory interpretation of the children's Supplemental Security Income (SSI) Program is arbitrary, capricious and manifestly contrary to the enabling statute. In October 1972, Congress enacted Title XVI of the Social Security Act "establishing a national program to provide supplemental income to individuals who . . . are disabled . . . and are determined . . . to be eligible on the basis of . . . income and resources." P.L. 92-603, §§ 1601, 1602, 42 U.S.C. §§ 1381, 1381a. The SSI program specifically covers needy disabled children as well as adults:

> An individual shall be considered to be disabled for purposes of this title . . . if he is unable to engage in any substantial gainful activity by reason of any medically determinable physical or mental impairment which can be expected to result in death or which has lasted or can be expected to last for a continuous period of not less than twelve months *(or, in the case of a child under the age of 18, if he suffers from any medically determinable physical or mental impairment of comparable severity)*. (Emphasis added.)

P.L. 92-603, § 1614(a)(3)(A), 42 U.S.C. § 1382c(a)(3). The grant of SSI benefits to a needy disabled person is not only important for the limited federal monetary assistance provided (currently $368.00/month maximum for an individual assuming no deductions for actual or deemed income, but also because receipt of SSI normally makes an individual eligible for Medical Assistance (Medicaid) under Title XIX of the Social Security Act. 42 U.S.C. § 1396(a)(10)(A)(i). In many instances this Medical Assistance is even more valuable to the claimant than the cash assistance because it provides access to essential medical care. Denial of Supplemental Security Income may well cause denial of medical care needed to ameliorate a disabling condition.

Under the Secretary's regulations, a disabled child can receive SSI benefits only if he or she has a medically determinable physical or mental impairment which is in the "Listing of Impairments," 20 C.F.R., Part 404, Subpart P, Appendix 1, or which is determined by DHHS to "medically equal" an impairment included in this Listing. 20 C.F.R. § 416.924. By comparison, an adult SSI applicant whose condition is not found to meet or equal one of those set forth in the Listings is *not* disqualified from benefits. Rather DHHS will go on to determine his or her overall residual *functional* capacity. This determination of residual functional capacity "is a medical assessment" of physical abilities, mental impairments and other impairments such as skin impairments, epilepsy, disorders of vision or hearing, manipulative limitations, etc. 20 C.F.R. § 416.945(a). Then DHHS determines whether the adult claimant is disabled based upon that residual functional capacity, as well as age, education and work experience. 20 C.F.R. §§ 416.920, 416.945.

By contrast, DHHS makes no such assessment of the residual functional capacity of a child—and its disabling impact on the child—where DHHS finds that the child does not have a condition which meets or is "medically equal" to a listing in the Listing of Impairments. The significance of terminating the analysis of children's disability claims at the stage of meeting or equaling the Listings is amply demonstrated by the Secretary's statistics for assessment of adult claims. Every year for the last five years, roughly 25% of all adults initially granted disability benefits did not meet or equal a Listing. These adults were granted benefits based upon the disabling impact of their residual functional capacity. No such assessment is made for children.

Moreover, the Secretary's definition of "medically equal" specifically excludes consideration of overall functional capacity:

> As in determining whether the listing is met, it is incorrect to consider whether the listing is equaled on the basis of an assessment of *overall*

> functional impairment. The level of severity in any particular listing section is depicted by the given set of findings and not by the degree of severity of any single medical finding—no matter to what extent that finding may exceed the listed value.
>
> The mere accumulation of a number of impairments also will not establish medical equivalence. When an individual suffers from a combination of unrelated impairments, the medical findings of the combined impairments will be compared to the findings of the listed impairment most similar to the individual's most severe impairment. The functional consequences of the impairment (*i.e.*, RFC), irrespective of their nature [or] extent, cannot justify a determination of equivalence. (Emphasis in original.)

Social Security Ruling 83-19. Joint Appendix 236, 239-240.

The Secretary argues that:

> Nor can it credibly be maintained that the Secretary's regulations are arbitrary and capricious. The criteria in the special Part B Listing for children in fact do take into account functional and developmental consequences of impairments and their impact on ability to do age-appropriate activities where those factors are germane to particular impairments. In other words, the considerations that respondents would require the Secretary to consider on an individualized basis were taken into account in the formulation of the Part B Listing in the first place. As a result, the criteria in the Listing *already* embody the level of impairment severity that, in the Secretary's judgment, has an impact on development in a child comparable to the impact of an impairment on an adult's ability to work. (Emphasis in original.)

Brief for the Petitioner, p. 18. This is extremely misleading. It begs the question. Of course the Listings occasionally mention the functional consequences of impairments. But if an adult's impairments do not meet or equal one of the Listings, the Secretary then assesses his overall residual functional capacity. For a child this assessment is precluded by the Secretary's own interpretation quoted above.

Furthermore, the courts have imposed upon the Secretary the duty in adult SSI cases to consider a variety of factors not addressed by the Listing of Impairments. Two examples are the evaluation of disabling effects of pain and the "treating physician's rule." Section 223(d)(5)(A) of the Social Security Act provides, in relevant part:

> An individual's statement as to pain or other symptoms shall not alone be conclusive evidence of disability as defined in this section; there must be medical signs and findings, established by medically acceptable clinical or laboratory diagnostic techniques, which show the existence of a medical impairment that results from anatomical, physiological, or psychological abnormalities which could reasonably be expected to produce the pain or other symptoms alleged and which, when considered with all evidence required to be furnished under this paragraph (including statements of the individual or his physician as to the intensity and persistence of such pain or other symptoms which may reasonably be accepted as consistent with the medical signs and findings), would lead to a conclusion that the individual is under a disability. Objective medical evidence of pain or other symptoms established by medically acceptable clinical or laboratory techniques (for example, deteriorating nerve or muscle tissue) must be considered in reaching a conclusion as to whether the individual is under a disability.

42 U.S.C. § 423(d)(5)(A). Nevertheless, the Adult Listings do not treat pain in any comprehensive manner, and the Childhood Listings do not specifically address pain at all. In order to fill this gap for adults, the courts have superimposed various rules regarding the evaluation of pain to effect this statutory mandate. The precedent in the Third Circuit is illustrative, requiring:

> (1) that subjective complaints of pain be seriously considered, even where not fully confirmed by objective medical evidence, *Smith v. Califano*, 637 F.2d 968, 972 (3d Cir. 1981); *Bittel v. Richardson*, 441 F.2d 1193, 1995 (3d Cir. 1971); (2) that subjective pain "may support a claim for disability benefits," *Bittel,* 441 F.2d at 1195, and "may

> be disabling," *Smith*, 637 F.2d at 972; (3) that when such complaints are supported by medical evidence, they should be given great weight, *Taybron v. Harris*, 667 F.2d 412, 415 n.6 (3d Cir. 1981); and finally (4) that where a claimant's testimony as to pain is reasonably supported by medical evidence, the ALJ may not discount claimant's pain without contrary medical evidence. *Green v. Schweiker*, 749 F.2d 1066, 1070 (3d Cir. 1984); *Smith*, 637 F.2d at 972.

*Ferguson v. Schweiker*, 765 F.2d 31, 37 (3rd Cir. 1985). No comparable rules can be applied in claims for SSI for children because under the Secretary's challenged regulations disabling pain is simply not relevant.

Likewise, in adult disability claims, the courts have long enunciated the "treating physical rule" to the effect that:

> the expert opinion of a claimant's treating physician regarding his "medical disability, i.e., diagnosis and nature and degree of impairment, is . . . binding on the fact-finder unless controverted by substantial evidence." *Schisler v. Heckler*, 787 F.2d 76, 812 (2d Cir. 1986).

*Hildalgo v. Bowen*, 822 F.2d 294, 296-97 (2nd Cir. 1987).

The circuit courts have further adopted a "corollary" to the treating physician's rule, as follows:

> A corollary to the treating physician rule is that the opinion of a non-examining doctor by itself cannot constitute the contrary substantial evidence required to override the treating physician's diagnosis. *See Havas*, 804 F.2d at 786; *Strickland v. Harris*, 615 F.2d 1103, 1109 (5th Cir. 1980); *Martin v. Secretary of Health, Education and Welfare*, 492 F.2d 905, 907-08 (4th Cir. 1974); *Landess v. Weinberger*, 490 F.2d 1187, 1190 (8th Cir. 1974); *Meffort v. Gardner*, 383 F.2d 748, 759 (6th Cir. 1967).

*Id.* at 297. Largely because the Secretary's analysis of SSI claims for children ends with the issue of whether a child meets or equals a Listing, the Secretary applies the converse of the "treating physician rule" in children's cases. 20 C.F.R. § 416.926. As clearly set forth in Social Security Ruling 83-19:

> Decisions of equivalence are the responsibility of a physician designated by the Secretary. In most instances, the designated physician is a physician in the State agency. A medical advisor at a hearing or a member of the Appeals Council's (AC) medical support staff (including medical consultants) may also make the physician's decision in the determination of medical equivalence.
>
> As with any other medical opinion concerning impairment severity for titles II and XVI disability purposes, judgments of the examining physician are not controlling on the issue of equivalence. In every instance, the decision as to equivalence is to be made by a program physician based upon the individual medical findings in the particular case.

Joint Appendix at 240. Hence for children seeking SSI, the opinion of a non-examining physician on the ultimate issue of medical equivalence takes precedence over those of treating physicians, thereby turning the "treating physical rule" on its head.

## *II. MANY DISABLED INDIVIDUALS ARE DENIED SSI AS CHILDREN AND THEN GRANTED SSI AS ADULTS ON THEIR EIGHTEENTH BIRTHDAY WITH NO CHANGE IN THEIR IMPAIRMENTS.*

In our practices, NOSSCR members repeatedly see that the inevitable effect of the Secretary's challenged regulation is to deny indigent disabled children SSI—and often therefore Medical Assistance—although their disabilities are of "comparable severity" to those of adults who would be granted benefits. This can best be seen in those cases in which a child turns eighteen (18) years old during the course of the notoriously lengthy administrative proceedings. It is not unusual for the Secretary to deny a child SSI disability benefits prior to her eighteenth (18th) birthday, but to award them as of that date. Because the child starts receiving monthly benefits and because this result is often mandated by the Secretary's challenged regulation, it is understandable that very few of these cases are appealed to court.

### A. Lisa Wills

One of the few reported court decisions involving this scenario is that of Lisa Wills. In *Wills v. Secretary of Health and Human Services,* the district court stated that the issue presented was whether Lisa Wills, then nineteen (19) years of age, suffered from problems which "were sufficiently disabling to entitle Lisa to SSI before her eighteenth birthday." 686 F. Supp. 171, 172 (W.D. Mich. 1987). The court noted that:

> Lisa became eighteen during the administrative pendency of her SSI application. She was awarded benefits as an adult commencing on her birthday. That decision is not before the court.

*Id.* at 172, n.1. One unfamiliar with the Secretary's regulations might wonder what had befallen Lisa on her eighteenth birthday to render her condition so disabling as to be recognized as such by the Secretary. The simple answer is that all that befell Lisa was her eighteenth birthday and the application of the more flexible adult SSI regulations. In fact Lisa had suffered since infancy from a rare genetic enzyme defect which had caused mild retardation and central nervous system defect contributing to learning and behavioral difficulties. *Id.* at 172.

Lisa Wills was fortunate in that the reviewing court found that there was no substantial evidence to support the Secretary's finding that she did not meet a Listing as a child. The court therefore reversed the Secretary's final administrative decision denying her benefits. *Id.* at 176. Nevertheless her case demonstrates that, as the Secretary interprets and enforces his regulations, a child who is denied children's SSI may have the exact impairments which cause the Secretary to grant her adult SSI when she reaches the age of eighteen (18).

Lisa Wills' case is not an isolated example. Again and again we see similar situations of disabled children denied SSI benefits until their eighteenth birthday (thereby frustrating the very purpose of the SSI children's program) and then granted SSI benefits as of their eighteenth birthday with no change in their impairments. Even for the few comparatively fortunate children like Lisa Wills who ultimately prevail in federal court, the Secretary's inflexible and arbitrary regulations mean the denial of SSI benefits during the critical period that they were intended to be received and often the consequent denial of Medical Assistance during that period.

### B. Steven Martinez

Many disabled individuals and their families give up along the way, frustrated by the Secretary's seemingly interminable procedures and stymied by the double standard which the Secretary denies to this Court that he applies. The case of Steven D. Martinez exemplifies the Secretary's actual practice. Steven's mother filed an application for children's SSI benefits for Steven in early May 1985 alleging that he was disabled. Steven was then seventeen (17) years old. He suffered from severe bilateral sensorineural hearing loss and congenital abnormality of the right hand with severe loss of grip strength and absence of the right thumb and fourth and fifth fingers. In addition, he had received a penetrating injury to his rectum and bladder which necessitated surgery and a temporary colostomy. Steven's claim was denied initially and on reconsideration, and his mother requested a hearing before an administrative law judge. In June 1986, over thirteen (13) months after Steven's mother filed his claim, the administrative law judge issued a decision denying it.

On appeal, the Secretary acting through the Appeals Council remanded the case "for additional evaluation because the claimant had attained age eighteen (18) before the date of the decision." In October 1987, almost two and a half years after the initial filing, Steven's claim was again denied by an administrative law judge. On appeal, the Secretary again remanded the case. A supplemental hearing was held in late October 1988, some three and a half years into the process. That hearing resulted in a final "favorable" decision on December 27, 1988.

The "favorable" decision in Steven Martinez' case again illustrates the illegality of 20 C.F.R. § 416.924. This final decision finds Steven to be disabled and eligible for SSI as of April 15, 1986, the day he turned eighteen (18), but not before. No intervening injury or illness struck Steven on April 15, 1986. His impairments of April 15, 1986, were clearly of "comparable severity" to those he suffered in 1985 when he applied. Indeed if anything, his condition had improved by 1986 because he had a longer recovery time since his temporary colostomy. When the Secretary's administrative law judge considered primarily the impact on his long-term hearing loss and congenital hand deformity, he appropriately found Steven's residual functional capacity to be so diminished that he was disabled as an adult. However, since none of Steven's impairments met a Listing, 20 C.F.R. § 416.924 barred him from receiving SSI as a child.

## C. Leon Gable

Leon Gable was born on November 28, 1969, and suffers from defective intellectual development, the side effect of seizure medication (sluggishness, blurred vision and uncontrolled bowel movements), limited social ability and impaired ability to deal with stress. In December 1986, his mother filed an application for child's SSI benefits on his behalf. In July 1987, his mother also filed an application for "disabled adult child's" benefits for Leon under Title II of the Social Security Act. Both claims were denied initially and on reconsideration. Leon's mother sought and obtained a hearing before a Social Security administrative law judge. Almost two years after the child's SSI claim was filed, the ALJ issued a decision denying that claim, pursuant to 20 C.F.R. § 416.924, finding that "the evidence fails to establish conclusively a history of impaired intellectual functioning below that (I.Q. of 69 or less) prescribed by the Listings."

However, with regard to Leon's claim for disabled adult child's benefits under Title II of the Social Security Act, the ALJ reached a different result, because only claimants for childhood SSI benefits are required to meet or equal a Listing. The ALJ considered the testimony of a "vocational expert" who had appeared at the hearing. This vocational expert testified that Leon was adversely affected by limited social awareness, limited social ability, poor ability to deal with stress, a history of seizures and impaired intellectual capacity. The vocational expert opined that an individual with Leon's combination of impairments was unlikely to function in any job. Using the standard for a disabled adult child, in which residual functional capacity is assessed, the ALJ found Leon to be under a disability since Sept. 1, 1983 (when he was 13 years of age). This entitled him to disabled adult child benefits after age 18, but not to SSI benefits as a child!

On administrative appeal, the Secretary, acting through the Appeals Council, affirmed the decision of the administrative law judge, stating that he had correctly applied the law.

NOSSCR could multiply examples from around the country of children who have been denied SSI benefits by the Secretary until the date of their eighteenth (18th) birthday and granted benefits as of that birthday with no change in the severity of their impairments. However, we do not mean to suggest that 20 C.F.R. § 416.924 is illegal only with regard to this subgroup of children's SSI claimants who turn eighteen (18) during the Secretary's extended administrative processes. It is also illegally applied to young children who are denied children's SSI benefits who, we are confident, would have to be awarded benefits if their residual functional capacity were assessed in a manner comparable to that assessment for adult claimants. We specifically bring to this Court's attention the arbitrary and irrational results in the case of children turning eighteen (18) because of the Secretary's own recognition of their disparate, non-comparable treatment, and not in any way to sanction the Secretary's illegal treatment of younger claimants.

## *III. THE REASONS ASSERTED BY THE SECRETARY FOR HIS DISPARATE TREATMENT OF DISABLED CHILDREN ARE NEITHER LAWFUL NOR RATIONAL NOR MANDATED BY PRAGMATIC CONCERNS.*

The Secretary argues that "the concept of comparability does not rigidly require uniformity insofar as the subjects to be compared 'are different in a fundamental way.'" Brief for the Petitioner, p. 24. But surely the statutory grant of benefits to children with impairments of comparable severity requires like results where there are identical impairments as in the cases cited above. Denial of childhood benefits in situations of comparable severity is the very essence of a regulatory framework that is arbitrary, capricious and manifestly contrary to the statute. *Atkins v. Rivera*, 477 U.S. 154, 162 (1986).

The Secretary further argues that the combined effect of multiple impairments is considered throughout the disability determination process. Brief for the Petitioner, p. 28, n.19. However, for children this process only extends to the determination of whether or not they have a severe impairment that meets or equals a specific listing. By the Secretary's edict, these combined effects will only be "compared to the findings of the listed impairment most similar to the individual's most severe impairment. The functional consequences of the impairments (i.e., FRC), irrespective of their nature or extent, cannot justify a determination of equivalence." SSR 83-19, Joint Appendix, p. 240. Hence, by the Secretary's regulations, Steve Martinez' functional limitations did not render him disabled for SSI purposes until he turned eighteen (18), then rendered him disabled.

Of course no listing of afflictions can ever be comprehensive, nor do all impairments necessarily impact all individuals in the same way. Indeed, as the Listings have been promulgated and revised, the Secretary previously acknowledged that they were not comprehensive and were not intended to preclude assessment of functional limitations in those cases where the Listings were not equaled or met. *See Marcus v. Bowen,* 696 F. Supp. 364, 373-76 (N.D. Ill. 1988).

The Secretary asserts:

> The regulations focus, however, not on the individual child's ability to function as such, but on the impact of the impairment on his physical, mental, and emotional growth and development. An assessment of functional abilities will normally be subsumed in applying these standards.

Brief for the Petitioner, p. 42. This self-contradictory language obfuscates rather than clarifies. If disability is not the impairment of function of an individual, what is it? In some cases, the child's impairment of physical, mental and/or emotional growth will be demonstrated by the child meeting or equaling a specific Listing. But because the Listings cannot be comprehensive, and because the overall functional consequences of impairments irrespective of their nature or extent cannot justify a determination of equivalence, the Secretary's regulation violates the Social Security Act. The Secretary goes on to argue:

> Simply put, an assessment of residual functional capacity or functional impairment cannot exist in a vacuum. The relevant question is, functional capacity to do *what*? With respect to adults, the Secretary is instructed to inquire into an individual's functional capacity to engage in "substantial gainful activity," *i.e.*, to work. Ability to work thus provides a single, objective benchmark against which a person's individual nonmedical attributes—his age, education, and previous work experience—can be assessed. As the Secretary has recognized from the outset of the program, however, the assessment of disability in children "cannot properly be associated with an inability to work, since children are not ordinarily expected to engage in such activity." J. A. 90. (Emphasis in original.)

Brief for the Petitioner, p. 43. This is simply disingenuous. Obviously assessment of residual functional capacity or functional impairment cannot exist in a vacuum. But there is no mystery as to against what it should be assessed. The Secretary has acknowledged that the appropriate issue is, as already noted, "the impact of the impairment on his [the child's] physical, mental and emotional growth and development." Brief for the Petitioner, p. 42. Indeed, since filing his Brief for the Petitioner with the Court, the Secretary has published a notice of proposed rulemaking which would revise the Listings of Impairments for children under age eighteen (18) with mental disorders. *Federal Register*, Vol. 54, No. 155, August 14, 1989, pp. 33, 238 *et seq*. In the new proposed mental Listings for children, the Secretary would evaluate various functional limitations "which are applicable to children," such as "motor development, cognitive/communicative function, and social function" and "function in the school setting." *Id*. at 33, 242. For the severely impaired child who does not meet or equal a Listing, an assessment of limitation of function in these areas is essential to determine whether that child has impairments of comparable severity to those of adults who would be granted benefits.

As the Leon Gable case exemplifies, the Secretary can apply functional criteria to children who do not meet or equal the Listings. Using this criteria, the Secretary found Leon to be disabled at age 13. The Secretary is not unable to apply comparable criteria, but rather is unwilling to award SSI benefits to comparably impaired children.

The Secretary opines:

> Moreover, as noted above, if, as respondents allege, there are any "gaps" in the Secretary's Part B Listing (Br. in Opp. 24)—that is, if experience reveals that the Listing overlooks certain impairments that have a severe impact on childhood growth and development, or inadequately gauges the impact of a specific impairment on childhood development—the solution is not to jettison the entire regulatory framework. Rather, as the district court observed, the proper remedy is to challenge particular Part B listings (or the absence of such listings) on judicial review of the denial of disability benefits.

Brief for the Petitioner, p. 42. Respondents are not seeking "to jettison the entire regulatory framework" and have not asked the courts to do so. Rather, because there are, and must be, gaps and inadequacies in any set of Listings, respondents ask that the Secretary be ordered to apply an assessment of residual functional capacity to children whose impairments do not meet or equal one of the Listings in a manner comparable to that assessment for adults.

The Secretary's argument regarding the challenge to particular Listings or the absence thereof is not only unrealistic, but is a complete misstatement of what the district court said. The district court never suggested that an appellant could challenge a particular Listing or absence thereof on judicial review. Rather, it stated:

> Plaintiffs' argument may well be valid, in many cases; but errors in applying the regulations in some cases do not demonstrate invalidity of the regulations themselves. Part B of the Secretary's listings of impairments, 20 C.F.R. § 416.925, is not facially invalid or incomplete, seems to provide the necessary flexibility, and, in my view, permits the award of benefits in conformity with the intent of Congress. If these criteria are being misapplied or misinterpreted, the remedy lies in the appeal process in individual cases, not in a class-action decree.

*Zebkey v. Heckler,* 642 F. Supp. 220, 222 (E.D. Pa. 1986).

The reality is that such an attack on the adequacy or nonexistence of a specific Listing would likely be precluded by the courts' limited scope of review. The standard for judicial review of the denial of individual claims is set forth in Section 205(g) of the Social Security Act, 42 U.S.C. § 405(g), which provides in relevant part:

> The findings of the Secretary as to any fact, if supported by substantial evidence, shall be conclusive, and where a claim has been denied by the Secretary or a decision is rendered under subsection (b) of this section which is adverse to an individual who was a party to the hearing before the Secretary, because of failure of the claimant or such individual to submit proof in conformity with any regulation prescribed under subsection (a) of this section, the court shall review only the question of conformity with such regulations and the validity of such regulations.

Applying this test to Social Security appeals, this Court has stated that substantial evidence is "more than a mere scintilla. It means such relevant evidence as a reasonable mind might accept as adequate to support a conclusion." *Richardson v. Perales,* 402 U.S. 389, 401 (1971). As the Secretary correctly notes, Congress has given him authority to publish such criteria as Listings. Brief for the Petitioner, p. 21. A direct attack on a specific Listing or lack thereof would implicate the courts in what the Secretary claims is implicated here: substituting their medical judgment for that of the Secretary. The Secretary points to no case in which such an attack has been mounted, much less one that has been successful. One can imagine the Secretary's reaction if, on judicial review, one were to ask a court, for example, to rule that the standard for growth impairment under Listing 100.03A should be a drop in height of 20 percentiles rather than the current regulatory 25 percentiles. *See* Joint Appendix, p. 208. He would, properly, respond that such a judgment is his, not the court's, to make.

One cannot expect the courts to substitute their medical judgment for that of the Secretary. Nor is the answer to ask the courts to do so, on an individual basis, to remedy gaps and flaws in the Listings. Rather, the answer is for this Court to direct the Secretary to use comparable methodology to assess children's impairments as he does to assess adults' impairments. That is the only way to effectuate Congress's clear mandate that the Secretary grant SSI benefits to children who suffer from any medically determinable physical or mental impairment of comparable severity to that of an adult who would be granted such benefits.

## CONCLUSION

Congress has clearly and specifically mandated that the Department of Health and Human Services grant SSI benefits to children who suffer from any medically determinable physical or mental impairment of comparable severity to that of an adult who would be granted such benefits. Instead the Secretary of DHHS holds children to a more restrictive standard of disability than adults, by requiring them to present an impairment that meets or equals a Listing and by ignoring impairment of their overall residual functional capacity. The necessary result of this disparate treatment is to deny SSI and Medical Assistance to many of the children whom Congress intended to benefit from these programs. The Secretary's arguments that children are treated in a comparable manner to adults ignore the inevitable results of this regulatory framework and are belied by his actions. The arbitrary and capricious results are not mandated by any inability to perform the evaluations mandated by Congress. Real children in real need with real and serious problems suffer real harm as a result. These children will not receive the statutory benefits they desperately need unless and until this Court upholds the Third Circuit and directs the Secretary to make fully comparable assessments of the impairments of disabled children.

* * *

## EXAMPLE 2

**Author** Chesley N. Blevins, Jackson Walker L.L.P.
**Case** *Boerjan v. Rodriguez*, 436 S.W.3d 307 (Tex. 2014)

On behalf of the Texas Mining and Reclamation Association (TMRA), and as its General Counsel, I have been asked to file this amicus. The amicus was prepared by Trey Powers, TMRA's Executive Director and a salaried employee.

TMRA is tremendously concerned with the San Antonio Fourth Court of Appeals' ruling in this matter. TMRA is an industry trade association which represents the interests of the mining industry in Texas. Our membership of some 120 companies includes mining companies (Lignite Coal, Uranium, Sand, Gravel, Rock, etc.) as well as numerous contracting companies who support mining activities. There are currently 45 permitted coal and uranium mines in the state of Texas, located from the Rio Grande to near Texarkana. The annual economic impact of these operations to the Texas economy is over $2.3 billion. In addition, there are over 1,000 Texas aggregate, sand, and rock mining operations, located in all areas of the state, and contributing an additional $5.5 billion annually to the state's economy.

The abbreviated facts of the case are as follows:

- While trespassing on the privately-owned Jones Ranch in South Texas, an immigration smuggler lost control of his vehicle and crashed, the result being the loss of life of two illegal immigrants that were hidden in the vehicle; and
- Heirs of the descendants brought claim for wrongful death, asserting the actions of a petitioner employee caused the crash and thus the death of the illegal immigrants.

Several TMRA member mining companies operate in the South Texas region where illegal immigration and trespassing on private lands are prevalent. It is well known that a portion of this illegal activity includes the transport of drugs by often violent smugglers. To avoid public highways and Border

Patrol checkpoints, these criminals cut fences and drive on private ranch roads.

TMRA believes the very basis of private land ownership and private property rights vests an owner with basic rights to protect their land and business operations—at the very least to question individual(s) who do not have permission to be on the ranch. In this case, we understand the Mestena Security guard stopped and questioned the assailant, who then fled at a dangerous and reckless rate of speed, which ultimately caused the crash and resulting deaths.

Specifically as this case relates to TMRA Mine Operator members, we would like the Court to understand the following:

1. Mine Operators in Texas often own or lease several thousand acres which are included within permit areas approved by the Railroad Commission of Texas and/or the Texas Commission on Environmental Quality.
2. The Mine Operators, as permittees, have very broad duties and obligations set out in their permits and/or in the statutory and regulatory requisites relating to those permits.
3. These obligations to state and federal agencies include not only protecting the environment, but assuring certain levels of health and safety to workers and the public. As such, security and monitoring of all persons in and out of mine-permitted land is imperative.
4. Because the very nature of mining, recovering and/or processing these resources, including uranium and coal, can create hazardous conditions, the duties and obligations on these permittees mandate a higher, more strict, level of vigilance, oversight and protection than might fall on most landowners.

Should the Court ultimately uphold the Court of Appeals' Opinion, a very troubling precedent would be set whereby mining companies could be rendered helpless in patrolling and protecting their business operations. Moreover, and of great importance, tying the hands of these Mine Operators might well lead to putting the public at risk from these operations and cause properly issued state and federal permits and permit terms to be violated. This would almost certainly lead to severe disruptions to the industry, necessitate increased liability insurance, and cause other undue and costly harm.

Considering the above facts and argument, we respectfully ask that the Court overturn the ruling of the Fourth Court of Appeals and uphold private property rights in the State of Texas.

## EXAMPLE 3

**Author** James F. Buchanan, Welder Leshin LLP
**Case** *Boerjan v. Rodriguez*, 436 S.W.3d 307 (Tex. 2014)

The John G. and Marie Stella Kenedy Memorial Foundation has requested that I file this *amicus* in support of the Petition for Review of Philip Boerjan and Mestena Uranium, LLC and Mestena Operating, LLC, formerly known as Mestena Operating, Ltd. and Mestena, Inc. The Foundation requests that copies of this letter be circulated to the chambers of the Justices of the Supreme Court for consideration of the pending Petition for Review. In accordance with Rule 11, Texas Rules of Appellate Procedure, I certify that copies of this *amicus* letter have been served on all counsel for the parties. The Kenedy Memorial Foundation will pay the attorney's fee of the undersigned for the preparation of this *amicus* letter.

### *I. STATEMENT OF INTEREST*

The John G. and Marie Stella Kenedy Memorial Foundation is a 501(c)(3) non-profit corporation established in 1960 to primarily support Catholic educational, charitable and religious activities. Seventy percent of the support is to South Texas entities. At least 10% of the Foundation's support is for non-sectarian charities in Texas.

The Foundation derives the bulk of its income from the Kenedy Memorial Foundation Ranch in Kenedy County. The Kenedy Memorial Foundation Ranch consists of three parts, stretching some 60 miles along U.S. Highway 77. The La Parra Division, the northernmost, is approximately 23,000 acres east of U.S. Highway 77, while the Rita Division is approximately 36,000 acres west of U.S. 77, and the Jaboncillos is approximately 176,900 acres east of U.S. 77. The La Parra and the Jaboncillos Divisions are separated by ranchland which belongs to the Kenedy Trust. The U.S. Border Patrol "Sarita" Station is located on U.S. 77 between the La Parra and the Jaboncillos Divisions.

One of the missions of the Kenedy Memorial Foundation is to maintain its portion of the Kenedy Ranch as a natural asset that honors the role of the Kenedy family in both the development and preservation of South Texas. In

1997-98, the Kenedy Memorial Foundation received the prestigious Texas Parks and Wildlife Department's Outstanding Lone Star Steward Award in recognition of outstanding efforts in the conservation and enhancement of wildlife habitat in Texas.

There are frequent incursions onto the Rita, Jaboncillos and La Parra Divisions by trespassers, both illegal aliens and drug and human smugglers seeking to avoid the U.S. Border Patrol Sarita checkpoint. The decision of the San Antonio Court of Appeals is of concern, because it appears to create additional duties owed by occupiers of agricultural land to these trespassers, and is contrary to current Texas law.

## *II. BACKGROUND*

In 2007, one morning before sunrise, Jose Francisco Maciel was illegally transporting Oscar Vasquez-Lara and at least three other undocumented aliens in his pickup truck across the Jones Ranch in Brooks County in order to avoid the U.S. Border Patrol Falfurrias checkpoint. A Mestena Operating employee flashed the lights of his truck and stopped Maciel. After a brief discussion, Maciel sped off. A short while later, Maciel's truck was found in the brush. Maciel lost control of his truck which rolled over, ejecting Vasquez-Lara. In addition, plaintiffs' decedents were ejected and fatally injured.

## *III. ARGUMENT*

The Court of Appeals applied a standard negligence analysis to the case: "a duty, a breach of that duty, and damages proximately caused by the breach of duty. *See Doe v. Boys Club of Greater Dallas,* 907 S.W.2d 472, 477 (Tex. 1995)." The Court of Appeals went further in its analysis of the duty owed to plaintiffs' decedents: "Every person has a duty to exercise reasonable care to avoid a foreseeable risk of injury to others." *Midwest Emp'rs. Cas. Co. ex rel. English v. Harpole,* 293 S.W.3d 770, 776 (Tex.App.—San Antonio 2009, no pet.) (quoting *Lukasik v. San Antonio Blue Haven Pools, Inc.,* 21 S.W.3d 394, 403 (Tex.App.—San Antonio 2000, no pet.)). The Court of Appeals held, in part: "The Rodriguezes do not have to prove the decedents were engaged in entering the United States illegally or eluding immigration officers to show the Mestenas had a duty to exercise reasonable care not to harm the decedents." *Rodriguez v. Boerjan;* 2012 W.L. 3764933 (Tex. App.—San Antonio 2012).

However, for all of its consideration of the duty owed to plaintiffs' decedents, the Court of Appeals erred. In its opinion, there is not one mention of the status of plaintiffs' decedents as trespassers. That puts the Court of Appeals' decision at odds with existing Texas law, Chapter 75, Limitation of Landowners' Liability, Texas Civil Practice and Remedies Code. Section 75.007(b) provides:

> An owner, lessee, or occupant of land does not owe a duty of care to a trespasser on the land and is not liable for any injury to a trespasser on the land, except that an owner, lessee, or occupant owes a duty to refrain from injuring a trespasser willfully, wantonly, or through gross negligence.

Texas law prior to the enactment of §75.007 provided a trespasser is a person who enters the property of another without right, lawful authority, or express or implied invitation, permission or licensee. *Park v. Troy Dodson Constr. Co., 761*\ S.W.2d 98, 100 (Tex.App.—Beaumont 1988, writ denied); *See* Tex. Civ. Prac & Rem. Code §75.007(a). The fact that a person does not know that the conduct is trespassing is irrelevant. *Williams v. Bill's Custom Fit, Inc.,* 821 S.W.2d 432, 435 (Tex.App.—Waco 1991, no writ).

In general, prior to May 11, 2011, an owner, lessee or occupier of land had no duty toward a trespasser, other than to refrain from injuring them willfully, wantonly, or through gross negligence. *Carlisle v. J. Weingarten, Inc.,* 152 S.W.2d 1073, 1074 (Tex. 1941). A trespasser enters land of another without any legal right and without any implied assurance of safety from the owner or occupier of the land. An owner, lessee or occupant of the land is justified under the Penal Code in using force against the trespasser in defense of person or property, and there is no liability to the trespasser. Tex. Civ. Prac & Rem. Code §75.007(d). Texas Penal Code §9.41 (a) provides: "A person in lawful possession of land or tangible moveable property is justified in using force against another when and to the degree the actor reasonably believes force is immediately necessary to prevent or terminate another's trespass on the land or unlawful interference with the property."

Thus, the Court of Appeals' decision, seemingly creating a new duty of care to trespassers, is at odds with Texas law at the time of the incident made the basis of the suit and under current statutory law.

Another disturbing aspect of the Court of Appeals' decision is equating the current invasion of private agricultural land in South Texas by undocumented aliens and smugglers of aliens and drugs, who are often dangerous, to Depression Era trespassing on trains. The conditions, which are set forth in Exhibits B-H to the Brief of *Amicus Curiae* of South Texas Property Rights Association, Texas and Southwestern Cattle Raisers Association, Texas Cattle Feeders Association, Texas Wildlife Association, Independent Cattlemen's Association of Texas, Exotic Wildlife Association, Texas Independent Ginners Association and Texas Poultry Federation in Support of Petitioners, chronicle an alarming increase in criminal activity and in the apprehension of aliens by immigration and other law enforcement authorities in the Rio Grande Valley sector of the Customs/Border Patrol which encompasses Kenedy County.

Based on the foregoing facts and arguments, the John G. and Marie Stella Kenedy Memorial Foundation requests the Supreme Court of Texas grant Petitioners' Petition for Review and reverse the opinion of the Court of Appeals so this opinion does not contribute to confusion over settled law established by the Texas Legislature.

## EXAMPLE 4

**Authors** Andrew L. Frey, Kenneth S. Geller, Lauren R. Goldman, Michael S. Rayfield, Mayer Brown LLP; Miguel A. Estrada, Amir C. Tayrani, Robert E. Johnson, Gibson, Dunn & Crutcher LLP

**Case** *R.J. Reynolds Tobacco Co. v. Brown,* 134 S. Ct. 2726 (2014) (cert. denied)

### BRIEF OF PHILIP MORRIS USA INC. AS AMICUS CURIAE IN SUPPORT OF PETITIONER

### INTEREST OF AMICUS CURIAE

*Amicus curiae* Philip Morris USA Inc. ("PM USA") is a defendant in thousands of pending *Engle* progeny cases that will be directly affected by the disposition of these two petitions for certiorari, and has filed its own petition for certiorari in *Philip Morris USA Inc. v. Barbanell,* No. 13-1180, which it has asked the Court to hold pending the resolution of these two petitions.

If the decisions below are allowed to stand, each of the thousands of *Engle* progeny cases pending in state and federal courts throughout Florida will be infected by the same due process error that petitioner R.J. Reynolds Tobacco Co. ("Reynolds") asks this Court to remedy here. Like Reynolds, PM USA will be denied any ability to contest the tortious conduct elements of the plaintiffs' defect and negligence claims in those cases—and will thus be unable to dispute, for example, that the PM USA cigarettes smoked by each plaintiff contained a defect or that its conduct toward each plaintiff was negligent. Instead, those elements will be conclusively established by highly generalized findings rendered in the now-decertified *Engle* class action—even though those findings cannot be shown to be relevant to any particular progeny plaintiff who now stands to benefit from them.

Only this Court can provide PM USA and the other *Engle* defendants with relief from that massive and unprecedented due process violation. Although the Florida District Court of Appeal in *Brown* was gravely "concerned" by the due process implications of its holding, *Brown* Pet. App. 18, it considered itself bound to follow the course charted by the Florida Supreme Court in *Engle* and subsequently reaffirmed in *Philip Morris USA Inc. v. Douglas,* 110 So. 3d 419 (Fla.), *cert. denied,* 134 S. Ct. 332 (2013). And, in *Walker,* an Eleventh Circuit panel—in a decision issued after most of the cert-stage briefing in *Douglas* was completed—likewise deemed itself bound to defer to the Florida Supreme Court under an erroneous theory of full faith and credit that was not even advanced by the plaintiffs in that case. Now that the Eleventh Circuit has declined en banc rehearing, the due process question is fully ripe for this Court's review.

## STATEMENT

**A.** The due process flaws in the *Brown* and *Walker* trials are obvious and elementary: plaintiffs will be permitted to take the defendant's property under the guise of a tort judgment without proving each of the elements that state law concededly prescribes before such a deprivation can take place. In both cases—but for different and mutually inconsistent reasons—this deprivation is to take place under the perceived compulsion of *Engle v. Liggett Group, Inc.,* 945 So. 2d 1246 (Fla. 2006) (per curiam), an anomalous class-certification decision that this Court never reviewed.

Confronted with a sprawling, statewide class of Florida smokers, the Florida Supreme Court concluded in *Engle* that "continued class-action treatment" was "not feasible because individualized issues . . . predominate[d]." 945 So. 2d at 1268. Rather than decertify the class altogether, however, the court decided for "pragmatic" reasons to decertify the class only prospectively, retroactively certifying an issues class and authorizing class members to "initiate individual damages actions" in which "the Phase I common core findings will have res judicata effect." *Id.* at 1269. The court adopted this procedure even though the class members themselves had virtually nothing in common: they had smoked different brands of cigarettes with different designs and different alleged defects at various points over a fifty-year period.

In *Douglas,* 110 So. 3d 419, the Florida Supreme Court was squarely presented with the *Engle* defendants' argument that federal due process prohibits plaintiffs from relying on the Phase I findings to establish elements of their particular claims because it is impossible to determine whether the *Engle* jury actually decided those issues in their favor. In addressing that argument, the Florida Supreme Court acknowledged that the *Engle* class's theories of liability "included brand-specific defects"—*i.e.,* defects that applied only to some cigarettes and thus only some class members—as well as theories that could apply to all class members. *Id.* at 423. The court concluded that, as a result of the class's alternative theories of liability and the generality of the Phase I findings, the findings would be largely "useless" to *Engle* progeny plaintiffs if issue preclusion applied because that doctrine requires proof that an issue was "actually decided" in the prior proceeding. *Id.* at 433.

The Florida Supreme Court nevertheless held that progeny plaintiffs could rely on a heretofore-unknown doctrine of *offensive* "claim preclusion" to establish in their favor any issue that "might . . . have been" decided against the defendants by the Phase I jury. *Douglas,* 110 So. 3d at 432 (internal quotation marks omitted). The court held that this novel approach to preclusion comports with due process because claim preclusion, unlike issue preclusion, "has no 'actually decided' requirement." *Id.* at 435.

**B.** Reynolds's petitions for certiorari in *Brown* and *Walker* seek review of two of the thousands of *Engle* progeny actions that remain pending in Florida state and federal court.

*Brown* was filed as an *Engle* progeny suit in Florida state court. The trial court did not require the plaintiff to demonstrate that the *Engle* Phase I jury had actually decided issues relevant to Mr. Brown's smoking history, but nonetheless instructed the jury that the *Engle* findings conclusively established the conduct element of his claims. *Brown* Pet. App. 10-11. On appeal, the Florida Fourth District Court of Appeal affirmed, explaining that it was "concerned the preclusive effect of the *Engle* findings violates Tobacco's due process rights" but that it was "compelled to follow the mandate of the [state] supreme court." *Id.* at 18. The Florida Supreme Court held the case pending its decision in *Douglas* and thereafter declined jurisdiction. *Walker* is a consolidated appeal from two *Engle* progeny actions tried in the United States District Court for the Middle District of Florida. As in *Brown,* the district court instructed the juries in both cases that the plaintiffs could rely on the *Engle* Phase I findings to establish the conduct elements of their claims and that the juries were not required to make any finding on those elements. *Walker* Pet. App. 16.

On appeal, Reynolds argued that permitting the plaintiffs to rely on the Phase I findings to establish elements of their claims violated federal due process and that the doctrine of offensive claim preclusion adopted by the Florida Supreme Court in *Douglas* was a constitutionally inadequate ground for affording such broad preclusive effect to the findings. The Eleventh Circuit, however, declined to address the constitutionality of *Douglas*'s unprecedented theory of claim preclusion. Instead, it read *Douglas* as having conducted the very examination of the *Engle* record that *Douglas* had expressly conceded could *not* produce any usable findings under the doctrine of issue preclusion. *Walker* Pet. App. 23. Indeed, whereas the Florida Supreme Court felt compelled to adopt a previously unknown version of claim preclusion to justify using the *Engle* findings in progeny trials, the Eleventh Circuit ascribed to the Florida Supreme Court an analysis that satisfied traditional issue-preclusion requirements, despite that court's express disclaimer of any such analysis.

According to the Eleventh Circuit, "[t]he Supreme Court of Florida looked through the jury verdict entered in Phase I to determine what issues the jury decided." *Walker* Pet. App. 18. Regardless of any doubts the Eleventh Circuit might have had about the accuracy of the Florida Supreme Court's supposed examination of the *Engle* record, the court concluded that it was required to "give full faith and credit to the decision in *Engle*, as interpreted in *Douglas*," and was not permitted to undertake its own independent examination of the issues "actually decided" in *Engle*. *Id.* at 17, 23. The Eleventh Circuit reached that conclusion even though the plaintiffs themselves had not invoked the Full Faith and Credit Act in defense of the district court's judgment.

Reynolds filed petitions for certiorari in both *Brown* and *Walker*.

## SUMMARY OF ARGUMENT

The due process violations implicated in these petitions span thousands of cases and threaten defendants with staggering liability to plaintiffs who may never have proved the essential elements of their claims in any proceeding. This Court is the only forum in which PM USA and the other *Engle* defendants can obtain relief from the ongoing, serial deprivation of their constitutional rights by Florida's state and federal courts.

In *Engle*, the Florida Supreme Court retroactively certified an issues class action that encompasses plaintiffs who share little in common except their use of some brand or brands of defendants' cigarettes during some portion of a fifty-year period and their subsequent development of a smoking-related illness. Because many of the alternative theories of liability pursued by the class applied only to limited subsets of class members, the Florida Supreme Court recognized that the generalized findings rendered by the class-action jury would be "useless" to *Engle* progeny plaintiffs under traditional preclusion principles. *Douglas,* 110 So. 3d at 433. To salvage the Phase I findings, the court therefore adopted a wholly unprecedented doctrine of offensive claim preclusion—even though no *claim* is being precluded in the progeny litigation—that binds a defendant with respect to any issue that "*might* . . . have been litigated and determined" against it in the prior lawsuit. *Id.* at 432 (emphasis added). This "radical departure" from common-law preclusion principles, *id.* at 439 (Canady, J., dissenting), permits *Engle* progeny plaintiffs to invoke the Phase I findings to establish any issue the *Engle* jury "might"—or might *not*—have decided in their favor. Relying on the sweeping preclusive effect of those findings, *Engle* progeny plaintiffs have already secured total judgments exceeding $450 million—and more than 95% of the progeny cases still remain to be tried.

Based on a gross misreading of *Douglas,* the Eleventh Circuit declined to examine the constitutionality of the Florida Supreme Court's novel theory of offensive claim preclusion. According to the Eleventh Circuit, the Florida Supreme Court had applied traditional issue-preclusion principles and determined, based on an examination of the *Engle* record, that the *Engle* jury actually decided "all common liability issues for the class." *Walker* Pet. App. 14 (internal quotation marks omitted). In fact, the Florida Supreme

Court expressly declined to undertake any such record-based examination of *Engle* because it was apparent to the court from the face of the record that application of the "actually decided" requirement would render the Phase I findings "useless." *Douglas,* 110 So. 3d at 433. It was for that reason that the Florida Supreme Court invoked claim preclusion, which "has no 'actually decided' requirement." *Id.* at 435.

Moreover, even if the Eleventh Circuit's reading of *Douglas* were correct, its deference to that decision would still reflect a fundamental misunderstanding of full faith and credit. The "actually decided" inquiry is one of constitutional magnitude because it would violate due process for a federal court to give preclusive effect to a state court jury's findings on issues that the jury did not actually decide. The Eleventh Circuit was therefore required to undertake an independent examination of the *Engle* record to identify those issues actually decided by the Phase I jury. Its failure to do so—in deference to the Florida Supreme Court's supposed record-based inquiry—is an inexcusable abdication of its constitutional obligations.

The implications of these decisions transcend the *Engle* progeny setting. Like the Florida Supreme Court in *Engle,* courts across the country are increasingly deploying the issues-class device to manage complex litigation. *See, e.g.,* 7AA Charles Alan Wright et al., *Federal Practice and Procedure* § 1790 & nn.18-20 (3d ed. 2005). The Florida Supreme Court's decisions in *Engle* and *Douglas* provide a roadmap for other courts to facilitate classwide treatment of inherently individualized tort claims through the combination of issues-class certification and offensive claim preclusion. This Court should grant review to prevent the proliferation of this unprecedented and unconstitutional "abrogation of . . . well-established common-law protection[s]." *Honda Motor Co. v. Oberg,* 512 U.S. 415, 430 (1994).

## ARGUMENT

### *I. REVIEW IS NECESSARY TO FORESTALL A MASSIVE DUE PROCESS VIOLATION SPANNING THOUSANDS OF PENDING CASES.*

In both *Brown* and *Walker,* the lower courts upheld damages awards against Reynolds in the absence of any assurance that the plaintiffs had proved each element of their claims. In upholding those awards, the state and federal forums devised inconsistent theories of preclusion. In the state courts, preclusion applies because, under *Douglas,* it does not matter whether or not the *Engle* jury actually decided any facts relevant to a particular progeny case; preclusion applies in state courts because the *Engle* jury *might* have decided such facts. In federal court, by contrast, preclusion is based on the demonstrably false notion that *Douglas* performed a traditional issue-preclusion analysis and identified particular facts that were *actually* decided by the *Engle* jury. Thus, whereas the state courts have embraced a new and radical preclusion regime that defies traditional norms of justice, the federal courts preclude defendants from litigating key facts by purporting to "defer" to a state preclusion rule that the state courts themselves expressly disclaim.

Respondents make much of the fact that this Court has declined to address the *Engle* progeny morass on several previous occasions. All but one of those petitions, however, arose from the lower state courts at a time when it was still possible that the Florida Supreme Court could reject, as a matter of state law, the abusive use of preclusion that has characterized this issues class. *Douglas,* where the highest state court first made clear that state law has indeed discarded the traditional safeguards of preclusion doctrine, represents the only previous instance where this Court denied review in a progeny case following exhaustion of all potentially available state processes. It was not clear at that time, however, that the Eleventh Circuit would deny all relief as well. Although the panel decision in *Walker* was issued before the Court considered *Douglas* at conference, the petition and brief in opposition had already been filed, and the possibility of panel or en banc rehearing remained. Now that such remedies have likewise proved illusory, vindication of the *Engle* defendants' due process rights can only come from this Court.

### A. The *Engle* Progeny Litigation Threatens The Defendants With Massive, Serial Deprivations Of Their Due Process Rights.

For centuries, the common law has required that a plaintiff seeking to rely on the preclusive effect of prior litigation to establish the elements of a claim demonstrate that the prior finder of fact actually decided the "'precise question'" on which preclusion is sought. *De Sollar v. Hanscome,* 158 U.S. 216, 221 (1895) (quoting *Russell v. Place,* 94 U.S. 606, 608 (1877)). In *Fayerweather v. Ritch,* 195 U.S. 276 (1904), this Court held that the "actually decided" requirement is mandated by the Constitution because it would violate due process to accept as a "conclusive determination" a verdict "made without any finding of the fundamental fact." *Id.* at 297, 299. As this Court recognized in *Fayerweather,* the "actually decided" requirement is an essential safeguard against arbitrary deprivations of property because it ensures that a defendant is held liable only where the plaintiff has established *every* element of his claim against the defendant—either in the current proceeding or in some prior proceeding. *See Logan v. Zimmerman Brush Co.,* 455 U.S. 422, 433 (1982) (due process guarantees the right to "have [the] merits" of a claim "fairly judged").

In contrast to the traditional common-law preclusion standard, the Florida Supreme Court's novel claim-preclusion theory permits *Engle* progeny plaintiffs to rely on the Phase I findings to establish any issue "which *might* . . . have been" decided in their favor by the *Engle* jury, *Douglas,* 110 So. 3d at 432 (internal quotation marks omitted)—without requiring the plaintiffs to demonstrate based on an examination of the *Engle* record that those issues were *actually* decided in their favor.

The Eleventh Circuit in *Walker* acknowledged that the Florida Supreme Court's version of claim preclusion is "unorthodox and inconsistent with the federal common law." *Walker* Pet. App. 23. In fact, the doctrine of offensive claim preclusion is unprecedented in our legal tradition. As traditionally understood, claim preclusion is available only when there has been a final judgment that "'puts an end to *the cause of action,*'" *Nevada v. United States,* 463 U.S. 110, 130 (1983) (emphasis added) (quoting *Comm'r v. Sunnen,* 333 U.S. 591, 597 (1948)). A "verdict" or "finding" that leaves issues to be determined later "is not sufficient" for claim-preclusion purposes.

*Oklahoma City v. McMaster,* 196 U.S. 529, 532-33 (1905); *see also G. & C. Merriam Co. v. Saalfield & Ogilvie,* 241 U.S. 22, 28-29 (1916); Restatement (Second) of Judgments § 13 cmt. b (1982).

"Claim preclusion," as its name suggests, applies only where a *claim* is being precluded—that is, where it merges into a final judgment, barring further litigation on that claim entirely. Under those circumstances, it does not matter what the jury actually decided in reaching the final judgment; the judgment itself demonstrates that the claim has been fully resolved against the losing party. Thus, if claim preclusion did apply in the *Engle* progeny litigation, the progeny plaintiffs' claims would be completely barred.

But, in fact, no claim is being precluded in the progeny litigation; rather, the plaintiffs' claims are being *litigated,* and the question is whether preclusion applies to particular issues central to those claims. In such circumstances, it is critical to know whether the prior proceedings resulted in an actual decision on those issues, and what that decision was—otherwise, a party could be precluded from litigating issues that may not have been decided at all or may even have been decided in the precluded party's *favor* in the prior proceeding.

The Florida Supreme Court's formulation of an "offensive" version of claim preclusion to give sweeping preclusive effect to the Phase I findings is nothing more than issue preclusion stripped of its due process safeguards. The court's novel invocation of claim preclusion makes it possible for *Engle* progeny plaintiffs to recover without proving the essential elements of their claims in their individual suits or demonstrating that those issues were actually decided in their favor in *Engle.* The result is an "arbitrary and inaccurate" procedure that deprives the defendants of their property in the absence of any assurance that a factfinder has ever found each element of the plaintiffs' claims. *Honda Motor Co.,* 512 U.S. at 430.

### B. Only This Court Can Remedy This Unprecedented Violation Of Due Process.

As a federal court sitting in diversity, the Eleventh Circuit was required to accept the rule of claim preclusion adopted in *Douglas* as an authoritative statement of Florida preclusion law, just as the court was required to accept laws passed by the Florida legislature as controlling on state-law questions.

*See Erie R.R. Co. v. Tompkins*, 304 U.S. 64 (1938). But federal courts have an independent duty to determine whether state laws are constitutional when, as here, they are invoked by one party as a basis for depriving another party of its property in a federal proceeding. That constitutional obligation applies with equal force to state statutes and common law: when a party invokes state judge-made doctrines in federal court, federal courts can no more "defer" to state courts on the question of constitutionality than they can defer to state legislatures on the same question with respect to statutes.

In *Walker*, however, the Eleventh Circuit declined to address the constitutionality of the rule of offensive claim preclusion adopted by the Florida Supreme Court in *Douglas* and invoked by the *Engle* progeny plaintiffs as the basis for depriving Reynolds of its property. Instead of discharging its obligation to determine the constitutionality of that rule of preclusion, the Eleventh Circuit dodged the question by relying on a factually and legally flawed application of the Full Faith and Credit Act—and, in so doing, guaranteed that no other panel of the Eleventh Circuit will be able to address the merits of the *Engle* defendants' federal due process argument. As a result, this Court is the only remaining forum in which the *Engle* defendants can vindicate their due process rights.

The Eleventh Circuit premised its full-faith-and-credit analysis on a fundamental misreading of *Douglas*. The Florida Supreme Court expressly declined to examine the *Engle* record to determine the issues actually decided by the *Engle* jury because, as the court explained, application of the "actually decided" requirement would render the Phase I findings "useless." 110 So.3d at 433. In the Eleventh Circuit's view, however, the Florida Supreme Court had supposedly conducted just such an inquiry in *Douglas* and had determined that the *Engle* jury was asked to decide only "'all common liability issues for the class,' not brand specific defects." *Walker* Pet. App. 19 (quoting *Douglas*, 110 So.3d at 423). At a minimum, that astounding misreading of *Douglas* warrants summary reversal. See *Walker* Pet. 21.

More fundamentally, where federal due process rights are at stake, a federal court is not permitted simply to take a state court at its word that federal constitutional guarantees are being adequately safeguarded. Although federal courts sitting in diversity must accept the Florida Supreme Court's interpretations of state preclusion law, they have an independent duty to determine whether those state preclusion rules are *constitutional. See Kremer v. Chem. Constr. Corp.*, 456 U.S. 461, 481 (1982). Thus, even if the Florida Supreme Court had examined the *Engle* record in *Douglas* to determine the issues actually decided by the Phase I jury, the Eleventh Circuit still would have been required to undertake its own independent examination of the *Engle* record. The "actually decided" inquiry is one of constitutional dimension because it would violate due process for a federal court to give preclusive effect to the verdict of a state court jury on issues that the jury did not actually decide. *See Fayerweather*, 195 U.S. at 307. A federal court therefore must determine for itself what issues the state court jury actually decided, rather than deferring to the state court's examination of the record. After all, *Walker* is not simply a collateral attack on a state court judgment; it is an independent proceeding in federal court that could lead to a deprivation *by the federal court* of Reynolds's property without due process if preclusion is unconstitutionally applied.

To be sure, the lower federal courts do not follow a uniform approach when asked to decide whether giving preclusive effect to a state court judgment would violate due process. The Eleventh Circuit's deference to the Florida Supreme Court's supposed examination of the *Engle* record—and refusal to undertake an independent examination of the issues actually decided by the Phase I jury—deepened an existing circuit split on the question [of] whether federal courts are required to defer to a state court's determination that its own proceedings complied with due process. In accordance with this Court's precedent, the Sixth Circuit has correctly held that a federal court asked to afford preclusive effect to a state court judgment must undertake an independent review of the state court proceeding to ensure that giving preclusive effect to the judgment would not violate due process. *See Gooch v. Life Investors Ins. Co.*, 672 F.3d 402, 420-22 (6th Cir. 2011) (conducting an independent examination of the adequacy of a state court class-action settlement even though the state supreme court had previously upheld the settlement as adequate). This obligation, the Sixth Circuit explained, "flows from the Supreme Court's observation that 'a court adjudicating a dispute may not be able to predetermine the res judicata effect of its own judgment.'" *Id.* at 420 (quoting *Phillips Petroleum Co. v. Shutts*, 472 U.S. 797, 805 (1985)); *see also Stephenson v. Dow Chem. Co.*, 273

F.3d 249, 257 (2d Cir. 2001), *aff'd in relevant part by an equally divided Court,* 539 U.S. 111, 112 (2003) (same, in context of prior federal class action); *cf. State v. Homeside Lending, Inc.*, 826 A.2d 997, 1017 (Vt. 2003).

In contrast, the Ninth Circuit in *Epstein v. MCA, Inc.*, 179 F.3d 641 (9th Cir. 1999), refused to conduct such an examination when asked to give preclusive effect to a state class-action settlement, concluding that the parties resisting the full-faith-and-credit effect of the judgment lacked the "right to challenge collaterally the adequacy of representation." *Id.* at 647. According to the Ninth Circuit, it was required under the Full Faith and Credit Act to defer to the state court's own determination of that issue. *Id.* at 650.

Like the Ninth Circuit, the Eleventh Circuit in *Walker* declined to undertake an independent examination of the *Engle* record to determine whether giving preclusive effect to the Phase I findings would deny Reynolds its due process rights, reasoning that "we cannot refuse to give full faith and credit to the decision in *Engle* because we disagree with the decision in *Douglas* about what the jury in Phase I decided." *Walker* Pet. App. 18. Thus, in addition to addressing the due process question that hangs over all the *Engle* progeny litigation, granting certiorari in *Walker* would enable this Court to resolve that split and make clear that a state court's rulings cannot supersede a federal court's independent obligation to ensure that giving preclusive effect to state court proceedings does not violate due process.

## *II. THE ISSUE PRESENTED BY THESE PETITIONS IS ONE OF SYSTEMIC IMPORTANCE TO THE JUDICIAL SYSTEM.*

The due process violation at issue in these cases has profound consequences for both the *Engle* defendants and for other class-action defendants in state and federal courts across the country.

In the absence of this Court's review, the constitutional error that both the Florida Supreme Court and the Eleventh Circuit have failed to correct will infect every one of the thousands of *Engle* progeny cases currently pending in Florida's state and federal courts. These suits implicate immense potential liability and represent a substantial portion of the docket in one of the Nation's largest States. The due process violations in *Brown* and *Walker* will assuredly be repeated in each of those cases, exposing PM USA and the other *Engle* defendants to liability to plaintiffs who may never have proved the essential elements of their claims in any court.

Moreover, the implications of these decisions transcend the *Engle* setting. It is already becoming increasingly common for courts to invoke the issues-class device—under either Federal Rule of Civil Procedure 23(c)(4) or state-law analogues—to bypass well-established and constitutionally compelled restraints on the arbitrary deprivation of property. *See* Principles of the Law of Aggregate Litigation ch. 2 (2010); 7AA Wright et al., *supra,* § 1790 & nn.18-20. The *Engle* progeny litigation is likely to accelerate that trend because the Florida Supreme Court's decision in *Douglas* provides a roadmap for other courts to use the combination of issues certification and preclusion law to facilitate classwide adjudication of inherently individualized claims: Class counsel need only present an issues-class jury with a mix of classwide and non-classwide theories and *all* of those issues will then be deemed conclusively established in favor of the class members in their subsequent individual actions as long as the class-action jury finds for the plaintiffs on *any* one of those issues.

Particularly given these broader implications, *Brown* and *Walker* involve an unusually large number of the considerations that, even in isolation, have justified this Court's review. *See, e.g., Richards v. Jefferson Cnty.,* 517 U.S. 793, 797 (1996) (extreme application of preclusion); *Honda Motor Co.,* 512 U.S. at 420-21 (departure from common-law protections; issue limited to a single State); *FTC v. Jantzen, Inc.,* 386 U.S. 228, 229 (1967) (hundreds of cases affected); Stephen M. Shapiro et al., *Supreme Court Practice* 269-70 (10th ed. 2013) (citing cases) (large financial stakes). Absent review, the constitutional violation in these cases will be endlessly replicated both in the thousands of pending *Engle* progeny cases and in the copycat issues-class actions that will inevitably be filed against other industries in courts across the country—confronting the *Engle* defendants and other targets of the plaintiffs' bar with massive potential liability based on findings that a prior jury "might," or might not, have made. Due process and fundamental fairness require far more.

## CONCLUSION

The petitions for a writ of certiorari should be granted.

## EXAMPLE 5

**Authors** Walter Dellinger, Irving L. Gornstein, Jonathan D. Hacker, Anton Metlitsky, O'Melveny & Myers LLP

**Case** *Hollingsworth v. Perry*, 134 S. Ct. 2175 (2014)

### BRIEF FOR WALTER DELLINGER AS AMICUS CURIAE IN SUPPORT OF RESPONDENTS ON THE ISSUE OF STANDING

### INTEREST OF AMICUS CURIAE

Walter Dellinger is the Douglas B. Maggs Professor Emeritus of Law at Duke University, and a partner at O'Melveny & Myers LLP. Professor Dellinger has throughout his career studied the scope of the Article III jurisdiction of federal courts, including issues relating to Article III standing. He is committed to the public interest and to the enforcement of proper limits on the scope of judicial power. Based on his study of the applicable precedent and principles, he believes that the proponents of Proposition 8 had no standing to appeal the judgment of the district court in this case.

### INTRODUCTION AND SUMMARY OF ARGUMENT

In 2008, petitioners Dennis Hollingsworth, Gail J. Knight, Martin F. Gutierrez, and Mark A. Jansson (the proponents) proposed an initiative known as Proposition 8 that would amend the California Constitution to provide that only marriages between a man and a woman would be valid in California. The voters approved that initiative, and Proposition 8 became California law.

Two same-sex couples subsequently brought suit against the Governor, the Attorney General, and other state officials in federal district court, alleging that Proposition 8 violated their rights under the Equal Protection and Due Process Clauses of the Fourteenth Amendment to the United States Constitution. The state officials answered the complaint and continued to enforce Proposition 8, but they did not defend its constitutionality. The district court allowed the proponents to intervene to defend Proposition 8. After a trial, the district court issued a judgment holding Proposition 8 unconstitutional.

The state officials declined to appeal the district court's judgment. After the proponents sought to appeal to the Ninth Circuit, that court certified to the California Supreme Court two questions related to the proponents' standing. As relevant here, the California Supreme Court held that initiative proponents are authorized under state law to represent the state's interest in enforcement of a law enacted through an initiative when the state Attorney General refuses to defend the law. Based on that determination, the Ninth Circuit held that the proponents here have standing in federal court to defend Proposition 8's constitutionality.

That holding is incorrect. The proponents did not have Article III standing to appeal from the district court's judgment holding Proposition 8 unconstitutional because they have only a generalized interest in the enforcement of that law, and the Court has repeatedly held that such an interest is not sufficient to establish a case or controversy under Article III. The Court should therefore vacate the court of appeals' judgment and remand with directions to dismiss the proponents' appeal.

**I.** To satisfy the requirements of Article III, parties appealing from a district court judgment must show that they have a personal stake in the outcome of the appeal. A generalized interest in the enforcement of a law is not sufficient to create Article III standing, and that is true regardless of the parties' level of ideological commitment to the law's enforcement.

The proponents had certain personal rights in the initiative process that arguably gave them a personal interest in ensuring that Proposition 8 became valid California law. Once the California Supreme Court held that Proposition 8 was valid California law, however, the proponents had no more interest in the enforcement of that law than any other citizen. And that generalized interest in Proposition 8's enforcement was not sufficient to give them standing to defend that law.

The state had a continuing interest in defending Proposition 8. But the state, through its officials, declined to appeal.

**II.** Relying on the California Supreme Court's determination that state law confers on an initiative's proponents the authority to represent the state's own interest in the enforcement of an initiative when state officials decline to defend it, the Ninth Circuit held that the proponents had Article III standing to appeal. But a private party having only a generalized interest in enforcement of a law does not possess Article III standing, and neither Congress nor a state has authority to confer standing on private parties when they otherwise would not have it. *See Lujan v. Defenders of Wildlife*, 504 U.S. 555 (1992); *Doremus v. Bd. of Educ.*, 342 U.S. 429 (1952). The rule against generalized-grievance standing is one of substance, not semantics: It ensures that federal courts stay within their constitutionally prescribed role. Accordingly, neither Congress nor a state can transform a generalized interest in a law's enforcement from an insufficient basis for Article III standing into a cognizable Article III injury simply by relabeling it as the state's interest.

If the rule were otherwise, the Article III principle that federal courts cannot serve as a forum for the airing of generalized grievances would be drained of any practical meaning. For example, the Court has held that a doctor ethically opposed to abortion does not have standing to appeal the invalidation of a law restricting abortions, and taxpayers who have standing in state court to challenge official action without showing a personal injury do not have standing to appeal to this Court. Under the Ninth Circuit's theory, each of these cases would have come out the other way if the state had designated the party's generalized interest in enforcement to be the state's interest. Indeed, under the Ninth Circuit's ruling, a state could authorize any citizen of the state to enforce or defend any state law in any court, so long as it makes clear that the citizen is representing the state's interest rather than his own.

**III.** The Ninth Circuit relied on *Karcher v. May*, 484 U.S. 72 (1987), and *Arizonans for Official English v. Arizona*, 520 U.S. 43 (1997), as support for its novel standing theory. But those cases merely recognize that when agents of the state have been delegated authority to represent the state's interest, the agents have Article III standing to do so. Those decisions do not suggest that states can confer standing on non-agents who have nothing more than a generalized interest in a law's enforcement.

Other decisions of this Court, including *Vermont Agency of Natural Resources v. United States ex rel. Stevens,* 529 U.S. 765 (2000), confirm that agents can assert the sovereign's interest in federal court. But they also indicate that a mere delegation of authority is not enough.

The Proposition 8 proponents are not agents of the state or the people. Under common-law agency principles, an agent has a fiduciary duty to the principal and is subject to the principal's control. The proponents do not satisfy either of those requirements. They do not take an oath to support the state and federal constitution or otherwise assume a duty to serve the state's interest. They are also not subject to the state's or the people's control, such as through election or removal. Neither the state nor the people exercise any control over the arguments proponents make, or over their decisions to appeal, settle, or let matters lie. The proponents remain entirely free to pursue their own ideological agenda, and are accountable to no one other than themselves. And the proponents can apparently continue to pursue their own agenda in litigation challenging Proposition 8 years and even decades after its enactment.

A rule that a state may delegate representation of its own interests only to actual agents is necessary to keep the federal judiciary within its constitutionally prescribed role. When a party has a fiduciary duty to the state and is subject to its control, a federal court can be sure that the agent is pressing the state's interests rather than his own ideological agenda. When a party lacks a fiduciary duty and is not subject to state control, there can be no such guarantee. The court is then at risk of serving as a forum for the airing of an ideological grievance, a role that is outside the purview of Article III.

The agency rule also promotes the Constitution's structural concern with government accountability. When an agent decides to appeal, the people can hold him or his superiors accountable for the decision. But allowing non-agents to make that decision—and all subsequent litigation decisions in the case—would blur the lines of accountability. State officials would be shielded from the electoral consequences of their decision not to appeal. And they would also be able to blame unaccountable private parties for the decision to appeal without absorbing the political consequences for that decision.

The Ninth Circuit's rule also raises serious administrability concerns. For example, a federal court would have no way to know what to do when proponents disagree on such matters as whether to appeal or what to argue. No such concerns exist under the agency rule, because governments routinely assign the authority to resolve any such conflicts to a single high-ranking officer.

The agency rule does not prevent the state from ensuring a defense for its initiatives. Among other options, it can authorize any citizen to bring a state court action to determine an initiative's constitutionality before it takes effect, which would bind the Attorney General and other state officials. It can require the state Attorney General, in the event she has doubts about an initiative's constitutionality, to initiate an action or seek an advisory opinion in state court to test its constitutionality before it becomes effective. It can require the Attorney General to defend the initiative in federal court and to take all necessary appeals to do so. Or it could establish an independent officer, removable for cause by a high-ranking state official, to defend initiatives when the Attorney General declines to do so. The one thing a state cannot do is conscript federal courts to serve as a forum for the resolution of a generalized grievance by a private party who has nothing more than an ideological interest in a law's enforcement.

Because the proponents lacked standing to appeal, this Court should vacate the court of appeals' judgment. But it should not disturb the district court's judgment. An Article III case or controversy existed in the district court because the plaintiffs sought marriage licenses and the defendant state officials declined to provide them absent a court order. *See INS v. Chadha,* 462 U.S. 919, 939-40 (1983). In similar circumstances, the Court has left intact judgments that were the product of a case or controversy.

The proponents challenge the breadth of the district court's injunction to the extent it gives relief to non-parties. Such arguments may be open to future litigants with Article III standing. But because no party with standing appealed, issues relating to the actual scope of the injunction and the district court's remedial authority to issue it are not properly before the Court.

## ARGUMENT

### *I. THE PROPONENTS' GENERALIZED INTEREST IN ENFORCEMENT OF PROPOSITION 8 IS NOT SUFFICIENT TO GIVE THEM ARTICLE III STANDING*

**A.** The Proposition 8 proponents lacked Article III standing to appeal the district court's judgment to the Ninth Circuit and to petition for this Court's review. The proponents have nothing more than a generalized interest in the enforcement of Proposition 8. That interest is insufficient to establish Article III standing. And state law cannot confer Article III standing on a private party who otherwise lacks it. The proponents' lack of standing follows from three bedrock Article III principles.

First, the Constitution does not give federal courts an unrestrained power to decide every constitutional question that a party wishes to have them resolve. Instead, it confines federal courts to resolving constitutional questions only when they are presented in "Cases" or "Controversies." U.S. Const, art. III, § 2. The case-or-controversy limitation is indispensable to ensuring "the proper—and properly limited—role of the [federal] courts in a democratic society." *Allen v. Wright,* 468 U.S. 737, 750 (1984). Allowing federal courts to decide constitutional questions outside of cases or controversies "would be inimical to the Constitution's democratic character." *Ariz. Christian Sch. v. Winn,* 131 S. Ct. 1436, 1442 (2011).

Second, because the rule against generalized-grievance standing is required by Article III, it cannot be altered by Congress or the states. *See Raines v. Byrd,* 521 U.S. 811, 820 n.3 (1997) (Congress cannot "erase Article III's standing requirements by statutorily granting the right to sue to a plaintiff who would not otherwise have standing"); *Orr v. Orr,* 440 U.S. 268, 277 n.7 (1979) (states "cannot confer standing before this Court on a party who would otherwise lack it"). That means that neither Congress nor the states can confer standing on parties who have nothing more than a generalized interest in a law's enforcement.

Third, Article III's standing requirements apply not only to plaintiffs, but to all parties who seek to invoke the jurisdiction of a federal court. Thus, a party who intervenes as a defendant in a district court and then seeks to appeal must establish Article III standing to appeal. *Arizonans,* 520 U.S. at 64; *Diamond,* 476 U.S. at 62.

## *II. A STATE CANNOT CONFER STANDING BY DENOMINATING A PRIVATE PARTY'S GENERALIZED INTEREST AS THE STATE'S INTEREST*

**A.** The Ninth Circuit did not hold that the proponents' generalized interest in application and enforcement of Proposition 8 gave them a personalized interest sufficient to establish Article III standing. Instead, it held that the state itself had an Article III interest in defending Proposition 8, which the state then validly conferred on the proponents. In reaching that conclusion, the court relied on the California Supreme Court's holding that California law "confers on the official proponents of an initiative the authority to assert the state's interests in defending the constitutionality of that initiative, where the state officials who would ordinarily assume that responsibility choose not to do so." Pet. App. 38a; *see* Pet. App. 352a-402a (California Supreme Court opinion) (holding that California law authorizes initiative proponents to represent the state's interest in enforcement of voter-enacted initiatives).

The Ninth Circuit's reasoning cannot be squared with the basic Article III principles described above. The principle that a private party cannot assert a generalized interest in enforcement of the law as Article III injury is one of substance, not semantics—it ensures that courts "stay within their constitutionally prescribed sphere of action." *Steel Co.,* 523 U.S. at 102 n.4. Accordingly, just as the state cannot transform a generalized grievance into a personal interest by a law "that denominates it as such," *Lujan,* 504 U.S. at 576-77, neither can it transform a generalized interest insufficient to establish Article III standing into a cognizable Article III injury simply by relabeling it something else. States cannot, through labels alone, confer Article III standing on a private party where standing would not otherwise exist. *Cf. Orr,* 440 U.S. 268 at n.7; *Doremus,* 342 U.S. at 434.

**B.** If the rule were otherwise, the principle that a generalized interest in enforcement of the law is insufficient to create an Article III case or controversy would be drained of any practical meaning, because the states would be able to transform any generalized grievance into an Article III injury.

## *III. AGENTS OF THE STATE CAN REPRESENT THE STATE'S INTERESTS, BUT PROPONENTS ARE NOT AGENTS OF THE STATE*

A state may, of course, appoint an agent to represent its interests, as this Court has recognized. But that is far from what happened here. Under established common-law agency principles, an agent of the state has a fiduciary duty to serve the state's interest and is subject to the state's (or people's) control. *See* Restatement (Third) of Agency § 8.01 ("An agent has a fiduciary duty to act loyally for the principal's benefit in all matters connected with the agency relationship."); *id.* § 1.01 cmt. f(l) ("A relationship of agency is not present unless the person on whose behalf action is taken has the right to control the actor."). The proponents are not agents of the state because they do not owe a fiduciary duty to the state and they are not subject to its control in any respect. Requiring such an agency relationship will ensure that the courts decide concrete controversies, and not merely ideological, generalized grievances. To allow citizens with only a generalized grievance and no agency responsibilities to sue would be contrary to Article III principles and this Court's precedents. *Cf. Whitmore,* 495 U.S. at 163-64 (adopting common-law limits on "next friend" status to prevent circumvention of Article III's generalized-grievance rule).

* * *

*Vermont Agency of Natural Resources v. United States ex rel. Stevens,* 529 U.S. 765, 773 (2000), confirms that the government can authorize an agent to represent its interest in federal court. At the same time, it indicates that a mere delegation of authority to represent the state's interest to a private party does not suffice.

In *Stevens,* the court examined a qui tam provision that authorized a person to bring a civil action "for the person *and for the United States Government.*" 31 U.S.C. § 3730(b) (emphasis added). That provision clearly delegates to private plaintiffs the authority to assert the government's interest. If that were enough to confer standing, the opinion could have ended there with a statement to that effect. Instead, however, the Court examined two bases for standing that would have been unnecessary to consider had the delegation of authority to represent the government's interest been enough by itself.

The Court first examined whether standing could be upheld on the theory that a qui tam plaintiff "is simply the statutorily designated *agent* of the United States." 529 U.S. at 772 (emphasis added). The Court rejected that possibility because qui tam plaintiffs do not satisfy traditional agency standards: They lack a fiduciary duty because they can sue on their own behalf as well as on behalf of the government. *Id.* And they are not subject to government control, because they are entitled to a hearing if the United States decides to dismiss the suit, and the government cannot settle the suit without a judicial finding of fairness. *Id.* The implication of that discussion is that qui tam plaintiffs would have Article III standing to assert the government's interest if they were properly regarded as agents, but that a mere delegation of authority to represent the government's interest does not confer standing.

* * *

## *IV. THE STATE CAN ENSURE DEFENSE OF ITS INITIATIVES WITHOUT PUTTING IT IN THE HANDS OF PRIVATE PARTIES WHO HAVE NOTHING MORE THAN A GENERALIZED INTEREST IN A LAW'S ENFORCEMENT*

The Ninth Circuit concluded that recognizing the standing of proponents to defend an initiative when state officials do not is necessary to protect the initiative process. Pet. App. 38a-39a. That conclusion is incorrect. There are a variety of ways for a state to guarantee a defense of its initiatives without conscripting federal courts to adjudicate the grievances of private parties who have nothing more than a generalized interest in an initiative's enforcement.

First, because state courts are not bound by the Article III case-or-controversy requirement, *ASARCO*, 490 U.S. at 617, a state can authorize initiative proponents, after an initiative is approved but before it takes effect, to file suit in state court against the Attorney General for a binding determination that the initiative is constitutional. *Cf.* Pet. App. 393a

("[P]rivate citizens have long been authorized to bring a mandate action to enforce a public duty involving the protection of a public right in order to ensure that no government body impairs or defeats the purpose of legislation establishing such a right.").

Second, the state could require the Attorney General, before an initiative about which she has constitutional doubt takes effect, to initiate a declaratory judgment action in state court to resolve the constitutionality of the initiative, or seek an advisory opinion from the state's highest court. *Cf.* Neb. Rev. Stat. 84-215 (if the Attorney General concludes that an act of the legislature is unconstitutional and any state official fails to implement the act in reliance on that opinion, then "the Attorney General shall . . . file an action in the appropriate court to determine the validity of the act"); Mass. Const., Art. LXXXV (amending the Massachusetts Constitution to provide: "Each branch of the legislature, as well as the governor or the council, shall have authority to require the opinions of the justices of the supreme judicial court, upon important questions of law, and upon solemn occasions").

Third, the state could require the Attorney General or another state official to defend the constitutionality of enacted initiatives and to take all available appeals to do so. Indeed, state law could authorize any initiative to include that requirement as one of its provisions.

Fourth, without requiring the Attorney General to offer a defense of the initiative, the state could require the Attorney General to enforce it and take all possible appeals, while allowing the proponents or others to participate as amici curiae to defend the initiative on the merits. Such a procedure fully complies with Article III. *See INS v. Chadha,* 462 U.S. 919, 931 & n.6, 939-40 (1983).

Fifth, the state could create an independent office responsible for defending initiatives in cases in which the Attorney General declines to do so. The state could, for example, allow state courts to appoint such an officer and subject him to removal for cause by the Governor or Attorney General. *Cf. Morrison v. Olson,* 487 U.S. 654 (1988).

These options—and there are likely others—taken separately or together, would ameliorate the concern that the California initiative process could be undermined by state officials' refusal to defend the constitutionality of initiatives. The one option states cannot pursue is the constitutionally unacceptable one of conferring on private parties who have only a generalized interest in enforcement of an initiative the right to invoke the jurisdiction of a federal court.

## *V. THE COURT OF APPEALS' JUDGMENT SHOULD BE VACATED, BUT THE DISTRICT COURT'S JUDGMENT SHOULD BE ALLOWED TO STAND*

Because the proponents did not have standing to appeal to the Ninth Circuit, the Court should vacate the judgment of the court of appeals. *See Diamond,* 476 U.S. at 71; *Karcher,* 484 U.S. at 83. The district court's judgment, however, should not be vacated. Because the plaintiffs sued for marriage licenses in the district court, and the state defendants refused to provide them absent a court order, a case or controversy existed in the district court. *See Chadha,* 462 U.S. at 939-40. In the past, when this Court has dismissed for lack of standing to appeal, it has left intact the judgment of the last court in which there was a case or controversy. *See Diamond,* 476 U.S. at 71; *Karcher,* 484 U.S. at 83. There is no reason not to follow the same course here.

The proponents argue that the district court issued an injunction that exceeded its remedial authority because it ordered a statewide injunction against the enforcement of Proposition 8, rather than limiting the scope of the injunction to the named plaintiffs. Pet. Br. 18. Such arguments may be open to future litigants with Article III standing. But because no party with standing appealed the district court's judgment, issues relating to the district court's injunction and the scope of the court's remedial authority are not properly before this Court.

## CONCLUSION

The court of appeals' judgment should be vacated, with instructions to dismiss petitioners' appeal for lack of jurisdiction.

## EXAMPLE 6

**Authors** Patrick Morrisey, Attorney General; Elbert Lin, Solicitor General; Jennifer S. Greenlief and J. Zak Ritchie, Assistant Attorneys General; Office of the Attorney General of West Virginia

**Case** *Christie v. NCAA*, 134 S. Ct. 2866 (2014) (cert. denied)

### BRIEF OF *AMICI CURIAE* STATES OF WEST VIRGINIA, WISCONSIN, AND WYOMING IN SUPPORT OF PETITIONERS

### INTRODUCTION AND INTEREST OF *AMICI CURIAE*

Certiorari is warranted because the Third Circuit's decision below conflicts with two lines of this Court's precedent concerning federal-state relations. In upholding the Professional and Amateur Sports Protection Act ("PASPA"), 28 U.S.C. § 3701 *et seq.*, the Third Circuit radically expanded the doctrine of federal preemption by holding that Congress may enact a free-standing "law of preemption" that does nothing more than dictate State law, without affirmatively setting forth a federal regulatory or deregulatory scheme. In addition, the Third Circuit disregarded this Court's anti-commandeering jurisprudence by creating a false distinction between impermissible "affirmative" commands on the States and permissible "negative" commands.

*Amici curiae* are States that submit this brief in support of Petitioners Christopher J. Christie, David L. Rebuck, and Frank Zanzuccki because the Third Circuit's decision fundamentally alters the nature of federal-state relations. The concern of *Amici* States—the States of West Virginia, Wisconsin and Wyoming—is not *what* Congress regulates but *how* it does so. Even where it has Article I authority to act, Congress may not force the States to act as the vehicle for implementing federal policy and thereby shift to the States the political accountability for its actions. Whether it does so by affirmative or negative command is irrelevant. In either case, it is engaged in unconstitutional commandeering and not lawful preemption under the Supremacy Clause.

Importantly, *Amici* States take no position on the wisdom of the state and federal sports wagering laws in this case. Some States may support the expansion of gambling, while others oppose it. *Amici* States file this brief because they agree that the Third Circuit's decision raises serious federalism concerns for all States.

## REASONS FOR GRANTING THE PETITION

This Court has long explained that our system of dual sovereignty limits Congress's ability to directly regulate a State's regulation. It may "encourage a State to regulate in a particular way" by "hold[ing] out incentives to the States as a method of influencing a State's policy choices." *New York v. United States,* 505 U.S. 144, 166 (1992). Moreover, where Congress seeks "to regulate matters directly" through an affirmative federal regime, the Supremacy Clause authorizes "pre-empt[ion] [of] contrary state regulation." *Id.* at 178. But Congress may not simply "regulate state governments' regulation," *id.* at 166, as "the Constitution has never been understood to confer upon Congress the ability to require the States to govern according to Congress's instructions," *id.* at 162.

The petition should be granted because the Third Circuit has failed to respect these limits on federal power. Over a dissent, the Third Circuit rejected the argument that PASPA violates this Court's anti-commandeering jurisprudence. Applying an "affirmative/negative command distinction," the court upheld PASPA because it does not "impose an affirmative requirement that the states act," but rather "only *stops* the states from doing something." Pet. App. 40a, 52a. Instead, the court explained, PASPA is a permissible "standalone" federal "law of pre-emption" that "simply operates to invalidate contrary state laws." *Id.* at 30a n.9, 52a, 36a.

As shown below, the Third Circuit's decision confuses preemption and anti-commandeering and, in so doing, dramatically departs from this Court's jurisprudence on both. *First,* this Court's preemption cases make clear that if Congress enacts an affirmative federal regime, it may also enact an express preemption clause to protect that regime from contrary action by the States. But this Court has never recognized that the Supremacy Clause permits

Congress to enact free-standing "law[s] of preemption" that merely prohibit state laws when there is no affirmative federal regime to protect. *Second,* this Court's anti-commandeering cases do not recognize or support an "affirmative/negative command distinction." To the contrary, the political accountability principles at the core of those cases apply with equal force whether Congress compels or forbids States from acting.

If permitted to stand, the Third Circuit's decision threatens the constitutional balance of power between States and the federal government. This Court's review is needed to reinforce the proper line between permissible preemption and impermissible commandeering.

## *I. THE THIRD CIRCUIT'S DECISION CONFLICTS WITH TWO LINES OF THIS COURT'S PRECEDENT CONCERNING FEDERAL-STATE RELATIONS.*

### A. The Third Circuit's View of Preemption Is Inconsistent With This Court's Case Law.

**1.** In this Court's cases, the preemption of state law is something that occurs, pursuant to the Supremacy Clause, when necessary to protect the integrity of the federal government's own affirmative efforts to govern directly. As this Court has often explained, it has in its cases found state law preempted in three circumstances. *First,* Congress might "enact[] a statute containing an express preemption provision." *Arizona v. United States,* 132 S. Ct. 2492, 2500-01 (2012). *Second,* "state laws are preempted when they conflict with federal law." *Id.* at 2501. *Third,* "the States are precluded from regulating conduct in a field that Congress, acting within its proper authority, has determined must be regulated by its exclusive governance." *Id.* The consistent strand throughout the cases is the existence of valid federal law seeking to govern the country directly. *See Hodel v. Va. Surface Min. & Reclamation Ass'n, Inc.,* 452 U.S. 264, 290 (1981) ("A wealth of precedent attests to congressional authority to displace or pre-empt state laws regulating private activity affecting interstate commerce *when these laws conflict with federal law.*" (emphasis added)).

In cases of conflict or field preemption, the affirmative federal law is central to the Court's analysis. The question in every one of those cases, after all, is whether the existence of some affirmative federal law *implies* the displacement of a particular state law. For conflict preemption, this requires close scrutiny of the federal law to determine whether it makes compliance with the challenged state law "'a physical impossibility,"' *Arizona*, 132 S. Ct. at 2501 (quoting *Florida Lime & Avocado Growers, Inc. v. Paul,* 373 U.S. 132, 142-43 (1963)), or whether the state law '"stands as an obstacle to the accomplishment and execution of the full purposes and objectives of Congress,'" *id.* (quoting *Hines v. Davidowitz*, 312 U.S. 52, 67 (1941)). For field preemption, a court must determine whether the federal law is "so comprehensive[] that it has left no room for supplementary state legislation" *R.J. Reynolds Tobacco Co. v. Durham Cnty., N.C.*, 479 U.S. 130, 140 (1986).

In cases of express preemption, the focus tends instead to be on a specific preemption clause—often a single sentence in a statute—but there is always an overarching affirmative federal law, as well.

As this Court has said, an express preemption clause makes explicit what courts infer in finding conflict or field preemption: that certain state laws contravene an affirmative federal regime. *See Whiting,* 131 S. Ct. at 1977 (describing an "express preemption clause" as "the best evidence of Congress' preemptive intent" (internal quotations omitted)). Rather than relying on the courts to later discern whether a state law interferes with an affirmative federal law, Congress is permitted by the Supremacy Clause simply to enact "a statute *containing* an express preemption provision" that makes clear which state laws must give way to the new federal regime. *Arizona,* 132 S. Ct. at 2500-01 (emphasis added); *see also Easterwood,* 507 U.S. at 664 (noting that a federal statute may "contain[]" an express preemption clause); *Sprietsma,* 537 U.S. at 62 (same). When added to an affirmative federal law, an express preemption clause serves to protect that federal scheme from state laws that would impose inconsistent rules.

This Court's cases illustrate this use of express preemption clauses not only as part of federal regulatory regimes, but also *deregulatory* regimes. For example, in 1978 Congress enacted the Airline Deregulation Act ("ADA"), turning in that industry from complex government regulation to "maximum reliance on competitive market forces." *Morales,* 504 U.S. at 378 (internal quotations omitted). And "[t]o ensure that the States would not undo federal deregulation with regulation of their own, the ADA included a pre-emption provision, prohibiting the States from enforcing any law relating to rates, routes, or services of any air carrier." *Id.* at 378-79 (internal quotations omitted). Similarly, Congress "deregulated trucking" in 1980. *Rowe,* 552 U.S. at 368. Then in 1994, Congress sought to ensure that the States would not "undo federal deregulation" and thus adopted a law "preempting state trucking regulation." *Id.* (internal quotations omitted). In both cases, Congress adopted a federal deregulatory regime and added an express preemption clause to protect that regime by prohibiting action by the States.

All of these cases—whether concerning express, conflict, or field preemption—reflect this Court's description of the Supremacy Clause as a rule of priority between federal and state law. It is, of course, well known that the Constitution "establishes a system of dual sovereignty between the States and the Federal Government." *Gregory v. Ashcroft,* 501 U.S. 452, 457 (1991). But "[f]rom the existence of two sovereigns follows the possibility that [state and federal] laws can be in conflict or at cross-purposes." *Arizona,* 132 S. Ct. at 2500. The Supremacy Clause, this Court has explained, "provides a clear rule that federal law 'shall be the supreme Law of the Land; and the Judges in every State shall be bound thereby, any Thing in the Constitution or Laws of any State to the Contrary notwithstanding.'" *Id.* (quoting U.S. Const., art. VI, cl. 2).

**2.** The Third Circuit, however, has adopted a radically different understanding of preemption. In its analysis, the Supremacy Clause is not merely a rule of priority between state and federal laws "in conflict or at cross-purposes," *id.,* but rather grants Congress free-wheeling power to pass "stand-alone" federal "law[s] of pre-emption" that "simply operate[] to invalidate contrary state laws," Pet. App. 30a n.9, 52a, 36a. The Third Circuit found preemption even though "all [the] federal law does is supersede state law." *Id.* at 31a.

Contrary to the Third Circuit's assertion, that is neither a "straightforward" nor "everyday" view of preemption. *Id.* at 30a n.9, 38a n.11. Citing the express preemption clause in this Court's *American Trucking* decision as a "classic" example, *id.* at 30a, the Third Circuit asserts in support of its position that "numerous federal laws are framed to prohibit States from enacting or enforcing laws contrary to federal standards, and these regulations all enjoy different preemptive qualities," *id.* at 38a n.11. *See also id.*

at 43a (asserting that New Jersey's argument "imperil[s] a plethora of acts currently termed as prohibitions on the states"). But it misunderstands the nature of express preemption clauses in this Court's cases. They are not "standalone" "law[s] of pre-emption," *id.* at 30a n.9, 52a, but rather, as explained above, are parts of larger federal schemes. The express preemption clause at issue in *American Trucking*, for example, protects an elaborate federal regulatory scheme for motor carriers from inconsistent state law.

As Judge Vanaskie notes in dissent, "the majority opinion does not cite any case that sustained a federal statute that purported to regulate the states under the Commerce Clause where there was no underlying federal scheme of regulation or deregulation." Pet. App. 72a n.4. It cites two court of appeals decisions, *see id.* at 38a n.11, but neither is availing. The express preemption clause in *Farina v. Nokia Inc.*, 625 F.3d 97 (3d Cir. 2010), is part of the federal deregulatory regime for wireless carriers, and the clause in *MacDonald v. Monsanto Co.*, 27 F.3d 1021 (5th Cir. 1994), is integral to the federal regime for insecticides, fungicides, and rodenticides.

*Hodel* and *FERC v. Mississippi*, 456 U.S. 742 (1982), are also preemption cases involving the protection of federal regulatory schemes. In both those cases, Congress protected the federal regime not by excluding the States, but by permitting them to remain in the field under certain conditions. *See Printz v. United States*, 521 U.S. 898, 925-26 (1997) ("In *Hodel* we . . . concluded that the Surface Mining Control and Reclamation Act of 1977 did not present [a Tenth Amendment] problem . . . because it merely made compliance with federal standards a precondition to continued state regulation in an otherwise pre-empted field."); *FERC*, 456 U.S. at 765 ("PURPA should not be invalid simply because, out of deference to state authority, Congress adopted a less intrusive scheme and allowed the States to continue regulating in the area on the condition that they consider the suggested federal standards.").

In sum, despite its claims to the contrary, the Third Circuit's position is no less than "revolutionary." Pet. App. 37a. This Court's cases make clear that if Congress enacts an affirmative federal regime, it may also enact an express preemption clause to protect that regime from contrary action by the States. But this Court has never recognized—as the Third Circuit now has—that the Supremacy Clause endows Congress with the substantive authority to enact free-standing "law[s] of preemption" that prohibit state laws when there is no affirmative federal regime to protect. *Id.* at 52a. The Supremacy Clause has been held to give primacy to valid federal laws over contrary state laws, but it has never been construed as a license to Congress to prohibit state lawmaking whenever and however it desires. *See New York,* 505 U.S. at 178 ("The Constitution instead gives Congress the authority to regulate matters directly and to preempt contrary state regulation.").

3. Implicitly acknowledging the unprecedented nature of its ruling, the Third Circuit contends in the "[a]lternative[]" that PASPA does in fact impose an affirmative federal regime. Pet. App. 48a; *see also id.* at 52a ("PASPA does impose a federal standard directly on private individuals"). This assertion, however, does little to salvage the decision.

*First,* even in taking this alternative position, the Third Circuit refuses to acknowledge that the preemption of state law *requires* an affirmative federal regime. At most, it accepts for the sake of argument that "preemptive schemes *normally* either impose an affirmative federal standard or a rule of non-regulation." *Id.* at 51a (emphasis added). That is still at significant odds with this Court's many preemption cases, which consistently preempt state law only where it contravenes an affirmative federal regime.

*Second,* PASPA simply does *not* impose an affirmative federal regime. The Third Circuit asserts that PASPA seeks "to ban gambling pursuant to a state scheme." *Id.* at 51a. But that is not a *federal* regulatory or deregulatory regime over sports wagering. That is nothing more than an attempt by Congress to control (and prohibit) *state* regulation of sports wagering. As the dissent explains, "PASPA provides no federal regulatory standards or requirements of its own." *Id.* at 72a. Nor do "other federal statutes relating to sports gambling . . . aggregate to form the foundation of a federal regulatory scheme that can be interpreted as preempting state regulation of sports gambling." *Id.* at 73a.

## B. The Third Circuit Decision Also Conflicts With This Court's Anti-Commandeering Jurisprudence.

PASPA is not a permissible "law[] of preemption," Pet. App. 52a, but rather unlawful commandeering by Congress of state legislatures. This Court has made clear that Congress may not "regulate state governments' regulation." *New York,* 505 U.S. at 166. Yet that is precisely what PASPA does; it directly prohibits States (with a few grandfathered exceptions) from licensing or otherwise officially sanctioning sports wagering within their borders.

Just as it radically departed from this Court's preemption case law, however, the Third Circuit also fundamentally misconstrued this Court's anti-commandeering jurisprudence. The Third Circuit applied an "affirmative/negative command distinction," Pet. App. 40a, determining that it is one thing to "tell[] the states what to do" and altogether another to "bar[] them from doing something they want to do," *id.* at 38a. But that is not the test for commandeering under this Court's cases. Rather, as explained below, this Court has made clear that the anti-commandeering doctrine exists to ensure that the state and federal governments each remain directly accountable for their own actions. What matters is whether Congress has obscured its responsibility by forcing state governments to carry out federal policy rather than doing so itself. And that can occur—contrary to the Third Circuit's conclusion—whether Congress issues an affirmative or a negative command to a State.

1. *The political accountability principles at the core of this Court's anti-commandeering cases do not accord with the Third Circuit's "affirmative/negative command distinction."*

**a.** This Court has explained that the anti-commandeering doctrine flows directly from the Framers' decision to adopt a structure of dual sovereignty. In drafting the Constitution, the Framers deliberately rejected a system of government in which Congress would "employ state governments as regulatory agencies." *New York,* 505 U.S. at 163. Indeed, that was the model under the Articles of Confederation, and "[t]he inadequacy of th[at] governmental structure was responsible in part for the Constitutional Convention." *Id.* At the Convention, two proposals "took center stage," *id.* at 164, and the Framers "explicitly chose a Constitution that confers upon Congress the power to regulate individuals, not States." *Id.* at 166.

The point of the new governmental structure was to establish dual sovereigns, with each directly responsible to its citizens for its own actions. The Framers determined that "[t]he new National Government 'must carry its agency to the persons of the citizens . . . [and] address itself immediately to the hopes and fears of individuals." *Id.* at 163 (quoting *The Federalist* No. 16, at 116 (Alexander Hamilton) (Clinton Rossiter ed., 1961)). Likewise, "a State's government [would] represent and remain accountable to its own citizens." *Printz,* 521 U.S. at 920 (1997). The "great innovation of th[e] design" was "'a legal system unprecedented in form and design, establishing two orders of government, each with its own direct relationship, its own privity, its own set of mutual rights and obligations to the people who sustain it and are governed by it.'" *Id.* (quoting *U.S. Term Limits, Inc. v. Thornton,* 514 U.S. 779, 838 (1995) (Kennedy, J., concurring)).

The anti-commandeering doctrine safeguards this system of dual sovereignty and clear accountability. When state and federal governments act separately and directly on their citizens, each is publicly exposed as responsible for its actions, and each must bear the electoral consequences of those actions. If the citizens of a State do not agree with a certain state policy, for example, "they may elect state officials who share their view." *New York,* 505 U.S. at 168. And if that view is contrary to the national view, it "can always be pre-empted under the Supremacy Clause," and then "federal officials [will] suffer the consequences if the decision turns out to be detrimental or unpopular." *Id.* But where Congress commandeers and forces States to implement federal policy, "it may be state officials who will bear the brunt of public disapproval, while the federal officials who devised the regulatory program may remain insulated from the electoral ramifications of their decision." *Id.* at 169.

Contrary to the Third Circuit's suggestion, these concerns about misplaced political blame were not simply an afterthought in this Court's anti-commandeering jurisprudence. *See* Pet. App. 35a, 48a n.15. Rather, this Court has stressed that maintaining clear lines of political accountability is the touchstone of the anti-commandeering doctrine. Although commandeering can be a way for Congress to save a few federal dollars, it does not matter whether the States must actually "absorb the costs of implementing a federal program." *Printz,* 521 U.S. at 930. Nor is the importance of the federal program, *New York,* 505 U.S. at 178, or a State's consent, *id.* at 182, relevant. The critical question is whether the federal government has put States "in the position of taking the blame for [the federal program's] burdensomeness and for its defects." *Printz,* 521 U.S. at 930.

As this Court has noted, the focus on maintaining direct accountability "may appear 'formalistic'" but that is the nature of our Constitution, which places great emphasis on "the form of our government." *New York*, 505 U.S. at 187. Our system of dual sovereignty, requiring each government to remain accountable to its citizens, is as much a part of the Constitution as the substantive limits on Congress's power. And it is equally, if not more, significant. The separation of the state and federal governments "is one of the Constitution's structural protections of liberty," *Printz*, 521 U.S. at 921, providing an important "'double security'" against tyranny and the abuse of power, *id.* at 922 (quoting *The Federalist* No. 51, at 323 (James Madison)). By keeping them strictly apart, "'[t]he different governments will control each other, at the same time that each will be controlled by itself.'" *Id.*

**b.** The Third Circuit's "affirmative/negative command distinction" fails to recognize that federal laws prohibiting state action—particularly ones restricting or conditioning a State's ability to issue licenses—can result in precisely the sort of misplaced blame that the anti-commandeering doctrine aims to prevent. When a State denies an individual his driver's license, building permit, medical license, or fishing license, the individual is unlikely to blame Congress, which did not enact some form of direct national regulation. For the average American, who is not familiar with every nuance of the United States Code, the more obvious culprits are the state officials who stand between the citizen and the desired license.

Consider the following example. A 65-year-old citizen of West Virginia wants to lawfully fish. He goes to his county clerk's office and submits his information and fee to obtain a fishing license. Unbeknownst to him, the federal government, in an effort to prevent overfishing, has prohibited state governments from issuing fishing licenses to individuals over the age of 50. Congress, however, has not adopted any direct national regulation of fishing. Our would-be fisherman is denied his license. Because there is no federal regulatory regime that might have alerted him to Congress's involvement, it is unlikely that he will think to blame the federal government. More likely, he will fault the clerk who delivers the bad news or the

West Virginia Division of Natural Resources, which is responsible for issuing fishing licenses.

This human propensity to "shoot the messenger" has long been recognized. Sophocles wrote in *Antigone* that "[n]o one likes the bringer of bad news." Sophocles, *Antigone* (c. 441 B.C.), *reprinted in* Sophocles: *The Complete Plays* 352 (Paul Roche transl., Signet Classics 2001). Shakespeare wrote in *Antony and Cleopatra* that "[t]he nature of bad news infects the teller." William Shakespeare, *Antony and Cleopatra* (c. 1606), *reprinted in The Unabridged William Shakespeare* 1135 (William George Clark & William Aldis Wright eds. 1989). English law historically protected town criers because of the people's tendency to lash out at these bearers of the King's news. Any harm to a town crier—shooting the messenger, so to speak—was considered treason. *See "Top town crier to be crowned as Hebden Bridge hits 500,"* [Internet address].

Importantly, this Court has shown that it does not matter, for purposes of the anti-commandeering doctrine, that a little research might reveal the federal government's involvement. In *Printz,* this Court found that Congress had improperly shifted political accountability to state chief law enforcement officers ("CLEOs") by requiring them to conduct background checks during handgun sales. The Court reasoned: "[I]t will be the CLEO and not some federal official who stands between the gun purchaser and immediate possession of his gun." 521 U.S. at 930. Thus, "it will likely be the CLEO, not some federal official, who will be blamed for any error (even one in the designated federal database) that causes a purchaser to be mistakenly rejected." *Id.* This Court did not suggest that the gun purchaser should have researched whether the CLEO was in fact acting at Congress's direction. Nor did the Court find it relevant that the challenged federal law—the Brady Act—was a very high-profile piece of federal gun-control legislation of which many Americans were surely aware.

### 2. *This Court's anti-commandeering cases have never adopted an "affirmative/negative command distinction."*

**a.** Discussing *New York* and *Printz,* the Third Circuit asserts that this Court's cases support its novel limitation on the anti-commandeering doctrine, *see* Pet. App. 39a-46a, but it is wrong. In *New York,* this Court stated that "the

Constitution has never been understood to confer upon Congress the ability to require the States to govern according to Congress's instructions." 505 U.S. at 162. Congress may not "conscript state governments as its agents," *id.* at 178, or "regulate state governments' regulation," *id.* at 166. None of this language even begins to suggest that Congress runs afoul of the anti-commandeering doctrine only where it compels affirmative action by the States. Indeed, a federal law prohibiting state action would fall squarely within the scope of all these statements.

The Third Circuit claims that "it is hard to see how Congress can 'commandeer' a state, or how it can be found to regulate how a state regulates, if it does not require it to do anything at all." Pet. App. 39a-40a. The court's confusion is perplexing, to say the least. Restraining a State's actions can exert just as much control over the State as does dictating its actions. If Congress were to prohibit a State from issuing fishing licenses, for example, it would be directly mandating at least part of what the State's fishing policy shall be.

To be sure, *New York* and *Printz* did include some statements specifically barring Congress from compelling affirmative state action. *See New York,* 505 U.S. at 188 (finding it "clear" that Congress "may not compel the States to enact or administer a federal regulatory program"); *Printz,* 521 U.S. at 933 (same). But the reason for those seemingly narrow statements is that the offending federal law in both cases required affirmative state action. Those statements concerned the particular statutes in the two cases and nothing more.

More important is the fact that the laws at issue in *New York* and *Printz*—as well as any number of other affirmative commands—could just as easily be written as prohibitions on state action. Instead of requiring States to enact certain regulations governing the disposal of radioactive waste, as was rejected in *New York,* Congress could put limitations on the ability of States to license the disposal of such waste. And instead of requiring state law enforcement officers to conduct background checks during handgun sales, as in *Printz,* Congress could prohibit those same state officers from issuing handgun permits if they have not performed a background check.

This Court thus could not have intended in those cases to limit the anti-commandeering doctrine to "affirmative" requirements, as that would have robbed those decisions of any real meaning. Congress could continue to govern in exactly the same objectionable way—making States implement a federal restriction on the activity in question rather than doing so itself—by slightly rewriting the offending laws. The Third Circuit quarrels with whether the specific law in *Printz* could actually be recast as a prohibition without also imposing an affirmative condition, *see* Pet. App. 43a, but it has no answer to the general principle that many affirmative commands can be easily recast as prohibitions.

**b.** The Third Circuit also places great weight on *South Carolina v. Baker,* 485 U.S. 505 (1988), and *Reno v. Condon,* 528 U.S. 141 (2000), but neither is an anti-commandeering case. Those cases did not involve attempts by Congress to control the States' actions as sovereigns governing their own citizens—the issue central to commandeering—but rather concerned federal laws regulating the actions of States like private individuals participating in a market. *Condon* involved the federal Driver's Privacy Protection Act (DPPA), which regulated the behavior of States and private actors in the market for drivers' personal information. *Id.* at 149-151 ("The DPPA regulates the States as the owners of databases."); *id.* at 149 (describing "drivers' personal information" as "an article in interstate commerce"). *Baker* involved a regulation of States and private actors in the bond market. 485 U.S. at 510 (explaining that the law "covers not only state bonds but also bonds issued by the United States and private corporations"). Whatever lessons those cases may have regarding federal regulation of a State's actions, they have no application to the anti-commandeering doctrine.

Noting that DMVs are "uniquely state institutions," the Third Circuit challenges this characterization of *Condon,* arguing that States are not engaged in market activity when they "obtain information through the[ir] DMVs." Pet. App. 47a. But the court misunderstands what was at issue in *Condon.* The issue there was not whether the States could *obtain* information from their DMVs, but rather their "*sale* or *release* of that information in interstate commerce" for use by private "insurers, manufacturers, direct marketers, and others." *Condon,* 528 U.S. at 671 (emphases added). This latter activity, the *Condon* Court explained, was market activity "property subject [to] congressional regulation." *Id.*

## *II. THE THIRD CIRCUIT'S DECISION HARMS STATES AND OUR SYSTEM OF DUAL SOVEREIGNTY.*

If permitted to stand, the Third Circuit's decision threatens to greatly expand the federal government's power. Like every other State in the union, West Virginia requires state-issued licenses, permits, or authorizations for a wide-ranging variety of occupations and activities. Some form of state approval is required for matters as varied as becoming an auctioneer or a veterinarian, manufacturing frozen desserts or dealing ginseng, building a house, or driving a car. *See* Business for West Virginia, Apply for Licenses/Permits, http://www.business4wv.com/b4wvpubhc/default.aspx?pagename=applyforlicense#results. If there is some nexus to interstate commerce, the Third Circuit would permit Congress to pass "standalone" laws that restrict West Virginia's ability to issue these licenses, permits, or authorizations. Pet. App. 30a n.9.

Significantly, with the ability to shift political blame to the States, Congress could act with far less fear of repercussions at the voting booth, especially on issues that strike at the core of American life and for which the federal government would very likely want to avoid responsibility. For instance, with the recent controversy over long-term brain damage in football players, Congress could decide that American children should not be playing the sport. But rather than enact what could be extremely unpopular restrictions at the national level, the federal government could prohibit the States from authorizing or licensing youth football leagues. In the interest of national security, Congress might decide that the Department of Justice requires greater ability to monitor the Internet. But to deflect the backlash for its invasion of privacy, federal legislators could restrict the States from issuing business licenses to Internet service providers unless those companies agreed to provide the FBI unrestrained access to their subscriber databases. To save money on health insurance costs, Congress could determine that Americans should avoid eating particular foods. But to try to avoid being blamed, it could bar States from allowing the sale of buttered popcorn at movie theaters or extra-large sodas at sports stadiums. And if studies began to show detrimental effects from the ingestion of large amounts of caffeine, Congress could even decide to regulate the consumption of coffee. But because the federal government would not want to be seen as interfering with such an integral part of so many morning routines, Congress might instead stop States from licensing businesses that sell drinks that exceed a certain caffeine content.

In each case, when the permit or license is denied, at least some (if not all) of the blame will fall wrongly on the States, even if a particular State would prefer as a matter of policy to have acted otherwise. Just as in *Printz,* it will be the State, or a state official, and "not some federal official" who is interfering with day-to-day life. 521 U.S. at 930. And just as in *Printz,* there would be legitimate concerns about misplaced blame even though these are high-profile issues and the relevant laws would be available to anyone diligent enough to seek them out and read them.

The injury to state sovereignty would be unprecedented. The genius of our system of dual sovereignty is that the States can act as a voice for change or dissent, even in the face of a national policy. Our system of government "promotes innovation by allowing for the possibility that 'a single courageous State may, if its citizens choose, serve as a laboratory; and try novel social and economic experiments without risk to the rest of the country.'" *Gonzalez v. Raich,* 545 U.S. 1, 42 (2005) (O'Connor, J., dissenting) (quoting *New State Ice Co. v. Liebmann,* 285 U.S. 262, 311 (1932) (Brandeis, J., dissenting)). If Congress disagrees and has the Article I authority to act, it may establish a federal regime and preempt contrary state law. And when Congress does so, it is understood that the federal government has simply overridden the States and that individual States do not necessarily agree with the national policy. But under the Third Circuit's view, Congress could avoid taking ownership and force the States to advance its policy view, whatever that may be under the political party then in power, in a way that makes individual States seem responsible.

## EXAMPLE 7

**Authors** Burton Craige and Narendra K. Ghosh, Patterson Harkavy LLP; J. Edward Bell III, Bell Legal Group

**Case** *CTS Corp. v. Waldburger*, 134 S. Ct. 2175 (2014)

### BRIEF OF JERRY ENSMINGER, THE ESTATE OF CHRISTOPHER TOWNSEND, MIKE PARTAIN, KRIS THOMAS, AND THE ESTATE OF ROSANNE WARREN AS AMICI CURIAE IN SUPPORT OF RESPONDENTS

### QUESTION PRESENTED

Whether 42 U.S.C. § 9658 preempts periods of repose such as that found in N.C. Gen. Stat. § 1-52.

[In a footnote to the brief, this statement was made: Pursuant to Supreme Court Rule 37.6, counsel for amici state that they authored this brief in its entirety and that no party or counsel for any party, nor any other person or entity other than amici or their counsel made a monetary contribution intended to fund the preparation or submission of this brief. Respondents have provided amici with written consent to the filing of this brief, and petitioner has consented to the filing of this brief by a blanket agreement filed with the clerk of this Court.]

### INTEREST OF *AMICI CURIAE*

Jerry Ensminger, the Estate of Christopher Townsend, Mike Partain, Kris Thomas, and the Estate of Rosanne Warren submit this brief as *amici curiae* in support of respondents. *Amici* lived on or near Marine Corps Base Camp Lejeune in Jacksonville, North Carolina, at various points between the 1950s and 1985. During this period, drinking water provided through Camp Lejeune's Tarawa Terrace and Hadnot Point water systems was highly contaminated with multiple human carcinogens. The toxic exposure had devastating consequences for these *amici*, and for many other Marines and their families.

Jerry Ensminger joined the United States Marines after graduating from high school in 1970. Ensminger and his wife were assigned to Camp Lejeune in 1973. In 1975, while the couple was living in the base's Tarawa Terrace neighborhood, Ensminger's wife became pregnant with their second child. The family moved away from Camp Lejeune in December 1975, and their daughter Janey was born in South Carolina on July 30, 1975. In 1982, the Ensmingers returned to Camp Lejeune. Although the family lived off-base, Janey frequently visited the base, often spending time at the base swimming pools. Janey was thus exposed to Camp Lejeune's carcinogenic water both *in utero* and as a young child. In the summer of 1983, Janey fell ill and was ultimately diagnosed with acute lymphocytic leukemia. After a grueling course of chemotherapy, Janey died on September 24, 1985, at age nine. Jerry Ensminger had no reason to suspect that Camp Lejeune's water could have contributed to his daughter's death until 1997, when he saw a news report about possible contamination on base. When he contacted the Marine Corps and the Navy, officials assured him that the contamination was minor and could not have been responsible for Janey's illness and death. Not satisfied by these assurances, he began his own investigation and uncovered years of evidence suppression and deceit by the military regarding the contamination at Camp Lejeune.

Tom Townsend joined the Marines in 1949 at age 18. He and his wife Ann had a healthy son in 1955 and a healthy daughter in 1962. Assigned to Camp Lejeune in 1965, they were living in a neighborhood served by the base's Hadnot Point water system when their third child was conceived. Christopher Townsend was born on March 16, 1967, in the Camp Lejeune naval hospital. The baby struggled immediately after birth, and was diagnosed with serious heart defects. Over the following weeks, Christopher was treated in the Camp Lejeune naval hospital, and twice admitted into the naval hospital in Bethesda, Maryland. On June 27, 1967, Christopher Townsend died after living just three and a half months. An autopsy revealed that he died of congenital malformation of the heart. Tom Townsend only realized that his wife and infant son may have been exposed to toxic water at Camp Lejeune in 1998, after reading an article in a magazine. He would eventually work with Jerry Ensminger to uncover countless documents demonstrating the extent of the contamination and the scope of the government's efforts to suppress the evidence. Townsend currently has a claim under the Federal Tort Claims Act ("FTCA") pending before the Department of the Navy on behalf of his son's estate.

Mike Partain is the grandson and son of Marine officers whose combined service includes World War II, the Korean War, and the Vietnam War. Conceived in 1967 and born in 1968 at Camp Lejeune, Partain was exposed to the base's carcinogenic drinking water *in utero* and as an infant. Partain lived a seemingly normal life until April 2007, when, on his eighteenth wedding anniversary, he was diagnosed with male breast cancer. He underwent a right mastectomy and eight rounds of active chemotherapy, followed by a year of oral chemotherapy. Male breast cancer is exceptionally rare and its occurrence peaks in men aged 71 years. Partain developed the disease at age 39, has no family history of breast cancer, and lacks the genetic mutation common in most male breast cancer victims. Partain was unaware of his exposure to carcinogenic chemicals in Camp Lejeune's water until two months after his diagnosis, when his father viewed a CNN report featuring Jerry Ensminger's congressional testimony about Camp Lejeune's contamination. Partain volunteered as an advocate for those poisoned at Camp Lejeune, and has identified an ever-expanding cluster of male breast cancer victims who were similarly exposed to Camp Lejeune's toxic drinking water. Partain currently has a claim under the FTCA pending with the Department of the Navy.

Kris Thomas is the son of a United States Marine. Born in 1958, Thomas lived in Camp Lejeune's Tarawa Terrace from approximately 1965 to 1970, just a few streets down from Mike Partain. Thomas's father was stationed at Camp Lejeune. In 1970, the Thomas family moved off base, but he regularly visited the base. Thomas enjoyed swimming and frequented Camp Lejeune's pools, waterways, and ponds. Thomas also attended school on base and received medical treatment at the base hospital. As an adult, Thomas served as a Church of God minister until 2004, when he was diagnosed with male breast cancer. He had surgery to remove the carcinoma and affected lymph nodes, and then underwent several months of chemotherapy. His treatment required him to resign from the ministry. Thomas only realized that he and his family had been exposed to carcinogens at Camp Lejeune when his wife read an article about Mike Partain's advocacy in a local newspaper in October 2007. Thomas currently has a claim under the FTCA pending before the Department of the Navy.

Rosanne Warren was born in 1971. Her mother, Patricia Warren, had worked on Camp Lejeune's Hadnot Point throughout her pregnancy. Through the early 1980s, Rosanne would frequently visit and stay with family friends in Tarawa Terrace while her mother was working. When she was twelve years old, Rosanne began suffering from serious kidney problems, which required multiple stent implants. Despite her medical problems, Rosanne attended college, and went on to receive a degree in medical technology. In her mid-20s, Rosanne was diagnosed with cervical cancer. She underwent chemotherapy, radiation, and surgical removal of her uterus. Despite aggressive treatment, the cancer returned in her hip and kidney. Rosanne died in 2000, at age 28. Her mother Patricia did not learn that she and her daughter had been exposed to carcinogens at Camp Lejeune until 2008, when a friend told her about a community meeting discussing the issue. Patricia Warren is currently pursuing an FTCA claim on behalf of her daughter's estate before the Department of the Navy.

*Amici's* interest in this case is substantial because its resolution could impact their claims against the government, as well as those of other victims of the Camp Lejeune contamination. Many of these victims are pursuing FTCA claims before the Navy. Some are pursuing FTCA claims in federal court. Those claims have been consolidated and are on appeal before the Eleventh Circuit. *See Bryant v. United States; Camp Lejeune Water Contamination Litigation v. United States,* No. 12-15424 (11th Cir., argued Jan. 17, 2014). In the Eleventh Circuit, the United States contends that North Carolina's statute of repose shields the government from all liability for injuries to the Camp Lejeune victims. Its argument in the Eleventh Circuit as to CERCLA preemption is nearly identical to the one it now makes to this Court as *amicus curiae. See* Brief of the United States, *Camp Lejeune Water Contamination Litigation,* No. 12-15424 (11th Cir. filed Feb. 11, 2013).

*Amici* also have a strong interest in ensuring that individuals with a long-latency cancer due to toxic contamination can pursue recovery in states with similar periods of repose. *Amici* have experienced cancer's devastating impact on individuals, families, and communities. If state statutes are permitted to bar victims of long-latency cancers from pursuing claims against those who caused their suffering, many victims will have no effective legal recourse, regardless of how clearly they were wronged.

Finally, *amici* know firsthand the extent to which perpetrators will attempt to hide their wrongs from victims. The Navy has required that Camp Lejeune test its water systems annually since 1963, but no records exist of any such tests until 1980. Although Camp Lejeune officials received reports of the water contamination as early as 1980, they did not begin closing wells on base until November 1984. For over two decades, the United States failed to notify potential victims of their exposure to contaminated water, suppressed information regarding the extent of the contamination, and refused to provide medical support. It took an act of Congress in 2007 for the military to begin formally notifying all exposed personnel and their families. Had Camp Lejeune officials notified these individuals more promptly, the suffering of countless victims could have been reduced through preventive care, aggressive monitoring, and early treatment.

## SUMMARY OF THE ARGUMENT

Camp Lejeune's water supply was contaminated with dangerous carcinogens for decades. Although the military had reason to know of the contamination, it did nothing to address the problem. Once the government finally began closing contaminated wells, it concealed the scope of the contamination for many years. *Amici* and countless others have had their lives devastated because of exposure to Camp Lejeune's contaminated water. Because cancer often develops many years after an individual is exposed to carcinogens, most of these victims did not know of their injuries until many years after they left Camp Lejeune. Those who developed injuries more immediately did not know that Camp Lejeune's water could have been the cause until the government's deception was exposed.

In 1986, Congress enacted legislation ensuring that individuals who develop long-latency diseases because of exposure to hazardous waste would have the opportunity to bring suit, regardless of state limitation periods.

This legislation was intended to address claims such as those arising from Camp Lejeune's water contamination. Petitioner and the United States as *amicus,* however, argue that the federal law has no effect on North Carolina's statute of repose. Their interpretation contravenes both the text and the intent of the 1986 legislation. If adopted, it would prevent the victims of Camp Lejeune from having any legal recourse, and would reward entities that conceal their misconduct. *Amici* and others similarly situated should not be excluded from the law's protection.

## ARGUMENT

### *I. EXTENSIVE WATER CONTAMINATION AT CAMP LEJEUNE LASTED FOR DECADES, WAS CONCEALED BY THE GOVERNMENT, AND AFFECTED THOUSANDS OF MARINES AND CIVILIANS.*

### A. The government exposed Marines and their families to toxic water for decades.

Founded in 1941, Camp Lejeune is the largest Marine Corps base on the East Coast. On approximately 220 square miles adjacent to Jacksonville, North Carolina, the base typically serves more than 100,000 service members, military families, and civilian personnel. *Amici* and their families once lived on or near this base.

The government maintained a cavalier attitude toward waste disposal at Camp Lejeune for much of the mid-twentieth century. Although the base had a hazardous waste dump since 1959, military officials permitted the disposal of waste at other locations throughout the base. Mike Magner, *A Trust Betrayed: The Untold Story of Camp Lejeune and the Poisoning of Generations of Marines and Their Families* 33-34, 55-59 (Da Capo Press 2014). Waste was generally either dumped onto the land or into ditches dug by Marines. *Id.* at 33-34. These wastes included industrial cleaning solvents, gasoline, oil, mustard gas, battery acid, heavy metals, and pesticides. *Id.* at 55-59, 87-90. In addition, as much as one million gallons of fuel from the base's fuel depot leaked into the soil, forming large pools of diesel and gasoline floating on top of the aquifer closest to the surface. *Id.* at 87, 209-11.

Camp Lejeune is supplied by on-base water wells. Since at least 1963, the Navy recognized that it was "responsible for the protection and the purity of the water during its distribution on its premises." Dep't of Navy, Manual of Naval Preventative Medicine ("NAVMED"), P-5010 § 5-23 (August 1963) [.], *available at* [Internet address]. It likewise recognized that "ground waters are becoming polluted with increasing frequency and the resulting hazards require special surveillance," particularly from "chemical pollutants originating either from sewage or industrial effluents." *Id.* § 5-32, Appendix A. Accordingly, the Navy required that a "complete chemical analysis of the water supply shall be made annually[,]" with the additional requirement that "[i]f the supply is from wells, water from each well is analyzed." *Id.* § 5-32(5)(a). Despite these requirements, there is no indication that Camp Lejeune's water systems or wells were tested in the years before 1980.

In 1974, Camp Lejeune officials acknowledged that they understood the risk posed by industrial pollutants. That year, the Camp Lejeune Base Commander issued an order recognizing that "organic solvents were hazardous materials," and that "improper disposal practices create hazards such as the contamination of drinking water." U.S. Marine Corps, Camp Lejeune Base Order 5100.13B (June 27, 1974), *available at* [Internet address]. Knowing the source of the base's drinking water and the extent and nature of the waste disposed at the base, military officials had many reasons to suspect that the water system was already contaminated. *See* Magner, *supra,* at 55-59.

Officials would eventually have definitive proof. In the wake of impending federal water quality regulations, base officials had water samples independently evaluated in 1980 and 1981. *Id.* at 45-47. These evaluations repeatedly revealed that Camp Lejeune's drinking water was highly contaminated, and generated numerous written warnings to military officials. *Id.* The first report from October 1980 stated: "heavy organic interference . . . you need to analyze for chlorinated organics." *Id.* at 46. Another from 1981 flatly stated: "water highly contaminated with other chlorinated hydrocarbons (Solvents)!" *Id.* at 46. Despite these warnings, the military made no effort to shut down wells, improve water quality, or notify Marines and their families of the dangerous contaminants in their drinking water.

In 1982, tests revealed that the base's water was contaminated with the cleaning solvents Trichloro-ethylene ("TCE") and Perchloroethylene ("PCE"). *Id.* at 51-52. A sample from the Hadnot Point system contained 1,400 parts per billion ("ppb") of TCE. *Id.* at 53. At the time, the Navy's Bureau of Medicine and Surgery ("BUMED") Instructions limited the concentration of chlorinated hydrocarbons such as TCE and PCE in drinking water to maximums ranging from 3ppb to 100 ppb. *See* Dep't of Navy, BUMED Instruction 6240.3C at 6 (Dec. 13, 1972), *available at* [Internet address]. Although water test results were reported up the chain of command, the military made no effort to further investigate or address the problem. Magner, *supra,* at 51-53.

It was not until late 1984 that military officials took any action. In November and December of that year, three wells were closed after tests revealed TCE concentrations ranging from 300ppb to 1,600 ppb, along with elevated levels of benzene and other industrial contaminants. *Id.* at 69-70. Approximately one month after these wells were taken out of service, an on-base elementary school water fountain was found to contain 1,100 ppb of TCE. *Id.* at 71. Additional tests then revealed TCE contamination levels in some wells as high as 18,900 ppb. *Id.* Camp Lejeune finally closed its contaminated wells in 1985. *Id.*

The Agency for Toxic Substances and Disease Registry ("ATSDR") has conducted multi-year studies on Camp Lejeune's water contamination. *See* Morris L. Maslia, et al., *Analyses and Historical Reconstruction of Groundwater Flow, Contaminant Fate and Transport, and Distribution of Drinking Water Within the Service Areas of the Hadnot Point and Holcomb Boulevard Water Treatment Plants and Vicinities, U.S. Marine Corps Base Camp Lejeune, North Carolina* (March 2013) ("ATSDR Hadnot and Holcomb Report"), *available at* [Internet address]; Morris L. Maslia, et al., *Analyses of Groundwater Flow, Contaminant Fate and Transport, and Distribution of Drinking Water at Tarawa Terrace and Vicinity, U.S. Marine Corps Base Camp Lejeune, North Carolina: Historical Reconstruction and Present-Day Conditions* (March 2009) ("ATSDR Tarawa Terrace Report"), *available at* [Internet address]. These studies performed historical reconstruction calculations to estimate the monthly levels of contaminants in the drinking water provided to on-base family housing units. ATSDR Tarawa Terrace Report, *supra,* at A2; ATSDR Hadnot and Holcomb Report, *supra,* at A2.

The ATSDR's studies demonstrate that Camp Lejeune's Tarawa Terrace and Hadnot Point water systems were highly contaminated with multiple known human carcinogens from the 1950s to 1985. ATSDR Tarawa Terrace Report, *supra,* at A70; ATSDR Hadnot and Holcomb Report, *supra,* at A100-01. Because Camp Lejeune's water systems had different degrees of contamination, individuals living on base during the contaminated period experienced varying levels of exposure.

### B. The government concealed the nature and scope of Camp Lejeune's contamination.

After exposing its Marines, civilian personnel, and their families to poisonous water for decades, the government compounded its malfeasance by making every effort to prevent these victims, including *amici,* from learning that they had been exposed to dangerous carcinogens.

After they closed contaminated wells in 1984 and 1985, military officials downplayed the extent of the contamination through euphemistic language that obscured the problem and deceived the victims. For example, around the time the wells were shut down, Camp Lejeune's waste disposal practices had begun attracting media attention. Although the base's drinking water had been highly contaminated for years, base officials represented to the media that "people had not been directly exposed to the pollutants[,]" and characterized the closure of wells as "precautionary measures." Jerry Allegood, *Civilians, military investigating waste dumps at Camp Lejeune,* Raleigh News & Observer, Sept. 15, 1985, at 29A. In requesting residents of the Tarawa Terrace neighborhood to reduce their water usage, Camp Lejeune's base commander indicated that two wells had been shut down "because of minute (trace) amounts of several organic compounds." Magner, *supra,* at 73. The notice stated that "[t]here are no definitive State or Federal regulations regarding a safe level of these compounds, but as a precaution, I have ordered the closure of these wells for all but emergency situations[.]" *Id.* Contrary to these assertions, Camp Lejeune's water had previously contained as much as 300 times the TCE levels then permitted by the Navy. See BUMED Inst. 6240.3C at 6.

The military would continue its deceptive conduct for many years to come. It resisted turning over files to the ATSDR, Magner, *supra,* at 100; fought a proposed ATSDR study of infants born at Camp Lejeune, *id.* at 104; and refused to fund surveys to locate children born on the base, *id.* at 107. It misled the Environmental Protection Agency ("EPA") as to when water tests had been conducted and what those tests revealed. William R. Levesque, *Camp Lejeune water contamination history detailed in documents,* Tampa Bay Times, October 16, 2009, *available at* http://www.tampabay.com/news/military/veterans/camp-lejeune-water-contamination-history-detailed-in-documents/1044542. In 2010, a news reporter revealed that the Navy and Marine Corps had simply failed to turn over many relevant documents to the ATSDR, including one estimating that over one million gallons of fuel had leaked into the ground from the Hadnot Point fuel farm. Magner, *supra,* at 211. Military officials went so far as to advocate delaying the mailing of health questionnaires to ensure that they did not coincide with the release of the movie *A Civil Action,* which addressed the relationship between TCE contamination and childhood leukemia in Woburn, Massachusetts. *Id.* at 110. Indeed, military officials' resistance was so egregious that the EPA investigated whether their deceptive conduct warranted criminal charges for obstruction of justice. *Id.* at 167-68.

Even after being publicly reprimanded by members of Congress, the military refused to notify all affected Marines until forced to do so by the John Warner National Defense Authorization Act of 2007, Pub. L. No. 109-364, § 318(b), 120 Stat. 2083 (2006). This law also required the Navy to fund comprehensive studies evaluating the impact of pre-natal, childhood, and adult exposure to Camp Lejuene's contaminated water. *Id.* § 318(a).

### C. Camp Lejeune's toxic water devastated countless lives.

The chemicals found in Camp Lejeune's water included TCE, PCE, benzene, and vinyl chloride ("VC"). See Frank J. Bove, et al., Evaluation of mortality among marines and navy personnel exposed to contaminated drinking water at USMC base Camp Lejeune: a retrospective cohort study, Environmental Health 2014 13:10 ("Marine Cohort Study"), available at [Internet address]. These chemicals can be absorbed into the body through ingestion, skin exposure, and inhalation. *Id.* at 2. For example, an individual taking a ten-minute shower can absorb as much TCE through inhalation as he or she would by drinking two liters of the same water. *Id.* By the time Camp Lejeune began shutting down contaminated wells, its drinking water contained levels of these volatile organic compounds that were hundreds of times greater than what is considered safe for humans. As many as one million people could have been exposed to Camp Lejeune's contaminated water.

TCE, benzene, and VC are known human carcinogens; PCE is considered a "likely" human carcinogen. ATSDR Hadnot and Holcomb Report, *supra*, at A16. Exposure to these chemicals is associated with a wide variety of cancers and diseases, including leukemia, breast cancer, bladder cancer, kidney cancer, cervical cancer, liver cancer, non-Hodgkin's lymphoma, and multiple myeloma. See ATSDR, Reported health effects linked with trichloroethylene (TCE), tetrachloroethylene (PCE), benzene, and vinyl chloride (VC) exposure, *available at* [Internet address] (collecting scientific studies). In utero exposure to TCE and PCE is associated with childhood leukemia, major heart defects, neural tube defects, and fetal death. *Id.*

Individuals exposed to Camp Lejeune's contaminated water have significantly elevated rates of cancer mortality. A recent study compared the mortality rates of all Marines posted at Camp Lejeune between 1975 and 1985 to that of Marines posted at California's Camp Pendleton during the same period. See Marine Cohort Study, *supra*. The study found that Camp Lejeune Marines were more likely to die from several causes, including "kidney cancer, liver cancer, esophageal cancer, cervical cancer, multiple myeloma, Hodgkin lymphoma, and [Amyotrophic Lateral Sclerosis]." *Id.* at 13. Marines with high cumulative exposures to Camp Lejeune's contaminants had substantially higher cancer mortality rates. For example, Camp Lejeune Marines with high exposure to contaminated water were 580% more likely to die of cervical cancer than Camp Pendleton Marines, while Camp Lejeune Marines with low to no exposure to contaminated water were 112% more likely to die of cervical cancer than Camp Pendleton Marines. *Id.* at 9.

Children born to women exposed to the contaminated water during their pregnancy also experienced higher rates of juvenile diseases and disorders. A 2013 epidemiological study evaluated whether *in utero* and infant exposures to the base's contaminated water were associated with a defined set of birth defects and childhood cancers. Perri Z. Ruckart, et al., *Evaluation of exposure to contaminated drinking water and specific birth defects and childhood cancers at Marine Corps Base Camp Lejeune, North Carolina*, Environmental Health 2013, 12:104, *available at* [Internet address]. The study found that children exposed to contaminated water *in utero* were more likely to be born with neural tube disorders such as spina bifida and anencephaly, and were more likely to develop childhood hematopoietic cancers such as childhood leukemia and childhood non-Hodgkin's lymphoma. *Id.* at 1-2.

Many cancers caused by exposure to VC, TCE, PCE, and benzene do not manifest until decades after exposure to the chemical. "The time between first exposure to a cancer-causing agent and clinical recognition of the disease is called the latency period. Latency periods vary by cancer type, but for some cancers may be 15 to 20 years or longer." Centers for Disease Control and Prevention, Workplace Safety and Health Topics, Cancer Clusters, available at http://www.cdc.gov/niosh/topics/cancer/clusters.html (last visited March 27, 2014). In a congressional hearing on Camp Lejeune, Dr. Michael L. Gros, a Navy obstetrician, testified that after exposure to the toxins found in Camp Lejeune's water, "[t]he cancerous effects do not appear until 10 to 15 years[.]" Poisoned Patriots: Contaminated Drinking Water at Camp Lejeune: Hearing before the H. Comm. on Energy and Commerce, 110th Cong. 12, 15 (June 12, 2007) (statement of Michael L. Gros, M.D.).

In 2012, recognizing the weight of the scientific evidence, Congress enacted the Janey Ensminger Act, Pub. L. No. 112-154, 126 Stat. 1165 (Aug. 6, 2012). Under the Act, if a veteran or veteran's family member was exposed to Camp Lejeune's contaminated water for more than thirty days and later develops one of a number of listed diseases, there is a rebuttable presumption that the disease was caused by the individual's exposure. 38 U.S.C. § 1710(F). The Act establishes a presumption of causation for fifteen illnesses or conditions: breast cancer, kidney cancer, multiple myeloma, renal toxicity, female infertility, scleroderma, non-Hodgkin's lymphoma, lung cancer, bladder cancer, leukemia, myelodysplastic syndromes, hepatic steatosis, miscarriage, and neurobehavioral effects. *Id.*

While helping many of Camp Lejeune's victims, the Act provides only limited relief. Because victims are only "eligible for hospital care and medical services," *id.*, the Act provides no benefit to Tom Townsend, whose infant son died years before the Act's passage. It likewise provides limited benefit to individuals such as Kris Thomas, who was treated for his breast cancer several years before the Act's passage, but who has been unable to return to his career as a minister due to the side effects of treatment. Because the Act covers only veterans and their family members, individuals such as Rosanne Warren, who was not a family member of a veteran who served on active duty at Camp Lejeune, would not benefit from the Act in any way.

## *II. CERCLA'S UNIFORM DISCOVERY RULE WAS INTENDED TO ADDRESS SITUATIONS EXACTLY LIKE THOSE EXPERIENCED BY THE VICTIMS OF CAMP LEJEUNE'S CONTAMINATED WATER.*

### A. As amended, CERCLA was intended to protect the rights of those suffering from long-latency diseases.

In 1980, Congress enacted CERCLA "in response to the serious environmental and health risks posed by industrial pollution." *Burlington N. & Santa Fe Ry. Co. v. United States*, 556 U.S. 599, 602 (2009). CERCLA established a twelve-person study group "to determine the adequacy of existing common law and statutory remedies in providing legal redress for harm to man and the environment caused by the release of hazardous substances into the environment[.]" 42 U.S.C. § 9651(e).

The study group published its report in July 1982. *See* Superfund Section 301(E) Study Group, 97th Cong., Injuries and Damages From Hazardous Wastes—Analysis and Improvement of Legal Remedies (Comm. Print 1982) ("Study Group Report"). The report recognized that "[t]he most common mode of human exposure to waste chemicals is through groundwater." Study Group Report at 13. It likewise recognized: Exposure to certain hazardous wastes may result in cancer, neurological damage, and in mutagenic and teratogenic changes. Most of these types of injuries have long latency periods, sometimes 20 years or longer. With long latency periods, a rule which starts the running of the statute from the time of exposure will defeat most actions before the plaintiff knows of his injury. *Id.* at 28. The report therefore recommended:

> that all states that have not already done so, clearly adopt the rule that an action accrues when the plaintiff discovers or should have discovered the injury or disease and its cause. The Recommendation is intended also to cover the repeal of the statutes of repose which, in a number of states have the same effect as some statutes of limitation in barring plaintiff's claim before he knows that he has one.

*Id.* at 241.

Rather than wait for action from the states, Congress amended CERCLA in 1986 to "address[ ] the problem identified in the 301(e) study." H.R. Conf. Rep. No. 99-962 (1986), *reprinted in* 1986 U.S.C.C.A.N. 3276, 3354. Congress's solution established a minimum "federally required commencement date" ("FRCD") that applies to state causes of action for "personal injury, or property damages, which are caused or contributed to by exposure to any hazardous substance, or pollutant or contaminant, released into the environment from a facility[.]" 42 U.S.C. § 9658(a). The FRCD applies "[i]f the applicable limitations period for such action (as specified in the State statute of limitations or under common law) provides a commencement date which is earlier than the [FRCD]." *Id.* The FRCD is "the date the plaintiff knew (or reasonably should have known) that the personal injury or property damages referred to in subsection (a)(1) of this section were caused or contributed to by the hazardous substance or pollutant or contaminant concerned." *Id.* § 9658(b)(4)(A).

The FRCD is a simple and effective solution to the problems identified by the Study Group Report. It permits certain claims to be brought when an individual has discovered both an injury and its cause, regardless of whether the period for filing suit has passed under state law.

### B. Petitioner's position would terminate with prejudice the claims of individuals, such as the Camp Lejeune victims, who suffer from long-latency diseases.

If not for the FRCD, claims arising from the Camp Lejeune contamination would accrue pursuant to the same North Carolina statute that would otherwise bar respondents' claims in this case. That statute provides:

> [F]or personal injury or physical damage to claimant's property, the cause of action . . . shall not accrue until bodily harm to the claimant or physical damage to his property becomes apparent or ought reasonably to have become apparent to the claimant, whichever event first occurs. Provided that no cause of action shall accrue more than 10 years from the last act or omission of the defendant giving rise to the cause of action.

N.C. Gen. Stat. § 1-52(16). Petitioner mistakenly argues that this provision is not subject to the FRCD.

If the FRCD does not override N.C. Gen. Stat. § 1-52(16), the North Carolina statute could bar all claims from individuals suffering from diseases with latency periods longer than ten years. But the Study Group Report's detailed discussion of the problem posed by long-latency injuries never mentioned a latency period less than ten years—indeed, it frequently addressed latency periods as long as thirty and forty years. *See, e.g.*, Study Group Report at 55 ("ten-to-forty year latency period"); *id.* at 240 (Given "the delayed impact on different organs or the central nervous system, the latency period for the appearance of injury or disease is likely to be extended for thirty years or more[.]"); *id.* at 242 ("carcinogenic, mutagenic, and teratogenic effect may not manifest themselves until 20 or 30 years later"). Petitioner essentially argues that although Congress enacted the FRCD to address the problem, it intended to exclude entirely from its solution the handful of states that provided limitation periods similar to North Carolina's. This argument is as incoherent as it is inhumane.

The FRCD was enacted to ensure that the courthouse doors would be open to individuals like the victims of the Camp Lejeune contamination. Mike Partain was exposed to Camp Lejeune's water *in utero* and as an infant, but did not develop breast cancer until he was 39 years old. Kris Thomas was exposed throughout his childhood, but did not develop breast cancer until he was 45 years old. If petitioner's arguments are credited, these individuals will have no legal recourse. As recognized by United States District Court Judge Terrence Boyle:

> [T]hose exposed to the water at Camp Lejeune could not have connected their illnesses to the alleged contamination until studies and investigations began revealing such causation in 2007. Thus, to apply the statute of repose in this case would bar all potential claims from the over 500,000 marines and their families affected. Indeed, it would bar the overwhelming majority of claims involving any cancer.

*Jones v. United States,* 751 F. Supp. 2d 835, 841 (E.D.N.C. 2010).

### C. Petitioner's position would absolve polluters of liability if they hide their misconduct and succeed in delaying its discovery.

The arguments of petitioner and the United States are especially disturbing given the government's attempts to cover up its misconduct at Camp Lejeune. If the government had closed Camp Lejuene's wells when it first learned they were contaminated, Janey Ensminger and Rosanne Warren might be alive today. If the government had been forthcoming as to the scope of the problem leading to well closures, these families may have pursued claims against the government within North Carolina's statutory periods. If the government had promptly notified those who were exposed to the toxic water, countless other families may have been able to reduce the impact of their exposure through preventive care and early treatment.

Instead of being forthright about its mistakes, the military chose another approach: deception and delay. Today, it seeks the fruits of that strategy. Because it successfully prevented military families from learning the truth about Camp Lejeune's contaminated water for so many years, the United States argues that these families should be time-barred from filing any claims against it. While ordinary statutes of limitation can be tolled to account for such misconduct, those with periods of repose are not generally subject to equitable tolling. *See NCUA Bd. v. Nomura Home Equity Loan, Inc.,* 727 F.3d 1246, 1255 (10th Cir. 2013). Should the United States' argument prevail, companies and government bodies responsible for environmental disasters in North Carolina will have every incentive to use the military's strategy here: conceal their misconduct for as long as necessary to invoke periods of repose. By enacting the FRCD, Congress determined that entities should bear the economic costs caused by their toxic contamination. When the FRCD was used to impose liability on private enterprises, the United States embraced its remedial purpose:

> By increasing the likelihood that persons harmed by hazardous materials will obtain compensation for their injuries, the FRCD provision furthers CERCLA's purpose of "inducting" companies generating, transporting, dumping and storing, etc., hazardous wastes "voluntarily to pursue appropriate environmental response actions with respect to inactive hazardous waste sites." H.R. Rep. No. 1016, 96th Cong., 2d Sess. Pt. 1, at 17 (1980). As the Study Group Report emphasized, "the economic cost of injury should be carried by the industry or enterprise that creates [it], because efforts to reduce the cost will result in greater care and more safety and protection of the public." Study Group Report 248.

Brief for the United States on Petition for a Writ of Certiorari, *Freier v. Westinghouse Elec. Corp.*, No. 02-1036 (U.S. filed March 12, 2003) (quotation marks and record citations omitted) (discussing the constitutionality of the FRCD). The government's position in *Freier* predated the lawsuits from the Camp Lejeune victims. Faced with the prospect of having to absorb the economic costs of its own misconduct, the government has reversed course. It now contends that states can circumvent the FRCD through statutes of repose, and that entities can avoid the economic cost of their injuries by hiding their misconduct. The government's current position directly conflicts with the text and purpose of the FRCD.

Camp Lejeune's Marines were willing to give their lives to defend the United States. In return, the United States government recklessly exposed these Marines and their families to poisoned water for decades, and then concealed the facts that could have mitigated the devastating consequences. The government now asks this Court to reward its reckless misconduct and intentional deception by narrowly construing a remedial statute so as to block victims' claims for relief. But the FRCD was designed to ensure that all citizens would be able to pursue claims based on latent diseases caused by exposure to hazardous materials, regardless of the vagaries of state periods of limitation. *Amici* and others similarly situated should not be excluded from CERCLA's protection.

## EXAMPLE 8

**Authors** Andre M. Mura, Center for Constitutional Litigation, P.C.; Mary Alice McLarty, American Association for Justice

**Case** *Mutual Pharmaceutical Co. v. Bartlett*, 133 S. Ct. 2466 (2013)

### *AMICI CURIAE* BRIEF OF THE AMERICAN ASSOCIATION FOR JUSTICE AND PUBLIC JUSTICE IN SUPPORT OF RESPONDENT

### INTERESTS OF *AMICI CURIAE*

The American Association for Justice ("AAJ") and Public Justice submit this brief as amici curiae in support of Respondent Karen L. Bartlett.

AAJ is a voluntary national bar association whose trial-lawyer members primarily represent individual plaintiffs in civil suits, including personal injury actions, consumer lawsuits, and employment-related cases. Many AAJ-member attorneys represent consumers who have been harmed by dangerous prescription drugs, including consumers who live in New Hampshire. AAJ believes that holding drug makers accountable justly compensates those they have harmed and provides drug companies with a strong incentive to minimize the risk of harm to consumers.

AAJ has also appeared as an amicus curiae in litigation concerning whether federal regulation of prescription drugs and medical devices preempts traditional state-law causes of action. AAJ believes that state tort litigation generally complements and furthers the purposes of the federal regulatory scheme and, therefore, that few state tort claims should be held to be preempted by federal law.

Public Justice is a national public interest law firm dedicated to pursuing justice for victims of corporate and government wrongdoing. Through involvement in precedent-setting and socially significant litigation, Public Justice seeks to ensure that tort law compensates those injured by wrongful conduct and deters similar conduct in the future. As part of its work, Public Justice has represented consumers injured by prescription drugs and litigated many tort cases involving preemption defenses, including as co-counsel for

Gladys Mensing in *PLIVA, Inc. v. Mensing,* 131 S. Ct. 2567 (2011). Public Justice is concerned that if tort remedies against generic drug manufacturers are limited through improper application of preemption principles, injured patients will be left without compensation and generic manufacturers will not have adequate incentive to ensure that their drugs are safe.

## INTRODUCTION AND SUMMARY OF ARGUMENT

Petitioner Mutual Pharmaceutical Company, Inc., a generic manufacturer of a non-steroidal anti-inflammatory drug (NSAID) with the nonproprietary name sulindac, seeks a ruling that Congress, in enacting and amending the Federal Food, Drug, and Cosmetic Act (FDCA), 21 U.S.C. §§ 301 *et seq.,* intended to deprive injured parties like Respondent of long-standing compensation for defective drugs.

Congress has not expressly preempted state tort actions against prescription drug manufacturers, even as it has periodically enlarged the Food and Drug Administration's (FDA's) power to administer federal law. *See Wyeth v. Levine,* 555 U.S. 555, 566-67 (2009). Petitioner argues, however, that preemption may be inferred because it is "impossible" for drug manufacturers to comply with both state law and federal law; and because state law "stands as an obstacle to the accomplishment and execution of the full purposes and objectives of Congress" as expressed in the FDCA. *See Crosby v. Nat'l Foreign Trade Council,* 530 U.S. 363, 372-373 (2000).

The question is ultimately one of congressional intent. When "'Congress has legislated ... in a field which the States have traditionally occupied, . . . [courts] start with the assumption that the historic police powers of the States were not to be superseded by the Federal Act unless that was the clear and manifest purpose of Congress.'" *Levine,* 555 U.S. at 565 (quoting *Medtronic, Inc. v. Lohr,* 518 U.S. 470, 485 (1996); some internal quotation marks omitted). That is particularly true as to matters of health and safety, which traditionally are areas of State concern. *Lohr,* 518 U.S. at 485. The presumption against preemption has added force in this context. *Hillsborough Cnty. v. Automated Med. Labs., Inc.,* 471 U.S. 707, 719 (1985).

Strictly as a matter of impossibility preemption, there is no basis to infer a conflict. Nothing in federal law prohibits a drug manufacturer from complying with a state-law judgment obligating it to pay compensation to a patient injured by a drug found to be unreasonably dangerous on the record in the case. Indeed, federal law does not even require a manufacturer, whether brand-name or generic, to sell a non-life-saving drug that has met FDA approval. *See* 21 U.S.C. § 356c; 21 C.F.R. § 314.161. Federal law permits both brand-name and generic manufacturers independently to stop selling a drug. *See id.*

As for obstacle preemption, Petitioner has not preserved that affirmative defense for this Court's review. *See* Resp't Br. 39-40. Had it been properly preserved, however, the argument would nonetheless fail on the merits. State-law liability based on significant new evidence that a drug is unreasonably dangerous if taken for its approved uses *parallels* the federal-law duty not to market a misbranded drug. In this circumstance, state law complements federal law's purposes and objectives. The United States' discussion of conflict preemption in a hypothetical case concerning what it calls a "pure" design-defect claim contains two significant errors. First, the United States' account of post-marketing regulation fails either to acknowledge the agency's shortcomings, which hamper its ability to monitor the safety and efficacy of prescription drugs, or to credit product-liability litigation for providing a critical layer of consumer protection. The *Levine* Court made no such mistake. It recognized that the FDA lacks the resources to monitor the safety profiles of the more than 11,000 drugs on the market; and that the FDA is a largely reactive institution that depends on the press, manufacturers, *and* litigation to uncover safety hazards. *See* 555 U.S. at 578-79 & n.11.

Second, the United States errs in suggesting that an injured plaintiff must "prove that the manufacturer knew or should have known of new and scientifically significant evidence that rendered the drug 'misbranded' under federal law"; or that States must rewrite their tort laws accordingly. U.S. Br. 12, 16 & n.3. If the FDCA, by operation of the Supremacy Clause, is read to displace design-defect claims absent such evidence, then such evidence will be required only as a consequence of preemption. Because the burden of establishing the affirmative defense of preemption rests with the defendant, the defendant manufacturer should be required to prove that all of plaintiffs evidence of defect had already been considered by the FDA and had been found insufficient to render a drug misbranded. Further, the States need not rewrite their tort laws to accommodate possible preemption defenses. The Supremacy Clause displaces contrary state law, but it does not require any affirmative action by the States. The United States' contrary suggestion fails to appreciate this feature of our federalism.

## ARGUMENT

### *I. CONGRESS DID NOT INTEND TO DEPRIVE PERSONS INJURED BY UNREASONABLY DANGEROUS DRUGS OF LONG AVAILABLE COMPENSATION.*

### A. Even a State-Law Prohibition Against the Sale of a Particular Unreasonably Dangerous Drug Would not Pose an Impossibility Conflict with Federal Law When Federal Law Does not Require Drug Manufacturers to Sell Drug Products.

**1.** In order to show 'impossibility,' a defendant must prove that "compliance with both federal and state [law] is a physical impossibility," *Florida Lime & Avocado Growers, Inc. v. Paul,* 373 U.S. 132, 142-43 (1963). Such 'impossibility' can only exist when two statutes impose "directly conflicting duties"—"as they would, for example, if the federal law said, 'you must sell insurance,' while the state law said, 'you may not.'" *Barnett Bank of Marion Cnty., NA v. Nelson,* 517 U.S. 25, 31 (1996). But "physical impossibility" does not exist where state law merely authorizes an action that federal law forbids. *Michigan Canners & Freezers Ass'n, Inc. v. Agricultural Marketing & Bargaining Bd.,* 467 U.S. 461, 478 n.21 (1984) ("Because the Michigan Act is cast in permissive rather than mandatory terms—an association may, but need not, act as exclusive bargaining representative—this is not a case in which it is impossible for an individual to comply with both state and federal law.").

Petitioner cannot make that demanding showing here. It cannot show that state law *requires* anything that federal law *forbids,* or vice-versa—the only circumstances in which compliance with state and federal law is physically impossible. *See Barnett Bank,* 517 U.S. at 31; *Michigan Canners,* 467 U.S. at 478 n.21

The district court in this case concluded that New Hampshire's "strict products liability requires[]" "that manufacturers compensate consumers for the damage caused by unreasonably dangerous products, not necessarily that they remove such products from the market." 2010 WL 3092649, at *8 (D. N.H. Aug. 2, 2010) (JA 305) (citing 5 Louis R. Frumer & Melvin I. Friedman, *Products Liability* § 57.01[4], at 57-9 (2010) for the proposition that "almost all of the opinions which have addressed the issue have found that there is no common law duty to recall or retrofit" unreasonably dangerous products). The court of appeals' decision, though not explicit on this point, at least implicitly endorsed the district court's understanding that New Hampshire design-defect liability obligates a defendant to pay damages. *See* Pet. App. 10a-lla (noting that "the decision [of a manufacturer] to make the drug and market it is wholly its own").

A state-law obligation to compensate injured parties, standing alone, does not "directly" conflict with any FDCA requirement. Federal law does not forbid the payment of compensatory damages; therefore, it is not physically impossible to comply with both state and federal law. *See Barnett Bank,* 517 U.S. at 31; *Michigan Canners,* 467 U.S. at 478 n.21. This remains true even if the payment of damages once, twice, or even multiple times might induce a manufacturer to stop selling its product; "[a]n occurrence that merely motivates an optional decision does not qualify as a requirement." *Bates v. Dow Agrosciences LLC,* 544 U.S. 431, 443 (2005).

Even assuming for argument's sake that a design-defect claim were premised on the violation of an underlying duty not to sell an unreasonably dangerous drug, however, it still would not be physically impossible for a manufacturer to comply with both state law and federal law. This is because federal law expressly *permits* both brand-name and generic manufacturers to stop selling a non-life-saving drug. *See* 21 U.S.C. § 356c; 21 C.F.R. § 314.161. That decision, moreover, is one that manufacturers can make independently of the FDA, *see id.*—in other words, "unilaterally," *see Mensing,* 131 S. Ct. at 2581. And it is one manufacturers make with some frequency; "studies show[] that anywhere from one-third to one-half of generic drugs no longer have a marketed brand-name equivalent." *Id.* at 2584 (Sotomayor, J., dissenting) (citing Brief for Marc T. Law, *et al.* as Amici Curiae 18). Thus, even if this Court understood state law to be saying, "You must stop selling your drug," federal law does not say, "You must sell your drug." It says only: "You *may* sell your drug." Under *Michigan Canners,* this is insufficient to establish physical impossibility. *See* 467 U.S. at 478 n.21 (in case where state law was permissive and federal law mandatory, compliance with federal and state law was not physically impossible).

2. Petitioner takes a decidedly different view of state and federal law. A manufacturer can only avoid liability for design defect, Petitioner argues, by redesigning its drug. That obligation, Petitioner maintains, conflicts with federal law, which does not permit a manufacturer to do so unilaterally; and in any event, a redesign is impossible here because sulindac is a one-molecule drug. Pet'r's Br. 30-36.

The impossibility conflict Petitioner describes is premised on a misunderstanding of design-defect law. Design-defect liability does not turn on the capacity to redesign a drug. Neither distributors nor retailers have control over the design of the product, yet both have been held liable for defective design. *See Tobin v. Astra Pharm. Prods., Inc.,* 993 F.2d 528 (6th Cir. 1993) (distributor; applying Kentucky law); Restatement (Second) of Torts § 402A cmt. f (1965) ("The rule stated in this Section applies to any person engaged in the business of selling products for use or consumption. It therefore applies to any manufacturer of such a product, to any wholesale or retail dealer or distributor, . . ."). This establishes that the power to redesign a product is not an element of the cause of action. It is not impossible, then, to comply with both federal law, which does not permit a manufacturer to unilaterally alter a drug's design, and state law, which extends liability to a manufacturer of a defectively designed drug without regard to whether it may redesign its drug. Because state law does not require what federal law forbids, there is no impossibility conflict here.

3. Petitioner and the United States suggest that *Mensing* and *Levine* foreclose the argument that state-law design-defect claims do not conflict with federal law because a manufacturer is not required to make its drug. A close

reading of these cases suggests, however, that the Court did not examine this argument.

Consider first *Mensing:* The injured plaintiff in that case did not argue that the manufacturer there "could not show impossibility because federal law merely permitted them to sell generic drugs; it did not require them to do so." 131 S. Ct. at 2588 n.8 (Sotomayor, J., dissenting). Accordingly, neither the majority nor the dissent in *Mensing* considered the argument. Instead, the majority's holding rested on its understanding that federal law did not permit a unilateral labeling change, but that state law required a labeling change. *See id.* at 2573 (noting that this understanding of state law was "undisputed"). This clash of mandatory duties—*must* and *must not*—does not exist here, for the reasons just discussed.

Consider next *Levine:* The Court in that case did not have occasion to consider the stop-selling argument outlined here. In *Levine,* the Court concluded, in view of the record before it, that the brand-name manufacturer in that case had failed to establish, by clear evidence, that the FDA would not have approved a labeling change. 555 U.S. at 572-73. It therefore was not impossible for the manufacturer to comply with both federal labeling requirements and any state-law obligation to provide adequate warnings of health risks. *Id.* Given this conclusion, there was no reason for the *Levine* Court to consider any alternative argument against impossibility preemption, and none was advanced. *See id.*

* * *

Impossibility preemption is a demanding defense because "respect for the States as 'independent sovereigns in our federal system' leads us to assume that 'Congress does not cavalierly preempt state-law causes of action.'" *Levine,* 555 U.S. at 565-66, n.3 (quoting *Lohr,* 518 U.S. at 485); *see generally, Nw. Cent. Pipeline Corp. v. State Corp. Comm'n,* 489 U.S. 493, 515 (1989) ("conflict-preemption analysis must be applied sensitively in this area, so as to prevent the diminution of the role Congress reserved to the States while at the same time preserving the federal role"). Its demands should be particularly weighty here, given the long-standing co-existence of state tort liability and federal drug-safety law; and given that preemption would leave injured persons such as Respondent without a remedy. *Bruesewitz v. Wyeth LLC*, 131 S. Ct. 1068, 1080 (2011) (recognizing the Court's long-standing "doubt that Congress would quietly preempt product-liability claims without providing a federal substitute").

Petitioner cannot satisfy this stringent test in this case. As discussed, it can readily comply with both state and federal law obligations, and it may do so unilaterally, meaning, "without the Federal Government's special permission and assistance." *Mensing*, 131 S. Ct. at 2581. Petitioner's belief that it was the clear and manifest purpose of Congress to wipe out long-standing product-liability suits for defective design therefore cannot be credited.

### B. Design-Defect Claims Based on Significant New Evidence That a Drug Is Unreasonably Dangerous Complement the Purposes and Objectives of the FDCA.

Petitioner argues that design-defect liability stands as an obstacle to the accomplishment and execution of the full purposes and objectives of Congress, as expressed in the FDCA. But as Respondent demonstrates, Petitioner failed to preserve that argument for this Court's review. Resp't Br. 39-40.

Even had it been preserved, however, Petitioner's obstacle preemption argument would fail on the merits. State-law liability based on significant new evidence that a drug is unreasonably dangerous if taken for its approved uses *parallels* the federal-law duty not to market a misbranded drug. That federal duty is "triggered" (U.S. Br. 32) where there is significant new evidence that a drug is dangerous to health if taken in a manner consistent with its labeling. *See* 21 U.S.C. § 352(j). In these circumstances, state tort law complements the purposes and objectives of the FDCA.

**1.** This conclusion follows from the structure and purpose of federal law. Congress, in enacting and amending the FDCA, intended for drug manufacturers like Petitioner—not the FDA—to maintain front-line responsibility for drug safety "at all times." *See Levine*, 555 U.S. at 570-71 ("[T]hrough many amendments to the FDCA and to FDA regulations, it has remained a central premise of federal drug regulation that the manufacturer bears responsibility for the content of its label at all times."). This responsibility extends to all prescription drug manufacturers, whether brand-name or generic. *See* U.S.

Br. 5 (noting that new drug applicants for brand-name drugs and abbreviated new drug applicants for generic versions of brand-name drugs must "promptly report to FDA serious adverse events associated with use of its drug in humans and periodically submit certain new information that may affect FDA's previous conclusions about the drug's safety or effectiveness").

The structure and purpose of the FDCA and its animating regulations also demonstrate that FDA approval of a drug is not intended to "represent a singular moment of clarity about risks and benefits associated with a drug." Inst. of Med. of the Nat'l Acads., *The Future of Drug Safety, Promoting and Protecting the Health of the Public* 27 (2007); *see Levine,* 555 U.S. at 575 (rejecting the argument that, although "the FDCA requires the FDA to determine that a drug is safe and effective under the conditions set forth in its labeling, the agency must be presumed to have performed a precise balancing of risks and benefits and to have established a specific labeling standard that leaves no room for different state-law judgments"); *see id.* at 592 (Thomas, J., concurring in the judgment) (FDA approval "does not represent a finding that the drug, as labeled, can never be deemed unsafe by later federal action, or as in this case, the application of state law.") Risks and benefits emerge over time as a drug is introduced into the population; accordingly, "[a]ll consumers of prescription drugs serve as guinea pigs for the pharmaceutical industry." Richard A. Merrill, *Compensation for Prescription Drug Injuries,* 59 Va. L. Rev. 1, 20 (1973). It is only after a drug is widely sold that "risks that are relatively rare, that manifest themselves only after an extended period of time, or that affect vulnerable subpopulations, begin to emerge." David A. Kessler & David C. Vladeck, *A Critical Examination of the FDA's Efforts To Preempt Failure-To-Warn Claims,* 96 Geo. L.J. 461, 466 (2008).

The FDA monitors these risks, but not by itself. "[S]tate law offers an additional, and important, layer of consumer protection that complements FDA regulation." *Levine*, 555 U.S. at 579. This added layer of consumer protection is essential:

> The FDA has limited resources to monitor the 11,000 drugs on the market, and manufacturers have superior access to information about their drugs, especially in the postmarketing phase as new risks emerge.

> State tort suits uncover unknown drug hazards and provide incentives for drug manufacturers to disclose safety risks promptly. They also serve a distinct compensatory function that may motivate injured persons to come forward with information.

*Id.* at 578-79.

**2.** The United States considers at length whether a hypothetical suit alleging what it calls a "pure" design-defect claim would conflict with the FDCA. This discussion fails to appreciate the FDA's limitations or state tort law's consumer-protection role. And it suggests (erroneously) that conflict preemption principles here require States to rewrite their tort laws to place new burdens of proof on injured plaintiffs—even though preemption is an affirmative defense which defendant manufacturers must establish.

**a.** The United States' account of the FDA's role in monitoring the safety profiles of drugs is deficient because it fails to acknowledge the agency's serious shortcomings in post-market regulation. *See* U.S. Br. 24-28. "The agency's powers and resources in new drug review, however inadequately they are perceived by some critics, appear cosmic when contrasted with the tools available for post-market regulation." Daniel Carpenter, *Reputation and Power: Organizational Image and Pharmaceutical Regulation at the FDA* 586 (Princeton Univ. Press 2010) (hereinafter Carpenter). In *this* area, the FDA's "weaknesses are glaring and are the subject of extensive study and lament in contemporary medicine and politics." *Id.*

Three recent, independent studies of the FDA, cited by the Court in *Levine,* exposed these glaring weaknesses. FDA Science Board, *Report of the Subcommittee on Science and Technology: FDA Science and Mission at Risk* 2, 6 (2007) ("[T]he Agency suffers from serious scientific deficiencies and is not positioned to meet current or emerging regulatory responsibilities"); Inst. of Med. of the Nat'l Acads., *The Future of Drug Safety: Promoting and Protecting the Health of the Public* 193-94 (2007) ("The [FDA] lacks the resources needed to accomplish its large and complex mission. . . . There is widespread agreement that resources for postmarketing drug safety work are especially inadequate and that resource limitations have hobbled the agency's ability to improve and expand this essential component of its mission"); GAO, *Drug Safety: Improvement Needed in FDA's Postmarket Decision-making and Oversight Process* 5 (GAO-06-402, 2006) ("FDA lacks a clear and effective process for making decisions about, and providing management oversight of, postmarket safety issues"), *cited approvingly in* 555 U.S. at 578-79 n.11.

The United States ignores this aspect of *Levine*, and does not engage these studies. But they remain highly relevant. More recent reporting, moreover, only reinforces their central conclusion: The FDA is incapable of carrying out its mission. As reported by Marcia Angell, a former editor-in-chief of The New England Journal of Medicine,

> [T]here is growing evidence that the Center for Drug Evaluation and Research (CDER, pronounced "cedar"), the part of the agency that regulates prescription drugs, has become the servant of the industry it regulates. This has resulted in the sale of drugs of uncertain benefits, some with serious side effects, and in the agency's failure to respond promptly to evidence that a drug is dangerous. Marcia Angell, *FDA: This Agency Can Be Dangerous*, N.Y. Review of Books, Sept. 30, 2010, at 66 (hereinafter Angell).

Angell describes the FDA's 2005 review of the COX-2 inhibitor Bextra, which the United States now suggests also included a review of all NSAIDs (including sulindac), *see* U.S. Br. 24. She lays bare conflicts of interest and deficiencies in the review process that the United States' account ignores. For example, Angell writes that a special FDA panel, consisting of two standing advisory committees, was convened to consider whether Vioxx, Bextra, and Celebrex were safe enough to remain on the market. The panel recommended that all three drugs remain on the market "perhaps with strong warnings on the labels and a moratorium on advertising directly to consumers." Angell, at 67.

About a week later, however, *The New York Times* revealed that ten of the thirty-two members of the panel had financial ties to the makers of the drugs. If their votes had been discounted, the panel would have recommended that only Celebrex stay on the market. In a departure from its usual practice, CDER, no doubt embarrassed, rejected the advice of the full panel and allowed only Celebrex to stay on the market. If not for the revelations in *The New York Times,* the decision would probably have gone the other way. *Id.*

According to Daniel Carpenter, of Harvard University, there exists also a structural "conflict of interest" in the FDA's post-market review process: "The very office of the FDA that approves new drugs—and which therefore has the least reputation-based incentives to revisit its past approval decisions—is also the office with legal authority over post-marketing." Carpenter, at 630. FDA officials have echoed this concern. *Id.* (quoting Office of Drug Safety epidemiologist David Graham as stating in testimony before Congress that "the new drug reviewing division that approved the drug in the first place and that regards it as its own child, typically proves to be the single greatest obstacle to effectively dealing with serious drug safety issues").

**b.** The United States also fails to credit product-liability litigation for providing a critical layer of consumer protection.

As already noted, state tort law complements federal law in two important ways: It serves a remedial function, and it plays a critical role in uncovering unknown drug hazards and providing incentives for drug manufacturers to disclose safety risks promptly. *Levine,* 555 U.S. at 578-79.

Some examples: There have been substantial delays between the time drug manufacturers had "reasonable evidence of an association of a serious hazard" with certain drugs, 21 C.F.R. §§ 201.57(c)(6)(i), 201.80(e), and when they either provided that information to the FDA, warned physicians and patients of emerging risks; or voluntarily withdrew the drug from the market. This has happened with Vioxx, Celebrex, Propulsid, Rezulin, Darvon, and Bextra. State tort litigation was instrumental in uncovering these hazards, or in providing a fuller understanding of the manufacturers' conduct. Also, state tort law has provided (and may yet provide) critical compensation to the tens of thousands of persons injured by these drugs.

The importance of product-liability law is also evident outside the context of pharmaceutical drugs. For example, the history of so-called blood-shield laws, which foreclosed strict liability and implied warranty causes of action against blood collection centers, illustrates the consequences of foreclosing product-liability claims. States widely enacted such laws on the premise that blood banks were so important that their work should not be hampered by litigation. George C. Conk, *Is There A Design Defect In The Restatement (Third) Of Torts: Product Liability?*, 109 Yale L.J. 1087, 1100 (2000). Shielded from strict liability, the blood banks lacked a key "incentive to pursue research and development of pasteurization techniques to reduce the risk of contracting hepatitis (and later HIV) from the blood supply. The blood shield laws thus allowed the blood industry to continue to make blood products that were avoidably unsafe, at tremendous cost to human life." *Id.* at 1100.

* * *

Statistics from 2005 to 2008 demonstrate that 47.9 percent of persons in the United States used at least one prescription drug in the last month reported; 21.4 percent used three or more; and 10.5 percent used five or more. Centers for Disease Control and Prevention, FastStats: Therapeutic Drug Use. Given the ubiquity of prescription drugs, and the FDA's limited resources, the public would be at serious risk of harm if the consumer protection provided by the tort system were found to be preempted.

**c.** Lastly, the United States errs in suggesting that conflict preemption principles require that an injured plaintiff "prove that the manufacturer knew or should have known of new and scientifically significant evidence that rendered the drug 'misbranded' under federal law" (U.S. Br. 12), or that States must now redefine "the scope of [their] tort duties" accordingly *(see* U.S. Br. 16 n.3).

State product-liability law already incorporates risk-benefit analysis, *see* Restatement (Second) of Torts § 402A, and juries may consider evidence of FDA approval in reaching a verdict, *e.g., Tobin,* 993 F.2d at 538. If, however, the FDCA, by operation of the Supremacy Clause, were read to displace design-defect claims absent evidence that a drug was misbranded under federal law, then the role of this evidence in product-liability litigation against a drug manufacturer would arise only as a result of the manufacturer's preemption defense. *Cf. Mensing,* 131 S. Ct. at 2588 n.ll (Sotomayor,

J., dissenting). Because the burden of establishing a preemption defense rests with defendants, the defendant manufacturer should be required to prove that all of plaintiffs evidence of defect had already been considered by the FDA and had been found insufficient to render a drug misbranded. *See Levine*, 555 U.S. at 571 (requiring defendant manufacturer to show clear evidence that the FDA would not have approved a labeling change).

The United States' suggestion that States must rewrite their tort law (*see* U.S. Br. 16 n.3) misapprehends our federalism. The Supremacy Clause, though it displaces contrary state law, does not require any affirmative action by the States. *Cf. Haywood v. Drown*, 556 U.S. 729, 752 (2009) (Thomas, J., dissenting) ("This historical record makes clear that the Supremacy Clause's exclusive function is to disable state laws that are substantively inconsistent with federal law—not to require state courts to hear federal claims over which the courts lack jurisdiction."). The preemption defense is available whether or not States explicitly anticipate it. *Cf. Bates*, 544 U.S. at 454 (recognizing that it would be "surprising" for state tort law to parallel federal requirements "in *identical* language" but that where some equivalency is required, defendants seeking to rely on preemption may ask for jury instructions on relevant federal standards (emphasis in original)).

## EXAMPLE 9

**Authors** J. Michael Weston, Lederer Weston Craig, PLC; Mary Massaron Ross and Hilary A. Ballentine, Plunkett Cooney

**Case** No. 13-1339, *Spokeo, Inc. v. Robins,* in the Supreme Court of the United States

### BRIEF OF DRI—THE VOICE OF THE DEFENSE BAR AS *AMICUS CURIAE* IN SUPPORT OF PETITIONER

### STATEMENT OF INTEREST OF *AMICUS CURIAE*

Amicus curiae DRI—the Voice of the Defense Bar, is a 22,500-member international association of defense lawyers who represent individuals, corporations, insurance carriers, and local governments involved in civil litigation. DRI is committed to enhancing the skills, effectiveness, and professionalism of defense lawyers around the globe. A primary part of DRI's mission is to make the civil justice system more fair, efficient, and consistent. See http://www.dri.org/About. To that end, DRI participates as amicus curiae in cases that raise issues of importance to its membership and to the judicial system. This is such a case.

DRI's interest in this case stems from its members' extensive involvement in civil litigation. DRI's members are regularly called upon to defend their clients in lawsuits brought merely to pursue public policies rather than to seek redress for a distinct and personalized injury. Left unreviewed by this Court, the Ninth Circuit's decision in this case will have a profound effect on businesses and individuals who may be subject to suits brought under the Fair Credit Reporting Act, 15 U.S.C. § 1681, *et seq.*, and other federal and state statutes providing for statutory damages because it broadens the doctrine of standing to allow the judiciary to resolve disputes in the absence of an actual injury. The Ninth Circuit's decision, which exacerbates an already-existing circuit split, would encourage the filing of lawsuits by non-injured plaintiffs. DRI has a strong interest in assuring that the many federal and state statutes which confer a statutory cause of action do not provide a "back door" for uninjured litigants to obtain relief in federal court.

The Ninth Circuit's alteration of the standing doctrine opens the floodgates of litigation in derogation of the Framers' intent to limit the jurisdiction of the judicial branch to "cases" and "controversies." This, in turn, directly affects the fair, efficient, and consistent functioning of our civil justice system and, as such, is of vital interest to the members of DRI.

The ability of plaintiffs to circumvent Article III's standing requirement and proceed in class action and other litigation absent actual injury presents an ongoing point of concern for DRI's members. The issue of standing and its outer limits is frequently studied and discussed by DRI's membership in a variety of contexts. *See, e.g.*, Nora Coleman, et al., *Stopped Before They Start: Dismissing No-Injury Class Actions,* DRI For Def 42 (December 2010) (providing strategies for attacking standing in no-injury class actions); Brian A. Bender, et al., *A Gathering Storm: New Developments in Climate Change Litigation*, DRI For Def. 50 (January 2010) (discussing noteworthy decisions involving proprietary standing and parens patriae standing); Jeffrey A. Holmstrand, *Statutory Consumer Fraud Act Claims: Enforcing the Reliance Requirement,* DRI For Def. 43 (October 2010) (recognizing the exponentially broadened exposure a defendant faces as a result of statutory consumer fraud act claims brought on behalf of large numbers of people, many or most of whom did not sustain any actual injury). DRI therefore has a unique vantage point to help this Court understand the importance of proper interpretation of federal statutory damages statutes in light of the constitutionally mandated standing requirements, not only from a legal standpoint, but also from practical and economic standpoints as well. Based on its members' extensive practical experience, DRI is uniquely suited to explain why this Court should review and ultimately reverse the Ninth Circuit's decision in this case.

Both the bench and the bar need guidance regarding the outer limits of Article III's standing requirement. The current lack of clarity in the law of standing, as exemplified by conflicting circuit decisions, may lead federal courts to inappropriately exercise power beyond the scope authorized by Article III. DRI has a strong interest in assuring that a uniform rule is adopted which recognizes Congress's right to create statutory causes of action while safeguarding the constitutionally mandated requirement to establish standing for everyone on whose behalf a claim is presented for litigation in federal court.

Left intact by this Court, the Ninth Circuit's decision will have a profound effect on defendants who may be subject to litigation and ultimately forced to pay high-dollar judgments, even in situations where the plaintiff has suffered no harm. This creates the potential for widespread abuse of statutory damages statutes in a way not intended by the legislature. As such, this case is of vital interest to DRI.

## SUMMARY OF ARGUMENT

The United States Constitution mandates that all persons presenting a claim for litigation in federal court have an actual "Case" or "Controversy" to invoke the power of the federal courts. U.S. Constitution, Article III, Section 2, Clause 1. Article III forms the underpinnings of a constitutionally required standing doctrine that cannot be abrogated by statutory language purportedly entitling any person to sue. *Allen v. Wright,* 468 U.S. 737, 750-51 (1984). Thus, the Legislature cannot confer standing on any person in the absence of a showing that the person satisfies the constitutional test for standing. That test requires the plaintiff to allege "personal injury fairly traceable to the defendant's allegedly unlawful conduct" that is "likely to be redressed by the requested relief." *Hein v. Freedom from Religion Foundation, Inc.,* 551 U.S. 587, 598 (2007), quoting *Allen v. Wright, supra,* at 751. This test comports with the long-standing precept that federal courts are courts of limited jurisdiction. *Owen Equipment & Erection Co. v. Kroger,* 437 U.S. 365, 274 (1978).

The Ninth Circuit's decision in *Robins v. Spokeo,* 742 F.3d 409 (9th Cir. 2014), marks a radical departure from the constitutional mandate that all persons presenting a claim for litigation in federal court satisfy Article III standing. In reviewing the uninjured plaintiffs claim brought under the Fair Credit Reporting Act (FCRA), 15 U.S.C. § 1681 *et seq.,* the Ninth Circuit held that the "creation of a private cause of action to enforce a statutory provision implies that Congress intended the enforceable provision to create a statutory right," and that "the violation of a statutory right is usually a sufficient injury in fact to confer standing." 742 F.3d at 412, citing *Edwards v. First Am. Corp.*, 610 F.3d 514, 517 (9th Cir. 2010). Turning the three-part test for Article III standing into a single-factor inquiry satisfied by the availability of a statutory remedy contradicts this Court's precedents and represents a grave misunderstanding of the standing doctrine mandated by Article III's limitation on the judiciary's power to only "cases" or "controversies." As this Court observed in *Lujan v. Defenders of Wildlife*, "[Statutory] broadening [of] the categories of injury that maybe alleged in support of standing is a different matter from abandoning the requirement that the party seeking review must himself have suffered an injury." 504 U.S. 555, 578 (1992), quoting *Sierra Club v. Morton*, 405 U.S. 727, 738 (1972). By holding that a plaintiff bringing suit under the FCRA satisfies Article III's injury-in-fact requirement by virtue of the bare statutory violation—here the transmission of allegedly inaccurate personal information—the Ninth Circuit's decision enables individuals who have suffered no "actual injury" to enter federal courts through the "back door," a practice which this Court has expressly disapproved. *Allee v. Medrano*, 416 U.S. 802, 828-29 (1974) (Burger, C.J., concurring).

Now is the time for the Court to rule on this significant issue. The federal circuits that have addressed this standing issue in the context of various federal statutes providing statutory damages have reached inconsistent results. In *David v. Alphin*, 704 F.3d 327, 338 (4th Cir. 2013), the Fourth Circuit held, and DRI submits correctly so, that a theory of Article III standing based solely on the deprivation of a statutory right "is a non-starter as it conflates statutory standing with constitutional standing." Accordingly, the Fourth Circuit affirmed the district court's decision that it did not have jurisdiction over plaintiffs' ERISA claims absent "both statutory *and* constitutional standing." *(Id.). See also Lexmark Intern., Inc. v. Static Control Components, Inc.*, 134 S. Ct. 1377, 1388, n. 4 (2014) (discussing "statutory standing"). The Second and Third Circuits have similarly recognized the importance of strict adherence to the constitutional standing requirement even in the context of federal statutes providing statutory damages. See *Kendall v. Employees Retirement Plan of Avon Prods.*, 561 F.3d 112, 121 (2d Cir. 2009); *Joint Stock Soc'y v. UDV North America, Inc.*, 266 F.3d 164, 176 (3d Cir. 2001) (Alito, J.); *Fair Housing Council of Suburban*

*Philadelphia v. Main Line Times,* 141 F.3d 439, 443-44 (3d Cir. 1998). But the Ninth Circuit reached the opposite conclusion (Pet. App. la), in part by looking to the Sixth Circuit, which has allowed claims brought under the FCRA to proceed absent proof of injury. *Beaudry v. TeleCheck Services, Inc.,* 579 F.3d 702, 705-07 (6th Cir. 2009). *See also Murray v. GMAC Mortgage Corp.,* 434 F.3d 948, 952-53 (7th Cir. 2006). These conflicting decisions leave both bench and bar with no clear directive on whether Congress can create constitutional standing. This Court should therefore grant review to resolve the disagreement among the circuits and provide guidance on whether a suit brought under the Fair Credit Reporting Act or other similar statutes relieves plaintiffs from satisfying Article III's standing requirement. Indeed, given the number of federal and state statutes providing for statutory damages, the implications of the Ninth Circuit's decision will reach well beyond this case and the Fair Credit Reporting Act. Failure to address and reverse the Ninth Circuit's decision will not only provide a vehicle for individuals with no actual injury to seek and possibly obtain relief, it will also result in the increase of costly litigation against businesses and individuals that was not intended by the Framers of the United States Constitution. Additionally, the Ninth Circuit's decision to excuse plaintiffs from showing Article III injury-in-fact undermines class certification standards and thereby encourages forum shopping. DRI believes that preserving the Legislature's right to create a statutory cause of action while simultaneously requiring a plaintiff to allege actual injury will safeguard the constitutionally derived balance of powers between and among the three branches of government, by maintaining the long-standing doctrine of standing, which is an indispensable element in our separation of powers.

## ARGUMENT

### *I. THIS CASE PRESENTS THE COURT WITH AN OPPORTUNITY TO RESOLVE CONFLICTING CIRCUIT DECISIONS AND CLARIFY THAT THE ACTUAL INJURY REQUIREMENT OF ARTICLE III, APPLIED IN THE CONTEXT OF THE FAIR CREDIT REPORTING ACT AND OTHER FEDERAL STATUTES GRANTING STATUTORY CAUSES OF ACTION, REQUIRES A PLAINTIFF TO SATISFY THE CONSTITUTIONAL STANDING REQUIREMENT.*

### A. The doctrine of standing is essential to maintaining the equilibrium between the separate but overlapping branches of government embodied in our federal Constitution and must apply to all suits brought pursuant to federal statutes conferring private rights of action—like the Fair Credit Reporting Act.

The United States Constitution establishes three distinct branches of government and grants to each the responsibility for exercising one of the three major types of governmental power. U.S. Const., art. I, § 1; art. II, § 2; art. III, § 1. This separation of powers was not intended to make each branch completely autonomous or result in a "hermetic division" of the branches, but rather to create separate but overlapping branches. *Bowsher v. Synar,* 478 U.S. 714, 748-49 (1986); *Mistretta v. U.S.,* 488 U.S. 361, 381 (1989); *Youngstown Sheet & Tube Co v. Sawyer,* 343 U.S. 579, 635 (1952) (Jackson, J., concurring). One of the safeguards developed to preserve this carefully crafted balance is the doctrine of standing. The doctrine assures that the "courts exercise power 'only in the last resort, and as a necessity,' and only when adjudication is consistent with a system of separated powers and [the dispute is one] traditionally thought to be capable of resolution through the judicial process." John G. Roberts, *Article III Limits On Statutory Standing,* 42 Duke L. J. 1219, 1223-1224 (1993), quoting *Allen v. Wright,* 468 U.S. 737, 750-51 (1984). This case falls at the heart of the limits on the judiciary's exercise of legislative power and presents the Court with the opportunity to clarify the standing doctrine as it applies to the Fair Credit Reporting Act and the Legislature's right to confer standing on a litigant.

Constitutional standing, a threshold requirement to any suit in federal court, is derived from Article III's limitation of the judicial power of the United States to the resolution of "Cases" and "Controversies." U.S. Constitution, art. III, § 2; *Hein v. Freedom From Religion Foundation, Inc.*, 551 U.S. 587, 598 (2007); *Lujan v. Defenders of Wildlife,* 504 U.S. 555, 560 (1992); *Friends of the Earth, Inc. v. Laidlaw Environmental Services,* 528 U.S. 167 (2000). It has been said that Article III requires a live contest in which to test legal differences. Felix Frankfurter, *A Note on Advisory Opinions,* 37 Harv. L. R. 1002, 1006 (1924). The issue of standing depends upon whether the party has alleged such a personal stake in the outcome of the controversy as to ensure that the dispute sought to be adjudicated will be presented in an adversary context and in a form historically viewed as capable of judicial resolution. Stated otherwise, it is incumbent upon a party to demonstrate more than just a commitment to vigorous advocacy. *Lujan, supra,* at 559-560. *See also Summers v. Earth Island Institute,* 129 S.Ct. 1142, 1148-49 (2009).

Those who seek to invoke the jurisdiction of the federal courts must therefore satisfy the threshold standing requirement imposed by Article III. *City of Los Angeles v. Lyons,* 461 U.S. 95 (1983). That means a plaintiff must demonstrate "a personal stake in the outcome" in order to assure the presence of that concrete adverseness which sharpens the presentation of issues necessary for the proper resolution of constitutional questions. *(Id.* at 101). Under such an approach, abstract injury is not enough. *(Id.).* A plaintiff must show that she sustained or is immediately in danger of sustaining some direct injury as a result of the challenged official conduct and the injury or threat of injury must be both real and immediate, not conjectural or hypothetical. *(Id.* at 102). The plaintiff must also demonstrate that the injury will likely be redressed by a favorable decision. *Friends of the Earth, Inc. v. Laidlaw Environmental Services, supra,* at 180-81.

The standing doctrine is a critical element of the separation-of-powers principle and the separation of powers is a fundamental method of protecting liberty. *DaimlerChrysler Corp. v. Cuno,* 547 U.S. 332, 340-342 (2006). Under the doctrine of the separation of powers, each branch of government has powers that belong to it and cannot be transferred to another branch of government. The doctrine of standing recognizes and honors those bounds.

When a court encroaches on Article III's standing requirement by permitting a suit to proceed based on a bare statutory violation—even though the plaintiff does not have an actual injury, on the theory that the statutory violation alone confers standing, it strips Article III of its power. That is exactly what the Ninth Circuit did in this case when it held that standing is demonstrated whenever there is a "violation of a statutory right [.]" 742 F.3d at 412. This holding not only undermines respect for the law, and particularly, our federal Constitution, it also renders it difficult for DRI's members to adequately represent their clients' interests. As a result of the Ninth Circuit's decision, DRI's members are unable to predict with any accuracy the outcome of suits brought by uninjured plaintiffs under the FCRA and other similar no-harm statutes. The current circuit split further exacerbates this problem.

### B. The Court's review is needed to resolve a circuit conflict—exacerbated by the Ninth Circuit's decision in this case—and engender uniformity on the issue of whether a statutory violation, unaccompanied by any actual injury, is enough to establish Article III standing.

This Court has long sought to achieve uniform pronouncements of federal law. "Both the Constitution's framers and the Supreme Court have stressed that the articulation of nationally uniform interpretations of federal law is an important objective of the federal adjudicatory process." Evan H. Caminker, *Precedent and Prediction: The Forward-Looking Aspects of Inferior Court Decisionmaking,* 73 Tex. L. Rev. 1, 38 (November 1994). Uniformity serves several "laudable goals," including "ensuring the predictability of legal obligations," garnering respect for judicial authority, and ensuring that "similarly situated litigants are treated equally." *(Id.* at 38-39). Given the desire for uniformity among the circuits, a decision of a circuit that "conflict[s] with the decision of another United States court of appeals on the same important matter" is deemed, for purposes of review on a writ of certiorari, a compelling consideration. See Supreme Court Rule 10(a). And many appellate circuits, including the Ninth Circuit, have expressly recognized the importance of ruling consistent with sister circuits on issues of federal law, viewing deviations from past decisions a last resort to be avoided. *See, e.g., KeltonArms Condo. Owners Ass'n v. Homestead Ins. Co.*, 346 F.3d 1190, 1192 (9th Cir. 2003); *Aldens, Inc. v. Miller*, 610 F.2d 538, 541 (8th Cir. 1979); *Alternative Sys. Concepts, Inc. v. Synopsys Inc.*, 374 F.3d 23, 31 (1st Cir. 2004); *Wagner v. Pennwest Farm Credit, AC A*, 109 F.3d 909, 912 (3d Cir. 1997).

The question raised in this case—whether federal statutes like the FCRA confer automatic standing to sue absent actual injury—is an issue of "exceptional importance" this Court should address. The Ninth Circuit's decision in this case exacerbates an already-existing circuit split on this issue and leaves DRI's members unable to predict accurately for their clients the outcome of suits brought under the FCRA and other similar statutes conferring statutory rights of action. Prior to this decision, the Second Circuit refused to allow a claim under ERISA to proceed absent actual injury. *Kendall v. Employees Retirement Plan of Avon Prods.*, 561 F.3d 112, 121 (2d Cir. 2009). That same year, the Sixth Circuit reached the opposite conclusion, holding that a plaintiff had Article III standing to bring an action under the FCRA absent any actual injury. *Beaudry v. TeleCheck Services*, 579 F.3d 702, 705-07 (6th Cir. 2009). The Seventh Circuit has taken a similar stance, albeit in a more generalized way. See *Murray v. GMAC Mortgage Corp.*, 434 F.3d 948, 952-53 (7th Cir. 2006). To the contrary, the Fourth Circuit held just last year (in the context of an ERISA action) that the mere violation of a statutory right does not satisfy Article III's standing requirement. *David v. Alphin*, 704 F.3d 327, 338-39 (4th Cir. 2013).

Intra-circuit splits of authority further add to the bar's confusion. Over a decade ago, the Third Circuit held that plaintiffs must allege actual injury—not just a statutory violation of the Lanham Act, 15 U.S.C. § 1051 *et seq.*,—in order to establish Article III standing. *Joint Stock Soc'y v. UDVNorth America*, 266 F.3d 164, 176 (3d Cir. 2001). This comports with the Third Circuit's earlier pronouncement in *Fair Housing Council of Suburban Philadelphia v. Main Line Times*, 141 F.3d 439, 443-444 (3d Cir. 1998), that "[t]he fact that a housing organization is able to show that a particular advertisement violates the [Fair Housing] Act is not sufficient to satisfy the requirements of Article III; a violation of the Act does not automatically confer standing on any plaintiff, even one who holds the status of a private attorney general." However, in 2009, the Third Circuit, in the context of the Real Estate Settlement Procedures Act of 1974 (RESPA), 12 U.S.C. § 2607(d)(2), held that "[a] plaintiff need not demonstrate that he or she suffered actual monetary damages, because 'the actual or threatened injury required by Art. III may exist solely by virtue of statutes creating legal rights, the invasion of which creates standing." *Alston v. Countrywide Financial Corp.,* 585 F.3d 753, 763 (3d Cir. 2009). At least one federal circuit court is deferring decision on this issue, waiting for guidance from this Court. In a recent opinion, the Eighth Circuit expressed its reluctance to address the "difficult constitutional question whether Congress can drill through this hard floor of injury *in fact* by creating an injury *in law* (i.e., a statutory cause of action requiring no showing that the plaintiff was personally and actually harmed) [.]" *Wallace v. ConAgra Foods, Inc.,*— F.3d —, 2014 WL 1356860, at *6 (8th Cir. 2014). It noted that "[t]his constitutional question recently reached the Supreme Court without yielding an answer." *(Id.,* at *7, n. 3 (citing *First Am. Fin. v. Edwards,* 567 U.S. —,— (132 S.Ct. 2356 (2012) (per curiam)).

Finally, the Ninth Circuit in this case held that the "creation of a private cause of action to enforce a statutory provision implies that Congress intended the enforceable provision to create a statutory right," 742 F.3d at 412, and that "the violation of a statutory right is usually sufficient injury in fact to confer standing." *Id.* (citing *Edwards v. First Am. Corp.,* 610 F.3d 514, 517 (9th Cir. 2010)). Because "the statutory cause of action does not require a showing of actual harm when a plaintiff sues for willful violations[,]" *id.,* the Ninth Circuit reasoned that actual harm was unnecessary to establish injury in fact. In so ruling, the Ninth Circuit recognized that its analysis essentially turns the three-part test for Article III standing—which requires a showing of causation and redressability—into a single-factor inquiry satisfied by the availability of a statutory remedy. *Id.* at 414. In a remarkable departure from this Court's jurisprudence, the Ninth Circuit rationalized that "[w]hen the injury in fact is the violation of a statutory right that we inferred from the existence of a private cause of action, causation and redressability will usually be satisfied." *Id.*

Clearly, application of the standing requirement to federal statutes creating private causes of action, like the Fair Credit Reporting Act, has caused much confusion amongst the federal circuits. The time is ripe for this Court to step in and reaffirm that the constitutional injury-in-fact requirement cannot be manufactured by Congress through enactment of a federal statute providing statutory damages for technical violations that result in no harm to plaintiffs. The current unpredictability created by the circuit split makes it difficult for DRI's members to accurately advise their clients on whether to litigate a suit brought under one of these statutes or settle. In addition, the lack of predictability makes it difficult for defense counsel, their clients, or any insurers covering the claim to properly place a value on the case for settlement purposes or to set reserves. This Court has the opportunity to restore uniformity to the nation's courts and clarify the outer limits, if any, of the constitutional standing requirement under federal and state statutes providing statutory damages. Failure to do so will have a devastating impact on the businesses and individuals DRI's members are regularly called upon to defend.

### C. Absent review and clarification by this Court, the relaxed standing requirement adopted by the Ninth Circuit will encourage needless litigation, dramatically increase costs for businesses and individuals, and encourage forum shopping.

The FCRA is just one of a myriad of federal statutes embracing this "no harm" approach to litigation. From the Telephone Consumer Protection Act to the Real Estate Settlement Procedures Act to the Truth in Lending Act, Congress has authorized suits based on a mere statutory violation. For example, the Telephone Consumer Protection Act, 47 U.S.C. § 227(3), allows a private right of action with an alternative-damages provision. Similarly, the Real Estate Settlement Procedures Act, 12 U.S.C. § 2607, prohibits kickbacks in certain mortgage-loan transactions. The Truth in Lending Act, 15 U.S.C. § 1640, contains an alternative-damages provision that has been interpreted to allow a consumer to bring a claim and receive damages upwards of $500,000 without any showing of actual injury or damages. *See, e.g., Gambardella v. G. Fox & Co.*, 716 F.2d 104 (2d Cir. 1983); *Purtle v. Eldridge Auto Sales, Inc.*, 91 F.3d 797 (6th Cir. 1996). Accordingly, absent review by this Court, the Ninth Circuit's decision may be used as a roadmap in suits well beyond those brought under the FCRA. The decision from the Ninth Circuit to narrow the standing doctrine to permit a suit in the absence of an actual injury could be applied to as many as fifteen federal statutes permitting suits based on mere statutory violations alone. *See, e.g.*, 15 U.S.C. § 1692 (Fair Debt Collection Practices Act); 29 U.S.C. § 1854 (Migrant and Seasonal Agricultural Worker Protection Act); U.S.C. § 1693m(a)(2) (Electronic Funds Transfer Act); 12 U.S.C. § 4907 (Homeowners Protection Law); 15 U.S.C. § 1681, *et seq.* (Fair and Accurate Credit Transactions Act).

These legislatively conferred statutory suits can be brought through any of a number of means, but are typically brought in the form of a class action, as in this case. "The impact of federal statutes that allow the award of statutory damages for violations that cause no harm is exponentially multiplied by the class-action mechanism of Federal Rule of Civil Procedure 23." Michael O'Neil, *Privacy and Surveillance Legal Issues, Leading Lawyers on Navigating Changes in Security Program Requirements and Helping Clients Prevent Breaches—The Transformation of the "Right to Privacy" and its Unintended Liability Consequences*, 2014 WL 10441, *6 (Aspatore Jan. 2014).

Relaxation of the standing requirement will broaden dramatically the composition of a class litigating a violation of the FCRA or other similar "no harm" statute. This, in turn, will dramatically increase the expense of defending a class action. Even before the Ninth Circuit's decision in this case, the attendant costs of a major lawsuit could sound the death knell for new companies and those suffering under today's current economic climate. Bradley J. Bondi, *Facilitating Economic Recovery and Sustainable Growth Through Reform of the Securities Class-Action System: Exploring Arbitration as an Alternative to Litigation*, 33 Harv. J. L. & Pub. Pol'y, 607, 612 (Spring 2010). With the new lax standing requirement announced by the Ninth Circuit, defendants may be forced to make payouts to hundreds or even thousands of unharmed class members. In addition, due to the violation of some statutory standard, a non-injured plaintiff might be deemed a "prevailing party" entitled to attorney fees.

The unwarranted economic burden this imposes on defendants cannot be overstated. As one legal scholar noted, "aggregated statutory damages claims can result in absurd liability exposure in the hundreds of millions—or even billions—of dollars on behalf of a class whose actual damages are often nonexistent." Sheila B. Scheuerman, *Due Process Forgotten: The Problem of Statutory Damages and Class Actions,* 74 Mo. L. Rev. 103, 104 (Winter 2009). Stated another way, a class judgment based on a statutory damages claim can have an "annihilating effect" on a defendant. *O'Neil, supra,* at *6. Defendants, unwilling to roll the dice, are placed under intense pressure to settle, even if an adverse judgment seems "improbable." See *Thorogood v. Sears, Roebuck and Co.,* 547 F.3d 42, 745 (7th Cir. 2008); *Matter of Rhone-Poulenc Rorer, Inc.,* 51 F.3d 1293, 1298 (7th Cir. 1995). *See also* Barry F. McNiel, *et al., Mass Torts and Class Actions: Facing Increased Scrutiny,* 167 F.R.D. 483,489-90 (updated 8/5/96). The Ninth Circuit's holding in this case, if left uncorrected by this Court, will only exacerbate these problems and proliferate more of these "blackmail settlements." *Rhone, supra* at 1298, citing Henry J. Friendly, *Federal Jurisdiction: A General View* 120 (1973).

Equally troubling, DRI's members will have no way to predict whether their clients will fall victim to these ills. Certainly, the Ninth Circuit's relaxation of class certification requirements will encourage potential class members to forum-shop, a practice looked upon with disfavor by the Court. *See Piper Aircraft Co v. Reyno,* 454 U.S. 235, 254 (1981); *Deposit Guaranty Nat. Bank, Jackson, Miss. v. Roper,* 445 U.S. 326 (1980). Beyond that, because of confusion among the federal circuits, DRI's members and clients have no way of knowing what standard a particular court will apply. DRI therefore has a strong interest in assuring that this Court adopts a clear standing rule that is capable of consistent application across the country.

Careful adherence to the standing doctrine serves to guard against the ills set forth above. Litigation brought by entrepreneurial class action attorneys attempting to serve as private attorneys general in lieu of the federal government harms the civil justice system, both because it creates enormous litigation costs with no attendant benefit and because it destabilizes the carefully calibrated equilibrium between the political branches of government and the judiciary. By limiting suits to the constitutional framework of a "case" or "controversy," standing assures that corporations and individuals will not be subject to academic litigation where the complaining party has suffered no real injury. And it also guards against plaintiff attorneys, and particularly class action attorneys, receiving exorbitant fees that may put a corporation out of business for a statutory violation unaccompanied by any cognizable injury. On the other hand, by allowing Congress to create a statutory cause of action, defendants are incentivized to conform their conduct to the law. Accordingly, it is imperative that this Court review the Ninth Circuit's decision.

## EXAMPLE 10

**Authors** Mark A. Behrens, Shook, Hardy & Bacon L.L.P.; Kate Comerford Todd and Sheldon B. Gilbert, National Chamber Litigation Center

**Case** No. 13-31048, *Dupre v. CBS Corp.*, in the United States Court of Appeals for the Fifth Circuit

# *AMICI CURIAE* BRIEF OF COALITION FOR LITIGATION JUSTICE, INC. AND CHAMBER OF COMMERCE OF THE UNITED STATES OF AMERICA IN SUPPORT OF DEFENDANTS-APPELLEES CBS CORPORATION, FOSTER WHEELER, L.L.C., AND GENERAL ELECTRIC COMPANY

## QUESTION PRESENTED

Whether Defendants-Appellees may be held liable for claims arising from exposure to asbestos insulation that was manufactured, supplied, and distributed by other companies, where Defendants-Appellees delivered uninsulated equipment to the Navy, and the Navy thereafter had that equipment insulated with asbestos.

## IDENTITY AND INTEREST OF *AMICI CURIAE* AND SOURCE OF AUTHORITY TO FILE

*Amici* are organizations that represent companies that have been named as defendants in asbestos lawsuits and their insurers. Accordingly, *amici* have a substantial interest in ensuring that tort law rules applied in the asbestos litigation are fair, follow traditional tort law rules, and reflect sound public policy.

Here, Plaintiffs are asking this Court to impose liability on makers of *uninsulated* turbines and boilers in "bare metal" form for harms from exposure to asbestos-containing external thermal insulation manufactured and sold by *third parties* and attached post-sale. The MDL court confirmed, "there is no evidence that Decedent was exposed to respirable dust from asbestos-containing insulation that was manufactured or supplied by Westinghouse—or that Decedent was in proximity when Westinghouse representatives were performing any work." *Dupre v. Eagle, Inc.*, 2012 WL 5395194, *1 (E.D. Pa. Oct. 2, 2012).

The MDL court properly granted summary judgment for the Defendants. *Amici* seek to use their broad perspective to educate the Court about the legal and policy implications of Plaintiffs' radical theory and why it should be rejected.

*Amici* file this brief with an accompanying Motion for Leave to File.

* * *

## INTRODUCTION AND SUMMARY OF ARGUMENT

Now into its fourth decade, the asbestos litigation is the "longest-running mass tort." Originally and for many years, asbestos litigation typically pitted a "dusty trades" worker "against the asbestos miners, manufacturers, suppliers, and processors who supplied the asbestos or asbestos products that were used or were present at the claimant's work site or other exposure location." James S. Kakalik et al., Costs of Asbestos Litigation 3 (Rand Corp. 1983). By the late 1990s, the asbestos litigation had reached such proportions that the United States Supreme Court noted the "elephantine mass" of cases, *Ortiz v. Fibreboard Corp.*, 527 U.S. 815, 821 (1999), and referred to the litigation as a "crisis." *Amchem Prods. Inc. v. Windsor*, 521 U.S. 591, 597 (1997). Mass filings pressured many primary historical defendants into bankruptcy, including virtually all manufacturers of asbestos-containing thermal insulation.

As a result of these bankruptcies, "the net . . . spread from the asbestos makers to companies far removed from the scene of any putative wrongdoing." Editorial, *Lawyers Torch the Economy, Wall St. J.*, Apr. 6, 2001, at A14, abstract at 2001 WLNR 1993314. One plaintiffs' attorney candidly described the asbestos litigation as an "endless search for a solvent bystander." *'Medical Monitoring and Asbestos Litigation'—A Discussion with Richard Scruggs and Victor Schwartz,* Mealey's Litig. Rep.: Asbestos, Mar. 1, 2002, at 33, 37 (quoting Mr. Scruggs). Most recently, this trend was described in a significant ruling that is achieving nationwide notoriety. *See In re Garlock Sealing Tech.*, LLC, 2014 WL 104021 (W.D.N.C. Jan. 10, 2014).

In an attempt to further stretch the liability of solvent manufacturers, some plaintiffs' counsel are promoting the theory that makers of uninsulated products in "bare metal form"—such as turbines, boilers, pumps, and valves—should have warned about potential harms from exposure to asbestos-containing external thermal insulation manufactured and sold by third parties and attached post-sale, such as by the U.S. Navy. "It is easy to see what is suddenly driving this novel theory: most major manufacturers of asbestos-containing products have filed bankruptcy and the Navy enjoys sovereign immunity." Mark A. Behrens, *What's New in Asbestos Litigation?*, 28 Rev. Litig. 501, 542 (2009). "As a substitute, plaintiffs seek to impose liability on solvent manufacturers for harms caused by products they never made or sold." Victor E. Schwartz, *A Letter to the Nation's Trial Judges: Asbestos Litigation, Major Progress Made Over the Past Decade and Hurdles You Can Vault in the Next,* 36 Am. J. of Trial Advoc. 1, 24-25 (2012).

Plaintiffs' theory is so extreme that almost no plaintiff raised it until recently. Indeed, the lack of older case law on point, after several decades of litigation and many hundreds of thousands of filings, by itself, speaks volumes about the theory's exotic nature and recent vintage.

Ordinarily, manufacturers are named in asbestos cases with respect to asbestos that was contained in their own products—not to hold them liable for products made by others. This is an important point to keep clear. Whether couched in terms of strict liability or negligence, or in terms of manufacturing defect, design defect or failure to warn, it is black-letter product liability law that manufacturers are not liable for harms caused by others' products except in very limited situations not present here. *See* James A. Henderson, Jr., *Sellers of Safe Products Should Not Be Required to Rescue Users from Risks Presented by Other, More Dangerous Products,* 37 Sw. U. L. Rev. 595, 602 (2008).

Plaintiffs' lawyers claim that liability should extend to makers of uninsulated products used on ships, such as the turbines and boilers at issue here, based upon the foreseeability that those products would be used in conjunction with asbestos-containing external thermal insulation made by others. But, as every first-year law student knows, foreseeability can be a Palsgraf-Yike slippery slope. Courts must draw a line limiting tort liability in order to avoid the unending slippery slope that a foreseeability standard would inevitably create. That line is logically drawn at the point where a plaintiff is harmed by a product that was neither made nor sold by the defendant.

Furthermore, Plaintiffs' theory represents unsound public policy. If adopted, Plaintiffs' third-party duty to warn theory would worsen the nearly four decades long asbestos litigation and invite a flood of new cases. Hundreds of companies made products that arguably were used in the vicinity of some asbestos insulation, which in earlier years was ubiquitous in industry and buildings. Many of these companies may have never manufactured a product containing asbestos (e.g., manufacturers of steel pipe and pipe hangers; makers of nuts, bolts, washers, wire, and other fasteners of pipe systems; makers of any equipment attached to and using the pipe system; and paint manufacturers), but they could nonetheless be held liable under Plaintiffs' theory.

Civil defendants in other types of cases would also be adversely affected, as the broad new duty rule sought here presumably would not be limited to asbestos litigation but could require manufacturers to warn about all conceivable dangers relating to hazards in others' products that might be used in conjunction with or near their own. For example, makers of bread or jam would be required to warn of peanut allergies, as a peanut butter and jelly sandwich is a foreseeable use of their products. Door or dry wall makers could be held liable for failure to warn about the dangers of lead paint made by others and applied to their products post-sale. As this Court can appreciate, the only limit on such an expansive legal requirement would be the imagination of creative plaintiffs' lawyers.

In addition, consumer safety could be undermined by the potential for over-warning and through conflicting information that may be provided by manufacturers of different components and by makers of finished products.

For these reasons, the Court should affirm the orders granting summary judgment to Defendants-Appellees.

## ARGUMENT

### I. *IT IS FUNDAMENTAL TORT LAW THAT MANUFACTURERS OUTSIDE THE CHAIN OF DISTRIBUTION CANNOT BE HELD LIABLE FOR HARMS CAUSED BY POST-SALE, THIRD-PARTY ADDITION OF ASBESTOS TO THEIR PRODUCTS*

Product liability law generally provides that any entity *which participates in the chain of distribution* of a product *is liable* for harms caused by *a defect* in *that product,* whether negligently or nonnegligently caused. *See* Restatement (Second) of Torts § 402A (1965); Restatement Third, Torts: Products Liability § 1 (1997); La. Rev. Stat. § 9:2800.54. Here, the Defendant makers of uninsulated "bare metal" turbines and boilers used on naval ships were *not* in the chain of distribution of the asbestos-containing external thermal insulation affixed to their products post-sale. Therefore, Defendants are not liable for Plaintiff's alleged asbestos-related injury. *See* James Henderson, Jr. & Aaron Twerski, *Doctrinal Collapse in Products Liability: The Empty Shell of Failure to Warn,* 65 N.Y.U. L. Rev. 265, 284 (1990) ("The [defendant's own] product must, in some sense of the word, 'create' the risk.").

As a comment to § 402A explains:

> On whatever theory, the justification for strict liability has been said to be that the seller, by marketing his product for use and consumption, has undertaken and assumed a special responsibility toward any member of the consuming public who may be injured by it; that the public has the right to and does expect, in the case of products which it needs and for which it is forced to rely upon the seller, that reputable sellers will stand behind their goods; that public policy demands that the burden of accidental injuries caused by products intended for consumption be placed upon those who market them, and be treated as a cost of production against which liability insurance can be obtained; and that the consumer of such products is entitled to the maximum of protection at the hands of someone, and the proper persons to afford it are those who market the products.

Restatement (Second) of Torts § 402A cmt. c (emphasis added). None of the interests support imposing liability on Defendants who did not market or sell the asbestos-containing insulation that caused the Plaintiff's harm.

For these reasons, asbestos third-party duty to warn claims like the one at issue here have been almost uniformly rejected by courts. The diverse and growing body of courts that have rejected these novel claims include the Supreme Courts of California and Washington; appellate courts in Maryland, Massachusetts, New York, and Pennsylvania; trial courts in Connecticut, Delaware (applying the law of Delaware and many other states), Maine, Minnesota, and New Jersey; federal district courts in Alabama, Delaware, Florida, Illinois, and New York; and state and federal courts applying maritime law, including the manager of the federal asbestos MDL and the Sixth Circuit Court of Appeals.

The Supreme Court of California's decision in *O'Neil v. Crane Co.* is perhaps the most significant of these decisions. The case involved a mesothelioma plaintiff allegedly exposed to asbestos in the late 1960s in the course of his job supervising individuals who repaired equipment in the engine and boiler rooms of a World War II-era naval ship. The plaintiff sued two companies that sold valves and pumps to the Navy. It was undisputed that the defendants never manufactured or sold any of the asbestos-containing materials to which the plaintiff was exposed. Instead, the plaintiff's asbestos exposures came from external insulation and replacement of internal gaskets and packing made by third parties.

The Supreme Court of California applied general principles of tort law, concluding that, while "manufacturers, distributors, and retailers have a duty to ensure the safety of their products . . . we have never held that these responsibilities extend to preventing injuries caused by *other* products that might foreseeably be used in conjunction with a defendant's product." *Id.* at 991 (emphasis in original). The court reasoned that requiring manufacturers to warn about the dangerous propensities of products they did not design, make, or sell would be contrary to the purposes of strict products liability. The court added, "[i]t is also unfair to require manufacturers of nondefective products to shoulder a burden of liability when they derived no economic benefit from the sale of the products that injured the plaintiff." *Id.* at 1006. The court rejected the notion that a manufacturer has a duty to warn about the dangers of products that it knew or should have known would be used alongside its own. *Id.* The court concluded that "expansion of the duty of care as urged here would impose an obligation to compensate on those whose products caused the plaintiffs no harm. To do so would exceed the boundaries established over decades of product liability law." *Id.* at 1007.

As stated, a number of decisions rejecting Plaintiffs' theory have been decided under maritime law. In *Lindstrom v. A-C Product Liability Trust,* 424 F.3d 488 (6th Cir. 2005), the leading admiralty case, the Sixth Circuit Court of Appeals confirmed that a manufacturer is not liable for asbestos-containing components and replacement parts it did not manufacture or distribute. Lindstrom was a merchant seaman who worked in the engine rooms of various ships and developed mesothelioma as an alleged result of maintenance work on pumps and valves. Lindstrom claimed that he was exposed to asbestos while replacing gaskets on pumps manufactured by Coffin Turbo Pump, Inc. But, as Lindstrom testified, the replacement gaskets themselves were not manufactured by Coffin Turbo. The Sixth Circuit affirmed summary judgment, holding: "Coffin Turbo cannot be held responsible for the asbestos contained in another product." *Id.* at 496. Furthermore, Lindstrom alleged exposure to asbestos packing that was attached to water pumps manufactured by Ingersoll Rand Company. The asbestos packing, however, was not manufactured by Ingersoll Rand. The court, again, held that Ingersoll Rand could not be held responsible for asbestos-containing material attached to Ingersoll Rand's products post-manufacture. *Id.* at 497. Numerous other maritime decisions are in agreement:

- *Stark v. Armstrong World Indus., Inc.,* 21 Fed. Appx. 371, 381 (6th Cir. 2001) ("In essence, [plaintiff] seeks to have Foster Wheeler and CE [two boiler manufacturers] held responsible because their equipment is integrated into the rest of the machinery of the vessel, much of which uses and may release asbestos. This form of guilt by association has no support in the law of products liability.").
- *In re Asbestos Prods. Liab. Litig. (No. VI) (Sweeney v. Saberhagen Holdings, Inc.),* 2011 WL 346822, *7 (E.D. Pa. Jan. 13, 2011) ("We find that maritime law applies to this action and that Plaintiffs' evidence is

insufficient to survive summary judgment under that standard in that he cannot establish any threshold exposure to asbestos-containing parts manufactured or distributed by Crane. Rather, the evidence establishes that any asbestos-containing parts of Crane valves to which Plaintiff may have been exposed would have been replacement parts manufactured and distributed by companies other than Crane."), *report and recommendation adopted,* 2011WL 359696 (E.D. Pa. Feb. 3, 2011).

- *In re Asbestos Litig. (Wesley K. Davis),* 2011 WL 2462569, *5 (Del. Super. Ct. New Castle County June 7, 2011) ("Consistent with *Lindstrom* . . . . the Court declines to hold that Crane became liable for exposures to other manufacturers' asbestos products by supplying asbestos gaskets or packing with its new valves without providing any specifications, instructions, or recommendations regarding replacement parts or insulation.").
- *Conner v. Alfa Laval, Inc.,* 842 F. Supp. 2d 791, 801 (E.D. Pa. 2012) (Robreno, J.) ("Therefore, this Court adopts *Lindstrom* and now holds that, under maritime law, a manufacturer is not liable for harm caused by, and owes no duty to warn of the hazards inherent in, asbestos products that the manufacturer did not manufacture or distribute. This principle is consistent with the development of products-liability law based on strict liability and negligence, relevant state case law, the leading federal decisions, and important policy considerations regarding the issue.").
- *Floyd v. Air & Liquid Sys. Corp.,* 2012 WL 975615 (E.D. Pa. Feb. 8, 2012) ("This Court has recently adopted the so-called 'bare metal defense' under maritime law, holding that a manufacturer has no liability for harms caused by—and no duty to warn about hazards associated with—a product it did not manufacture or distribute."), and 2012 WL 975756 (E.D. Pa. Feb. 10, 2012).
- *Abbay v. Armstrong Int'l, Inc.,* 2012 WL 975837, *1 (E.D. Pa. Feb. 29, 2012) (Robreno, J.) ("Plaintiff has alleged exposure to asbestos-containing insulation used in conjunction with Elliott turbines. This Court has held that [under maritime law] a manufacturer cannot be liable for injuries from products that it did not manufacture or supply.").

- *In re Asbestos Litig. (Harold and Shirley Howton)*, 2012 WL 1409011, *6 (Del. Super. Ct. New Castle County Apr. 2, 2012) ("The court finds under Maritime law Defendant does not owe a duty [to] Plaintiff for asbestos-containing parts used with or added to its products after sale."), *appeal refused sub nom. Crane Co. v. Howton*, 44 A.3d 921 (Del. Super. Ct. New Castle County 2012).
- *Various Plaintiffs v. Various Defendants*, 856 F. Supp. 2d 703, 709 (E.D. Pa. 2012) ("This Court recently found that the so-called 'bare metal defense' is recognized under maritime law, holding that a manufacturer has no liability for harms caused by—and no duty to warn about hazards associated with—a product it did not manufacture or distribute.").
- *Cabasug v. Crane Co.*, 2013 WL 6212151, *13 (D. Haw. Nov. 26, 2013) ("under maritime law, a manufacturer is not liable for harm caused by, and owes no duty to warn of the hazards inherent in, asbestos-containing replacement parts that the manufacturer did not manufacture or distribute.").

## *II. COURTS OUTSIDE OF THE ASBESTOS CONTEXT HAVE REFUSED TO EXTEND LIABILITY TO MANUFACTURERS OF PRODUCTS THAT ARE USED IN CONJUNCTION WITH PRODUCTS BY THIRD PARTIES THAT CAUSE HARM*

For years, courts in non-asbestos cases have refused to impose liability on manufacturers of products that are used in conjunction with harm-causing products made by others. For example, in *Rastelli v. Goodyear Tire & Rubber Co.*, 591 N.E.2d 222 (N.Y. 1992), New York's highest court "decline[d] to hold that one manufacturer has a duty to warn about another manufacturer's product when the first manufacturer produces a sound product which is compatible with the defective product of another manufacturer." *Id.* at 225-226. The plaintiff's decedent was killed while inflating a truck tire, manufactured by Goodyear, when a multi-piece tire rim made by a different company separated explosively. Plaintiff's decedent claimed that Goodyear had a duty to warn against its tire being used in conjunction with allegedly defective multi-piece tire rims made by others because Goodyear was *aware* that the defective rim could be used with its product. The *Rastelli* court rejected plaintiff's foreseeability-based theory and found that there could be no liability because "Goodyear had no control over the production of the subject multi-piece rim, had no role in placing that rim in the stream of commerce, and derived no benefit from its sale. Goodyear's tire did not create the alleged defect in the rim that caused the rim to explode." *Id.* at 226.

Additional cases from the Eleventh Circuit, Supreme Courts of Texas and Hawaii, a California Court of Appeal, and a Michigan appellate court held that liability does not extend to car or tire manufacturers for defects found in other manufacturers' products.

In *Brown v. Drake-Willock International, Ltd.,* 530 N.W.2d 510 (Mich. App. 1995), *appeal denied,* 562 N.W.2d 198 (Mich. 1997), the court held that dialysis machine manufacturers owed no duty to warn hospital employees of the risk of exposure to formaldehyde supplied by another company even though the dialysis machine manufacturers had recommended the use of formaldehyde to clean the machines. The court held: "The law does not impose upon manufacturers a duty to warn of the hazards of using products manufactured by someone else." *Id.* at 515.

Additional cases have held that a manufacturer or distributor of a paint sprayer were not liable for a user's burn injuries where a solvent sold by a third party and used to clean the sprayer ignited, *see Dreyer v. Exel Indus., S.A.,* 326 Fed. Appx. 353, 358 (6th Cir. 2009); a metal forming equipment manufacturer was not liable for a defective wood planking used in conjunction with its product, *see Toth v. Economy Forms Corp.,* 571 A.2d 420, 423 (Pa. Super. Ct.), *appeal denied,* 593 A.2d 422 (Pa. 1990); a crane manufacturer had no duty to warn about rigging it did not manufacture, integrate into its crane, or place in the stream of commerce, *see Walton v. Harnischfeger,* 796 S.W.2d 225, 226 (Tex. App. 1990); a hydraulic valve manufacturer was not liable for a defective log splitter used in conjunction with its product, *see Childress v. Gresen Mfg. Co.,* 888 F.2d 45, 46, 49 (6th Cir. 1989); an airplane manufacturer was not liable to passengers for circulatory problems caused by seats installed post-sale, *see In re Deep Vein Thrombosis,* 356 F. Supp. 2d 1055, 1068 (N.D. Cal. 2005); a manufacturer of a truck cab and chassis was not liable when a dump bed and hoist made by a third party were added post-sale without a back-up alarm and resulted in an injury, *see Shaw v. General Motors Corp.,* 727 P.2d 387,

390 (Colo. App. 1986) ("The burden of guarding against the injury suffered here should appropriately be placed upon the entity that designed the final product, arranged for the acquisition of all the component parts, and directed their assembly."); a water heater manufacturer had no duty to warn of dangers of misplacing a temperature control device it did not manufacture, *see Cleary v. Reliance Fuel Oil Assocs.*, 17 A.D.3d 503, 506 (N.Y. App. Div.), *appeal denied,* 836 N.E.2d 1149 (N.Y. 2005); a manufacturer of a garbage packer mounted on a truck chassis made by another company was not liable for a defect in the chassis, *see Sanders v. Ingram Equip., Inc.*, 531 So. 2d 879, 880 (Ala. 1988); and a manufacturer of electrically powered lift motors used in conjunction with scaffolding equipment had no duty to warn of risks created by scaffolding made by others, *see Mitchell v. Sky Climber, Inc.*, 487 N.E.2d 1374, 1376 (Mass. 1986).

Similarly, courts in non-asbestos cases have refused to impose liability on manufacturers for harms caused by replacement parts sold by third parties. For example, in *Baughman v. General Motors Corp.*, 780 F.2d 1131 (4th Cir. 1986), the Fourth Circuit refused to hold an automobile manufacturer liable for a mechanic's injuries when a tire mounted on a replacement wheel exploded. Plaintiff contended that even though the vehicle's manufacturer did not place the replacement wheel into the stream of commerce, the vehicle was nevertheless defective because the manufacturer failed to adequately warn of the dangers with similar wheels sold by others. The Fourth Circuit rejected this argument, stating:

> Where, as here, the defendant manufacturer did not incorporate the defective component part into its finished product and did not place the defective component into the stream of commerce, the rationale for imposing liability is no longer present. The manufacturer has not had the opportunity to test, evaluate, and inspect the component; it has derived no benefit from its sale; and it has not represented to the public that the component part is its own.

*Id.* at 1132-33 (emphasis added); *see also Cousineau v. Ford Motor Co.*, 363 N.W.2d 721, 727-28 (Mich. Ct. App. 1985) (truck manufacturer not liable for injuries caused by defective replacement wheel made by another company); *Hansen v. Honda Motor Co.,* 480 N.Y.S.2d 244, 245-46 (N.Y. App. Div. 1984) (motorcycle manufacturer not liable for defective replacement wheel manufactured by another company).

Other decisions are in agreement. *See Fricke v. Owens-Corning Fiberglas Corp.,* 618 So. 2d 473, 475 (La. App. 1993) (previous owner of mustard vat tank showed that it was not manufacturer of vinegar in vat at time of accident and thus did not owe any duty to worker to warn users of dangers regarding vinegar/acetic acid); *Fleck v. KDI Sylvan Pools,* 981 F.2d 107, 118 (3d Cir. 1992) (it would be "unreasonable" to impose liability on a manufacturer of a "safe pool" for injuries sustained as a result of a lack of depth warnings on a replacement pool liner made by another manufacturer), *cert, denied sub nom. Doughboy Recreational, Inc., Div. of Hojfinger Indus., Inc. v. Fleck,* 507 U.S. 1005 (1993); *Exxon Shipping Co. v. Pacific Res., Inc.,* 789 F. Supp. 1521, 1526 (D. Haw. 1991) (chain manufacturer not liable for defectively designed replacement chain made by another even though the replacement part was "identical, in terms of make and manufacture, to the original equipment").

## *III. IMPOSITION OF LIABILITY ON A DEFENDANT FOR AN ASBESTOS PRODUCT MADE OR SOLD BY A THIRD PARTY WOULD REPRESENT UNSOUND PUBLIC POLICY*

"[C]ourts must be mindful of the precedential, and consequential, future effects of their rulings, and limit the legal consequences of wrongs to a controllable degree." *In re New York City Asbestos Litig. (Holdampf v. A.C.&S., Inc.),* 840 N.E.2d 115, 119 (N.Y. 2005) (quoting *Hamilton v. Beretta U.S.A. Corp.,* 750 N.E.2d 1055 (N.Y. 2001)). That policy would be significantly undermined by the theories Plaintiffs are promoting here. *See* Thomas W. Tardy, III & Laura A. Frase, *Liability of Equipment Manufacturers for Products of Another: Is Relief in Sight?,* Harris Martin's Columns—Raising the Bar in Asbestos Litigation, May 2007, at 6.

In the real world of product design and usage, virtually every product is connected in some manner with many others in ways that could conceivably be anticipated if courts were willing to extend foresight far enough. Such a duty rule would lead to "legal and business chaos—every product supplier would be required to warn of the foreseeable dangers of numerous other manufacturers' products." John W. Petereit, *The Duty Problem With Liability Claims Against One Manufacturer for Failing to Warn About Another Manufacturer's Product,* Toxic Torts & Env'tl L. 7 (Defense Research Inst. Toxic Torts & Env'tl L. Comm. Winter 2005).

"For example, a syringe manufacturer would be required to warn of the danger of any and all drugs it may be used to inject, and the manufacturer of bread [or jam] would be required to warn of peanut allergies, as a peanut butter and jelly sandwich is a foreseeable use of bread." Tardy & Frase, *supra,* at 6. Packaging companies might be held liable for hazards regarding contents made by others.

We will not belabor this exercise because similar scenarios could be developed for virtually any product. If a manufacturer's duty were defined by foreseeable uses of *other* products, the chain of warnings and liability would be so endless, unpredictable, and speculative as to be worthless. No rational manufacturer could operate under such a system. Manufacturers also cannot be expected to have R&D facilities to identify potential dangers with respect to all products that may be used in conjunction with or in the vicinity of their own products.

Consumer safety also could be undermined by the potential for overwarning and through conflicting information on different components and finished products. *See* David C. Landin *et al., Lessons Learned from the Front Lines: A Trial Court Checklist for Promoting Order and Sound Public Policy in Asbestos Litigation,* 16 Brook. J.L. & Pol'y 589, 630 (2008) (urging courts to reject the duty Plaintiffs seek here); *see also* Victor E. Schwartz & Russell W. Driver, *Warnings in the Workplace: The Need for a Synthesis of Law and Communication Theory,* 52 U. Cin. L. Rev. 38, 43 (1983) ("The extension of workplace warnings liability unguided by practical considerations has the unreasonable potential to impose absolute liability. . . .").

"Further, '[i]f business [entities] believe that tort outcomes have little to do with their own behavior, then there is no reason for them to shape their behavior so as to minimize tort exposure.'" Paul Riehle *et al., Product Liability for Third Party Replacement or Connected Parts: Changing Tides From the West,* 44 U.S.F. L. Rev 33, 61-62 (2009) (quoting Stephen J. Carroll *et al., Asbestos Litigation* 129 (RAND Corp. 2005)).

## IV. IMPOSITION OF LIABILITY ON "BARE METAL" PRODUCT MAKERS FOR INSULATION PRODUCTS MADE BY OTHERS WOULD WORSEN ASBESTOS LITIGATION AND IS UNNECESSARY BECAUSE TRUSTS EXIST TO PAY FOR HARMS CAUSED BY EXPOSURE TO ASBESTOS INSULATION BY BANKRUPT COMPANIES

"For decades, the state and federal judicial systems have struggled with an avalanche of asbestos lawsuits." *In re Combustion Eng'g, Inc.,* 391 F.3d 190, 200 (3d Cir. 2005). So far, the litigation has forced approximately 100 employers into bankruptcy, and has had devastating impacts on defendant companies' employees, retirees, shareholders, and surrounding communities. *See* Joseph E. Stiglitz *et al., The Impact of Asbestos Liabilities on Workers in Bankrupt Firms,* 12 J. Bankr. L. & Prac. 51 (2003).

Plaintiffs' theory would worsen the asbestos litigation and lead to a flood of claims against solvent makers of uninsulated "bare metal" products for harms caused by exposures to asbestos-containing thermal insulation products made by others. This is especially problematic because the influx of asbestos claims shows no signs of abating. A 2012 review of asbestos-related liabilities reported to the Securities and Exchange Commission by over 150 publicly traded companies showed that "[s]ince 2007, filings have been fairly stable." Mary Elizabeth C. Stern & Lucy P. Allen, NERA Economic Consulting, *Asbestos Payments per Resolved Claim Increased 75% in the Past Year—Is This as Dramatic as it Sounds?,* 7 (Aug. 2012); *see also* Jenni Biggs *et al., A Synthesis of Asbestos Disclosures from Form 10-Ks—Updated* 1 (Towers Watson June 2013) (mesothelioma claim filings have "remained near peak levels since 2000."). "Typical projections based on epidemiology studies assume that mesothelioma claims arising from occupational exposure to asbestos will continue for the next 35 to 50 years." Biggs *et al., supra,* at 5. Industry analysts predicted last year that another 28,000 mesothelioma claims will be filed. *Id.* at 1.

Furthermore, it is important to remember that trusts have been established to pay claims involving exposures to asbestos products made by bankrupt entities. *See* Lloyd Dixon *et al., Asbestos Bankruptcy Trusts: An Overview of Trust Structure and Activity with Detailed Reports on the*

*Largest Trusts* (Rand Corp. 2010). Over sixty trusts have been established to collectively form a *$36.8 billion* privately-funded asbestos personal injury compensation system that operates parallel to, but wholly independent of, the civil tort system. U.S. Gov't Accountability Office, GAO-11-819, *Asbestos Injury Compensation: The Role and Administration of Asbestos Trusts* 3 (Sept. 2011).

In fact, one study concluded: "For the first time ever, trust recoveries may fully compensate asbestos victims." Charles E. Bates & Charles H. Mullin, *Having Your Tort and Eating it Too?*, 6:4 Mealey's Asbestos Bankr. Rep. 1 (Nov. 2006); *see generally* William P. Shelley *et al., The Need for Transparency Between the Tort System and Section 524(g) Asbestos Trusts,* 17 Norton J. Bankr. L. & Prac. 257 (2008). For example, it is estimated that mesothelioma plaintiffs in Oakland, California (Alameda County) will receive an average $1.2 million from active and emerging asbestos bankruptcy trusts, *see* Charles E. Bates *et al., The Naming Game,* 24:15 Mealey's Litig. Rep.: Asbestos 1 (Sept. 2, 2009), and could receive as much as $1.6 million. *See* Charles E. Bates *et al., The Claiming Game,* 25:1 Mealey's Litig. Rep.: Asbestos 27 (Feb. 3, 2010).

## CONCLUSION

If the Court finds it has jurisdiction over this appeal, the Court should affirm the orders granting summary judgment to Defendants-Appellees.

## EXAMPLE 11

**Authors** U.S. Solicitor General Paul D. Clement, Counsel of Record; Peter D. Keisler, Assistant Attorney General; Gregory G. Garre, Deputy Solicitor General; Daryl Joseffer, Assistant to Solicitor General; Douglas N. Letter, August E. Flentje, Attorneys, Department of Justice; Lawrence H. Norton, General Counsel, Richard B. Bader, Associate General Counsel. David Kolker, Assistant General Counsel, Steve N. Hajjar, Attorney, Federal Election Commission; Howard M. Radzely, Solicitor, Katherine E. Bissell, Associate Solicitor, Nora Carroll, Senior Attorney, Department of Labor

**Case** *Davenport v. Washington Education Association*, 551 U.S. 177 (2007)

## QUESTION PRESENTED

Under Washington law, a labor organization "may not use agency shop fees paid by an individual who is not a member of the organization to make contributions or expenditures to influence an election or to operate a political committee, unless affirmatively authorized by the individual." Wash. Rev. Code Ann. § 42.17.760 (West 2006). The question presented is whether such an affirmative-authorization or opt-in requirement violates the First Amendment rights of the labor organizations.

## INTEREST OF THE UNITED STATES

This case presents a First Amendment challenge to a state law that requires labor unions to obtain the permission of nonmembers before using compelled agency shop fees to make contributions or expenditures to influence elections. The United States has a substantial interest in the validity of such a provision. The Federal Election Commission is charged with enforcing federal election laws, including laws that generally prohibit unions from using nonmembers' agency shop fees for political activities. 2 U.S.C. 441b

(2000 & Supp. IV 2004). In addition, the Secretary of Labor is responsible for helping "to foster, promote, and develop the welfare of the wage earners of the United States." 29 U.S.C. 551.

## SUMMARY OF ARGUMENT

The First Amendment does not prevent a State from establishing an opt-in requirement for use of nonmembers' agency shop fees for political purposes. The decision below went far astray and interpreted a statute that furthers First Amendment values as violating the Amendment. That decision has far-reaching consequences and should be reversed.

**I.** The opt-in provision at issue in this case requires only that unions obtain nonmembers' consent before using their compelled agency shop fees for political purposes. That requirement—the simple proviso that a "member must say 'yes,' instead of failing to say 'no,'" 05-1657 Pet. App. 10a—not only fails to raise any constitutional concern, but actually promotes First Amendment interests by protecting the freedom of speech and association of workers who chose not to join the union and may well oppose its political activities. The First Amendment requires that those workers be given an opportunity to "opt out"; and those same values are furthered, not threatened, by requiring that they affirmatively "opt in." In addition, such an affirmative-authorization requirement protects all participants in the political process from the distorting effects that result from permitting a speaker to amplify its voice with the money of others who do not actually support its message.

**II.** Far from abridging unions' freedom of speech, Washington's opt-in requirement leaves unions free to speak on any topic of their choosing, at any time or place, and in any manner. Nor does it restrict the amount of money unions can raise or spend on speech. The requirement certainly does not abridge union members' freedom of association, because union members remain free to associate and pool their (own) funds, to determine the content of their shared message and the means of communicating it, and to organize their internal affairs as they see fit. It simply requires a union to obtain nonmembers' affirmative consent before using their coercively collected fees for political purposes.

Nor do the administrative costs of securing nonmembers' consent unconstitutionally burden unions' First Amendment rights. The costs of requesting affirmative authorization are relatively modest—a mailing or perhaps a phone call—and are likely less than the costs faced by every other organization that seeks to use other peoples' money for speech. While other organizations must solicit and collect donations without the government's assistance, Washington gives unions a significant advantage by (i) permitting them to impose agency shop fees on nonmembers and use those fees for political purposes (with nonmembers' affirmative authorization), and (ii) collecting those fees for the unions through payroll deductions. The union has no constitutional entitlement to additional advantages. And, of course, the unions face no possibility of suffering any net harm—if the costs of obtaining affirmative consent outweigh the funds generated, the unions can simply not pursue consent. But they lack any a priori entitlement to those funds and therefore can state no claim to constitutional injury from burdens on their ability to collect them.

In situations where Congress or a state legislature has given unions a statutory right to enter into collective bargaining agreements permitting unions to collect and use agency shop fees, this Court has held that unions may constitutionally use the fees for political purposes unless a dissenter objects to such use. But nothing in this Court's precedents suggests that the government may not insist that nonmembers affirmatively consent to the use of their dues for political purposes. The Washington Supreme Court fundamentally erred by treating the constitutionally required procedures for protecting dissenters' rights as a constitutional ceiling, rather than a floor, on the protections the government may afford individuals who decline to join a union.

**III.** The constitutionality of Washington's affirmative-authorization requirement is underscored by this Court's decisions upholding campaign-finance laws that impose more burdensome requirements on unions. Under federal law, unions generally may not finance federal political activities with general treasury funds derived from nonmembers' fees, or even from members' dues, regardless of whether the member or nonmember would consent to that use. Instead, unions must: establish separate segregated funds; solicit separate voluntary contributions to those funds; and observe strict limits on their solicitation of contributions from nonmembers. Because the constitutionality of those federal restrictions is well-settled, it follows a fortiori that Washington's more modest affirmative-authorization requirement is constitutional as well.

## ARGUMENT

This Court long ago established that the First Amendment prohibits unions from using for political purposes fees collected under a state-imposed union-shop or agency-shop arrangement from nonmembers who object to the union's political activities. In many States, that constitutional prohibition is given effect by permitting nonmembers to opt out of any regime in which their dues are used for political purposes. The basic question in this case is whether the Constitution prohibits a State from imposing an opt-in requirement that prevents a union from using nonmembers' fees for political purposes unless workers affirmatively authorize it. The answer is clearly no. Far from violating the First Amendment, such a requirement actually advances First Amendment values by safeguarding the interests of nonmembers in not having to pay for union political activities with which they disagree. The added protections afforded nonmembers in no way intrude on the First Amendment interests of unions. Indeed, unions have no First Amendment interest at all in using nonmembers' dues for political activities with which they disagree.

### *I. WASHINGTON'S AFFIRMATIVE-AUTHORIZATION REQUIREMENT PROMOTES THE LEGITIMATE FIRST AMENDMENT INTERESTS OF NONMEMBERS AND THE INTEGRITY OF THE ELECTION PROCESS*

**A.** Union-shop and agency-shop arrangements directly impact the First Amendment interests of workers who are compelled by state law to pay dues or fees to the union. As this Court has recognized, because "[u]nions traditionally have aligned themselves with a wide range of social, political, and ideological view points," *Lehnert v. Ferris Faculty Ass'n*, 500 U.S. 507, 516 (1991), "[a]n employee may very well have ideological objections to a wide variety of activities undertaken by the union." *Abood v. Detroit Bd. of Educ.*, 431 U.S. 209, 222 (1977). In order to further the government's interest in labor peace, the government may nonetheless authorize union-shop or agency-shop arrangements. *Railway Employees' Dep't v. Hanson*, 351 U.S. 225, 233-235 (1956). But as this Court has emphasized, "allowing the union shop at all" is "a significant impingement on First Amendment rights." *Ellis v. Brotherhood of Ry. Clerks*, 466 U.S. 435, 455-456 (1984); see *Chicago Teachers Union v. Hudson, Local No. 1*, 475 U.S. 292, 301 (1986); *Abood*, 431 U.S. at 222. As a result, "[t]here can be no doubt that it is within the police power of a State to prohibit the union * * * shop." *Hanson*, 351 U.S. at 233; accord *Lincoln Fed. Labor Union v. Northwestern Iron & Metal Co.*, 335 U.S. 525, 531 (1949).

If the government authorizes a union or agency shop, employees may be required to pay only their fair share of "the work of the union in the realm of collective bargaining," work from which all employees benefit. *Hanson*, 351 U.S. at 235. The First Amendment prohibits the government from requiring workers to support a union's political activities over their objection. *Hudson*, 475 U.S. at 301-302; *Abood*, 431 U.S. at 234. Thus, union- or agency-shop fees "must (1) be 'germane' to collective-bargaining activity; (2) be justified by the government's vital policy interest in labor peace and avoiding 'free riders'; and (3) not significantly add to the burdening of free speech that is inherent in the allowance of an agency or union shop." *Lehnert*, 500 U.S. at 519.

**B.** The federal and state governments have adopted various approaches to balancing their interest in promoting labor peace with their interest in protecting workers who would prefer not to associate with a union. The National Labor Relations Act, 29 U.S.C. 151 *et seq.*, generally authorizes private-sector employers and unions to enter into union-shop or agency-shop agreements, 29 U.S.C. 158(a)(3), but also permits States to ban such arrangements, 29 U.S.C. 164(b). See *NLRB v. General Motors Corp.*, 373

U.S. 734, 742-744 (1963). Approximately half of the States have enacted "right-to-work" laws restricting or prohibiting private-sector union or agency shops. See Employment Standards Admin., U.S. Dep't of Labor, *State Right-to-work Laws* (last modified Dec. 2005)[Internet address]; 05-1657 Pet. App. 35a-36a n.3 (collecting state laws).

Federal and state governments have also adopted a variety of approaches to union and agency shops in the context of public-sector employment. The federal government, for example, does not permit federal employers and unions to enter into union-shop or agency-shop arrangements at all. See generally 5 U.S.C. 7102 (granting each employee the right to "refrain" from "assist[ing] any labor organization"). In contrast, Washington, like several other States, generally authorizes public-sector employers and unions to enter into agency-shop (but not union-shop) agreements. *E.g.*, Wash. Rev. Code Ann. §§ 41.56.122(1), 41.59.100 (West 2006).

In the statute at issue here, Washington mitigated the impact of the agency-shop arrangement on nonmembers' freedom of association and speech by requiring unions to obtain nonmembers' affirmative authorization before using their fees for political purposes. Wash. Rev. Code Ann. § 42.17.760. That provision grants workers greater procedural protection than the constitutional floor by requiring unions to obtain nonmembers' affirmative authorization before using their compelled agency shop fees for political purposes, instead of putting the burden on nonmembers to opt out. Although not constitutionally required, the provision directly serves First Amendment values by protecting the rights of nonmembers, while ensuring that the unions' political activities reflect the views of those who fund them.

Washington thereby struck a reasonable balance between the two competing government interests. It chose to permit agency shops notwithstanding their "significant impingement on First Amendment rights" of workers, *Ellis*, 466 U.S. at 455-456, but conditioned that permission on the modest, and highly germane, requirement that unions obtain nonmembers' affirmative authorization before using their fees for political purposes, Wash. Rev. Code Ann. § 42.17.760. That requirement ensures that nonmembers' contributions to the political activities of the unions are made knowingly and voluntarily, in part by "remind[ing] those persons that they are giving money for political purposes and counteract[ing] * * * inertia." *Michigan*

*State AFL-CIO v. Miller*, 103 F.3d 1240, 1253 (6th Cir. 1997). Striking such a balance between competing government interests is a quintessentially appropriate exercise of the State's police power in this area.

C. As the Washington Supreme Court recognized, the affirmative-authorization requirement also "protect[s] the integrity of the election process from the perception that elected officials are improperly influenced by monetary contributions and the perception that individuals have an insignificant role to play." 05-1657 Pet. App. 12a. This Court has long recognized the government's authority to protect against the corruption or appearance of corruption that can accompany unions' political contributions, as well as the potential that workers' union dues or fees will be used to support political causes that they oppose. *FEC v. National Right to Work Comm.*, 459 U.S. 197, 208 (1982) (*NRWC*); see pp. 25-27, infra. Washington law directly promotes that weighty interest by ensuring that any spending of nonmember dues on political activities actually reflects the will of the nonmembers because, like the contributions of nonmembers in virtually any other context, they involve the affirmative authorization of the workers.

## *II. THE AFFIRMATIVE-AUTHORIZATION REQUIREMENT DOES NOT ABRIDGE FREEDOM OF SPEECH OR ASSOCIATION, BUT INSTEAD PROMOTES IT*

The Washington law at issue in no way impedes the First Amendment rights of unions. Indeed, unions receive preferential treatment under Washington law compared with other speakers. Washington requires only that unions obtain affirmative authorization from nonmembers before using their fees for political purposes—a practical requirement faced by everyone else who seeks to use other peoples' money for speech. Even so, unions are still favored vis-a-vis other speakers. Other groups must identify and seek out contributors, and even if they receive an affirmative pledge of support, they still face uncertain prospects of collecting. By contrast, Washington law authorizes unions to impose fees on nonmembers and requires employers to collect those fees through payroll deductions, which almost certainly increases the amount collected while reducing the union's collection costs. *See, e.g.*,

Wash. Rev. Code Ann. §§ 41.56.122(1), 41.59.100. The First Amendment does not entitle unions to even more preferential treatment.

### *III. THIS COURT'S CAMPAIGN-FINANCE DECISIONS UNDERSCORE THE CONSTITUTIONALITY OF THE AFFIRMATIVE-AUTHORIZATION REQUIREMENT*

The Washington Supreme Court's decision invalidating the State's opt-in requirement is also fundamentally out of step with this Court's decisions upholding more burdensome campaign-finance laws against First Amendment challenges. That disconnect provides an additional basis for overturning the decision below.

**A.** Under the Federal Election Campaign Act of 1971 (FECA), 2 U.S.C. 431 *et seq*., it is unlawful for a union or corporation "to make a contribution or expenditure in connection with any election" for federal office. 2 U.S.C. 441b(a). Although a union or corporation may establish "a separate segregated fund [SSF] to be utilized for political purposes," 2 U.S.C. 441b(b)(2) (Supp. IV 2004), such an SSF generally may not use "dues, fees, or other moneys required as a condition of membership in a labor organization or as a condition of employment," 2 U.S.C. 441b(b)(3)(A); see 11 C.F.R. 114.5(a)(1). Rather, the SSF operates as an opt-in requirement, barring a union or corporation from using workers' contributions for political purposes unless an employee affirmatively contributes funds to the SSF. See *ibid*.

Moreover, in addition to that opt-in requirement, it is generally unlawful for a union or its SSF to "solicit contributions * * * from any person other than its members and their families." 2 U.S.C. 441b(b)(4)(A)(ii). The only exception is that unions and their SSFs, like corporations and their SSFs, may "make 2 written solicitations for contributions during a calendar year" from employees and certain other individuals. 2 U.S.C. 441b(b)(4)(B); see 11 C.F.R. 114.6(a).

Such solicitations are carefully regulated to ensure that contributions are voluntary. Solicitations of a nonmember must be made by mail to the person's residence, and must be designed to prevent the labor organization or corporation conducting the solicitation from determining which recipients do not contribute or contribute $50 or less. 2 U.S.C. 441b(b)(4)

(B). All potential donors, including union members, must also be informed of "the political purposes of [the] fund" and their "right to re fuse to * * * contribute without any reprisal." 2 U.S.C. 441b(b)(3)(B) and (C); see 11 C.F.R. 114.6(c). The Federal Election Commission's regulations protect the anonymity of solicited nonmembers by requiring contributions to be sent to a custodian, who must keep detailed records of contributions and make various disclosures to the Commission. 11 C.F.R. 114.6(d).

To protect the voluntariness and anonymity of contributions, the Commission has also forbidden the use of payroll deductions to collect contributions from nonmembers. 11 C.F.R. 114.6(e)(1). Unions and SSFs may use employers' payroll deduction systems to facilitate members' regular contributions (11 C.F.R. 114.5(k)(1)), but even when such systems are used "there must be an affirmative authorization by the contributor in order to permit the deduction." FEC Advisory Opinion 2001-04, 1 Fed. Election Camp. Fin. Guide (CCH) ¶ 6360.

Like the Washington statute, Section 441b therefore permits a union to use a nonmember's wages for political purposes only if the nonmember has affirmatively authorized that use. Moreover, Section 441b is more restrictive than the Washington statute in several important respects. Under Washington law, a union may fund political activities with its general treasury funds, including funds derived from members' dues and nonmembers' agency shop fees (with the nonmembers' consent). Under federal law, however, a union may not do so with respect to federal elections. Instead, it must: incur the costs of establishing an SSF with a custodian who is subject to record-keeping and reporting obligations; solicit separate political contributions from members and nonmembers alike; and refrain from using payroll deductions to collect any contributions from nonmembers.

**B.** Significantly, the constitutionality of Section 441b is well-settled. This Court has upheld the constitutionality of Section 441b in decisions that indicate, a fortiori, that Washington's less burdensome affirmative-authorization requirement is constitutional. For example, in *NRWC*, in which this Court upheld Section 441b's solicitation limits, the Court explained that Section 441b "protect[s] the individuals who have paid money into a corporation or union for purposes other than the support of candidates from having that money used to support political candidates to whom they may be opposed." 459 U.S. at 208. The Court further explained that Section 441b protects the public against unions' and corporations' ability to amass "substantial aggregations of wealth" that may "be used to incur political debts from legislators" but may not reflect contributors' actual support for an organization's message. *Id.* at 207.

Although *NRWC* involved a corporation without capital stock rather than a union, this Court drew no distinction between the different types of organizations in upholding Section 441b's solicitation limits in light of the long history of congressional regulation of unions' and corporations' political contributions and expenditures. 459 U.S. at 208; see *Pipefitters Local Union No. 562 v. United States*, 407 U.S. 385, 401-414 (1972) (detailing history of regulation of union political activity and long-standing rule that unions' participation can be limited to voluntary contributions to an SSF).

This Court later drew on *NRWC* in upholding Section 441b's ban on political contributions, noting that the statute protects "individuals who have paid money into a corporation or union for [non-political] purposes" while also "permit[ing] some participation of unions and corporations in the federal election process by allowing them to establish and pay the administrative expenses" of SSFs. *FEC v. Beaumont*, 539 U.S. 146, 154, 162-163 (2003) (quoting *NRWC*, 459 U.S. at 201, 208). For those reasons, this Court upheld Section 441b's ban on political contributions, notwithstanding the "administrative burdens" required to establish and administer an SSF. *Id.* at 163; see *McConnell v. FEC*, 540 U.S. 93, 203-209 (2003) (upholding amendments that broadened Section 441b to prevent circumvention of its prohibitions); *Austin v. Michigan State Chamber of Commerce*, 494 U.S. 652, 660 (1990) (upholding state-law prohibition on corporate expenditures, in part because it "ensures that expenditures reflect actual public support for the political ideas espoused by corporations").

The Washington Supreme Court's decision in this case is irreconcilable with those cases. For example, because this Court recognized in *NRWC* that the government may limit solicitations of voluntary contributions, it follows that the government may condition the use of involuntary fees on nonmembers' consent. Similarly, because this Court recognized in *Beaumont* that the government may prohibit altogether the use of treasury funds for political activities, it follows that the government may condition the use of treasury funds derived from nonmembers' compelled fees for political activities on the nonmembers' consent.

C. Respondent errs in arguing (Br. in Opp. 17-18) that *NRWC* is distinguishable because it involved a contribution limit, as opposed to an expenditure limit. While "restrictions on political contributions have been treated as merely 'marginal' speech restrictions subject to relatively complaisant review under the First Amendment," restrictions on political expenditures are subject to strict scrutiny. *Beaumont*, 539 U.S. at 161. That distinction is irrelevant here because the Washington statute does not impose an expenditure limit within the meaning of this Court's cases.

The Washington law directly regulates neither contributions nor expenditures, but instead regulates the means by which the union solicits the subset of contributions facilitated by the State's agency-shop laws. In that sense, it is analogous to the solicitation restrictions upheld under a relatively deferential standard of review in *NRWC*. The effect of Washington's statutes, like the provisions upheld in *NRWC*, is to regulate political contributions (namely, by requiring nonmembers' affirmative authorization). Indeed, any effect the affirmative-authorization requirement might have on unions' political expenditures or contributions would result not from a State-imposed limit on unions' expenditures or contributions, but from a reduction in nonmembers' contributions to unions' political activities (or the minimal administrative costs of seeking authorization). Thus, the statute regulates at most contributions, not expenditures.

In *McConnell*, this Court analyzed as a contribution limit FECA's prohibition against political parties' spending of soft money. 540 U.S. at 138-139. Although the plaintiffs there argued that "provisions restrict[ing] not only contributions but also the spending and solicitation of funds raised outside of FECA's contribution limits" were expenditure limits subject to strict scrutiny, this Court disagreed. *Id.* at 138. The Court explained that "[t]he relevant inquiry is whether the mechanism adopted to implement the contribution limit * * * burdens speech in a way that a direct restriction on the contribution would not." *Id.* at 138-139. Because the limits on parties' spending of soft money did not "limit[] the total amount of money the parties can spend," but instead "simply limit[ed] the source and individual amount of donations," they were contribution rather than expenditure limitations. *Id.* at 139. The Washington affirmative-authorization requirement imposes direct limits on neither contributions nor expenditures, but simply regulates the terms by which a unique subset of funds—those facilitated by the state agency-shop laws—can be solicited. In essence, it says that consent to use those funds for political purposes must be solicited, and should not be presumed. Under *NRWC* and *McConnell*, therefore, the affirmative-authorization requirement is not an expenditure limit, but rather is subject to much more complaisant review.

## CONCLUSION

The judgment of the Supreme Court of Washington should be reversed and the cases remanded.

## EXAMPLE 12

**Authors** Charles F. Preuss and Alan J. Lazarus, Drinker Biddle & Reath, LLP

**Case** *Aguilar v. ExxonMobil Corp.*, in the *Lockheed Litig. Cases*, 192 P.2d 403 (2007) (review dismissed)

### BRIEF OF AMICUS CURME MATRIXX INITIATIVES, INC., IN SUPPORT OF THE POSITION OF RESPONDENTS

### INTEREST OF AMICUS CURIAE

Matrixx Initiatives, Inc. (Matrixx) is a Delaware corporation with its principal place of business in Phoenix, Arizona. Together with its wholly owned subsidiary, Zicam LLC, an Arizona Limited Liability Company, Matrixx is the seller and distributor of a line of cough, cold and allergy remedy products marketed under the Zicam® brand.

Matrixx is currently a defendant in several cases pending in California trial courts alleging personal injuries as a result of reactions to Zicam® Cold Remedy Nasal Gel, a homeopathic remedy sold over the counter. All of the cases are predicated on a theory of toxicity and causation generated by a single published poster presentation, later repeated in a published article. That theory—published as a conclusion without valid scientific support—is that intranasal application of the active ingredient in Zicam®, zinc gluconate (a substance classified by the FDA as Generally Recognized as Safe (GRAS)), causes smell loss in users of the product. The lead author of the poster and article has been disclosed as an expert in several lawsuits against Matrixx, including at least one in California.

A Scientific Advisory Board convened by Matrixx to study the conclusion, basis, and reasoning of the poster/article has determined that it presents, at best, an unproven hypothesis, resting on several unsupported assumptions. Matrixx has an interest in seeing that when it is hauled into California courtrooms to answer allegations that its product causes harm, appropriate scientific standards are applied to the scientific testimony and no unreliable and speculative opinions of causality are presented to the jury. Accordingly,

Matrixx is interested in confirming that trial courts are empowered under Evidence Code sections 801(b) and 803 to determine whether scientific evidence is founded upon data, reasoning, and methods, (i.e., foundation) that meets minimum standards of scientific reliability.

Matrixx therefore respectfully requests that this Court confirm the authority of trial courts to require that scientific evidence be grounded in reliable scientific data, reasoning and methodology. The decision and analysis of the court of appeal should be affirmed.

## INTRODUCTION/SUMMARY OF ARGUMENT

In affirming the trial court's exclusion of the testimony of plaintiffs' expert, the court of appeal addressed an issue of considerable importance in this State: What standards of scrutiny govern the admissibility of complex scientific opinion testimony, such as opinions concerning latent disease causation?

It is well-established since *People v. Kelly* (1976), 17 Cal.3d 24, that where scientific evidence is based on application of a new technique, theory or process, the proponent must establish foundational reliability by demonstrating that the technique, theory or process has achieved the status of general acceptance in the relevant scientific community. The reliability of the technique itself is considered established when it is generally accepted by scientists. But what if the expert claims to reliably apply an established technique? In these circumstances, what type of screening may the trial court exercise when faced with a credible challenge to the reliability of the methodology, data or analysis employed by a scientific expert witness? This appeal raises that question.

The court of appeal correctly recognized that the *Kelly* test was never intended to be, and is not, the sole tool to accomplish the goal of Evidence Code section 801 and general principles of evidence law—to assure that any and all scientific testimony or evidence is reliable. *People v. Leahy* (1994) 8 Cal.4th 587, 597. It cannot be, because the *Kelly* test is applied only in rare circumstances.

The trial court concluded that the causation expert for plaintiffs, Dr. Teitelbaum, lacked a reasonably reliable foundation for his opinion that occupational exposure to certain organic solvents causes certain diseases. The court of appeal concluded that the trial court had acted within the permissible discretion granted by Evidence Code section 801(b). The decision of the court of appeal is supported by Evidence Code sections 801 and 803, by the general rule that all expert testimony must be reliable, and by wise public policy.

In attacking the decisions of the lower courts, plaintiffs have staked out a rather extreme position. In their view, trial judges essentially have no discretion when it comes to the admission of expert testimony, once the expert displays his degree or recites relevant professional experience. Once qualified, all the expert must do to be permitted to offer his opinion to the trier of fact is point to an appropriate *type* of resource as the basis for the opinion. The trial judge is barred from reviewing the cited basis to see if it *could* logically support a non-speculative opinion; the court must accept the expert's word for that. AOB 1-2.

Thus, in plaintiffs' view, the trial judge has no authority to prevent qualified experts from offering opinions that *in fact* lack a reasonably reliable foundation. So long as a qualified expert has identified a basis for his opinion that categorically or structurally resembles the sort of data that experts in the field might examine on the subject, the trial court must allow the expert to tell the jury his opinion.

In contrast, defendants, virtually every court of appeal in this State, every federal court in the country, and virtually every state court in the country, believe that trial judges may or must, upon objection, make some type of threshold determination that the expert's opinion rests on a reliable foundation. While there is some variation in the particular criteria and procedures courts employ for this gatekeeping rule, all fundamentally agree that there must be *some* screening, *some* examination of the methods and reasoning of the expert, and *some* assurance of reliability before opinion testimony can be admitted. All agree that experts must be excluded if then-opinions lack an adequate foundation.

This case therefore squarely presents competing paradigms of how the courts should treat scientific opinion testimony. As such, it affords the Court the opportunity to deliver on the promise of its decision 11 years ago in *Leahy*, 8 Cal.4th 587—the promise of a coherent system for assuring that all scientific opinion testimony offered in California courtrooms meets the minimum standards of scientific reliability that the law requires. This Court should pick up where it left off in *Leahy* and explain that in cases not subject to the general acceptance threshold established in *Kelly,* trial courts are still empowered, and indeed required under Evidence Code sections 801 and 803, to make an assessment of whether the expert's opinion actually rests on a reasonable scientific foundation.

## DISCUSSION

### A. THE *KELLY* RULE

In *People v. Kelly* (1976) 17 Cal.3d 24, this Court adopted the *Frye* standard, holding that scientific evidence predicated on a novel theory, technique or process is not admissible in California courts unless the proponent demonstrates to the court that the predicate is generally accepted as reliable by the relevant scientific community. The Court held that such a showing is necessary because of the captivating effect that scientific evidence may have on a jury. The risk that a jury will get carried away by novel scientific evidence that has not been shown to be reliable presents too great a threat to rational decision making.

Thus, *Kelly* calls for strict scrutiny of novel scientific theory for essentially two reasons:

(1) The experimental or novel nature of many scientific theories, techniques or processes raises questions concerning their ability to reliably generate valid conclusions; and
(2) the trappings of science have the tendency to confer, in the minds of jurors, unwarranted persuasive power on expert scientists with impressive credentials who claim to demonstrate that science supports or compels their opinions.

Since then, the courts of appeal and this Court have taken a fairly narrow view of the type of scientific testimony to which the *Kelly* safeguards applies. *See People v. Venegas* (1998) 18 Cal.4th 47, 80 (*Kelly* rule is "intended to forestall the jury's uncritical acceptance of scientific evidence or techniques that is so foreign to everyday experience as to be unusually difficult for laypersons to evaluate."). Indeed, several courts have even taken the anomalous position that *Kelly* does not apply to "medical causation testimony," even if the causation theory is novel and the issue complex. *See, e.g., Roberti v. Andy's Termite & Pest Control, Inc.* (2003) 113 CalApp.4th 893, 903. These interpretations of *Kelly* leave a broad range of scientific expert opinion that is not regulated by *Kelly*'s special reliability safeguards. This sets the stage for the questions raised by plaintiffs' petition: Is there no inquiry into reliability of the scientific foundation in non-*Kelly* cases? Do any of the concerns posed by novel scientific theories exist when the expert is not using a technique that has not been generally accepted? Is there no mechanism under California law to prevent an expert who grossly abuses an established scientific method from poisoning the jury with unfounded and speculative opinions except vigorous cross-examination?

In non-*Kelly* cases, the concerns this Court has expressed over the significant impact unreliable scientific testimony may have on the jury do not disappear. New technique or old, modern scientific disease causation testimony is frequently complex and often impenetrable, no matter how skillful the presentation or cross-examination. The threat that a jury will be unduly awed or otherwise ill-equipped to separate the scientific wheat from chaff remains acute. Employing an established technique does not appreciably dim the scientific aura surrounding the expert's testimony, nor does it guarantee that the substantive (data and reasoning) or procedural (methodology) foundation for the opinion is scientifically sound and reliable. Experienced scientific witnesses can be quite adept at impressing a jury with their opinions, no matter how thin their support.

Indeed, it is even more true today than when *Kelly* was decided that the public is awed by science and scientists. In this post-gene mapping age, the newspapers regularly report increasingly remarkable advances in science and technology that easily escape the comprehension of the layperson. The quick march of scientific progress has become an afterthought. The danger that jurors will indulge leaps of faith, and accord undue weight to conclusions that purport to be scientifically derived has certainly not abated.

For all these reasons, the *Kelly* rule as interpreted by the courts is not by itself sufficient to protect against the intrusion of junk science into the courtroom. Some form of foundational screening is also needed for those cases where complex scientific testimony is proffered and the *Kelly* safeguards do not apply.

## B. THE COURTS' GENERAL SCREENING AUTHORITY UNDER CALIFORNIA LAW

With *Kelly* applying only in rare circumstances and scientific evidence becoming increasingly ubiquitous and complex, the courts' ability to prevent the admission of "junk science" has become crucial to those concerned with rational and reliable decision making in toxic tort and product liability lawsuits. *See Leahy,* 8 Cal.4th at 603 *(Kelly* screening prevents justice from becoming a matter of guesswork based on unreliable techniques and influenced by the vagaries of pseudoscience).

The solution has always resided in the courts' general obligation to ensure that expert testimony is reliable. That obligation stems from several sources. First, under Evidence Code section 350 and before that the common law, only relevant evidence is admissible; to be relevant, scientific testimony must be reliable. *People v. Harris* (1989) 47 Cal.3d 1047, 1094. *See also Leahy,* 8 Cal. at 598. Second, as an overarching principle of the law of evidence, all expert testimony must be reliable to be admitted into evidence. *People v. Stoll, supra,* 49 Cal.3d at 1140, 1161; *People v. Gardeley, supra,* 14 Cal.4th at 618. Third, the expert testimony provisions of the Evidence Code require the proponent to demonstrate that the opinion is grounded in reliable methods, data and reasoning.

Specifically, California Evidence Code sections 720, 801 and 803 govern the admissibility of expert testimony. Section 801 in pertinent part limits expert opinion to testimony

> (a) Related to a subject that is sufficiently beyond common experience that the opinion of an expert would assist the trier of fact; and

> (b) Based on matter . . . that is of a type that reasonably may be relied upon by an expert in forming an opinion upon the subject to which his testimony relates . . . .

Similarly, Evidence Code section 803 provides, in pertinent part, that "[t]he Court may, and upon objection shall, exclude testimony in the form of an opinion that is based in whole or in significant part on matter that is not a proper basis for such an opinion . . . ." (emphasis added). Taken together, sections 801(b) and 803 require that expert testimony have a reliable basis. California courts have consistently read these provisions to require trial courts to strictly scrutinize the foundations of expert opinion to determine its reliability, hence its relevance, and its admissibility. *See Korsak v. Atlas Hotels, Inc.* (1992) 2 Cal.App.4th 1516, 1523; *Pacific Gas & Elec. Co. v. Zuckerman* (1987) 189 Cal.App.3d 1113, 1134, 1136.

Recognizing their responsibilities, courts have not hesitated to exclude expert testimony they find to be lacking in reliable foundation. In *Zuckerman,* the court of appeal rejected the opinion of an expert as to the value of a gas storage field, finding his approach, data and reasoning fundamentally flawed. The flaws included extrapolating an inflation multiplier for net income from gross figures; extrapolating value of the stored gas field from a producing gas field; analogizing to a "comparable transaction" which was not truly comparable; and calculating the value of an underground storage reservoir by proportional reference to the value of the total surface area rather than the storage capacity. The court of appeal concluded that the absence of a reliable and adequate foundation rendered the opinions of the expert speculative and insubstantial. 189 Cal.App.3d at 1134-1136.

The court rejected the argument that such foundational flaws go to weight rather than admissibility, finding that it impermissibly seeks "to minimize judicial responsibility":

> The value of opinion evidence rests not in the conclusion reached but in the factors considered and the reasoning employed. . . . . Where an expert bases his conclusion upon assumptions which are not supported by the record, upon matters which are not reasonably relied upon by other experts, or upon factors which are speculative, remote

> or conjectural, then his conclusion has no evidentiary value[.] In those circumstances, the expert's opinion cannot rise to the dignity of substantial evidence. [189 Cal.App.3d at 1135]

*See also In re Marriage of Hewitson* (1983) 142 Cal.App.3d 874, 885-86 (excluding expert valuation testimony because the foundation—the value of shares of a publicly traded company—was unreliable as the basis for valuing rights in a closely held corporation).

Similarly, the courts have excluded engineering testimony for lack of a reliable foundation. For example, in *Hyatt v. Sierra Boat Co.* (1978) 79 Cal. App.3d 325, the trial court excluded opinion that the plaintiff was driving at excessive speed at the time of initial impact, which was based in part on evidence of its velocity at final impact. Because there was no evidence of the vehicle's deceleration between the initial and final impacts, the opinion had no reliable factual basis, and was therefore speculative and conjectural. 79 Cal.App.3d at 338-339.

The courts also have excluded causation testimony lacking reliable foundation in toxic tort and medical malpractice cases. In *Baptist v. WCAB* (1982) 137 Cal.App.3d 903, 908, the court held that disease causation testimony based on an epidemiology study which failed to support the expert's conclusion, in part because it contained "very considerable caveats" and "fundamental reservations," was "impermissibly conjectural and speculative." *See also Lockheed Litig. Cases* (2004) 115 Cal.App.4th 558, 564 (holding that an epidemiology study showing painters exposed to 130 different chemicals had an increased risk of cancer is not proper foundation for an opinion that any single chemical among the 130 is a cause of cancer; expressly interpreting section 801 to require "a reasonable basis for the particular opinion offered"); *Smith v. ACandS, Inc.* (1994) 31 Cal. App.4th 77, 93 (excluding asbestos exposure testimony where the expert's estimation of exposure levels was based on reviewing photographs of the site, an analytical method neither reasonably reliable nor generally practiced). In *Jennings v. Palomar Pomerado Health Sys., Inc.* (2003) 114 Cal. App.4th 1108, an expert's opinion that plaintiff's post-surgical infection was caused by the retractor left in plaintiff's abdominal cavity lacked an adequate foundation. The court found that the expert offered only an "ipso facto explanation," made certain critical assumptions which lacked evidentiary support, and there was no nexus between the suggested causal mechanism and the plaintiff's liability theory. 114 Cal.App.4th at 1116-1120. *See also Bushling v. Fremont Med. Center* (2004) 117 Cal.App.4th 493, 510-511 (medical malpractice experts' declarations were of no evidentiary value where they relied on assumptions lacking in evidentiary support).

If plaintiffs' vision of a limited role for the trial court is correct, then California courts like these have been acting in excess of their authority for decades. Avoiding the "abdication of responsibility" mentioned by the court in *Zuckerman,* these courts all examined the methods, data and reasoning of the proffered expert testimony and found the foundation for the expert's opinion unreliable and inadequate. Only if all these courts were wrong can plaintiffs be right and the decision below be error.

### C. THE SCREENING FRAMEWORK FOR SCIENTIFIC EVIDENCE ARISING FROM *LEAHY*

Any doubts about the courts' general responsibility to assure the reliable foundation of a scientific expert's testimony should have been laid to rest in 1994 when this Court decided *People v. Leahy, supra,* 8 Cal.4th 587. In *Leahy,* this Court reviewed in detail the then-recent decision of the U.S. Supreme Court in *Daubert v. Merrell Dow Pharms., Inc.* (1993) 509 U.S. 579. *Leahy* observed that the U.S. Supreme Court had interpreted Federal Rule of Evidence 702 to require federal trial courts to conduct rigorous reliability screening of scientific opinion testimony. "In the following portion of its opinion, the [*Daubert*] court expounded on the screening functions federal courts should perform under rule 702 to assure that 'any and all scientific testimony or evidence admitted is not only relevant, but reliable.'" *Leahy,* 8 Cal.4th at 597 (quoting *Daubert,* 509 U.S. at 590). So informed, the Court then analyzed the analogous provisions of the California Evidence Code, and concluded that "[s]ections 720 and 801, in combination, seem the functional equivalent of Federal Rules of Evidence, rule 702, *as discussed in* Daubert." 8 Cal.4th at 598 (emphasis added). By explicitly drawing this parallel, *Leahy* implicitly confirmed that section 801, like its federal counterpart, requires trial courts to assure themselves before admission "that any and all scientific testimony or evidence is . . . reliable."

8 Cal.4th at 597. *Leahy* thus supports the conclusion that once apprised of substantial questions concerning the reliability of the factual and analytical bases for an expert's opinion, trial courts must evaluate the reliability of that foundation.

By reaffirming that the *Kelly* rule remained viable for cases presenting novel scientific theories, processes or techniques, but also interpreting section 801 (along with section 720) to be the functional equivalent of the federal rule that requires the trial court to assure the reliability of the foundations for all scientific testimony, the Court suggested the structure of the approach trial courts should take in assessing the foundation of scientific testimony for reliability: (1) Where the challenged testimony is based on a novel scientific technique, the proponent must show both that the predicate technique is generally accepted and that the foundation is otherwise reliable. (2) When the challenged testimony is based on more established scientific methods, the proponent is required to show that it rests on a reliable foundation. Thus, satisfaction of the general acceptance standard is required for a novel scientific technique, but in other cases, only a general review of the reliability of the foundation for the opinion is required. The court of appeal properly concluded that the trial court had correctly applied general reliability screening principles to the foundation for Dr. Teitelbaum's opinion.

## D. *ROBERTI* MISINTERPRETED THE *LEAHY* OPINION

As shown above, both before and after *Leahy* courts of appeal have recognized and exercised the screening authority conferred by section 801. Moreover, two cases—one post-*Leahy (People v. Mitchell* (2003) 110 Cal. App.4th 772, 794) and one earlier *(People v. Johnson* (1993) 19 Cal.App.4th 778, 790)—have expressly drawn the parallel between California's Evidence Code provisions and Federal Rule of Evidence 702, both requiring a reliable foundation for scientific expert opinion. *Johnson* arrived at that conclusion independently, *Mitchell* did so by interpreting the language *of Leahy.*

In response to this long-standing consensus that reliability screening is appropriate, plaintiffs rely on one of the rare exceptions, *Roberti v. Andy's Termite & Pest Control, Inc.* (2003) 113 CalApp.4th 893. There the court of appeal described an interpretation of Evidence Code section 801 and *Leahy* at odds with the language of both. In *Roberti*, the defendant argued that

*Kelly* applied to the expert testimony that low-level exposures to a common pesticide caused plaintiff's autism, and if it did not, then "the foundational analysis applied in federal courts" should be applied. The court held that *Kelly* does not apply to "medical causation testimony." The court then read *Leahy* as a rejection of *Daubert*'s "threshold reliability analysis" and determined that threshold reliability screening is "not in keeping with California law." Thus, the court failed to recognize that *Daubert* had been rejected solely in the context of novel scientific evidence such as the horizontal gaze test at issue in *Leahy*. See 113 CalApp.4th at 905-906 (disagreeing with the interpretation of *Leahy* expressed in *People v. Mitchell*, *supra*, 110 Cal. App.4th at 783-784). In fact, as *Mitchell* correctly recognized, *Leahy* was far from a "rejection" of a threshold reliability requirement under California law—it found Rule 702 and its screening requirements to be functionally equivalent to the California rules governing admission of expert testimony.

*Roberti* may or may not turn out to be correct that something known as a "*Daubert*-style analysis" is not required under California law. As the court of appeal appeared to recognize below, it is unclear what the court meant by the quoted phrase. This Court has not yet had occasion to itemize the specific factors or process a trial court must or should utilize to fulfill its obligation under California law to assure that scientific testimony is scientifically sound. That California's expert testimony provisions are the "functional equivalent" of Federal Rule 702 does not necessarily mean that the reasoning process and adjudication method is identical to that applied in federal court. Indeed, the abuse of discretion standard suggests that courts may have considerable leeway in matching process to content, as the Supreme Court recognized in *Kumho Tire*. But *Roberti* simply ignored the plain language and the clear import of *Leahy*'s analysis, as well as the prior and contemporary consensus, when it failed to recognize that trial courts must evaluate the foundation of scientific testimony in some fashion before allowing it into evidence.

*Roberti*'s dissenting interpretation also tends to undermine this Court's salutary 29-year effort to protect juries (and consequently litigants) from the "vagaries of pseudoscience." *Leahy*, 8 Cal.4th at 603. Pseudoscience is not limited to the use of new and unproven scientific techniques; established techniques and mainstream methods can just as easily be distorted, manipulated, or exaggerated to reach the result desired by the expert's patron. To pretend otherwise undermines the goal of assuring that civil litigation is decided based on reliable evidence and not speculative conclusions—that justice not be decided on the basis of guesswork. *Leahy*, 8 Cal.4th at 803.

Ultimately, what *Roberti* teaches is the need for this Court to use this opportunity to clarify that California law authorizes trial courts to bar unreliable expert opinion testimony for lack of adequate foundation in those cases where *Kelly* is deemed not to apply. *Roberti* shows that there still are courts that view *Kelly* as the only available check to assure a minimum level of quality in the scientific testimony admitted in California courtrooms, courts that continue to cling to the outdated philosophy that all substantive flaws in the expert's foundation merely detract from the weight of the expert's testimony.

## E. PUBLIC POLICY REQUIRES THAT JUDGES BE ALLOWED TO EXCLUDE OPINIONS LACKING RELIABLE SCIENTIFIC SUPPORT

As we show below, the public policy concerns raised by plaintiffs are based on a distorted reading or misunderstanding of what screening means. Screening is merely an investigation of the reliability of the basis for the expert's opinion, nothing more.

In fact, meaningful judicial screening is sound public policy. Arguably meritorious cases and well-founded, non-speculative opinions have nothing to fear from judicial scrutiny, because they will easily pass muster or go unchallenged. Only cases and opinions that are fundamentally flawed, measurably overreaching, or invite juries to speculate are at risk. Freed from the necessity of awaiting trial to have the flaws of expert testimony exposed before the jury, defendants can seek to have unsupported cases disposed of earlier, and the cases that are found to have potential merit will be easier to compromise at an earlier stage. It is axiomatic that settlement on the eve of trial is inefficient. Earlier and more meaningful tests of the foundation of the causation proof will lead to more efficient settlements, for the parties and for the courts.

Plaintiffs' suggested laissez-faire approach to expert testimony, on the other hand, takes a toll on the business community and the public. Junk science is a real threat to reliable adjudication, as it offers juries a scientifically and factually illegitimate basis for imposing liability. It also feeds the cynical notion that experts for hire can operate largely unfettered out of California courtrooms and offer opinions to jurors they would never share with their peers—a notion fundamentally offensive to those that value science and the justice system. Moreover, lax regulation of scientific foundations means experts can offer opinions to jurors in California courtrooms that would not be permitted in federal courts and the courts of most other states.

There are also the more tangible consequences that flow from having materially looser standards in state court for the admission of scientific evidence. If junk science is largely insulated from judicial review and the chance of getting to a jury with a weak causation case is substantially greater in state court, that is naturally where plaintiffs will prefer to file. To avoid removal, they may join unnecessary defendants such as the blameless local retailer, taking advantage of our strict liability rules. Allowing permissive standards for the admission of expert testimony therefore enhances burdens on the state's judicial system. Differential standards between the state and federal trial courts within a state also heightens the risk of substantially different outcomes in the two forums.

The junk science problem is magnified in the context of mass tort or pattern litigation, and often found at its heart. Much of the Rule 702 case law leading up to the *Daubert* decision arose from the pattern litigation against Merrell Dow Pharmaceuticals arising from allegations that the morning sickness drug Bendectin caused structural birth defects. In case after case plaintiffs relied on a small group of experts willing to opine that there was a causal connection between the drug and infant deformities. They relied primarily on re-analyzed epidemiology, animal studies, in vitro tests, and case reports. Several juries were permitted to render verdicts for plaintiffs based on this evidence, inspiring hundreds of lawsuits. Virtually all of the verdicts for plaintiffs were ultimately overturned on appeal, and almost every court to review the scientific validity of the experts' foundations found them unreliable and inadequate to present a jury question on causation.

Despite the lack of reliable scientific support for the causation conclusions concerning Bendectin, the manufacturer was forced to deal with an overwhelming mass tort docket for years and forced to spend many millions of dollars in defense costs before the appellate process and the scientific community were able to expose the scientific shortcomings in the experts' causation theories. By that time the beneficial and innocent product had been withdrawn from the market because of the massive litigation risk. *See generally* Michael D. Green, Reexamining the Bendectin Litigation Story: Bendectin and Birth Defects: The Challenges of Mass Toxic Substances Litigation (1996); Richard Marcus, *Book Review,* 83 Iowa L. Rev. 231 (1997). The breast implant litigation is another example of a mass tort litigation where law led science, for years, until the real science—a cavalcade of epidemiological studies—accumulated and ultimately dispelled the persistent junk. *See generally* Marcia Angell, M.D., *Science On Trial* (1996).

Under plaintiffs' theory of judicial authority, there is no mechanism under California law to stem the tide of junk science or hasten the demise of similar product liability witch hunts.

Moreover, while large and healthy businesses can weather a litigation explosion ignited by junk science and survive, smaller businesses may face the prospect of ruin. A single overreaching theory or publication can incite a flood of lawsuits, generate intolerable settlement pressures, and ultimately threaten the viability of a small product manufacturer. The consequences for the small company could be devastating.

To illustrate: Suppose an irresponsible scientist with a hidden financial motive publishes an article suggesting that it is a scientific fact that the small company's pharmaceutical product causes some users to experience certain subjective personal injuries. The theory is actually based largely on anecdotal case reports and high-dose animal studies conducted on another chemical with some structural similarity. There are also human studies on the different chemical that were performed in the early part of the century, when the science was questionable, and the data was not rigorously analyzed. The theory of defect and causation contains several assumptions the scientist insists are reasonable and supported by his experiential observation, but they remain unproven.

To complicate the causation issue, it appears that the case reports are of even less value than usual. The condition the product is designed to treat also happens to be a common cause of the endpoint of concern, and consequently, an invariable confounder.

As soon as the poster is published, however, it receives widespread dissemination over the Internet by a competitor of the company with a slightly different product. It is then picked up and circulated by opportunistic members of the investment community who hold short positions in the company's stock. The story gets picked up in the media. Ultimately, the stock drops, lawsuits are filed, attorney-sponsored web pages pop up soliciting clients who could claim to have experienced harm after using the product, and many more suits follow. The small company is faced with mass tort litigation.

The insurance limits it thought were ample appear less so. Class actions are filed, then tag along securities class actions against the company and its executives. National and local lawyers must be retained in various different jurisdictions. All of the company's documents must be imaged and prepared for production, along with all of the company's computer databases, based on recent e-discovery orders issued on the East Coast. Plaintiffs' lawyers gravitate toward filing in jurisdictions with less rigorous admissibility standards and join the company's retailers to keep the cases in state court. This puts further pressure on the company's business relationships. The limited number of company employees find themselves swamped by litigation demands, interfering with the conduct of business. The company finds it hard to hire and retain key executives because of the litigation environment and pervasive concerns over whether the company will be able to survive long enough to allow real science to prevail and vindicate the company's product—or whether the company will collapse from the sheer weight of the litigation burden before the published hypothesis can be addressed on its scientific merit.

No epidemiological evidence is generated by plaintiffs or their expert, and therefore the case reports are not accompanied by any evidence that individuals who use the product are at increased risk. No evidence is generated that reliably shows a toxic dose of the active ingredient reaches the relevant organ and causes an adverse reaction. Yet, numerous lawsuits must be defended, and the wayward scientist is designated to testify in the various suits and paid handsomely for his opinions in all of the cases.

Several lawsuits are filed in California, some in federal court and some in state court. In federal court at least the company can be confident that it will obtain a fair hearing well before trial to determine whether the causation theory is supported by a valid scientific foundation. Perhaps if the expert is excluded in case after case the lawyers for plaintiffs will, sooner rather than later, lose their enthusiasm for the attacks on the company. At least in courts which practice threshold reliability screening. But will there be a meaningful and timely opportunity to challenge the foundation for the causation evidence in California state court cases?

For a small company faced with mass tort litigation predicated on what is arguably junk science, that may depend on the decision in this case.

The lesson from the Bendectin and breast implant litigation experiences is that a system that tolerates junk science and disables the courts from discovering and excluding it does not merely produce unjust and aberrational results on a case-by-case basis. Left unchecked, junk science can destroy beneficial products and ruin companies. A comparatively small company faced with a large litigation docket is particularly vulnerable. Even if the causation hypothesis ultimately proves to be scientifically unsupported, the process of fighting the cases may prove too much of a burden for the defendant to bear because trial courts defer questions of reliable scientific foundation to the jury. The company may succumb long before the product can be vindicated by the true science. But if trial courts are authorized to screen opinions for reliable foundation, then unnecessary trials can be avoided, the risk of speculative jury verdicts is minimized, and the scope of the litigation burdens can be significantly and timely reduced.

## F. THE PECULIAR NEED FOR RELIABILITY SCREENING IN TOXIC TORT CASES

### 1. *Why Screening Is Particularly Important for Complex Disease Causation Testimony*

Medical science research concerning the mechanisms of disease causation and the relationship between various diseases and various environmental influences is constantly evolving. Theories and suspicions of disease causation abound, but they remain hypothetical until proven through empirical testing. Many hypotheses are ultimately proven false or modified substantially when tested in the laboratory or the field. Thus, it is not uncommon that the opinions of expert scientists in the courtroom, offered to establish a causal connection between exposure (particularly low-level chronic exposures) to a certain substance and the development of a disease, *never* cross the line from the experimental to the demonstrable. This heightens the need for judicial intervention, a preliminary showing that the expert's analysis rests on reliable data, sound reasoning, and accepted scientific methods—a reliable foundation.

Like the new scientific techniques governed by *Kelly,* latent disease causation opinions threaten to overwhelm and confuse jurors. Biological processes are unseen and mysterious; generalized concerns over the impact of exposure to toxins in our industrial and increasingly environmentally conscious society are rampant. When the plaintiffs have been exposed to substances suspected of causing some deleterious effects in humans and/or some species of animals under *some* conditions of exposure, and plaintiffs have been diagnosed with a debilitating or life-threatening and poorly understood disease, jurors are naturally receptive to a suggested, temporally convenient causal explanation, no matter how speculative. The jury may be unduly impressed that the expert can point to scientific studies which, according to the expert, suggest that an exposure scenario like that claimed by the plaintiff may cause the consequences plaintiff experienced. Under these circumstances, the explanation proffered by a well-credentialed scientist has a powerful capacity to persuade, even if supported only by proof that the scientific community generally regards as flawed, inadequate, unreliable, or wrong. The need for some judicial intervention against the introduction of unreliable, experimental science in the courtroom is particularly acute in this context. *See Whiting v. Boston Edison Co.* (D. Mass. 1995) 891 F. Supp. 12, 24 (noting the potential for jurors to "blindly accept an expert's opinion that conforms with their underlying fears of toxic substances without carefully understanding or examining the basis for that opinion.").

In sum, testimony on disease causation in toxic tort litigation is an area plagued by junk science and a context where the reliability of the foundations for the experts' opinions are in most need of policing. There are compelling reasons to apply threshold reliability screening in those cases where the *Kelly* safeguards do not apply.

Indeed, *Roberti*'s rejection of any significant screening of disease causation testimony, under *Kelly* or otherwise, is ironic. The testimony in that case was expert opinion purporting to solve one of the great medical mysteries of the modern era, what causes autism. When experts in toxic tort cases claim to have an answer that has eluded and continues to elude the concentrated efforts of medical science, judicial skepticism is warranted and screening is critical. It is no accident that *Daubert, Joiner,* and many of the numerous federal and state court decisions applying them or applying *Frye* in civil litigation have been toxic tort cases and concern disease causation testimony. Disease causation opinion evidence in toxic tort cases, such as the testimony in *Roberti,* has truly been the apotheosis of the junk science problem.

### 2. *The Screening Required by California Law*

Viewed in context and through the prism of *Leahy, Kelly* and *Daubert* are symbiotic decisions which combine to offer a measure of protection against the insidious intrusion into the courtroom of illegitimate scientific opinions. In cases where the expert relies on a purportedly scientific technique, theory or process to reach his conclusion, *Kelly* requires in the first instance that the proponent satisfy the general acceptance test. In all cases where scientific evidence is challenged, Evidence Code sections 801, 803 and 350 charge the trial court with responsibility for ensuring that all scientific expert testimony—novel or otherwise—meets minimum standards of scientific reliability.

This Court has previously suggested this, in cases other than *Leahy.* In *People v. Stoll, supra,* 49 Cal.3d 1136, reversing the lower court, this Court held that an expert's diagnostic opinion that the defendant displayed no signs of sexual deviance, based on personality testing and a psychological interview, was not subject to *Kelly/Frye* scrutiny. *Id.* at 1140. However, the Court pointed out that the evidence was still required to satisfy traditional limits governing admission of expert testimony generally, including a basis consisting of professionally reasonable "matter." *Id.* Thus, the trial court's exclusion of the evidence was error, not only because *Kelly/Frye* was not applicable, but because the evidence also met "traditional standards for competent expert opinion, without need for additional screening procedures applicable to new, novel or experimental scientific evidence not previously accepted in court." *Id.* at 1161. *See also id.* at 1164-1165 (Lucas, C.J., dissenting) (noting "that expert testimony is subject to the overriding requirement of reasonable reliability" and that the *Kelly/Frye* test is merely a special application of the "reasonable reliability standard" to purported scientific evidence).

### 3. *Plaintiffs' Concerns Over Reliability Screening Are the Product of Their Misunderstanding of the Screening Process*

Plaintiffs complain that reliability screening like that performed by the trial court in this case results in the court improperly weighing the evidence, making unauthorized findings of fact, and invading the jury's sphere of authority. Moreover, they urge, because the evidentiary exclusion can be the death knell for the litigation, screening sometimes denies plaintiffs their right to a jury trial, and did so here.

Plaintiffs substitute imagination for the record. What the court of appeal did in this case is a far cry from the scenario plaintiffs describe. Moreover, the court was obviously sensitive to the limits of its role, specifically observing

> A court determining whether there is a reasonable basis for an expert opinion under Evidence Code section 801, subdivision (b), must examine the matter that the expert relied on in forming his or her opinion. This limited analysis involves reviewing the matter relied on and understanding the matter to the extent necessary to determine whether it can provide a reasonable basis ("reasonably may be relied upon" (Evid. Code, § 801, subd. (b))) for the expert's opinion. A court conducting this analysis must not weigh the probative value of the opinion, substitute its own opinion for the expert's opinion, or presume to be an expert. Rather, the analysis is limited to determining whether the matter relied on can provide a reasonable basis for the opinion or, on the other hand, reveals that the opinion is based on a leap of logic, conjecture, or artifice. (*See* Evid. Code, § 801, subd. (b); *Lockheed*

*Litigation Cases, supra,* 115 Cal.App.4th at p. 564.) [126 Cal.App.4th at 285 (opinion superseded by Grant of Review).].

Plaintiffs' concerns are based on a fundamental misunderstanding of what screening entails and what the trial court did. Screening is simply performing the same type of analysis of the foundation of the expert's opinion that a trial court applies in the summary judgment context to determine whether the record discloses a triable issue, in neither situation is the court weighing the evidence, other than determining whether it is sufficiently substantial to permit the jury to accept it. On summary judgment, the court determines whether there is sufficient evidentiary basis to support a finding in favor of the non-moving party. In resolving a foundation objection, the court determines whether "there is a reasonable basis for [the] expert opinion." Again, the issue is not whether the opinion is right, or persuasive; it is whether the opinion is actually supported by the analysis and evidence relied on by the expert, "or, on the other hand, [whether] the opinion is based on a leap of logic, conjecture, or artifice."

In sum, in screening the opinion, the court is not deciding anything other than whether a reasonable scientist applying the scientific method could reasonably reach the conclusion drawn by the expert based on the evidence cited and the reasoning process employed. This is no more the finding of facts than the analysis this Court performs when it reviews a record for substantial evidence.

Plaintiffs also urge that it is improper for judges not trained in science to pass judgment on what is and is not valid science. This argument undervalues the training, experience, and intelligence of jurists. More importantly, however, it ignores that judges trying to understand the expert's opinion and how he or she got there are *uniquely qualified to* determine whether the opinion is sufficiently supported to be helpful to the trier of fact. Expert testimony must "assist the trier of fact to understand the evidence or to determine a fact in issue." Evidence Code § 801(a). If the judge is unable to see how the expert's reasoning logically flows from reliable data to conclusion, then a jury will presumably be equally or more mystified. An expert's opinion assists the trier of fact in deciding a fact at issue only if it is accompanied by a logical and understandable explanation showing how the data leads to the expert's conclusion. Otherwise, the opinion amounts to nothing more than a statement by the expert as to how the case should be decided, which is harmful rather than helpful, because it impermissibly tends to shift the jury's responsibility to find the facts to the expert witness. *Jennings, supra,* 114 Cal.App.4th at 1120; *Summers v. A.L. Gilbert Co.* (1999) 69 CalApp.4th 1155, 1182-1183. Screening assures the jury can properly do its job, and judges are well qualified to perform that task.

Indeed, in this case, the primary flaw in the foundation of Dr. Teitelbaum's opinion was his failure to explain how the data he cited actually supported his opinion. He failed to explain how a study of complex multi-solvent exposures could demonstrate an increased risk as to any single solvent, when the presence of all of the other solvents was a potentially plausible explanation for the increased risk. He failed to explain how and why it was appropriate to extrapolate between high- and low-dose exposures and between humans and the animal species involved in the animal experiments. He failed to explain why case reports predicated solely on temporal coincidence were probative of causation, particularly in the absence of supporting epidemiology data or controls. Under the circumstances, exclusion of the evidence for these manifold shortcomings in its foundation was the proper course, and certainly a permissible exercise of the court's discretion.

## CONCLUSION

The stakes in toxic tort litigation, and thus the consequences when juries are seduced by the sway of pseudoscience in the emotionally charged, sympathy-laden atmosphere of a trial fixing responsibility for a catastrophic disease, are often dramatic. A prior trial in this coordinated litigation resulted temporarily in an award of $760 million, despite the flaws in the causation theory so severe that they later led to the exclusion of the expert's testimony.

At this point in the evolution of California law it should be clear that the trial courts are required to ensure that experts offer only reliable and non-speculative science to the jury. But *Roberti* demonstrates that the philosophy that foundational flaws in the expert's testimony "go to the weight" of the testimony lingers.

This Court in this case should ensure that the lower courts properly understand their role and responsibility in assuring that the scientific evidence proffered in California courtrooms is scientifically valid and reliable. Judicial scrutiny of foundation is critical because absent a valid scientific basis for the expert's opinion, he or she is offering not scientific evidence, but personal opinions, subjective belief, hypothesis, or speculation.

For the foregoing reasons, Matrixx respectfully urges this Court to affirm the decision of the Court of Appeal and confirm that the Court meant what it said in *Leahy*—that California law not only permits but requires trial courts to assure themselves that the scientific evidence presented to the jury is relevant and reliable.

## EXAMPLE 13

**Authors** Debra P. Fourlas and Barbara A. Darkes, McNees Wallace & Nurick LLC

**Case** *Lake Adventure Community Association v. Dingman Township Zoning Hearing Board,* 79 A.3d 708 (Pa. Commw. Ct. 2013)

### BRIEF *AMICUS CURIAE* ON BEHALF OF PENNSYLVANIA RECREATION VEHICLE AND CAMPING ASSOCIATION AND RECREATION VEHICLE INDUSTRY ASSOCIATION, IN SUPPORT OF APPELLEE, LAKE ADVENTURE COMMUNITY ASSOCIATION, INC.

### *I. INTRODUCTION*

*Amici,* the Recreation Vehicle Industry Association ("RVIA") and the Pennsylvania Recreation Vehicle and Camping Association ("PRVCA") are nonprofit industry trade organizations (nationwide and statewide, respectively) that represent member businesses involved in the manufacture and marketing of recreational vehicles ("RVs"). As trade organizations, they are familiar with all aspects of the recreational vehicle industry, including manufacturing, applicable standards and regulations, consumer demand, and safety issues. RVIA and PRVCA respectfully offer this brief *amicus curiae* for the aid of the Court in understanding the effects on the industry and the public that are implicated in this case.

### *II. COUNTER-STATEMENT OF QUESTION INVOLVED*

Is a township zoning ordinance provision invalid which denies campground access to a class of vehicles based solely on the state's requirement that those vehicles have special permits for highway travel, where the ordinance burdens industry and consumers and where there is no substantial relationship between the highway permit requirement and the goals underpinning the zoning provision? (Answered in the affirmative by the trial court)

## *III. COUNTER-STATEMENT OF FACTS*

The Lake Adventure Community is a non-residential campsite community in Dingman Township, Pike County, Pennsylvania. See *Lake Adventure Community v. Dingman Twp.*, 37 A.3d 83, 2012 Pa. Commw. Unpub. LEXIS 14, *1 (Pa. Cmwlth. 2012). The Lake Adventure Community Association ("LACA") operates the community and owns a number of the campsites. *Id.*

Lake Adventure is a recreational community. Both the Township's zoning ordinance and LACA's covenants preclude use of any sites for residences, and both the Township and LACA enforce that restriction. *See, e.g., Lake Adventure Community Ass'n v. Anderson,* 34 D. & C.4th 178 (C.P. Pike 1996) (action by both Dingman Township and LACA to enjoin lot owner's use of site as residence). There are about 1800 lots at Lake Adventure. See *Lake Adventure Community,* 2012 Pa. Commw. Unpub. LEXIS 14 at *1. However, even at the peak of vacation season, only about 60% of the properties are occupied on any given day. Reproduced Record ("R.") 168a (testimony of A. Berkey).

LACA allows placement of recreational vehicles up to 400 square feet in size in their set-up mode on the lots at Lake Adventure. One type of 400 square foot vehicle is known colloquially as a "slide-out" because it travels over the road at eight to eight and one-half feet wide, but once the vehicle is on site, one side slides out to make the vehicle twelve feet wide while in use. R. 223a-224a, 479a-480a (testimony of J. Soard). Newer vehicles in this size range developed in response to customer demand are known as "12-wides" because they are made in one piece and travel over the road at their full width. See R. 37a (testimony of R. Ferri). Once on site, 400 square foot slide-outs and 12-wides are identical in appearance and occupancy capacity. See Trial Court Opinion, No. 1896-2011-Civil (10/1/12) at 4 ("There are no distinguishable differences between 400 square feet vehicles allowed in LACA and the 400 square feet vehicles requiring a highway permit other than the size of the vehicle while it's being transported"); R. 464a (testimony of K. Arnoul) (no visible distinction between a slide-out and a 12-wide on site); 493a (testimony of J. Soard) (no difference in square footage). However, the 12-wides are faster to place or move; a 12-wide can be placed on site or made ready to leave the site in under one hour, while a slide-out requires substantial work to set up or close down, occupying up to four days. R. 494a-495a (testimony of J. Soard). *See also* R. 165a (testimony of A. Berkey); 472a (testimony of K. Arnoul). In addition, 12-wides are structurally stronger because they do not require the lengthy roof and floor hinges that are part of the construction of the slide-outs. R. 217a-220a (testimony of J. Soard). Further, 12-wides are subject to stringent manufacturing requirements that do not apply to the slide-outs. R. 218a-220a (testimony of J. Soard).

Virtually all manufacturers in the United States have now stopped making 400 square foot units with slide-outs and are making 12-wides instead. R. 220a-221a, 493a (testimony of J. Soard). One manufacturer, located not far from Lake Adventure, presently makes slide-outs only for use at Lake Adventure, apparently due to the ordinance at issue in this case. "Nobody else buys them anywhere in the country." *Id. See also* R. 475a (testimony of K. Arnoul) (only one manufacturer still makes slide-outs; they are obsolete).

Thus, the 12-wides are newer, and they are made with "greener," more energy-efficient utility fixtures. R. 87a-88a (testimony of R. Ferri). The new toilets, for example, use 1.6 gallons of water per flush compared to about 3-3.6 gallons in the older slide-outs. See R. 83a-85a (testimony of R. Ferri); 138a-139a (testimony of C. Niclaus). In one "full flow demand test" at Lake Adventure, a 2010 12-wide used only 49 gallons of water compared to 80.3 gallons for a 1998 slide-out of the same size. R. 90a-91a (testimony of R. Ferri). Industry-wide, water saved with the new fixtures is consistently at least 20%. R. 139a (testimony of C. Niclaus).

Because they travel at eight and one-half feet wide, slide-outs do not require any special highway permit from the Commonwealth. R. 496a (testimony of J. Soard). 12-wides do. *Id.* The Dingman Township zoning ordinance as currently enacted allows recreational vehicles up to 400 square feet, but only if they do not require a special highway permit. Trial Court Opinion, No. 1896-2011-Civil (10/1/12) at 2. Thus, the ordinance allows 400 square foot slide-outs at Lake Adventure but prohibits 12-wides, based solely on the latter's need for a state highway permit from PennDOT while en route to Lake Adventure. Notably, the roads accessing Lake Adventure are all state roads, not county or township roads. Trial Court Opinion, No. 1896-2011-Civil (10/1/12) at 5.

The demographics of consumers purchasing 12-wides reveal that buyers are generally aged 55 and up, have disposable income, and have grown families that do not accompany them to the campsites. R. 254a-255a, 257a (testimony of D. Burroughs). See *also* R. 485a & Exh. A-7 (testimony of J. Soard) (since 2005 average age of buyers has increased from 58.6 to 61.8). About 90% of the 12-wides manufactured nationwide are one-bedroom units. R. 253a (testimony of R. Burroughs). Although many are equipped with low-ceilinged lofts, most buyers use them for storage rather than extra sleeping space. R. 255a (testimony of R. Burroughs). Research suggests that typical occupancy of the units follows what is known as the "6-4-2" rule—"six for drinks, four for dinner, and two to sleep." *Id.*

Because they are vehicles, not houses, and are neither designed nor intended for occupancy as permanent residences, recreational vehicles depreciate like automobiles and wear out, and thus have a shorter useful life than a home would have. See R. 183a (testimony of G. Romanik). *See also* R. 257a (testimony of D. Burroughs) (replacement frequency depends on usage and needs, like replacement of a car); 475a-476a (testimony of K. Arnoul) (most slide-outs in Lake Adventure are visibly leaning and walls are coming apart). Because almost no manufacturers are continuing to make slide-outs, owners of 400 square foot slide-outs will need to replace their worn-out slide-out units with 12-wides if they want to have the same square footage. *Accord* R. 183a-184a (testimony of G. Romanik) (owners replacing large units at Lake Adventure will have to downgrade if they cannot replace their old units with 12-wides); 230a (testimony of J. Soard) (the current Dingman Township ordinance forces consumers replacing their units to buy models that have no structure standards). The Dingman Township zoning ordinance in its present form would preclude the replacement of worn-out slide-outs with 12-wides. Thus, despite ostensibly allowing RVs up to 400 square feet in size, the ordinance would result in a phase-out of 400 square foot vehicles over time as the slide-outs wear out and cannot be replaced with 12-wides. *Id.*

No other known zoning ordinance in the United States has a similar recreational vehicle placement restriction based on a highway permit requirement for transport. R. 497a (testimony of J. Soard).

## IV. SUMMARY OF ARGUMENT

Dingman Township's stated intent in its zoning ordinance provision governing recreational vehicles is to preserve the recreational character of the parks where those vehicles are placed, and thus to avoid residential use of the vehicles that could over-burden the utility infrastructure on which they depend. However, the Township's present ordinance allows placement of vehicles known as "slide-outs" while prohibiting other same-sized vehicles known as "12-wides" based solely on the state's requirement that 12-wides need a special highway permit for transport.

The ordinance is not substantially related to the Township's goal. 12-wides are newer, more efficient users of water and energy, more strongly constructed, and actually much easier to move on and off a camping site than the older slide-outs. Virtually no slide-outs are being manufactured any longer because of all the inherent advantages of 12-wides, which have the same square footage and occupancy capacity.

Further, by resting its restriction on the highway permit requirement, the ordinance defines this class of recreation vehicles in a way that is inconsistent with the definitions applied throughout Pennsylvania and the rest of the United States. Thus, the ordinance creates an impermissible and unjustified burden on commerce. The trial court correctly invalidated the restriction against 12-wides in Dingman Township, and its decision should be affirmed.

## V. ARGUMENT

### A. Applicable Law

A zoning ordinance is unconstitutional and invalid if it is unreasonable, arbitrary, or not substantially related to the police power interest it purports to serve. See *Larock v. Bd. of Supervisors,* 961 A.2d 916, 925 (Pa. Cmwlth. 2008) (citing *Hanson Aggregates Pa., Inc. v. College Twp. Council,* 911 A.2d 592, 595 (Pa. Cmwlth. 2006)). An ordinance is unreasonable and not substantially related to the police power if it is unduly restrictive or exclusionary, e.g., if it totally excludes an otherwise legitimate use, either on its face or by application. *Id. See also Main St. Dev. Group, Inc. v. Tinicum Twp.,* No. 09-03130-29-5, 2010 Pa. Dist. & Cnty. Dec. LEXIS 349, *15 (C.P. Bucks May 19, 2010) (where an ordinance has an exclusionary result or purpose, that ordinance cannot be considered substantially related to the general welfare) (citing *C&M Devs., Inc. v. Bedminster Twp. Zoning Hearing Bd.*, 573 Pa. 2, 820 A.2d 143 (Pa. 2002)).

Thus, despite a general presumption of validity, where a zoning ordinance totally prohibits a legitimate use, the burden shifts to the municipality to establish that the prohibition promotes the public health, safety, and general welfare. *Fernley v. Board of Supervisors,* 509 Pa. 413, 502 A.2d 585 (1985) (citations omitted). To pass constitutional muster, a zoning ordinance that totally excludes a legitimate use must bear a more substantial relationship to its stated public purpose than an ordinance that merely confines the use to a certain area within the municipality. *Id.*

### B. The zoning ordinance effectively eliminates 12-wides in Dingman Township.

In *Greenwood Twp. v. KEFO, Inc.*, 52 Pa. Cmwlth. 367, 416 A.2d 583 (1980), this Court examined a zoning ordinance with distance set-back restrictions that effectively precluded not only a specific proposed landfill, but also the establishment of any landfill anywhere in the township. *Id.*, 52 Pa. Cmwlth. at 371-72, 416 A.2d at 585. The township supervisors had made no independent evaluations of the specific landfill proposal or of landfills generally, nor had they consulted any experts, nor referred to any technical standards involving landfill operations, before formulating the ordinance; but they had referred to a plan of the proposed landfill site in drafting the distance restrictions, and they were aware at the time the distances were set that their application would completely eliminate the proposed site's use as a landfill. *Id.*, 52 Pa. Cmwlth. at 372, 416 A.2d at 585. This Court agreed with the trial court's conclusions that the obvious purpose of the ordinance's distance limitation was to stop the proposed landfill, and that the distance limitations were so restrictive that placement of a landfill anywhere in the township would be impossible. *Id.* The distance requirements therefore effected a *de facto* exclusion of landfill operations from the township. *Id.* (citations omitted).

Similarly, in this case, the Dingman Township ordinance effectively prohibits the use of 12-wides anywhere in the township. The Township's suggestion that 12-wides would qualify as mobile homes is in error.

The Township's zoning ordinance defines a mobile home as a "Manufactured Housing Unit," which is a "transportable, single-family dwelling *intended for permanent occupancy.*" R. 5a (zoning ordinance excerpt) (emphasis added). Moreover, the ordinance defines a "Manufactured Housing Park" as a "parcel of land under single ownership which has been planned and improved for the placement of two (2) or more mobile homes *for non-transient use.*" *Id.* (emphasis added). Thus, the 12-wides do not come within the Township's definition of manufactured housing units, and their placement in a mobile home park would be prohibited because they are designed for transient recreational use, not permanent occupancy.

Moreover, regardless of whether the Township's zoning ordinance would allow such a use, it would be precluded by other applicable laws and regulations. For example, HUD regulation 3282.8 exempts vehicles of 400 square feet and under from construction standards that otherwise apply to manufactured housing. *See* 24 C.F.R. § 3282.8(g); R. 216a (testimony of J. Soard). Thus, HUD regulations would not allow placement and use of a 12-wide in a mobile home park because a 12-wide would not meet construction standards required for manufactured housing.

Under Pennsylvania's Municipal Planning Code, "a mobile home is entitled to be treated under zoning like a conventional residence." *Hitchcock v. Zoning Bd. of Adjustment,* 140 Pa Cmwlth. 607, 612, 594 A.2d 820, 822 (1991) (citations omitted). "Placing a mobile home constitutes the erection of a dwelling." *Id.* 140 Pa. Cmwlth. at 613 n.3, 594 A.2d at 823 n.3 (citation omitted). Thus, by definition, a mobile home is a residence. A 12-wide is not. "One can ride in a motorhome, and one can take journeys with a travel trailer, but mobile homes are not for riding or traveling." *Id.* 140 Pa. Cmwlth. at 613, 594 A.2d at 823.

Contrary to the Township's argument, the law is clear that 12-wides, as recreational vehicles, could not be legally placed in a mobile home park. The Township's ordinance cannot, and does not purport to, regulate 12-wides as residential manufactured housing. By precluding the placement of 12-wides in recreation parks, Dingman Township has effectively prohibited their use anywhere in the township. There is no legal or factual justification to support such a drastic prohibition of an otherwise lawful use.

### C. There is no substantial relation between the ordinance and the interest it seeks to foster.

#### 1. *12-wides are the same size on site as slide-outs.*

There is apparently no dispute in this case that a 400 square foot slide-out and a 400 square foot 12-wide unit are the same size on site. As the trial court observed, "[t]here are no distinguishable differences between 400 square feet vehicles allowed in LACA and the 400 square feet vehicles requiring a special highway permit other than the size of the vehicle while it's being transported." Trial Court Opinion, No. 1896-2011-Civil (10/1/12) at 4. "[T]he vehicles with the highway permits are the same size as RVs already allowed in the campground when in set-up mode." *Id.* at 4-5. Thus, the ordinance does not constitute a valid size restriction.

#### 2. *12-wides have the same occupancy capacity as similarly-sized slide-outs, and per-unit occupancy is decreasing.*

Because they have the same on-site dimensions, slide-outs and 12-wides have the same occupancy capacity. See R. 493a (testimony of J. Soard) (no difference in square footage). In fact, based on consumer demand, design changes in newer models have reduced the average sleeping capacity in this category of RVs from 5.3 to 5.0 persons. R. 486a (testimony of J. Soard) & Exh. A-7. Moreover, the average number of actual occupants has stayed flat at 2.44 persons in both 2005 and 2010. R. 486a-487a (testimony of J. Soard) & Exh. A-7. The average number of expected days of recreational occupancy during the first year of ownership has also stayed relatively flat, having decreased slightly from 149 days to 144 days. R. 488a (testimony of J. Soard) & Exh. A-7.

Thus, there is nothing to indicate that a 12-wide will be occupied either by more people or for more days each year than a slide-out. If anything, there have been decreases in both statistics, as well as in the designed capacity of occupancy, during the time 12-wides have become popular.

### 3. *12-wide units provide substantial water, sewer and power usage efficiency savings over the obsolete slide-outs, thus fostering, not burdening, the Township's goal of reducing strain on Lake Adventure's infrastructure and the environment.*

12-wides are made with energy-efficient utility fixtures not found in the older slide-out models of the same size. The new toilets, for example, use 1.6 gallons of water per flush compared to about 3-3.6 gallons in the older slide-outs. See R. 83a-85a (testimony of R. Ferri); 138a-139a (testimony of C. Niclaus). In one "full flow demand test" at Lake Adventure, a 2010 12-wide unit used only 49 gallons of water compared to 80.3 gallons for a 1998 slide-out of the same size. R. 90a-91 a (testimony of R. Ferri). Industry-wide, water saved with the new fixtures is consistently at least 20%. R. 139a (testimony of C. Niclaus). Thus, the placement of 12-wides rather than slide-outs will lessen rather than add to the burden on Lake Adventure's water and septic systems. See Trial Court Opinion, No. 1896-2011-Civil (10/1/12) at 5 (acknowledging that 12-wides offer improvements over slide-outs related to water and sewer use which are "certainly beneficial to land use regulations").

Dingman Township's secondary goal of avoiding sewage problems does not support a zoning restriction against placement of recreation vehicles based on their need for a highway permit during transport. In *National Land Inv. Co. v. Easttown Bd. of Adjustment*, 419 Pa. 504, 215 A.2d 597 (1965), a township sought to avoid sewer problems and water pollution by mandating a minimum lot size. *Id.*, 419 Pa. at 525, 215 A.2d at 608. The ordinance was invalid. Because a legislative system of regulations and enforcement was available to control sewer and water quality, imposing a minimum lot size was "neither a necessary nor a reasonable method" for the township to "protect itself from the menace of pollution." *Id.*, 419 Pa. at 526, 215 A.2d at 609. "Zoning is a means by which a governmental body can plan for the future—it may not be used as a means to deny the future." *Id.*, 419 Pa. at 528, 215 A.2d at 610 (footnote omitted).

There are more direct and appropriate ways to limit the burden on a recreation park's sewer and water infrastructure than to preclude the placement of vehicles that require a highway permit for transport on state roads.

Indeed, the Township's primary goal is to assure that usage of the vehicles is recreational and not residential, with a resulting limitation on the burden to infrastructure. The Township can attain that goal simply by enforcing the provision of the ordinance forbidding use of recreational vehicles as residences. Indeed, LACA has a parallel restriction in its recorded covenants, and it also enforces its restriction. See *Lake Adventure Community Ass'n v. Anderson,* 34 D. & C.4th 178, 192 (C.P. Pike 1996) (granting LACA's motion for injunction to stop residential use of recreational vehicle by defendant); R. 68a, 122a (testimony of K. Arnoul) (LACA actively enforces its non-residence restriction). As a co-Plaintiff in *Anderson,* the Township is clearly aware of its own enforcement power.

*4. 12-wides are much easier to move than similarly sized slide-outs, thus fostering, not burdening, the Township's goal of avoiding permanent recreation vehicle placement.*

Although 12-wides require highway permits for transport on the roads because of their width, their one-piece construction actually makes them easier to move on and off site for camping and recreation. A 12-wide unit can be set up or closed down within one hour. R. 494a (testimony of J. Soard).

A slide-out unit, however, requires significant on-site finishing and installation requiring a "crew" of people, and can take one to four days, depending on the skill level of the people doing the work. R. 494a-495a (testimony of J. Soard). *See also* R. 472a (testimony of K. Arnoul). The floor is hinged along its length, as is the roof. Side walls, once pulled out, must be attached, siding added, and windows installed to make the unit weatherproof. R. 495a (testimony of J. Soard).

The Township's stated goal is preserving the recreational character of recreation vehicle parks. To foster that goal, the units placed in the camp should be relatively easy to move. 12-wides possess that characteristic. Slide-outs do not. See R. 504a (testimony of J. Soard) (the slide-outs at Lake Adventure were not purchased with an expectation that they would be moved on a regular basis). A zoning ordinance that allows such slide-outs while precluding 12-wides of the same length and square footage does not serve the goal of fostering the recreational character of Lake Adventure or other similar parks.

5. *12-wides are better constructed and safer than slide-outs.* Slide-outs have no structure standards for their construction. R. 224a (testimony of J. Soard). In addition, on site a slide-out is dependent on the ground (and thus on the condition of the ground) to support the pull-out portion. R. 223a, 225a (testimony of J. Soard). Further, to allow the sliding function, a slide-out must have a hinge the length of its roof and another hinge the length of its floor. R. 225a-226a (testimony of J. Soard). The hinges create weak points in the unit, as well as a risk of roof leaks. *Id.*

By contrast, 12-wides, because they exceed eight and one-half feet in width, must comply with industry structure standards that are not required for slide-outs. R. 493a-494a (testimony of J. Soard). 12-wides must meet construction standards for snow load, floor load, and wind load. R. 224a (testimony of J. Soard). They are stronger and more heavily constructed. *Id.* Because they are constructed in one piece, they do not have the weak points and leak hazards created by the hinges that must be used in constructing slide-outs. Thus, 12-wide units are much sturdier and safer than the obsolete slide-outs. An ordinance that allows the slide-outs while prohibiting 12-wides with the same square footage, based solely on the highway permit requirement applicable to 12-wides, hinders rather than fosters the safety advancements that improved manufacturing has created in the 12-wides.

6. *The ordinance is not substantially related to a valid exercise of the Township's police power.*

In *Geiger v. Zoning Hearing Bd*, 510 Pa. 231, 507 A.2d 361 (1986), a township zoning ordinance permitted placement of manufactured homes made in two sections, but precluded placement of permanently installed mobile homes manufactured in a single section. The ordinance was invalid because there was no justification for excluding homes manufactured and transported in one piece while allowing homes made and transported in two pieces. *Id.*, 510 Pa. at 237, 507 A.2d at 364. A "zoning ordinance should apply to all dwellings of the same or similar size, irrespective of any differences in basic construction." *Id.*, 510 Pa. at 238, 507 A.2d at 364. The ordinance's differentiation between one-piece and sectional manufactured housing was "arbitrary and discriminatory and unrelated to the police powers of the Township legislative body." *Id.*, 510 Pa. at 238, 507 A.2d at 365.

In this case, as the trial court observed, Dingman Township's stated purpose in amending the zoning ordinance was to preserve the non-residential character of Lake Adventure and other RV campgrounds. Trial Court Opinion, No. 1896-2011-Civil (10/1/12) at 4. The trial court correctly found that the highway permit provision is not a size restriction, since other units of the same size are permitted. *Id.* As the court explained: "The special highway permit provision regarding road transport has nothing to do with the land use or building structure but rather only applies to how the vehicle gets to the site." *Id.* at 5. Thus, the ordinance restriction has no substantial relationship to the goal it seeks to foster.

The Township's related purpose of avoiding overuse of the sewer and water infrastructure at Lake Adventure is similarly unrelated to the highway permit-based restriction in the zoning ordinance. In *General Battery Corp. v. Zoning Hearing Bd.*, 29 Pa. Cmwlth. 498, 502, 371 A.2d 1030, 1032 (1977), a zoning ordinance's total exclusion of a waste facility that was already "under the diligent control" of the DEP was invalid, in that the ordinance was not *prima facie* designed to protect the public health, safety and welfare. *See also Greenwood*, 52 Pa. Cmwlth. at 373, 416 A.2d at 586 (citing and discussing *General Battery*).

In this case, the Dingman Township zoning ordinance prohibits the use of 12-wides (and any other recreational vehicles that may require a highway permit for operation on Pennsylvania state roads) in the township. Like the waste facility in *General Battery* or the landfill in *Greenwood,* the operation of 12-wide units is governed by a Commonwealth agency, in this instance the Department of Transportation. Moreover, the construction of 12-wides, including both safety features *and dimensions,* is governed not only by nationally recognized industry standards but also by both state and federal regulations. Thus, like the zoning ordinances in *Greenwood* and *General Battery,* the ordinance here, which seeks to impose restrictions on use beyond those imposed by the applicable state and federal regulatory agencies, is not *prima facie* designed to protect the public health, safety and welfare. Indeed, the trial court expressly found, as a fact, that "[t]he highway permit restriction has no effect on promoting public health and safety." Trial Court Opinion, No. 1896-2011-Civil (10/1/12) at 5.

## D. Dingman Township's zoning ordinance unfairly burdens commerce, industry, property owners, and consumers.

As discussed above, virtually no one is still manufacturing the old slide-out style recreational vehicle. Consumers do not want that style unit, preferring the simpler 12-wides. 12-wides are manufactured to stricter standards and are more structurally sound. Moreover, no other municipality, either in Pennsylvania or elsewhere in the United States, has made the differentiation Dingman Township has made between slide-outs and 12-wides so as to preclude the placement of 12-wides where slide-outs are allowed, based merely on whether a highway permit is required for transport of the unit. R. 497a (testimony of J. Soard).

Application of the ordinance would prevent LACA, the property owners at Lake Adventure, and indeed the public at large from enjoying the economic and environmental benefits resulting from the improvements in efficiency and safety provided by 12-wides over the old slide-out model vehicles. In order to maximize the space available to them, owners would have to refrain from replacing their old slide-out units with safer, more efficient 12-wides. As a result, manufacturers would lose sales, burdening commerce, and owners would be at increased safety risk. There was also evidence that the unique restriction at Lake Adventure will have a detrimental effect on the resale value of the lots, thus burdening the owners' property rights. See R. 180a-185a (testimony of G. Romanik) & Exh. A-25.

By regulating the use of the nationally popular 12-wides in a way that is inconsistent with the rest of Pennsylvania and the United States, the Dingman Township ordinance burdens commerce, consumers, and manufacturers. As John Soard explained, basing the ordinance's restriction on the highway permit requirement changes the functional definition of a recreational vehicle to something different from what is applied everywhere else:

> . . . . That is what PRVCA . . .has an issue with because you have changed the definition of a recreation vehicle from state rules. PRVCA is especially looking at this because when you do that now you're creating an inconsistency somewhere in the state, which this happens to be Dingman Township, that could cause a consumer, at the Hershey RV show two weeks ago [for example,] to purchase a park trailer, all

> about coming up into Lake Adventure and realize they can't place in Lake Adventure.
>
> Now they have—now they have a unit that they can't use, they have to go somewhere else, they have to do whatever, because of the inconsistency in the state rules. That's something we don't as an association want to allow to have happening out there . . . .

R. 508a (testimony of J. Soard). Because there is no reasonable basis for the inconsistent regulation, the burden on commerce is unconstitutional.

12-wides are the newer, sounder, safer, more convenient generation of product. They are not a different category of RV from the obsolete slide-outs just because they need a highway permit. *Amici* PRVCA and RVIA respectfully urge this Court to affirm the trial court's decision striking the highway permit-based restriction on the placement of 12-wides in Dingman Township.

## *VI. CONCLUSION*

Based on the foregoing arguments, the Recreation Vehicle Industry Association and the Pennsylvania Recreation Vehicle and Camping Association, *amici curiae,* respectfully urge the Court to affirm the trial court's order invalidating that portion of the Township's zoning ordinance denying campground access to vehicles based on the requirement of a special highway permit.

## EXAMPLE 14

**Authors** William Pentelovitch and Emma G. Greenman, Maslon Edelman Borman & Brand, LLP

**Case** No. 62-CV-12-7718, *Minnesota Voters Alliance v. State of Minnesota*, in the Second Judicial District Court, Ramsey County, Minnesota

### BRIEF OF AMICUS CURIAE AMERICAN CIVIL LIBERTIES UNION OF MINNESOTA

### INTRODUCTION

The American Civil Liberties Union of Minnesota ("ACLU-MN"), is a not-for-profit, non-partisan, membership-supported organization dedicated to the protection of civil rights and liberties. It is the statewide affiliate of the American Civil Liberties Union and has more than 8,500 members in Minnesota. Its purpose is to protect the rights and liberties guaranteed to all Minnesotans by the state and federal constitutions and by state and federal laws. Since its founding, the ACLU-MN has engaged in constitutional and voting rights litigation, both directly and as *amicus curiae,* in a wide variety of cases.

While the ACLU-MN takes no position on whether the Secretary of State was authorized to set up an online voter registration system, if the Court determines that the Secretary of State was not authorized to do so, the ACLU-MN opposes Petitioners' request that the registrations of voters who availed themselves of the opportunity to register to vote online should be stricken from the voter rolls. It is the position of the ACLU-MN that in the event the Court determines the Secretary of State lacked authority to accept voter registrations online, the proper remedy is for this Court to order that the Secretary of State forward each online voter registration application to the county auditor of the county where the voter resides pursuant to Minnesota Statute § 201.061, subd. 1.

## ISSUES PRESENTED

1. Where a registrant has provided the Secretary of State all information statutorily required to register to vote, and has in good faith delivered the registration application in an online format specified by the Secretary of State, may the registrant's registration be revoked if the Court finds that the Secretary of State did not have proper authority to permit online voter registration?
2. If the Court finds that the Secretary of State created and accepted an online voter registration application without statutory authorization, is the proper remedy as to the online registrants to require the Secretary of State to forward their voter registration applications to the county auditor of the county in which each registrant resides?

## BACKGROUND

### *I. MINNESOTA VOTER REGISTRATION REQUIREMENTS*

To vote in Minnesota, an eligible voter must be registered to vote. MINN. STAT. § 201.018, subd. 2 (2013). An eligible voter may register in advance of an election by completing and submitting a voter registration application at least 20 days prior. *Id.* § 201.054, § 201.061, subd. 1. Minnesota Statute § 201.071 requires that the form of all voter registration applications be approved by the Secretary of State and contain spaces for the following information:

1. Voter's first, middle, and last name, and voter's previous name, if any;
2. Voter's current address, and voter's previous address, if any;
3. Voter's date of birth;
4. Voter's municipality and county of residence;

5. Voter's telephone number, if provided by the voter;
6. Date of registration;
7. Current and valid Minnesota driver's license or state identification number, or if the voter has no valid Minnesota driver's license or state identification, the last four digits of the voter's Social Security number; and
8. Voter's signature.

*Id.* § 201.071, subd. 1. The application must also include a certification that a voter meets the eligibility criteria to vote and include check boxes for the following questions: "(1) Are you a citizen of the United States?" and "(2) Will you be 18 years old on or before election day?" *Id.*

Although the form must include space for the above-mentioned information, § 201.071 expressly provides that a voter registration application is *not* deficient so long as it contains the following: name, address, date of birth, current and valid Minnesota driver's license or Minnesota state identification number or last four digits of the voter's Social Security number, and a signature. *Id.* Minnesota law mandates that "[n]o eligible voter may be prevented from voting unless the voter's registration application is deficient or the voter is duly and successfully challenged in accordance with Section 201.195 or 204C.12." *Id.* at subd. 3.

Minnesota law provides that an eligible voter registering in advance of election day may deliver his or her completed voter registration application by "submitting it in person or by mail to the county auditor of that county or to the Secretary of State's Office," *Id.* § 201.061, subd. 1. Mail registration is defined as an application delivered to the Secretary of State, county auditor, or municipal clerk by the U.S. Postal Service or a commercial carrier. *Id.* If a registration application is "improperly addressed or *delivered*" the provision provides the application "shall be forwarded within two working days after receipt to the county auditor of the county where the voter maintains residence." *Id.*

### *II. SECRETARY RITCHIE'S ONLINE VOTER REGISTRATION APPLICATION*

On September 26, 2013, Secretary of State Mark Ritchie began offering a voter registration application in an online format. The Online Voter Registration Form (hereinafter "Online Application") requires the registrant to provide the same information as required by the paper application, submitted in two electronic forms. *Voter Registration Application Step 1 of 2*, Office of the Minnesota Secretary of State (Nov. 26, 2013), https://mnvotes.sos.state.mn.us/ VoterRegistratiori/VoterRegistrationStepl.aspx. Form one contains two check boxes required by § 201.071, subd. 1 to confirm that the registrant is a U.S. Citizen and will be 18 years old by election day. *Id.* Form two requires the registrant to complete an electronic form containing the eight information fields required by § 201.071 and to certify that the registrant meets the eligibility criteria to vote. *Id.* at *Step 2 of 2,* [Internet address]. Online registrants provide their signature electronically pursuant to the Uniform Electronic Transactions Act and must acknowledge that the electronic signature is their legally binding signature. Online Application at *Step 2 of 2; see* MINN. STAT. § 325L.07(d) (2013) ("If a law requires a signature, an electronic signature satisfies the law.") Once submitted, an Online Application goes through the same verification process as paper applications, and if approved, the online registrant is added to the statewide voter registration list. *See* MINN. STAT. § 201.061, subd. 1.

## ARGUMENT

### *I. ONLINE REGISTRANTS SHOULD NOT BE REQUIRED TO RE-REGISTER IF THIS COURT HOLDS THAT ONLINE REGISTRATION WAS INSTITUTED WITHOUT PROPER AUTHORITY.*

The Minnesota Constitution and Minnesota law protect voters who register electronically in good faith from being disenfranchised if this Court finds Secretary Ritchie lacks the proper authority to accept online delivery of voter registration applications. Minnesota courts have long refused to disenfranchise eligible voters because of errors made by government officials interpreting or implementing Minnesota election laws. Moreover, Petitioners only challenge the method of delivery for voter registration applications and not the adequacy of the registration applications themselves. Verified Pet. Writ of Quo Warranto 1-3, ¶¶ 17-33. Minnesota's voter registration statute supplies no statutory authority for preventing the online registrants, whose registration applications are not legally deficient and whose eligibility has not been challenged, from voting.

### A. The Minnesota Constitution and Established Minnesota Law Direct That Online Registrants Should Not Be Disenfranchised by an Error of the Secretary of State.

The right to vote is enshrined and protected in two Articles of the Minnesota Constitution. The Bill of Rights of the Minnesota Constitution, Article 1 § 2, provides that "[n]o member of this state shall be disenfranchised." Minn. Const, art. 1, § 2. Article 7 provides the authority to create and implement election laws governing the franchise. Minn. Const, art. 7, § 1; *see McEwen v. Prince,* 147 N.W. 275, 276-77 (Minn. 1914). The Minnesota Constitution "secures to every person possessing the qualifications prescribed therein the right to vote." *Fitzgerald v. Morlock,* 120 N.W.2d 339, 345 (Minn. 1963) (construing Minn. Const, art. 7, § 1).

In furtherance of these constitutional principles, Minnesota courts have long held that errors made by government officials implementing or construing election laws should not be allowed to disenfranchise eligible voters. In cases going back almost to the state's founding, courts have made a "clear distinction between the provisions and prohibitions in the election laws which are personal to the elector and those which apply to election officers over whose conduct he has no control." *Sheehan v. Franken,* 161 N.W. 2d 453, 462 (Minn. 2009); *e.g., Fitzgerald,* 120 N.W.2d at 339; *Johnson v. Swenson,* 119 N.W.2d 723 (Minn. 1963); *Grimsrud v. Johnson,* 202 N.W. 72 (Minn. 1925); *Truelsen v. Hugo,* 91 N.W. 434 (Minn. 1902); *Hankey v. Bowman,* 84 N.W. 1002 (Minn. 1901); *Pennington v. Hare,* 62 N.W. 116 (Minn. 1895); *Taylor v. Taylor,* 10 Minn. 107 (Minn. 1865). These cases establish the rule that a voter's personal adherence to election requirements is mandatory; his or her vote may be properly rejected if the voter fails to comply with the requirements of election law. *Sheehan,* 767 N.W. 2d at

462 (Minn. 2009) (citing *Fitzgerald,* 120 N.W.2d at 345), But if the voter complies in good faith with the law, that voter's right to vote cannot be defeated by reason of "irregularities, ignorance, inadvertence, or mistake, or even intentional wrong on the part of the election officers," *Id.* (quoting *Fitzgerald,* 120 N.W.2d at 345).

The Minnesota Supreme Court has applied this rule to prevent eligible voters from being disenfranchised in a variety of circumstances. The issue most often arises in the context of disputed election results. *See Johnson,* 119 N.W.2d at 725-28 (holding ballots numbered and marked by election officials in violation of MINN. STAT. § 204.11, subd. 3 should be counted); *Grimsrud,* 202 N.W. at 73 (holding ballots prepared by a clerk and not marked as official ballots as required by law should be counted). Courts have applied this principle to a broader set of election-related challenges. In *Hankey v. Bowman,* the court upheld a Minnesota Governor's creation of three election districts and sustained the results of the election even after ruling the Governor did not have statutory authority to establish the election districts in the first place. 84 N.W. at 1004-05. The court held that the Governor established the districts under the color of authority, and voters should not be disenfranchised by setting aside the election. *Id.*

While Minnesota courts have not directly addressed the context of voter registration, this constitutionally derived rule should be applied broadly to Minnesota election laws regulating the franchise. *See Grimsrud,* 202 N.W. at 73 ("The right of franchise is an esteemed privilege of a citizen which should not be taken away or be denied, unless the statute regulating its exercise clearly indicates that the voter who has not complied with its essential prerequisites must be barred."). Moreover, the Minnesota Attorney General has provided guidance in line with the Minnesota Supreme Court's holdings. A 1962 Minnesota Attorney General Advisory Opinion addressed a question similar to the one at issue here: what happens to the registration of voters who registered pursuant to a procedure established by a city's registration commissioner, if that procedure was found to be unauthorized under the law. Op. Atty. Gen., 183Q, Oct. 24, 1962. The Attorney General stated that, "[i]n view of the fact that the voters in question here acted in good faith, in reliance upon persons acting under color of law, their names should not be summarily excluded from the registration list." *Id.*

Well-established precedent provides clear direction to this Court in the event that it accepts Petitioners' argument that the online registration applications were improperly delivered and that Secretary Ritchie did not have the statutory authority to accept electronically delivered applications. *See* Verified Pet. 2-3. Consistent with the prior holdings of Minnesota courts that ballots cast in good faith may not be disregarded, the online registration applications delivered by eligible voters in good faith should not be cast aside. If any error is found with the Secretary's authority to create and accept online voter registration applications, it is not because the registrants failed to comply with the registration rules. *Cf. Sheehan,* 767 N.W. 2d at 462 (Minn. 2009) (absentee ballots properly excluded because the absentee voters failed to comply with the requirements of the absentee ballot law). The error would be clearly attributable to Secretary Ritchie, a fact Petitioners concede. Verified Pet. at 144 ("The sole responsible party for this illegality would be the Secretary of State.").

An eligible voter who used the Online Application to successfully register has complied in good faith with Minnesota election law. *See* MINN. STAT. § 201. Petitioners do not dispute that the Online Application requires registrants to provide every piece of information required by statute, nor that online registrants complied with the mandatory requirements of providing a name, address, birthdate, valid Minnesota license, identification number or last four digits of his social security number, and a signature. *See* Verified Pet.; MINN. STAT. § 201.071, subd. 3. Moreover, even if this Court finds that Secretary Ritchie did not have the statutory authority to accept electronic signatures, online registrants relied in good faith on the express stipulation in the Online Application that registrants were providing their "legally binding signature." *See* Online Application at *Step 2 of 2.*

Petitioners contest Secretary Ritchie's interpretation of the method by which voter registration applications must be delivered under Minnesota Statute § 201.061 but do not dispute the adequacy of the registration applications submitted through the online system. *See* Verified Pet. at ¶¶ 17-33. Secretary Ritchie, Minnesota's top election official, concluded that he has the statutory authority to accept voter registration applications delivered via the Internet. Akin to the Minnesota Governor in *Hankey v. Bowman,* Secretary Ritchie acted under the color of law to set up the online registration application system. *See* 84 N.W. at 1004-05. If the Court finds Secretary Ritchie does not have the proper authority to implement online voter registration, then this Court should follow *Hankey;* the constitutional officer's erroneous misapplication of Minnesota election law should not defeat the online registrants' right to vote. *See Hankey,* 84 N.W. at 1004-05; *Sheehan,* 767 N.W. 2d at 462.

The same statutory provision that Petitioners rely on to challenge the online registration system contains a remedy for online registrants if this Court finds no authority for the Secretary of State's electronic registration system. Minnesota law requiring that an "improperly . . . delivered registration application shall be forwarded . . . to the county auditor of the county where the voter maintains residence" unambiguously applies in this case. MINN. STAT. § 201.061, subd. 1. Petitioners themselves state that "Section 201.061 embodies . . . the specific mandatory direction governing the delivery of voter registration applications." Verified Pet. at 29.

If the Petitioners succeed in convincing this Court that electronic transmission is an improper delivery method for voter registration applications, then this Court should follow the remedy prescribed by § 201.061 for improperly delivered registration applications. *See* MINN. STAT. § 201.061, subd. 1. Secretary Ritchie should be directed to forward the voter registration applications of each online registrant to the county auditor of the county where each registrant resides. *See id.* The county auditor should be required to accept the voter registration applications thus forwarded so that each online registrant will be registered in compliance with Minnesota law. *See id.* ("A registration that is received no later than 5:00 p.m. on the 21st day preceding any election shall be accepted.").

### B. There Is No Statutory Authority for Revoking the Registration of Online Registrants.

This Court has no authority under Minnesota election law to take the online registrants off the state's voter registration list or prevent online registrants from voting. Minnesota law provides only two reasons for preventing an eligible voter from voting: a deficient voter registration application or a successful challenge to the voter's eligibility or residence in accordance with law. MINN. STAT. § 201.071, subd. 3. Neither reason is present in this case.

Here the registrants' online applications were not deficient and Petitioners do not allege them to be deficient; the online voter registration applications contained all the information required by law to vote. *See id.* § 201.071, subd. 1, 3. Likewise, the online registrants have not been duly and successfully challenged based on their residency or eligibility to vote. *See id.* at subd. 1.

What Petitioners challenge here is not the adequacy of the online registrants' voter registration applications but the "*methods of delivery* for voter registration applications." Verified Pet. at 2 (emphasis added). Petitioners contend that Secretary Ritchie does not have the statutory authority to expand the delivery method for voter registration applications beyond those expressly listed in § 201.061: in person, U.S. mail, commercial carrier. *Id.* at 2, 8-16; *see* MINN. STAT. § 201.061, subd. 1.

However, even if this Court agrees with Petitioners and finds no statutory authority for online voter registration, the improper delivery of a registration application is not a legal justification for removing an online registrant from the registration rolls. *See id.* § 201.071, subd. 3. Because the online registrants' voter registration applications are neither deficient nor have the voters been lawfully challenged, the plain and unambiguous language of § 201.071 prohibits this Court from preventing the online registrants from voting. *See id.* Taking the online registrants off the voter rolls would do just that.

## *II. TAKING THE ONLINE REGISTRANTS OFF THE VOTER ROLLS WOULD VIOLATE 42 U.S.C. § 1971.*

Federal civil rights law prohibits the Secretary of State from removing the online registrants from the statewide voter registration list because of an error relating to their voter registration applications, when the error is not material to determining whether the registrants are qualified to vote. The method of delivering a registration application is not material to a voter's eligibility to vote under Minnesota law.

Federal law prohibits denying the right to register and vote based on errors or omissions that are not material to determining a voter's eligibility. Civil Rights Act of 1957, 42 U.S.C. § 1971(a)(2)(B). The law provides that no person acting under color of law shall:

> deny the right of any individual to vote in any election because of an error or omission on any record or paper relating to any application, registration, or other act requisite to voting, if such error or omission is not material in determining whether such individual is qualified under State law to vote in such election.

*Id.* The statute defines "vote" broadly to include "all action necessary to make a vote effective including, but not limited to, registration." *Id.* § 1971(e).

While this law was originally adopted to deal with practices that disenfranchised minority voters, the provision can and has been applied to a broader set of government actions that work to deny individuals the right to register to vote. *See Schwier v. Cox,* 439 F.3d 1285, 1286 (1lth Cir. 2006) (disclosure of social security numbers is not "material" to a voter registration system under § 1971(a)(2)(B)); *Washington Ass'n of Churches v. Reed,* 492 F. Supp. 2d 1264, 1270-71 (W.D. Wash. 2006) (state law making registration contingent on a voter's name matching to the Social Security Administration or Department of Licensing databases likely violated § 1971(a)(2)(B)).

Here, the removal of the online registrants from the voter registration list would meet all of the criteria for a violation of 42 U.S.C. § 1971(a)(2)(B). First, the Secretary of State at the direction of this Court would be acting under color of law to deny the right of each online registrant to remain registered, a prerequisite of voting. *See id.* Second, the names of the online registrants would be removed from the statewide registration system because of "an error or omission on any record or paper relating to . . . registration," namely that their registration records were created or updated by an improperly delivered registration application. *See id.*

Third, the "error or omission" of improper delivery of a voter registration application is not material to determining whether the online registrant was eligible to vote under Minnesota law. "Material" is not defined in § 1971. *See Florida State Conference of N.A.A.C.P. v. Browning,* 522 F.3d 1153, 1174 (1lth Cir. 2008) (opining that the term "material" could mean something between minimally relevant and outcome-determinative). But the Minnesota legislature has already delineated what is "material" to a person's eligibility to vote, a deficient voter registration application or a successful challenge to the voter's eligibility or residence. *See* MINN. STAT. § 201.071, subd. 1, 3. Any other errors in a registration application must not keep an eligible voter from voting. *See id*. Whether the Online Application was an improper method of delivering the voter registration application is not material to determining whether the online registrants were qualified to vote.

The remedy Petitioners seek would deny the online registrants the right to be registered and to vote because of the Secretary of State's decision to accept electronic delivery of voter registration applications, an error not material to determining whether a voter is eligible to vote under Minnesota law. Petitioners' requested remedy would violate federal civil rights law.

## CONCLUSION

If this Court finds that the Secretary of State did not have proper statutory authority to implement online voter registration, the proper remedy would be to order all electronically submitted registration applications be forwarded to the county auditor where each online registrant resides. Any remedy that removes the online registrants from voting rolls would be in violation of the Minnesota Constitution, Minnesota law, and federal law and must be rejected by this Court.

## EXAMPLE 15

**Authors** Paul D. Clement, Jeffrey M. Harris, Bancroft PLLC; John B. Bellinger III, Lisa S. Blatt, Ramon P. Marks, R. Reeves Anderson, Arnold & Porter LLP

**Case** *Kiobel v. Royal Dutch Petroleum Co.*, 133 S. Ct. 1659 (2013)

### BRIEF OF *AMICI CURIAE* BP AMERICA, CATERPILLAR, CONOCO PHILLIPS, GENERAL ELECTRIC, HONEYWELL, AND INTERNATIONAL BUSINESS MACHINES IN SUPPORT OF RESPONDENTS

* * *

### SUMMARY OF ARGUMENT

For the reasons set forth in the Second Circuit's opinion and Respondents' brief, the Court should hold that there is no cause of action under the ATS against corporate entities. But regardless of how this Court resolves that issue, the judgment below should be affirmed because the ATS [Alien Tort Statute]: (1) does not apply to extraterritorial conduct that occurred entirely in a foreign country; and (2) does not create a cause of action for civil aiding and abetting liability. Both issues are ripe for the Court's review. If corporate executives can still be sued for extraterritorial conduct or under broad aiding and abetting theories, a narrow ruling on corporate liability will not suffice to deter diplomatically problematic and investment-chilling lawsuits.

This Court has recognized that suits under the ATS pose a significant risk of interfering with United States foreign policy and create diplomatic friction. The Court accordingly has instructed the lower courts to proceed with great caution in their application of the ATS. Yet the lower courts have largely ignored that instruction, and ATS litigation has led to significant diplomatic disputes with foreign countries. The source of that friction is not the ATS in the abstract, but the ATS' extraterritorial application, as the United States explained to this Court in a 2008 amicus brief in *American Isuzu Motors v. Ntsebeza,* 553 U.S. 1028 (2008). In stark contrast, the United States now ignores these ongoing diplomatic complaints and urges the Court to avoid resolving the root causes of that friction.

The United States' approach would frustrate the purpose of the ATS. Congress enacted the ATS to ease diplomatic conflicts caused by a perceived inadequacy of state-law remedies for violations of the law of nations occurring here. The ATS has been converted from a salve to an irritant by the lower courts' misguided extraterritorial application of the statute.

The Court should clarify that the ATS, silent about any extraterritorial effect, does not extend abroad. This Court has recently and emphatically reaffirmed that a federal statute may not be applied to wholly extraterritorial conduct unless the text of the statute clearly compels that result. Nothing in the sparse text of the ATS supports—much less *clearly* supports—extending the statute to alleged torts that occurred entirely within the borders of a foreign nation. Indeed, the history and purpose of the statute confirm that it is solely intended to provide a remedy for: (1) torts committed against aliens that occurred on U.S. soil; or (2) torts that occurred on the high seas, such as piracy, which are by definition outside the territorial jurisdiction of *any* nation. The ATS has no application whatsoever to alleged injuries—such as the ones at issue here—suffered by a foreign citizen on foreign soil.

Extraterritorial application of the ATS not only offends basic precepts of our own law, it also violates international law. Territorial jurisdiction is one of the basic building blocks of international law. It serves to avoid confrontations between nations generated by conflicting and overlapping claims to jurisdiction. International law regards as illegitimate the assertion of jurisdiction over disputes that have no relation to the nation in which those disputes are adjudicated. The drafters of the ATS were well aware of the jurisdictional limits of international law, and those boundaries clearly informed the ATS' scope. Even in the criminal context, many nations—including the United States—regard as illegitimate the broad exercise of jurisdiction over events that occurred in another nation. It is thus hardly surprising that many countries—including close allies of the United States, such as the United Kingdom, Canada, and Australia—have repeatedly objected to ATS suits involving foreign conduct with no nexus to the United States.

The Plaintiffs' claims should also be dismissed for the separate and independent reason that the ATS does not confer jurisdiction over claims involving civil aiding and abetting liability. As with extraterritoriality, a cause of action for civil aiding and abetting liability is not cognizable unless Congress has clearly indicated its intent to create such liability. The fact that *criminal* aiding and abetting liability may exist is irrelevant. Congress has indicated a general preference for aiding and abetting liability in the criminal sphere. A comparable indication of congressional intent is missing in the civil context, as is the critical check of prosecutorial discretion.

At a minimum, the Court should hold that the *mens rea* standard for civil aiding and abetting liability under the ATS is *purpose*, rather than mere knowledge. A corporate defendant accused of aiding and abetting human rights abuses of a foreign government may not be held liable unless it acted with the purpose of causing those abuses.

## ARGUMENT

### *I. EXTRATERRITORIAL APPLICATION OF THE ATS CAUSES DIPLOMATIC FRICTION, CONTRARY TO THE PURPOSE OF THE ATS*

**A.** In *Sosa v. Alvarez-Machain,* this Court concluded that the ATS provides jurisdiction for federal courts to hear "a very limited category" of private claims "defined by the law of nations." 542 U.S. 692, 712 (2004). The Court admonished the lower courts to exercise "great caution" and restraint in expanding the scope of the ATS, explaining that "the potential implications for the foreign relations of the United States of recognizing such causes should make courts particularly wary of impinging on the discretion of the Legislative and Executive Branches in managing foreign affairs." *Id.* at 727-28.

The lower courts largely have ignored that admonition. Courts instead have condoned lawsuits under the ATS brought by foreign plaintiffs against U.S. and foreign corporations for conduct committed by foreign governments in foreign countries. These suits have precipitated the very diplomatic friction the ATS and *Sosa* sought to avoid. Before this litigation, the U.S. government had filed more than a dozen briefs emphasizing that such suits complicate relations with other nations.

Nonetheless, the United States now urges the Court to rule "narrow[ly]" on the issue of whether corporations are proper defendants under the ATS, and to ignore the broader, more troubling aspects of lower courts' ATS jurisprudence. Br. for the United States as Amicus Curiae ("U.S. Br.") at 6. That proposed course would do little to ameliorate foreign governments' concerns about the expanding scope of ATS liability, which has turned the federal judiciary into an international civil court to remedy wrongs anywhere in the world.

Two legal issues common in ATS litigation and present here—extraterritorial application of the statute and aiding and abetting liability—cause repeated diplomatic disagreements and inhibit international commerce. Those issues are what drive the most diplomatically problematic ATS suits. The resulting diplomatic friction is contrary to the original purpose of the ATS to redress violations of international law that "threaten[] serious consequences in international affairs" of the United States. *Sosa*, 542 U.S. at 715; *see also id.* at 761 (Breyer, J., concurring) (questioning "whether the exercise of jurisdiction under the ATS is consistent with those notions of comity that lead each nation to respect the sovereign rights of other nations by limiting the reach of its laws and their enforcement").

Curtailing ATS lawsuits against corporations by affirming the decision below will help rein in the expanding scope of ATS liability. But the Court should not stop at an incomplete solution that fails to address the root causes of the extraordinary diplomatic friction caused by ATS lawsuits—namely, the application of the ATS to allegedly tortious acts that occur in foreign countries, whether through direct acts or more commonly through allegations that corporate agents have aided and abetted the conduct of foreign governments.

**B.** This case exemplifies the sprawling geographic reach of the ATS post-*Sosa* and the resulting interference with U.S. foreign relations. Here, Nigerian plaintiffs seek to hold Dutch, British, and Nigerian corporations liable for aiding and abetting acts allegedly committed by the Nigerian government against its own citizens in Nigeria. Plaintiffs in this and numerous other ATS cases use ATS lawsuits against "corporations as proxies for what are essentially attacks on [foreign] government policy." Anne-Marie Slaughter & David Bosco, *Plaintiff's Diplomacy*, Foreign Affairs, Sept.-Oct. 2000, at 102, 107.

Foreign governments view ATS suits that impugn their own actions or the actions of their nationals to be unlawful infringements on their sovereignty. In the past decade, the governments of Australia, Canada, China, Colombia, El Salvador, Germany, Israel, Papua New Guinea, South Africa, Switzerland, and the United Kingdom have lodged protests with the State Department or filed briefs objecting to the extraterritorial application of the ATS, including in cases involving *amid* as defendants. For example, U.S. allies have criticized U.S. courts' "infringement in the conduct of foreign relations" and "interfere[nee] in the jurisdiction of [foreign] courts"—actions that "transgress thereby the sovereignty . . . and the will of [their] people." The United Kingdom and Australia have emphasized that merely limiting the number of actionable norms under the ATS is insufficient to assuage these concerns because "even if narrowly construed, the ATS remains a source of excessive extraterritorial jurisdiction."

The State Department has for years expressed to courts its concern that ATS litigation involving conduct in other countries interferes with U.S. foreign relations. *See, e.g.*, Letter from Legal Adviser William H. Taft, IV to Principal Deputy Assistant Attorney General Daniel Meron (Feb. 11, 2005), filed with United States Statement of Interest, *Presbyterian Church of Sudan v. Talisman Energy, Inc.*, No. 01-9882 (S.D.N.Y. Mar. 15, 2005) ("The Department of State shares . . . Canada's concerns about the difficulties that can arise from an expansive exercise of jurisdiction by the federal courts under the ATS.").8

The Departments of Justice and State have confirmed that diplomatic tension caused by extraterritorial application of the ATS "can and already has led to a lack of cooperation on important foreign policy objectives." Supp. Br. for United States as Amicus Curiae at 16, *Doe v. Unocal*, Nos. 00-56603 *et al.* (9th Cir. Aug. 25, 2004) ("U.S. *Unocal* Br.").

The "laundry list" of foreign government protests also "shows that something is palpably awry in the modern ATS juggernaut. The problem stems in large part from extension of the ATS to conduct occurring in foreign lands." *John Doe VIII v. Exxon Mobil,* 654 F.3d 11, 78 (D.C. Cir. 2011) (Kavanaugh, J., dissenting).

**C.** In light of numerous diplomatic objections, the United States in 2008 asked this Court to end ATS suits that "challeng[e] the conduct of foreign governments toward their own citizens in their own countries—conduct as to which the foreign states are themselves immune from suit—through the simple expedient of naming as defendants those private corporations that lawfully did business with the governments." Br. for United States as Amicus Curiae at 5, *Am. Isuzu Motors v. Ntsebeza,* No. 07-919, 2008 WL 408389 (Feb. 11, 2008) ("U.S. *Ntsebeza* Br."). "Such lawsuits," the United States explained, "inevitably create tension between the United States and foreign nations." *Id.*

In *Ntsebeza,* the United States argued that a court of appeals decision authorizing ATS claims against corporations for aiding and abetting a foreign state's activities outside the United States "represents a dramatic expansion of U.S. law that is inconsistent with well-established presumptions that Congress does not intend to authorize civil aiding and abetting liability or extend U.S. law extraterritorially." U.S. *Ntsebeza* Br. at 5. The United States criticized the lower court's disregard for the "serious risks to the United States' relations with foreign states and to the political Branches' ability to conduct the Nation's foreign policy." *Id.* at 18. The United States cited as evidence of the "international friction," *id.* at 14, diplomatic protests filed by Germany, South Africa, Switzerland, and the United Kingdom. *See id.* at la-14a. The United States had argued in numerous prior briefs that the extraterritorial application of the ATS for aiding and abetting the acts of a foreign government represents a "vast expansion of liability that would interfere with the Executive's conduct of foreign policy," Br. of United States as Amicus Curiae at 3, *Mujica v. Occidental,* Nos. 05-56056 *et al.* (9th Cir. Mar. 17, 2006), and that "the recognition of [extraterritorial] claims would directly conflict with Congress' purpose in enacting the ATS, which was to reduce diplomatic conflicts." Br. of United States as Amicus Curiae at 12, *Sarei v. Rio Tinto,* Nos. 02-56256 *et al.* (9th Cir. Sept. 28, 2006).

In contrast, the United States in this case urges the Court to rule "narrow[ly]," and ignore the broader issues at the root of this diplomatic tension. U.S. Br. at 6. That course should be avoided. While corporate liability remains an important and contentious issue in many ATS suits, resolution of the extraterritorial reach of the ATS and its application to aiding and abetting claims would go further in providing much-needed clarity to lower courts about the properly limited scope of the statute.

There is no obstacle to this Court resolving these pendent issues. Respondents raised the aiding and abetting issue below, and thus may defend the judgment on that basis, "whether or not [it] was relied upon, rejected, or even considered by the District Court or the Court of Appeals," *Washington v. Yakima Indian Nation,* 439 U.S. 463, 476 n.20 (1979), "provided the asserted ground would not expand the relief which has been granted." *Smith v. Phillips,* 455 U.S. 209, 215, n.6 (1982); *accord Whitley v. Albers,* 475 U.S. 312, 326 (1986). The decision below was a complete victory for the defendants, so the relief could not be expanded. And, as Respondents explain, whether the ATS can be applied to extraterritorial conduct is a question of jurisdiction that is properly before the Court. *See* Respondents' Br. 53.

Resolution now also makes prudent sense. The ATS is applied extraterritorially in almost every suit brought under that statute, and aiding and abetting liability is the key to litigating the conduct of foreign governments otherwise immunized from direct suit. Multiple circuits have considered and ruled on both issues. A narrow resolution of this case would lead to continued diplomatic friction, as Plaintiffs seek out new "proxies" (perhaps corporate directors and officers) by which to continue challenging the conduct and policies of foreign governments.

## *II. THE ATS DOES NOT APPLY TO PURELY EXTRATERRITORIAL CONDUCT*

The ATS should not be interpreted to reach extraterritorial conduct. The Second Circuit noted that this issue remains an open question, and—whether or not corporations can be held liable under the ATS—this Court should affirm on the alternative ground that the ATS does not apply extraterritorially against corporations or anyone else.

## A. Federal Statutes Are Presumed to Apply Only to U.S.-Based Conduct

**1.** Congress unquestionably has "the authority to enforce its laws beyond the territorial boundaries of the United States," but "[w]hether Congress has in fact exercised that authority ... is a matter of statutory construction." *EEOC v. Arabian Am. Oil Co.*, 499 U.S. 244, 248 (1991) *("Aramco")*.

As this Court recently and emphatically reaffirmed, Congress "ordinarily legislates with respect to domestic, not foreign matters." *Morrison v. National Australia Bank*, 130 S.Ct. 2869, 2877 (2010). It is well established that "legislation of Congress, unless a contrary intent appears, is meant to apply only within the territorial jurisdiction of the United States.'" *Aramco*, 499 U.S. at 248 (citing *Foley Bros. v. Filardo*, 336 U.S. 281, 285 (1949)). "When a statute gives no *clear indication* of an extraterritorial application, it has none." *Morrison*, 130 S.Ct. at 2878 (emphasis added); *see also Aramco*, 499 U.S. at 248 ("[U]nless there is the affirmative intention of the Congress, clearly expressed" to give a statute extraterritorial effect, "we must presume it is primarily concerned with domestic matters.") (citation omitted).

**2.** Applying these principles, this Court has repeatedly refused to construe ambiguous statutes as having extraterritorial application. The critical inquiry in each case was not the identity of the defendant, but the location where the alleged misconduct occurred.

Just two Terms ago, the Court held that Section 10(b) of the Exchange Act applied only to "transactions in securities listed on domestic exchanges, and domestic transactions in other securities," and thus did not extend to claims of securities fraud brought by Australians who purchased those securities from an Australian bank. *Morrison*, 130 S.Ct. at 2884-85. Similarly, in *Aramco*, the Court concluded that Title VII should not be construed to reach claims against an American corporation for alleged discrimination that occurred in Saudi Arabia. *Aramco*, 499 U.S. at 247-49. And in *New York Central Railroad v. Chisholm*, 268 U.S. 29 (1925), the Court held that a railroad worker who was injured in Canada, just 30 miles from the U.S.

border, could not bring a claim for benefits under the Federal Employers Liability Act ("FELA") because the statute "contains no words which definitively disclose an intention to give it extraterritorial effect." *Id.* at 31; *see also Hoffmann-La Roche,* 542 U.S. at 164-72 (holding that the Sherman Act does not apply to anticompetitive conduct by foreign companies that affects only foreign purchasers); *McCulloch v. Sociedad Nacional de Honduras,* 372 U.S. 10, 20-21 (1963) (finding "no basis for a construction which would exert United States jurisdiction over and apply its laws to the internal management and affairs of the vessels here flying the Honduran flag").

The fact that a statute makes some boilerplate reference to "foreign commerce" or "aliens" is insufficient to demonstrate that Congress intended it to apply to *actions* or *conduct* that occurred in a foreign country. For example, the FELA applies to common carriers engaged in "interstate or foreign commerce," 45 U.S.C. § 51, yet this Court held in *Chisholm* that the statute does not reach railroad accidents that actually *occurred* in Canada. *See* 268 U.S. at 31. The National Labor Relations Act also contains broad language that refers to "foreign" commerce, 29 U.S.C. § 152(6), but the Court concluded that this language was insufficiently "specific" to rebut the presumption against extraterritorial application of federal statutes. *McCulloch,* 372 U.S. at 19; *see also Hoffmann-La Roche,* 542 U.S. at 164-65 (holding that the Sherman Act does not apply to conduct that caused "independent foreign harm," even if there is some effect on domestic purchasers).

When Congress *does* intend for a statute to apply extraterritorially, it uses unmistakably clear language. For example, the Foreign Corrupt Practices Act prohibits foreign companies listed on an American stock exchange from "corruptly do [ing] any act *outside the United States* in furtherance" of the bribery of a foreign official. 15 U.S.C. § 78dd-2(i)(l) (emphasis added). Similarly, the Torture Victim Protection Act ("TVPA") grants jurisdiction over claims for torture and extrajudicial killing that were committed "under actual or apparent authority, or color of law, of any foreign nation." P.L. 102-256, § 2(a) (1992), *codified at* 28 U.S.C. § 1350, note. These statutes show that Congress chooses its words carefully when it intends for a statute to reach conduct that occurred within a foreign nation.

### B. Nothing in the Text or Purpose of the ATS Suggests that Congress Intended the Statute to Apply to Alleged Torts that Occurred Abroad

**1.** The ATS provides that "[t]he district courts shall have original jurisdiction of any civil action by an alien for a tort only, committed in violation of the law of nations or a treaty of the United States." 28 U.S.C. § 1350. Nothing in that rather cryptic 33-word sentence supports—much less *clearly* supports—extending the statute to alleged torts that occurred wholly within the borders of a foreign nation.

The word "alien" does not signal Congress' intent to apply the statute extraterritorially. *See Aramco,* 499 U.S. at 254-55 (holding that Title VII did not apply extraterritorially even though aliens were "included in the statute's definition of employee"). Congress may have chosen the word "alien" in order to *require* that an ATS plaintiff have a nexus to the United States. *See* Black's Law Dictionary (9th ed. 2009) (defining "alien" as "[a] person who resides *within the borders of a country* but is not a citizen or subject of that country" (emphasis added)). Similarly, the ATS' reference to a "violation of the law of nations" defines the types of claims that those aliens may bring. But since the law of nations protects aliens in this country, that phrase does not remotely suggest that aliens may seek relief in U.S. courts for alleged wrongs that occurred in a foreign country halfway around the world.

The history of the ATS reveals no "indication of a congressional purpose to extend its coverage," *Aramco,* 499 U.S. at 248, to extraterritorial conduct. To the contrary, the First Congress enacted the ATS in response to two highly publicized torts against foreign ministers that were committed *on U.S. soil.* In the "Marbois Affair" of 1784, the Secretary of the French Legion was assaulted on a street in Philadelphia. *See Sosa,* 542 U.S. at 716-17. Three years later, a constable entered the Dutch ambassador's home in New York City and arrested one of his servants. *Id.; see also Doe VIII,* 654 F.3d at 77 (Kavanaugh, J., dissenting). Both of these domestic incidents violated international law norms regarding the rights of ambassadors, and generated significant diplomatic friction with France and the Netherlands. *Id.* Yet, under the Articles of Confederation, the federal government "lacked authority to remedy or prevent violations of the law of nations." *Id.* at 76.

To address this problem, the Framers vested the Supreme Court with original jurisdiction over "all Cases affecting Ambassadors, other public ministers and Consuls." U.S. Const., art. III, § 2. The First Congress, in turn, enacted the ATS as part of the Judiciary Act of 1789 in order to ensure appropriate redress for aliens injured *in the United States* in violation of international law. As this Court has explained, "Congress intended the ATS to furnish jurisdiction for a relatively modest set of actions alleging violations of the law of nations." *Sosa,* 542 U.S. at 720. In enacting the ATS, "offenses against ambassadors" were "uppermost in the legislative mind." *Id.*

There is no indication whatsoever that Congress was concerned about torts that occurred on foreign soil. Indeed, in an opinion letter issued in 1795, Attorney General William Bradford noted that, insofar as "the transactions complained of originated or took place in a foreign country, they are not within the cognizance of our courts; nor can the actors be legally prosecuted or punished for them by the United States." 1 Op. Att'y Gen. 57, 58 (1795). The problem that led to the enactment of the ATS "was not that some faraway wrongdoer might violate the law of nations in some other country, but that violations had occurred and would occur within the United States that could, if unremedied, cause diplomatic or military hostility by other nations." *Sarei v. Rio Tinto,* — F.3d —, 2011 WL 5041927, at *55 (9th Cir. 2011) (Kleinfeld, J., dissenting). In sum, "[i]t would be very odd to think that the Congress of 1789 wanted to create a federal tort cause of action enforceable in U.S. court for, say, a Frenchman injured in London." *Doe VIII,* 654 F.3d at 77 (Kavanaugh, J., dissenting).

The history of the ATS shows some intent to provide a remedy for victims of piracy. *See Sosa,* 542 U.S. at 715, 720. That context is *sui generis,* however, because it involves offenses that—by definition—do not occur within the borders of *any* nation. On the high seas, "all nations have a common right, and exercise a common sovereignty." *The Apollon,* 22 U.S. at 371. Thus, the ATS "quite sensibly may be interpreted to extend to conduct on the high seas but not to conduct in foreign countries." *Doe VIII,* 654 F.3d at 79 (Kavanaugh, J., dissenting). Attorney General Bradford recognized this distinction in his 1795 opinion letter, noting that "crimes committed on the high seas *are* within the jurisdiction of the district and circuit courts of the United States," but acts that "took place in a foreign country" are not. 1 Op. Att'y Gen. at 58.

**2.** The D.C. Circuit and Ninth Circuit have each held, in deeply divided decisions, that the ATS does, in fact, apply to alleged torts that occurred in a foreign nation. *See Sarei,* 2011 WL 5041927, at *3-*5 (holding that the ATS "is not limited to conduct occurring within the United States or to conduct committed by United States citizens"); *Doe VIII,* 654 F.3d at 20-28. Neither decision is persuasive.

In *Sarei,* the Ninth Circuit found that the ATS contained the requisite indicia of extraterritorial application based simply on its references to "aliens" and the "law of nations." 2011 WL 5041927 at *4. That is not a faithful reading of *Morrison* or a faithful application of the presumption against extraterritorial effect. As explained above, the history of the ATS confirms that Congress intended to provide a remedy for torts against aliens that occurred *in the United States.* The reference to the "law of nations" simply defines the legal standards under which those claims will be evaluated.

The D.C. Circuit and the Ninth Circuit also concluded that the ATS must have extraterritorial application because "Congress expressly intended to include claims of piracy within the ambit of the [statute]." *Sarei,* 2011 WL 5041927, at *3-*4; *see Doe VIII,* 654 F.3d at 21-22. But, as noted above, the piracy context is unique. Providing a remedy for universally condemned conduct on the high seas, like providing a remedy for diplomatic affronts occurring here, eases diplomatic relations. Extending the statute further to foreign soil is categorically different and creates, rather than eases, such tensions. *See Doe VIII,* 654 F.3d at 79 (Kavanaugh, J., dissenting).

Finally, the D.C. Circuit held that, in applying the presumption against extraterritoriality, "the calculus can change where a U.S. citizen is a cause of the harm." *Id.* at 27. This Court, however, has never drawn such a distinction. To the contrary, this Court applied the presumption with full force in *Morrison, Aramco,* and *Chisholm,* even though U.S. citizens or corporations were defendants in each of those cases. *See Morrison,* 130 S.Ct. at 2875 (defendants included executives of a U.S. mortgage servicing company); *Aramco,* 499 U.S. at 247 (defendants were "two Delaware corporations"); *Chisholm,* 268 U.S. at 30 (defendant was "the New York Central Railroad").

* * *

Nothing in the text, purpose, or history of the ATS comes close to rebutting the well-established presumption against extraterritorial application of federal statutes. The ATS—which was carefully crafted to provide a remedy for aliens injured on U.S. soil or the high seas—has no application to alleged injuries suffered by foreign citizens that occurred in a foreign nation as a result of a foreign government's conduct.

### C. Extraterritorial Application of the ATS Contravenes International Law

The presumption against extraterritoriality is buttressed by the complementary principle that statutes should not be interpreted to regulate foreign persons or conduct if their prescriptions would conflict with principles of international law. *Spector v. Norwegian Cruise Line,* 545 U.S. 119, 143 (2005) (Ginsburg and Breyer, JJ., concurring); *Hartford Fire Ins. v. California,* 509 U.S. 764, 815 (1993) (Scalia, O'Connor, Kennedy, and Thomas, JJ., dissenting) (applying this doctrine to jurisdictional limits). The exercise of jurisdiction in this case would violate international law.

* * *

## *III. PLAINTIFFS CANNOT STATE A CLAIM UNDER THE ATS FOR AIDING AND ABETTING LIABILITY*

This Court should also affirm the judgment below on the alternative basis that the ATS does not support a cause of action for aiding and abetting. At a minimum, the Court should hold that, in order to recover under an aiding and abetting theory, an ATS plaintiff must show that the defendant acted with a specific *purpose* to bring about the abuse of human rights.

Aiding and abetting liability is the other key driver of the diplomatic tension caused by extravagant extensions of the ATS by lower courts. The ability to call into question the conduct of foreign governments and foreign officials immune from direct suit by the simple expedient of alleging corporate agents have aided and abetted the foreign nation's human rights violation is highly attractive to those interested in seeking financial recovery or in seeking to make a point about the conduct of foreign nations.

### A. The ATS Does Not Provide for Aiding and Abetting Liability

The creation of civil aiding and abetting liability is a legislative act separate and apart from the recognition of a cause of action against the primary actor. While Congress has enacted a general aiding and abetting statute applicable to all federal *criminal* offenses, *see* 2 U.S.C. § 2, it has not enacted any comparable provision for civil aiding and abetting liability. That omission is hardly surprising. In the criminal context, prosecutorial discretion can help divide the sheep from the goats. But there are no comparable checks on private litigants' ability to bring civil aiding and abetting claims. *See Sosa,* 542 U.S. at 727 (judicial caution required because a private cause of action under the ATS "permit[s] enforcement without the check imposed by prosecutorial discretion"); *Stoneridge Inv. Partners v. Scientific-Atlanta,* 552 U.S. 148, 158 (2008) (noting that, in the Private Securities Litigation Reform Act of 1995, 15 U.S.C. § 78t(e), Congress "directed prosecution of aiders and abettors by the SEC," but did not provide for private civil liability). To the contrary, in the civil context, considerations of who can pay or who is immune can overwhelm considerations of whether the degree of assistance merits punishment.

This Court accordingly has held that "when Congress enacts a statute under which a person may sue and recover damages from a private defendant for the defendant's violation of some statutory norm, there is no general presumption that the plaintiff may also sue aiders and abettors." *Central Bank of Denver v. First Interstate Bank of Denver,* 511 U.S. 164, 182 (1994); *see also id.* (noting that "Congress . . . has taken a statute-by-statute approach to civil aiding and abetting liability"). Because Congress has been "quite explicit in imposing civil aiding and abetting liability"—and because any recognition of civil aiding and abetting liability is a "vast expansion of federal law"—courts may not recognize an aiding and abetting cause of action in the absence of "congressional direction to do so." *Id.* at 183. That rule applies with even greater force where, as here, the expansion of civil liability would raise significant "risks of adverse foreign policy consequences." *Sosa,* 542 U.S. at 728.

The ATS' sparse text includes no "congressional direction" to federal courts to recognize civil aiding and abetting liability. As with the extraterritorial application of the statute, that should be the end of the matter. *See, e.g., Freeman v. DirecTV,* 457 F.3d 1001, 1004-05 (9th Cir. 2006) (rejecting civil aiding and abetting liability under the Electronic Communications Privacy Act because the statute applied only to a "person or entity providing an electronic communication service," and did not mention secondary liability). Congress knows how to provide for civil aiding and abetting liability, but simply did not do so in the ATS.

The Second Circuit and D.C. Circuit nonetheless concluded that plaintiffs can bring a civil aiding and abetting claim under the ATS. *See Doe VIII,* 654 F.3d at 28-32; *Khulumani,* 504 F.3d 254. In so holding, both courts relied exclusively on purported norms of international law regarding *criminal* aiding and abetting liability. For example, the courts relied on principles drawn from the Nuremberg war crimes tribunals, the International Criminal Tribunal for the Former Yugoslavia, the International Criminal Tribunal for Rwanda, and the International Criminal Court. *See Doe VIII,* 654 F.3d at 30-32; *Khulumani,* 504 F.3d at 270-79 (Katzmann, J., concurring). As explained above, however, this Court has drawn a bright-line distinction between criminal and civil aiding and abetting liability, and has made clear that the existence of criminal liability does not support creation of a civil cause of action. *See Central Bank,* 511 U.S. at 182.

Judge Hall also suggested that there was "no bar" to aiding and abetting liability under the ATS because there was "inconclusive evidence of Congress' intent to include or exclude aiding and abetting liability." *Khulumani,* 504 F.3d at 288 n.5 (Hall, J., concurring). But fully accepting Judge Hall's premise, the opposite conclusion follows. Under *Central Bank,* if the evidence of congressional intent is "inconclusive," the statute must be construed as excluding, not including, civil aiding and abetting liability.

## B. At a Minimum, Plaintiffs Must Plead that the Defendant Acted with the Purpose of Violating International Law

Even if the Court concludes that the ATS supports a cause of action for civil aiding and abetting liability, the Court should make clear that "the *mens rea* standard for aiding and abetting liability in ATS actions is *purpose* rather than knowledge alone." *Presbyterian Church of Sudan v. Talisman Energy*, 582 F.3d 244, 259 (2d Cir. 2009) (emphasis added); *but see Doe VIII*, 654 F.3d at 39 (rejecting the Second Circuit's "purpose" standard in favor of a more-lenient "knowledge" standard).

* * *

## EXAMPLE 16

**Authors** Laurence H. Tribe and Jonathan Massey
**Case** *Grutter v. Bollinger*, 539 U.S. 306 (2003).

## INTEREST OF AMICI CURIAE

Harvard University, Brown University, the University of Chicago, Dartmouth College, Duke University, the University of Pennsylvania, Princeton University, Yale University respectfully submit this brief amici curiae in support of respondents. For the last two-and-a-half decades, highly selective institutions have relied on the approval by five Justices of the favorable consideration of race and ethnicity in the admissions process in *Regents of the University of California v. Bakke*, 438 U.S. 265 (1978). *See id.* at 320 (opinion of the Court per Powell, J.); *id.* at 328 (opinion of Brennan, J., joined by White, Marshall, and Blackmun, J.J., concurring in the judgment in part and dissenting in part) (joining in Part V-C of Justice Powell's opinion). In *Bakke*, a number of private universities had filed a brief stressing the importance of admissions programs that treat "an applicant's membership in a minority racial group as a favorable factor in the consideration of his application." Brief of Columbia Univ. et al. as Amici Curiae, No. 76-811, at 4. Under this model, amici and other highly selective educational institutions consider an academically qualified student's race or ethnicity as one among many factors in a carefully designed, competitive admissions process that views each applicant as an individual and weighs the capacity of each to contribute to the class as a whole.

The 25 years since *Bakke* have seen extensive efforts by amici and other selective universities to encourage minority applications and expand minority admissions. The principle underlying *Bakke* has become the basis of well-settled reliance not only by amici, but also by students, alumni, high schools, and businesses. To abandon *Bakke* now would trigger wrenching disruption.

Amici's experience during the quarter century since *Bakke* has confirmed the wisdom of that decision. Amici's admissions policies have served compelling pedagogical interests by contributing to a diverse and inclusive educational experience, teaching students to view issues from multiple perspectives, and helping to break down prejudices and stereotypical assumptions. The policies prepare students to work productively in a multiracial environment after they graduate, and the policies meet the demands of business and the professions by preparing a generation of public and private leaders for an increasingly pluralistic national and global economy.

To be sure, the admissions process must not be used to separate, subordinate, or stigmatize students, or to exclude any student from any place in an entering class on account of that student's race. But a prohibition on such illegitimate practices does not justify jettisoning the genius of federalism or replacing the benefits of competition, experimentation, and heterogeneity with the dead hand of a stifling uniformity. So long as they do not employ these illegitimate practices, different universities should be free to craft their own distinctive approaches. Such a course would be especially appropriate if there were any uncertainty or ambiguity about the best means for promoting racial diversity. It is vital that the Constitution be understood to protect—not to eviscerate—the capacity of universities thoughtfully to determine how to fulfill their profound responsibility: educating a diverse array of talented students to reason rigorously, to bridge differences both real and imagined, and to emerge as effective citizens and leaders in a multiracial society.

Because Title VI of the Civil Rights Act of 1964 forbids institutions that receive federal funds from engaging in racial "discrimination," the ability of private colleges and universities to exercise their institutional competence could well be dramatically compromised by any new limits this Court might place on state university admissions criteria or procedures. Accordingly, amici urge this Court to interpret the Constitution and federal statutes to leave amici and other selective educational institutions with latitude to take race and ethnicity into account as positive factors in their individualized admissions processes.

## SUMMARY OF ARGUMENT

Academically selective universities have a compelling interest in ensuring that their student bodies incorporate the experiences and talents of the wide spectrum of racial and ethnic groups that make up our society. Amici should be free to compose a class that brings together many different kinds of students; that includes robust representation of students from different races and ethnicities; and that prepares graduates to work successfully in a diverse nation. Indeed, highly selective universities have long defined as one of their central missions the training of the nation's business, government, academic, and professional leaders. By creating a broadly diverse class, amici's admissions policies help to assure that their graduates are well prepared to succeed in an increasingly complex and multiracial society. The policies also make certain that no racial or ethnic group is excluded from that vital process. Nor have amici been educating students to meet a merely imagined need. Every major profession in America has made known a desire for diversity within its ranks. Businesses demand that the graduates of highly selective universities both be diverse and be prepared to work with colleagues from different backgrounds.

There is widespread agreement on these fundamental principles. Thus, even while opposing the particular programs in these cases, the United States recognizes that universities have an important—what it calls "paramount" (*U.S. Grutter* Br. 16)—interest in attracting students from a wide range of backgrounds, explicitly endorsing the "laudable goals of educational openness and diversity." *U.S. Gratz* Br. 16. The United States accepts that it is entirely legitimate for universities to concern themselves with "ensur[ing] that [they] are open to all individuals and that student bodies are educationally diverse and broadly representative of the public." *Id.* at 17. In particular, the United States acknowledges that "universities may adopt admissions policies that seek to promote experiential, geographical, political, or economic diversity. . . ." *U.S. Grutter* Br. 10.

The United States, to be sure, does not expressly include "racial diversity" within its general endorsement. But that reticence cannot reflect any sound limitation on the reach of the "diversity" that is relevant in these cases. It would be a strange, almost otherworldly, version of diversity that recognized the importance of all kinds of differences except racial ones. Certainly, American businesses, the professions, and the remaining elements of our society consider racial diversity to be of central importance. This Court should adhere to the principle of *Bakke*, which has been inextricably woven into the American social fabric over the past quarter century.

None of us favors a return to de facto segregation, or anything like it, in our leading universities. The principal issue in this case is the means by which racial and ethnic diversity should be achieved. This Court should respect the institutional competence and academic freedom of amici and of other highly selective universities, public and private, regarding the most appropriate means to achieve these agreed-upon ends. Rather than imposing a unitary, top-down model of how to be race-conscious enough without being too race-conscious, the Court should preserve the flexibility of universities to pursue carefully calibrated admissions policies designed to promote student diversity and the vital educational benefits that flow from it.

It is instructive to contrast the minority broadcast licensing preferences at issue in *Metro Broadcasting, Inc. v. FCC*, 497 U.S. 547 (1990). Those preferences necessarily depended for their success on the assumption that differences in the race of station owners would lead to differences in speech; otherwise, the programming at issue would have been unchanged. But the purposes of amici's admissions policies are served whether the views held by individual minority students, or by minority students on average, turn out to be very different or virtually indistinguishable from those of other students. The policies contemplate simply that being of a particular race, especially a race subject to historical and continuing prejudices, entails experiences that people of other races have not had and ought to understand better. These differences will vary from individual to individual, thus resulting in substantial differences within racial groups as well. Far from reflecting and perpetuating stereotypes, amici's admissions policies are consciously designed to dissolve them.

The critics of Michigan's admissions programs insist that mechanistic approaches—such as guaranteed admission for a specified percentile of high school graduates (as in California, Florida, and Texas)—or softer "race-neutral" proxies (like economic disadvantage) can be deliberately adjusted to replicate the racial and ethnic mix that explicit consideration of race in the admissions process would have achieved. According to the critics, the Constitution forbids overt consideration of race or ethnicity, even as part of a highly individualized admissions process. Instead, the university must be relegated to a purportedly "race-blind" approach—whose very aim, however, is to achieve the same diverse racial and ethnic mix.

Petitioners' proposed alternatives would be infeasible and ineffective. Although petitioners suggest that universities should consider factors like economic circumstances and personal hardships, the truth is that those factors are already taken into account in the typical selective admissions process. Petitioners' proposals for guaranteed admissions plans for the top GPA-achievers among the applicant pool are unworkable for relatively small private universities, which simply cannot promise to admit the top ten percent (or even the top one percent) of graduating high school seniors. Nor could graduate schools, with fewer available spaces and even more selective criteria, feasibly operate under such formulas.

Petitioners' proposals would also compromise the quality of student populations at selective universities. Thus, even if a policy of guaranteed admission for students graduating in a specified percentile of their high school class succeeded in admitting a certain number of minority students, it would likely compel the admission of so many other, non-minority applicants as to eliminate available spaces in the college class for those with unusual backgrounds, experiences, and other talents to contribute. Such alternatives are therefore fundamentally incompatible with the commitment to consider each applicant on his or her individual merit, taking into account all factors, not just test scores or class rank, that would militate for or against admission to a selective university. Whatever strict scrutiny properly requires, it should not force universities to achieve one vital interest (racial diversity) to the exclusion of another (treatment of students as individuals) and thereby compromise the constitutional imperative of academic freedom.

Nor should strict scrutiny be distorted to require amici to adopt disingenuous admissions policies—policies that would seek to accomplish with a wink and a nod the very diversity that petitioners contend amici are forbidden to achieve directly. Far more consistent with our constitutional traditions is an application of strict scrutiny that honors candor and transparency, that respects individualized evaluation, that recognizes the institutional competence of our nation's many and diverse educational institutions in framing their own learning strategies, and that can, as this Court has put it, distinguish between a "No Trespassing sign" and a "welcome mat." *Adarand Constructors, Inc. v. Pena*, 515 U.S. 200, 229 (1995). Such an application of strict scrutiny would regard the asserted ability of alternative methods to approximate the racial diversity that a sensibly designed program of race-based affirmative action can achieve not as proof that such a program should be struck down but as an inadvertent concession that the program is indeed constitutionally justified. Just as imitation is at times the sincerest form of flattery, so in this context petitioners' argument helps establish the breadth of the fundamental consensus that seeking a racially diverse student body, and attempting to graduate a class of future leaders able to operate effectively within a diverse and pluralistic society, represent neither "reverse discrimination" nor the patronizing use of race to perpetuate stereotypes of inferiority but simply educational measures within the competence and familiar domain of American universities.

Because petitioners' constitutional challenges to the admissions policies in both cases ignore these basic lessons and are deficient as a matter of law, the judgments of the court of appeals in No. 02-241 and of the district court in No. 02-516 should be affirmed.

## ARGUMENT

### *I. CONSIDERATION OF RACE AND ETHNICITY IN AN INDIVIDUALIZED ADMISSIONS PROCESS SERVES COMPELLING INTERESTS.*

### A. There Is a Broad Consensus on the Important Educational Benefits of Diversity.

It is appropriate to begin with the substantial common ground in this case: the United States acknowledges that "[e]nsuring that public institutions are open and available to all segments of American society, including people of all races and ethnicities, represents a paramount government objective." *U.S. Grutter* Br. 16 (emphasis added). Indeed, almost twenty-five years ago, this Court held that a university "has a substantial interest that legitimately may be served by a properly devised admissions program involving the competitive consideration of race and ethnic origin." *Regents of Univ. of Cal. v. Bakke*, 438 U.S. 265, 320 (1978) (Part V-C, opinion of Powell, J.); *see id.* at 272 (Brennan, White, Marshall, Blackmun, J.J., joining Part V-C); *see also Wygant v. Jackson Bd. of Educ.*, 476 U.S. 276, 286, 289 n.* (1986) (O'Connor, J., concurring in part and concurring in the judgment) (*Bakke* recognized the "compelling" nature of "a state interest in the promotion of racial diversity . . . in the context of higher education").

Tellingly, the United States does not ask this Court to overturn *Bakke. U.S. Grutter* Br. 15 n.4. In fact, the United States maintains that "this case requires this Court to break no new ground." *Id.* at 12. The best way to achieve that objective is to adhere to the core principle of *Bakke*. Since that decision, universities across the country have operated on the well-founded belief that they are free to give favorable consideration to race and ethnicity as part of their individualized admissions programs. To reverse course now, after a quarter century of reliance—to repudiate the importance of seeking racial inclusiveness through a carefully designed program consistent with *Bakke*—would be to upset deeply grounded expectations in a way utterly contrary to the doctrine of stare decisis. *See Dickerson v. United States*, 530 U.S. 428, 442-44 (2000); *Planned Parenthood v. Casey*, 505 U.S. 833, 861-69 (1992).

Amici's experience in the two-and-a-half decades since 1978 confirms the wisdom of *Bakke*'s premise. Selective universities across the country have built their communities mindful of the pedagogical value of multiracial diversity in educational programs. Students are both recipients and providers of the learning that takes place at universities, and amici thus have a vital interest in what students bring to the task of educating each other. In a recent survey, for example, 69 percent of Harvard Law School students and 73.5 percent of Michigan Law School students reported that having "students of different races and ethnicities" was a "clearly positive element of their educational experience." Diversity helps students confront perspectives other than their own and thus to think more rigorously and imaginatively; it helps students learn to relate better to people from different backgrounds; it helps students become better citizens. The educational benefits of student diversity include the discovery that there is a broad range of viewpoint and experience within any given minority community—as well as learning that certain imagined differences at times turn out to be only skin deep.

It is surely fitting for universities to undertake to prepare their students to live and work in a global economy within a multiracial world. The challenges of contemporary life demand that students acquire not just traditional forms of knowledge regarding science and the arts, but also techniques of bridging differences in perspective and in personal experience. Amici have concluded, as a matter of reasoned educational judgment, that their admissions policies are well adapted to such learning. This Court has no reason to distrust that judgment or to impose a set of uniform rules on the university admissions processes of the fifty states and of countless private institutions.

Amici have adopted admissions programs seeking racial and ethnic diversity as a natural part of a long and expanding policy of inclusion. Harvard, for example, has been pursuing the idea of student diversity for a period that dates to the nineteenth century. *See* Neil Rudenstine, *The President's Report 1993-1995: Diversity and Learning* 3-13. In its early stages, the concept of diversity was rooted primarily in geography. Thus, George Washington's will bequeathed funds for a national university so that "the youth of fortune and talents from all parts" might, "by associating with each other," be "enabled to free themselves in a proper degree" from "local prejudices and habitual jealousies."

Ultimately, amici embraced a broader vision of diversity. Thus, President Charles Eliot declared that students need to "feel that very wholesome influence which comes from observation of and contact with larger numbers . . . from different nations, States, schools, families, sects, parties, and conditions of life." The President's Report 1993-1995 at 10. As Eliot saw it, Harvard students should be children of the "rich and poor," the "educated and uneducated," rather than representing just one segment of American society. *Id.* Throughout the twentieth century, therefore, the University increasingly accepted students from public, rather than private, schools, and became increasingly, and then fully, coeducational. It also undertook to expand the enrollment of students from different ethnic groups, primarily of European origin, that had previously been represented at Harvard, if at all, in only small numbers. *Id.* at 24-25.

It is against this historical backdrop that selective universities ultimately developed their admissions policies with respect to African-Americans and other minority groups that have been subject to targeted exclusion from many of the benefits of American life. Far from adopting a theory for the convenience of the moment, amici simply recognized, as they had in the past, that students from these minority groups would bring valuable new experiences to the university community.

### B. Consideration of Race and Ethnicity Grows Naturally Out of the Needs of the Professions and of American Business.

Amici have a special interest in this pair of cases stemming from their distinctive responsibility, since colonial times, to educate leaders in all walks of life. As the United States has explained, "[a] university degree opens the doors to the finest jobs and top professional schools, and a professional degree, in turn, makes it possible to practice law, medicine and other professions." *U.S. Grutter* Br. 16. Highly selective academic institutions are keenly aware of a responsibility to train not only doctors, lawyers, and accountants, but also corporate, government, social, and academic leaders.

Every major profession in this country has sought greater diversity within its ranks. Businesses have demanded more minority managers and executives, as well as non-minorities who can work well with colleagues from diverse backgrounds. Leading corporations, business groups, professional organizations, and executives have repeatedly called for consideration of race and ethnicity in university admissions. In adopting their admissions policies, universities are responding to "the clearly articulated needs of business and the professions for a healthier mix of well-educated leaders and practitioners from varied racial and ethnic backgrounds. . . . [B]usinesses depend heavily on their ability to recruit broadly trained individuals from many racial backgrounds who are able to perform at the highest level in settings that are themselves increasingly diverse."

Commentators across the political spectrum have recognized and applauded the fact that "[t]he level of affirmative action in the United States in the private sector on grounds of race goes far beyond what is needed to keep firms out of hot water. It represents a sustained and consistent effort to change the dominant practices in the United States." Richard A. Epstein, *A Rational Basis for Affirmative Action: A Shaky But Classical Liberal Defense*, 100 MICH. L. REV. 2036, 2053 (2002). That is why there is broad support in the business community for consideration of race in university admissions. Holman W. Jenkins, Jr., *Why the Michigan Case Matters to Business*, WALL STREET JOURNAL, Jan. 22, 2003, at A15 (noting the "dozens of companies" filing briefs in support of Michigan in this case).

Empirical data have confirmed the value of amici's admissions programs in serving this interest. In a study of 45,000 students who matriculated in 1976 and 1989, Derek Bok, former president of Harvard, and William G. Bowen, former president of Princeton, have shown that minority students admitted under these programs were highly successful in completing rigorous academic programs, securing good jobs, and contributing to community life.

As this Court has noted, "[t]he Nation's future depends upon leaders trained through wide exposure to that robust exchange of ideas which discovers truth 'out of a multitude of tongues, [rather] than through any kind of authoritative selection.'" *Keyishian v. Board of Regents*, 385 U.S. 589, 603 (1967) (quoting *United States v. Associated Press*, 52 F. Supp. 362, 372 (D.D.C. 1943)). Amici's admissions programs are well adapted to achieving this paramount interest.

### C. The Interests in Diversity and Inclusion That Support Well-Designed Programs of Race-Specific Affirmative Action in University Admissions Do Not Reflect Impermissible Stereotyping.

The interests asserted by amici do not rest on a stereotypical assumption that all members of the same race have had the same or similar experiences, much less that they have the same fixed set of perceptions or beliefs. The interest in ensuring that minorities are not excluded from the professions and positions of future leadership does not hinge at all on any prediction that they will have particular views or philosophies, let alone that such views are monolithic.

Nor do the pedagogical benefits of diversity depend on stereotypical assumptions. Instead, those benefits rest upon a quite different expectation: that minority students will have had formative experiences that they would not have had as identically situated students of a different race. In the context of higher education, recognition of this real-world difference should be no more impermissible than recognition that gender plays a role, one that differs from individual to individual, in how young men and women grow up.

What those experiences are, and how each student has reacted to them, is part of what amici hope students will explore. Both minority and non-minority students will have the opportunity to reconsider preconceptions and prejudices in the course of obtaining a university education in a diverse environment. Indeed, one of the valuable lessons for non-minorities to discover is that members of a minority group do not all share the same views and opinions; far from it. Thus, amici's admissions policies are central elements in their strategy for breaking down racial and ethnic stereotypes. Openness to differing life experiences and perspectives, and the capacity to rethink what has been previously thought, are critical objectives of educational diversity in the first place.

The assumptions underlying the FCC station-ownership program in *Metro Broadcasting, Inc. v. FCC*, 497 U.S. 547 (1990), were very different. As devised, that program depended for its very existence on a conclusive presumption that minority station owners would make different broadcast programming choices from those that non-minority owners would make. *See id.* at 566-71. The FCC program also assumed that the views of minority owners about desirable programming would remain static—that is, remain distinctly "minority" views—during the entire period of ownership. Indeed, the FCC's presumption about minority tendencies was so rigid that it expected minority station owners, by reason of their race alone, to resist the market forces that had shaped broadcast programming up to that point. *See id.* at 626 (O'Connor, J., dissenting). Nothing approaching that sort of presumption is present in amici's admissions programs.

### D. Advancing the Interests in Diversity and Inclusion Is Not Tantamount to Attempting to Remedy Societal Discrimination.

Petitioners seek to equate the promotion of educational diversity with the pursuit of remedies for "societal discrimination," [*U.S.*] *Grutter* Br. 40; [*U.S.*] *Gratz* Br. 33, a mission this Court has described as too "amorphous" to support a number of race-based measures. *See Adarand Constructors*, 515 U.S. at 220; *City of Richmond v. J.A. Croson Co.*, 488 U.S. 469, 497-99 (1989) (plurality opinion); *Wygant*, 476 U.S. at 267 (plurality opinion). That the two goals are distinct is shown by the fact that Justice Powell rejected the interest in remedying societal discrimination in both *Bakke* and *Wygant*, but said in *Bakke* that he found educational diversity to be a compelling justification for considering race in university admissions. *See* 438 U.S. at 314. It has been suggested that the remedial interest is backward-looking and may at times even be punitive, while the educational diversity interest is forward-looking and inclusive. *See* Kathleen M. Sullivan, The Supreme Court, 1985 Term—Comment: *Sins of Discrimination: Last Term's Affirmative Action Cases*, 100 HARV. L. REV. 78 (1986). And, most important, the educational diversity interest is contextually limited by its link to the teaching mission of the university in a way that an interest in remedying societal discrimination could never be.

## *II. STRICT SCRUTINY IS SATISFIED BY PROPERLY DESIGNED UNIVERSITY ADMISSIONS POLICIES THAT CONSIDER RACE AND ETHNICITY.*

Strict scrutiny is, of course, a two-part test. Having established a compelling reason for consideration of race in decisionmaking as part of carefully calibrated procedures, an institution must also demonstrate that its use of race is "narrowly tailored" to the identified interest. *See Adarand Constructors*, 515 U.S. at 227; *see also Metro Broadcasting*, 497 U.S. at 617 (O'Connor, J., dissenting). This test is met by properly designed university policies that take race and ethnicity into account as part of the individualized and competitive admissions process.

### A. The Distinctive Educational Role of Universities Must Be Accommodated in the Application of Strict Scrutiny.

In addressing a university's choice of a specific admissions process, this Court should accord significant respect to the variety of ways in which our nation's institutions choose to compose their student bodies. Differences over the optimal means for promoting racial diversity suggest that the proper course is to allow each university to pursue its own admissions policy within constitutional constraints that are not so tight as to suffocate all possibilities for variation.

The judicially recognized and constitutionally grounded tradition of academic freedom, and the deeply ingrained practice of deference to educators' judgments on educational matters, combine to make it especially appropriate to defer to amici's well-supported assessment that individualized consideration of race and ethnicity in the admissions process is essential for selective universities to perform their broad educational function. *See Board of Regents v. Southworth*, 529 U.S. 217, 233 (2000); *University of Pennsylvania v. EEOC*, 493 U.S. 182, 199 (1990) (noting "importance of avoiding second-guessing of legitimate academic judgments"); *Regents of the University of Michigan v. Ewing*, 474 U.S. 214, 226 n.12, 227 (1985) ("Academic freedom thrives on . . . autonomous decisionmaking by the academy itself").

This Court has previously acknowledged "the vital role in a democracy that is played by those who guide and train our youth." *Sweezy v. New Hampshire*, 354 U.S. 234, 250 (1957). Academic freedom can and should be accorded a role in supporting a degree of judicial deference, particularly with respect to questions regarding the precise fit of the interests in diversity with the universities' other choices about their mission and the availability of alternative means to serve those interests. *See Bakke*, 438 U.S. at 314 (opinion of Powell, J.). Although strict scrutiny is properly demanding, it should not be applied so as to deprive university officials of responsibly exercised discretion to define what the university shall be, "what may be taught, how it shall be taught, and who may be admitted to study." *Id.* at 312 (opinion of Powell, J.) (*quoting Sweezy*, 354 U.S. at 263 (Frankfurter, J., concurring in result).

Nor have this Court's decisions created a paradigm of "strict scrutiny" so rigid as to rule out careful consideration of context. To be sure, this Court has at times spoken as though literally all decisions that consider an individual's race—even for such laudatory purposes as combatting or offsetting the lingering effects of discrimination against racial minorities—are to be equated with the constitutional anathema of racial segregation. In reality if not always in rhetoric, however, the Court has been far more nuanced in its understanding of the many and varied uses of race, making clear that strict scrutiny does not mean that all race-conscious measures are nearly certain to be doomed. "The point of carefully examining the interest asserted by the government in support of a racial classification, and the evidence offered to show that the classification is needed, is precisely to distinguish legitimate from illegitimate uses of race in government decisionmaking." *Adarand Constructors*, 515 U.S. at 227.

Thus, in *Adarand Constructors*, this Court distinguished between uses of race that literally segregate people into different physical locations or applicant pools on the basis of their race (a "No Trespassing" sign) and uses of race that serve principally to broaden and diversify the set of those who are invited in by rounding out a multi-variabled assessment of individuals (a "welcome mat"). 515 U.S. at 229. In this pair of cases, giving favorable consideration to minority race and ethnicity in individualized admissions processes that exclude no one from any place in an entering class on account of race is the proverbial "welcome mat" that does not use race in a segregative or constitutionally offensive way.

In this regard, there is an instructive parallel between legislative redistricting and university admissions. Each activity is part of a process for the formation of groups in the operation of a pluralistic system—whether for lawmaking or for the composition of a diverse student class. Moreover, just as there is usually no way for those drawing legislative district lines to avoid knowing the race and party affiliation of the residents of the voting districts that will be created, so too there is often no way for amici to avoid learning the race and ethnicity of their applicants as part of the individualized admissions processes on which amici rely. Through alumni interviews, application essays, and campus visits, amici gain a keen appreciation for the talents and backgrounds of their prospective students. To demand that amici close their eyes to the race and ethnicity of those students—alone among their many relevant characteristics—is as unrealistic as it is unjustified.

There are basic differences, of course, between forming a new legislative district and forming an entering college or law school class. Yet the two processes have enough in common that it is notable that this Court has not merely upheld redistricting that takes conscious and deliberate account of race but has actually concluded that "[s]trict scrutiny does not apply" invariably to such redistricting. *Bush v. Vera*, 517 U.S. 952, 958 (1996); *see also Easley v. Cromartie*, 532 U.S. 235, 241 (2001); *Hunt v. Cromartie*, 526 U.S. 541, 551 (1999). In view of this approach to redistricting, it would be surprising to conclude at the same time that, whenever a university class is formed with consciousness of race, strict scrutiny not only applies but proves fatal. That no such conclusion does follow, and that the contrasts in legal doctrine are not so surprisingly stark after all, is entailed by what is special about universities as places that educate their students, and expect their students to educate each other, to take their place in a multiracial world. This mission enables universities' individualized and competitive consideration of race to satisfy strict scrutiny, while similar uses of race by most other institutions would presumably fail to pass that test.

### B. Explicit Consideration of Race and Ethnicity in an Individualized Admissions Process Is Fully Capable of Satisfying the Narrow Tailoring Requirement.

The arguments raised by petitioners and their amici are beset by intractable contradictions. On the one hand, they complain that university admissions policies have impermissible collateral effects on those displaced by supposedly less qualified minorities. On the other, they contend that supposedly race-neutral alternatives can advance the same compelling interests in producing equally diverse and racially inclusive student populations. But if petitioners are correct that the alternatives will result in essentially the same levels of minority enrollments, then the impact on displaced non-minorities will, at minimum, be the same (and may even be worse, given the imprecise and overbroad nature of petitioners' alternatives). And if petitioners are not correct, as amici's experience strongly suggests, then their alternatives will not suffice. Either way, petitioners' arguments fail.

Moreover, petitioners' mechanistic, by-the-numbers proposals would threaten the ability of selective universities to ensure non-racial diversity in their student bodies—whether in terms of musical talents, unusual personal experiences, or other kinds of contributions. These proposals are anti-meritocratic and utterly contrary to amici's individualized admissions philosophies. Under petitioners' approach, the composition of an entering class will be changed for the worse, to the detriment of every student and the educational objectives of amici.

### 1. *Petitioners' Arguments Rest on a Misunderstanding of the Admissions Process at Selective Universities.*

An understanding of amici's admissions programs makes clear why petitioners' arguments are fundamentally misguided. The purpose of a university admissions process is not simply to identify the students who, if admitted, would be likeliest to earn the highest grade-point averages. Quite apart from the impossibility of reliably making that prediction, pursuit of so narrow a goal would be unlikely to yield a student body that any sensible university would wish to enroll. While amici continue to place the highest priority on academic rigor, they have always sought to enroll a broad cross section of students who can bring a critical mix of experiences and perspectives into the university community and who can leave it well prepared to serve as future leaders of our society.

The factors considered in amici's individualized admissions programs are extraordinarily varied, wide-ranging, and notoriously difficult to quantify. Although petitioners and the United States sometimes give the impression that university admissions officers consider just test scores, class rank, and race, little could be more misleading. At Harvard College, for example, every application is read individually by at least one admissions officer and often two or more. All applicants are further considered, and any who are serious contenders for admission are discussed by a multi-member admissions subcommittee. Candidates are reviewed and discussed yet again by the entire admissions committee, consisting of approximately 30 members, often supplemented by faculty members in relevant departments. All this review and discussion is necessary precisely because the admissions process seeks to form a class that is diverse along multiple dimensions, of which race is but one—a class that is more than the sum of its individual student parts.

Admission factors begin, of course, with the core academic criteria, including not just grades and test scores but teacher recommendations and state, regional, national, and international awards. In some cases, those criteria will be all but decisive, either positively (very rarely) or negatively (more often). In the vast majority of cases, however, they are not themselves decisive, and the process continues. Admissions officials give special attention to, among others, applicants from economically and/or culturally disadvantaged backgrounds, those with unusual athletic ability, those with special artistic talents, those who would be the first in their families to attend any college, those whose parents are alumni or alumnae, and those who have overcome various identifiable hardships. The committee also extends favorable consideration to applicants who write exceptionally well, to applicants who show a special dedication to public service, and to those who demonstrate unusual promise in a wide variety of fields.

These factors have a common feature: they provide evidence that particular students—all of whom have academic records very similar to many other highly capable students—are likely to add something distinctive to the university and, post-graduation, to the larger society. The decisions about whom to admit are typically made not head-to-head but sequentially, with an eye to the composition of the overall class. Each factor becomes part of the case for a particular applicant, just as other factors increase the chances for competing applicants. No one factor, including race, is dispositive, as empirical data make clear.

By the same token, the individualized admissions process means that simply eliminating the consideration of minority race and ethnicity would not significantly increase any given non-minority student's odds of gaining admission to an academically selective university. Data from a representative sample of selective colleges and universities demonstrate that the admissions rate for white students would rise by less than two percentage points, from roughly 25 percent to 26.5 percent.

### 2. *The Interest in Racial Diversity Cannot Be Served by Race-Neutral Reliance on Factors, Such as Economic Disadvantage, That Are Already Carefully Considered.*

Petitioners argue that race-conscious admissions decisions are unnecessary because suitable attention to race-neutral factors will do just as well. The United States urges (as one solution) that universities look to such factors as special economic hardship instead of race. *See U.S. Grutter* Br. 24-25. But the decisive fact is that all of the suggested race-neutral factors, and many more besides, already enter into admissions decisions. Consideration of those factors alone does not achieve the distinctly racial diversity that amici seek in their student bodies. To accomplish that goal, admissions committees must give favorable consideration to minority race in addition to those other factors, not instead of them.

To "tweak" the race-neutral factors emphasized by petitioners—for example, by deliberately tilting individual admissions toward "hardship" students in the hope of thereby selecting a large enough increment of minority students to make up for the losses that would result from race-blind admissions—would be disingenuous at best. Such an approach would in truth be a race-based policy and not a race-neutral alternative at all. Indeed, such programs, if adopted to assure increased minority enrollment, would be based on race in a causal sense and would thus raise obvious constitutional questions of their own. *See Shaw v. Reno*, 509 U.S. 630, 643-44 (1993); *Hunter v. Underwood*, 471 U.S. 222, 228-33 (1985). And no one is well served, especially in a university setting animated by respect for truth, by preferring covert processes to those that are candid, open, and forthright.

In any event, such programs would interfere with or profoundly alter what a university is seeking to achieve, not merely serve the goal in an alternative way. A race-neutral preference for economically disadvantaged students, for example, would admit many more whites than non-whites, because of sheer demographic realities. And, of course, the university interest in admitting minority students goes well beyond just admitting minority students from disadvantaged backgrounds.

### 3. *The Interest in Racial Diversity Cannot Be Served by the Newer Alternatives Involving Non-individualized Guaranteed Admissions.*

There are related, and no less serious, problems with plans—like those in Florida, Texas, and California—that guarantee admission to students who graduate in a certain percentile of their class. Available research suggests that the impact of these plans on minority admissions is quite limited and due in significant part to lingering racial segregation in secondary schools—itself a deeply problematic state of affairs.

Moreover, these proposals would plainly be impractical for relatively small, academically selective universities. For example, even if a college were to guarantee admission only to valedictorians in high schools across the country, the program simply could not work: according to the U.S. Department of Education, there are well over 30,000 high schools in the United States. In 2002, almost 2,900 valedictorians applied to Harvard, but the number of applicants offered admission to the freshman class was only 2,066. Over 1,600 applicants scored a perfect 800 on their verbal SATs, and over 2,100 scored a perfect 800 on the math portion. Harvard College could not accept all applicants in either category and would not wish to do so.

Nor could guaranteed admissions plans feasibly operate at the graduate level, where the pools of applicants are very different and the entering classes much smaller. Applicants to graduate schools are competing for far fewer spaces, making the problems of guaranteeing admission slots all but insurmountable. Notably, while petitioners and the United States endorse these plans, they make no real effort to show how the experience of a handful of large States would be transferable to other, very different, public and private institutions.

Practicalities aside, the allocation of guaranteed places is incompatible with the long-standing policies and practices of any truly selective university. Guaranteed admission plans would deny admissions officers the critical capacity to consider each applicant as an individual on his or her overall merits in the context of the admitted group as a whole. For example, a black student with lower class standing from a rigorous urban school may well be academically superior to black students who graduate at the top of smaller and less rigorous high schools. In Texas, for example, the average SAT scores of the top 10 percent of University of Texas students dropped from 1242 in 1996 to 1211 in 2000. The percentage of the class with scores under 1000 virtually doubled. In principle, a sensibly selective admissions program should take the strongest students, including the strongest minority students, a result that can be achieved only by amici's genuinely individualized procedures.

A practice of awarding of guaranteed places would thus diminish the ability of selective universities to achieve excellence and non-racial forms of diversity. Even if a "top 10 percent" program succeeded in admitting a significant number of minority students, it would likely compel the admission of so many other "guaranteed" students that it left too few places for those with more unusual talents and experiences to contribute. Squeezing the admissions process into so Procrustean a bed would conflict with the basic approach of selective university admissions as amici understand and have long embraced it. Whatever strict scrutiny properly requires, it should not force public or private universities to serve one vital interest (racial diversity) at the expense of another (individualized selection of students) and in the process sacrifice the constitutional imperative of respecting academic freedom.

### C. Consideration of Race Does Not Make an Admissions Plan a Quota.

Properly tailored admissions programs differ from quotas in the critical sense that they do not bar any slot to any individual based on his or her race but fully preserve "individual" consideration (*Bakke*, 438 U.S. at 319-20 (opinion of Powell, J.)), consistent with traditional principles of university admissions. Although amici consider minority race and ethnicity, the impact of that consideration always depends on the qualifications of all other applicants, including those who receive consideration for being, for instance, the first in their families to attend college or for having persevered in the face of illness or after losing a parent. The consideration of race remains at all times within the bounds of the overall, individualized admissions process.

The California-Davis policy in *Bakke* was quite different. As Justice Powell made clear, *see* 438 U.S. at 315-19, the problem with the California-Davis minority admissions program was not that it sought to enroll an increased number of minority students, or even that it quantified its aspiration candidly, but that the goal of admitting a particular number of qualified minority students effectively became the tail that wagged the dog. Because California-Davis established a prescribed floor for the number of qualified minority students to be admitted, the central admissions question became not how well a particular minority applicant matched up to the overall pool of medical school applicants, but whether he or she was qualified for one of the fixed number of slots set aside for minority applicants alone. No matter how outstanding the competing applicants from those groups might have been in a given year, they still could not gain admission to any of the reserved seats unless the university first found an absence of qualified minority candidates to admit.

A properly individualized admissions program does not suffer from this "set-aside" defect. Nor does an individualized admissions process become a "quota" simply because the number of admitted minority students may not vary radically from year to year. Amici's admissions committees do not have fixed targets for any group of admitted students, and the percentages for different groups change over time. Thus, over the past four years at Harvard College, the number of admitted students whose fathers did not attend any college has ranged from 220 to 228—or from a low of 10.6% of admitted students to a high of 11.0%, or a variation of approximately 3.8%. For the same academic years, the percentage of African-American students among the admitted applicants was as low as 8.76% and as high as 9.92%—approximately a 13% variation. That said, the makeup of any given class does tend to be relatively predictable, simply because the applicant pool tends to be relatively consistent. One would expect, for example, that the number of redheaded students in the entering class would be relatively constant from year to year—but that hardly demonstrates the existence of a "redhead quota."

### D. Race-Conscious Admissions Programs Are Not Open-Ended Commitments.

Petitioners contend that consideration of race and ethnicity will create an ever-expanding precedent that can have no temporal stopping point and that will lead to claims by other groups—whether social, religious, or ideological—for "fair" representation on our university campuses. That misconstrues amici's argument. Amici are not asserting that any group, including African-Americans, has a "right" to proportionate representation either in academia or in the professions—only that action by universities to achieve substantial and meaningful inclusion, if carefully tailored, violates no right on the part of others and no constitutional or statutory commitment of our society. The decision of a university as to which minority groups deserve favorable consideration in an individualized admissions process designed to foster such diverse representation, and the weight of such consideration, are necessarily and appropriately decisions to be made as a matter of educational judgment, taking into account both the university's sense of its mission and its best estimate of the leadership needs it will address—not as a matter of conflicting "rights."

Petitioners and their amici object, finally, that race-conscious university admissions programs have no identifiable time limit. *See U.S. Grutter* Br. 32-34. We question whether this is a cognizable constitutional complaint. Although this Court has at times expressed concern about temporal indefiniteness, it has never held that measures necessary to reach an intended objective—that is, measures otherwise properly tailored to serve a compelling interest—were to be struck down simply because such measures lack a clear exit strategy or a definite "sunset" provision. *See, e.g., Burson v. Freeman*, 504 U.S. 191 (1992) (First Amendment context). The proper constitutional concern would thus seem to be whether the selected means outlast the interest they are designed to serve, not whether they go on "too long" in some abstract, undefined sense. *Cf. Eldred v. Ashcroft,* 123 S. Ct. 769 (2003) (20-year extension of copyright terms held permissible).

In any event, even if there must be an ultimate end to the consideration of race in university admissions, it is surely premature to declare that the end is upon us. We are not so far removed from the days when segregation by race in education, and race discrimination in all sorts of vital opportunities relevant to educational performance, were for many a matter of law. *Brown v. Bd. of Education*, 347 U.S. 483 (1954); *Swann v. Charlotte-Mecklenburg Bd. of Education*, 402 U.S. 1 (1971); *Hills v. Gautreaux*, 425 U.S. 284 (1976). However devoutly we might wish it were otherwise, the effects of that history cannot be expected to play themselves out within a single generation. *See* Glenn Loury, *The Anatomy of Racial Inequality* 4 (2002). Progress toward a goal does not mean that the goal has been reached.

But progress there has been. Amici have seen a sharp rise in the number of applications filed by minority students during the past few decades. At the same time, the overall credentials of minority applicants—including the raw numbers on which others place so much emphasis—have increased as well. This is so, in fact, both on an absolute basis and in comparison with other applicants.

Average SAT test scores for minority students rose roughly 130 points at a group of liberal arts colleges studied in 1976 and 1995, and approximately 150 points at a group of research universities. Test scores for non-minority students rose as well, but by much smaller increments (about 30 points at the liberal arts colleges and 70 points at the research universities). If these trends continue, the interest in a racially diverse student body might gradually become decoupled from policies that give favorable consideration to minority race and ethnicity. But hoping that day will come sooner rather than later cannot be translated into a constitutional imperative that the nation's universities act as though that day has already arrived.

# EXCERPTS FROM FEDERAL AND STATE COURT APPELLATE RULES PERTAINING TO AMICUS BRIEFS

Provided below is a compilation of excerpts from federal and state appellate rules on amicus briefs concerning the issues discussed in this book. Four caveats are given with this compilation. First, the rules are obviously subject to change. Second, not reprinted below are: any internal court procedures relating to amicus briefs or any rules that apply generally to all briefs, including amicus briefs. Third, this compilation does not attempt to identify the format requirements for amicus briefs or associated filings, such as notices of appearance, docketing statements, disclosure requirements, and the like. Last, it is always advisable to consult an appellate practitioner familiar with the particular court to ensure compliance with all applicable rules and to determine how receptive the court may be to the planned amicus brief. An excellent resource for information about all federal and state courts, including amicus practice, is the APPELLATE PRACTICE COMPENDIUM by the Council of Appellate Lawyers, published by the American Bar Association.

## *FEDERAL RULES*

### U.S. Supreme Court Rule 37

1. An amicus curiae brief that brings to the attention of the Court relevant matter not already brought to its attention by the parties may be of considerable help to the Court. An amicus curiae brief that does not serve this purpose burdens the Court, and its filing is not favored. An amicus curiae brief may be filed only by an attorney admitted to practice before this Court as provided in Rule 5.
2. (a) An amicus curiae brief submitted before the Court's consideration of a petition for a writ of certiorari, motion for leave to file a bill of complaint, jurisdictional statement, or petition for an extraordinary writ may be filed if accompanied by the

written consent of all parties, or if the Court grants leave to file under subparagraph 2(b) of this Rule. An amicus curiae brief in support of a petitioner or appellant shall be filed within 30 days after the case is placed on the docket or a response is called for by the Court, whichever is later, and that time will not be extended. An amicus curiae brief in support of a motion of a plaintiff for leave to file a bill of complaint in an original action shall be filed within 60 days after the case is placed on the docket, and that time will not be extended. An amicus curiae brief in support of a respondent, an appellee, or a defendant shall be submitted within the time allowed for filing a brief in opposition or a motion to dismiss or affirm. An amicus curiae filing a brief under this subparagraph shall ensure that the counsel of record for all parties receive notice of its intention to file an amicus curiae brief at least 10 days prior to the due date for the amicus curiae brief, unless the amicus curiae brief is filed earlier than 10 days before the due date. Only one signatory to any amicus curiae brief filed jointly by more than one amicus curiae must timely notify the parties of its intent to file that brief. The amicus curiae brief shall indicate that counsel of record received timely notice of the intent to file the brief under this Rule and shall specify whether consent was granted, and its cover shall identify the party supported. Only one signatory to an amicus curiae brief filed jointly by more than one amicus curiae must obtain consent of the parties to file that brief. A petitioner or respondent may submit to the Clerk a letter granting blanket consent to amicus curiae briefs, stating that the party consents to the filing of amicus curiae briefs in support of either or of neither party. The Clerk will note all notices of blanket consent on the docket.

(b) When a party to the case has withheld consent, a motion for leave to file an amicus curiae brief before the Court's consideration of a petition for a writ of certiorari, motion for leave to file a bill of complaint, jurisdictional statement, or petition for an extraordinary writ may be presented to the Court. The motion, prepared as required by Rule 33.1 and as one document with the brief sought to be filed, shall be submitted within the time allowed for filing an amicus curiae brief, and shall indicate the party or parties who have withheld consent and state the nature of the movant's interest. Such a motion is not favored.

3. (a) An amicus curiae brief in a case before the Court for oral argument may be filed if accompanied by the written consent of all parties, or if the Court grants leave to file under subparagraph 3(b) of this Rule. The brief shall be submitted within 7 days after the brief for the party supported is filed, or if in support of neither party, within 7 days after the time allowed for filing the petitioner's or appellant's brief. Motions to extend the time for filing an amicus curiae brief will not be entertained. The 10-day notice requirement of subparagraph 2(a) of this Rule does not apply to an amicus curiae brief in a case before the Court for oral argument. An electronic version of every amicus curiae brief in a case before the Court for oral argument shall be transmitted to the Clerk of Court and to counsel for the parties at the time the brief is filed in accordance with guidelines established by the Clerk. The electronic transmission requirement is in addition to the requirement that booklet format briefs be timely filed. The amicus curiae brief shall specify whether consent was granted, and its cover shall identify the party supported or indicate whether it suggests affirmance or reversal. The Clerk will not file a reply brief for an amicus curiae, or a brief for an amicus curiae in support of, or in opposition to, a petition for rehearing. Only one signatory to an amicus curiae brief filed jointly by more than one amicus curiae must obtain consent of the parties to file that brief. A petitioner or respondent may submit to the Clerk a letter granting blanket consent to amicus curiae briefs, stating that the party consents to the filing of amicus curiae briefs in support of either or of neither party. The Clerk will note all notices of blanket consent on the docket.

   (b) When a party to a case before the Court for oral argument has withheld consent, a motion for leave to file an amicus curiae brief may be presented to the Court. The motion, prepared as required by Rule 33.1 and as one document with the brief sought to be filed, shall be submitted within the time allowed for filing an amicus curiae brief, and shall indicate the party or parties who have withheld consent and state the nature of the movant's interest.

4. No motion for leave to file an amicus curiae brief is necessary if the brief is presented on behalf of the United States by the Solicitor General; on behalf of any agency of the United States allowed by law to appear before this Court when submitted by the agency's authorized legal representative; on behalf of a State, Commonwealth, Territory, or Possession when submitted by its Attorney General; or on behalf of a city, county, town, or similar entity when submitted by its authorized law officer.
5. A brief or motion filed under this Rule shall be accompanied by proof of service as required by Rule 29, and shall comply with the applicable provisions of Rules 21, 24, and 33.1 (except that it suffices to set out in the brief the interest of the amicus curiae, the summary of the argument, the argument, and the conclusion). A motion for leave to file may not exceed 1,500 words. A party served with the motion may file an objection thereto, stating concisely the reasons for withholding consent; the objection shall be prepared as required by Rule 33.2.
6. Except for briefs presented on behalf of amicus curiae listed in Rule 37.4, a brief filed under this Rule shall indicate whether counsel for a party authored the brief in whole or in part and whether such counsel or a party made a monetary contribution intended to fund the preparation or submission of the brief, and shall identify every person other than the amicus curiae, its members, or its counsel, who made such a monetary contribution. The disclosure shall be made in the first footnote on the first page of text.

**Federal Rule of Appellate Procedure 29**

(a) **When Permitted.** The United States or its officer or agency or a state may file an amicus-curiae brief without the consent of the parties or leave of court. Any other amicus curiae may file a brief only by leave of court or if the brief states that all parties have consented to its filing.

(b) **Motion for Leave to File.** The motion must be accompanied by the proposed brief and state:

(1) the movant's interest; and

(2) the reason why an amicus brief is desirable and why the matters asserted are relevant to the disposition of the case.

(c) **Contents and Form.** An amicus brief must comply with Rule 32. In addition to the requirements of Rule 32, the cover must identify the party or parties supported and indicate whether the brief supports affirmance or reversal. An amicus brief need not comply with Rule 28, but must include the following:

(1) if the amicus curiae is a corporation, a disclosure statement like that required of parties by Rule 26.1;

(2) a table of contents, with page references;

(3) a table of authorities—cases (alphabetically arranged), statutes and other authorities—with references to the pages of the brief where they are cited;

(4) a concise statement of the identity of the amicus curiae, its interest in the case, and the source of its authority to file;

(5) unless the amicus curiae is one listed in the first sentence of Rule 29(a), a statement that indicates whether:

(A) a party's counsel authored the brief in whole or in part;

(B) a party or party's counsel contributed money that was intended to fund preparing or submitting the brief; and

(C) a person—other than the amicus curiae, its members, or its counsel—contributed money that was intended to fund preparing or submitting the brief and, if so, identifies each such person;

(6) an argument, which may be preceded by a summary and which need not include a statement of the applicable standard of review; and

(7) a certificate of compliance, if required by Rule 32(a)(7).

(d) **Length.** Except by the court's permission, an amicus brief may be no more than one-half the maximum length authorized by these rules for a party's principal brief. If the court grants a party permission to file a longer brief, that extension does not affect the length of an amicus brief.

(e) **Time for Filing.** An amicus curiae must file its brief, accompanied by a motion for filing when necessary, no later than 7 days after the principal brief of the party being supported is filed. An amicus curiae that does not support either party must file its brief no later than 7 days after the appellant's or petitioner's principal brief is filed. A court may grant leave for later filing, specifying the time within which an opposing party may answer.

(f) **Reply Brief.** Except by the court's permission, an amicus curiae may not file a reply brief.

(g) **Oral Argument.** An amicus curiae may participate in oral argument only with the court's permission.

## Second Circuit Local Rule 29.1

(a) Leave to File. The court ordinarily will deny leave to file an amicus brief when, by reason of a relationship between a judge assigned to hear the proceeding and the amicus curiae or its counsel, the filing of the brief might cause the recusal of the judge.

(b) Disclosure. The required disclosure statement under FRAP 29(c)(5) must appear in the first footnote on the first page of the brief.

## Third Circuit Local Rule 29.1

29.1 Time for Filing Amici Curiae Briefs on Rehearing

(a) In a case ordered for rehearing before the court en banc or before the original panel, if the court permits the parties to file additional briefs, any amicus curiae must file its brief in accordance with

Rule 29(e) of the Federal Rules of Appellate Procedure. In a case ordered for rehearing in which no additional briefing is directed, unless the court directs otherwise, any new amicus must file a brief within 28 days after the date of the order granting rehearing, and any party may file a response to such an amicus brief within 21 days after the amicus brief is served.

Before completing the preparation of an amicus brief, counsel for an amicus curiae must attempt to ascertain the arguments that will be made in the brief of any party whose position the amicus is supporting, with a view to avoiding any unnecessary repetition or restatement of those arguments in the amicus brief.

(b) The statement required by FRAP 29(c)(4) does not count toward the word limitations of FRAP 32(a)(7).

**Fifth Circuit Local Rules**

*Rule 29*

29.1 Time for Filing Motion. Those wishing to file an amicus curiae brief should file a motion within 7 days after the filing of the principal brief of the party whose position the amicus brief will support.

29.2 Contents and Form. Briefs filed under this rule must comply with the applicable FED. R. APP. P. provisions and with 5TH CIR. R. 31 and 32. The brief must include a supplemental statement of interested parties, if necessary to fully disclose all those with an interest in the amicus brief. The brief should avoid the repetition of facts or legal arguments contained in the principal brief and should focus on points either not made or not adequately discussed in those briefs. Any non-conforming brief may be stricken, on motion or sua sponte.

29.3 Length of Briefs. See FED. R. APP. P.29(d).

29.4 Denial of Amicus Curiae Status. After a panel opinion is issued, amicus curiae status will not be permitted if the allowance would result in the disqualification of any member of the panel or of the en banc court.

*Rule 31.2*

The time for filing the brief of the intervenor or amicus is extended until 7 days after the filing of the principal brief of the party supported by the intervenor or amicus.

**Sixth Circuit Local Rules**

*Rule 29.1*

An amicus curiae may request to participate in oral argument by motion stating the reason oral argument will aid the court.

*Rule 46*

(D) Attorneys for Amici Curiae. An attorney for an amicus curiae may participate in the case without being admitted to the bar of this court.

**Ninth Circuit Local Rule**

*Rule 29-1. Reply Brief of an Amicus Curiae*

No reply brief of an amicus curiae will be permitted.

Circuit Advisory Committee Note to Rule 29-1. The filing of multiple amici curiae briefs raising the same points in support of one party is disfavored. Prospective amici are encouraged to file a joint brief. Movants are reminded that the Court will review the amicus curiae brief in conjunction with the briefs submitted by the parties, so that amici briefs should not repeat arguments or factual statements made by the parties.

Amici who wish to join in the arguments or factual statements of a party or other amici are encouraged to file and serve on all parties a short letter so stating in lieu of a brief. If the letter is not required to be filed electronically, the letter shall be provided in an original.

*Rule 29-2. Brief Amicus Curiae Submitted to Support or Oppose a Petition for Panel or En Banc Rehearing or During the Pendency of Rehearing*

(a) When Permitted. An amicus curiae may be permitted to file a brief when the Court is considering a petition for panel or en banc rehearing or when the Court has granted rehearing. The

United States or its officer or agency, or a State, Territory, Commonwealth, or the District of Columbia may file an amicus curiae brief without the consent of the parties or leave of court. Subject to the provisions of subsection (f) of this rule, any other amicus curiae may file a brief only by leave of court or if the brief states that all parties have consented to its filing.

(b) Motion for Leave to File. The motion must be accompanied by the proposed brief and include the recitals set forth at FRAP 29(b).

(c) Format/Length.

  (1) A brief submitted while a petition for rehearing is pending shall be styled as an amicus curiae brief in support of or in opposition to the petition for rehearing or as not supporting either party. A brief submitted during the pendency of panel or en banc rehearing shall be styled as an amicus curiae brief in support of appellant or appellee or as not supporting either party.

  (2) A brief submitted while a petition for rehearing is pending shall not exceed 15 pages unless it complies with the alternative length limits of 4,200 words or 390 lines of monospaced text. Motions for leave to file an oversize brief are disfavored.

  (3) Unless otherwise ordered by the Court, a brief submitted after the Court has voted to rehear a case en banc shall not exceed 25 pages unless it complies with the alternative length limits of 7,000 words or 650 lines of monospaced text. Motions for leave to file an oversize brief are disfavored.

(d) Number of Copies.

  (1) If a petition for rehearing en banc has been granted and the brief is not required to be submitted electronically, an original and 20 copies of the brief shall be submitted.

  (2) For all other briefs described by this rule that are not required to be submitted electronically, an original shall be submitted.

The Clerk may order the submission of paper copies or additional copies of any brief filed pursuant to this rule.

(e) Time for Filing.

(1) Brief Submitted to Support or Oppose a Petition for Rehearing. An amicus curiae must serve its brief along with any necessary motion no later than 10 days after the petition or response of the party the amicus wishes to support is filed or is due. An amicus brief that does not support either party must be served along with any necessary motion no later than 10 days after the petition is filed. Motions for extensions of time to file an amicus curiae brief submitted under this rule are disfavored.

(2) Briefs Submitted During the Pendency of Rehearing. Unless the Court orders otherwise, an amicus curiae supporting the position of the petitioning party or not supporting either party must serve its brief, along with any necessary motion, no later than 21 days after the petition for rehearing is granted. Unless the Court orders otherwise, an amicus curiae supporting the position of the responding party must serve its brief, along with any necessary motion, no later than 35 days after the petition for panel or en banc rehearing is granted. Motions for extensions of time to file an amicus curiae brief submitted under this rule are disfavored.

(f) Circulation. Motions for leave to file an amicus curiae brief to support or oppose a petition for panel rehearing are circulated to the panel. Motions for leave to file an amicus curiae brief to support or oppose a petition for en banc rehearing are circulated to all members of the Court. Motions for leave to file an amicus curiae brief during the pendency of en banc rehearing are circulated to the en banc court.

Circuit Advisory Committee Note to Rule 29-2. Circuit Rule 29-2 only concerns amicus curiae briefs submitted to support or oppose a petition for panel or en banc rehearing and amicus curiae briefs submitted during the pendency of rehearing. The Court considers the filing of amicus curiae briefs related to petitions for rehearing or en banc review to be appropriate only when the post-disposition deliberations involve novel or particularly complex issues.

The Court will ordinarily deny motions and disallow stipulations for leave to file an amicus curiae brief where the filing of the brief would result in the recusal of a member of the en banc court. Any member of the Court who would be subject to disqualification in light of the amicus curiae brief may, of course, voluntarily recuse, thereby allowing the filing of the amicus curiae brief. (New 7/1/07)

*Rule 29-3. Motions for Leave to File Amicus Curiae Briefs*
A motion for leave to file an amicus brief shall state that movant endeavored to obtain the consent of all parties to the filing of the brief before moving the Court for permission to file the proposed brief.

Circuit Advisory Committee Note to Rule 29-3. FRAP 29(a) permits the timely filing of an amicus curiae brief without leave of the Court if all parties consent to the filing of the brief; obtaining such consent relieves the Court of the need to consider a motion. (New 1/1/12)

**Tenth Circuit Local Rule 29.1. Amicus briefs on rehearing.**
The court will receive but not file proposed amicus briefs on rehearing. Filing will be considered shortly before the oral argument on rehearing en banc if granted, or before the grant or denial of panel rehearing. Except by the court's permission, an amicus brief filed at the rehearing stage may be no more than 3,000 words in length and shall include a certification of the word count in conformance with Fed. R. App. P. 32(a)(7)(C). Proposed amicus briefs in support of the petition must be tendered within 7 days from the date the rehearing petition is filed. Proposed amicus briefs in opposition to rehearing are not allowed unless the court has directed that a response be filed. See Fed. R. App. P. 40(a)(3). In that event, any proposed amicus brief must be tendered on the due date for the response.

**Eleventh Circuit Local Rules**
***29-1 Motions for Leave.*** Motions for leave to file a brief of amicus curiae must comply with FRAP 27 and 11th Cir. R. 27-1, including the requirement

of a Certificate of Interested Persons and Corporate Disclosure Statement as described in FRAP 26.1 and the accompanying circuit rules.

***29-2 Amicus Brief.*** In addition to the requirements of FRAP 29(c), an amicus brief must contain items (a), (b), (d), (e), (h), (j), (k), (l), (m) and (n) of 11th Cir. R. 28-1.

***35-6 Motion for Leave to File Amicus Brief in Support of Petition for Rehearing En Banc.***

The United States or its officer or agency or a state may file an amicus brief in support of a petition for rehearing en banc without the consent of the parties or leave of court. Any other amicus curiae must request leave of court to file an amicus brief in support of a petition for rehearing en banc. The request must be made by motion accompanied by the proposed brief in conformance with 11th Cir. R. 35-5, except that subsections (f) and (k) may be omitted. The proposed amicus brief must not exceed 15 pages, exclusive of items required by 11th Cir. R. 35-5(a), (b), (c), (d), and (j). The cover must be green. An amicus curiae must file its proposed brief, accompanied by a motion for filing when necessary, no later than 10 days after the petition for rehearing en banc being supported is filed.

**35-9 En Banc Amicus Briefs.**

The United States or its officer or agency or a state may file an en banc amicus brief without the consent of the parties or leave of court. Any other amicus curiae must request leave of court by filing a motion accompanied by the proposed brief in conformance with FRAP 29(b) through (d) and the corresponding circuit rules. An amicus curiae must file its en banc briefs, accompanied by a motion for filing when necessary, no later than the due date of the principal en banc brief of the party being supported. An amicus curiae that does not support either party must file its en banc briefs, accompanied by a motion for filing when necessary, no later than the due date of the appellant's or petitioner's principal en banc brief. An amicus curiae must also comply with 11th Cir. R. 35-8.

**40-6 Motion for Leave to File Amicus Brief in Support of Petition for Panel Rehearing.**

The United States or its officer or agency or a state may file an amicus brief in support of a petition for panel rehearing without the consent of the parties or leave of court. Any other amicus curiae must request leave of court to file an amicus brief in support of a petition for panel rehearing. The request must be made by motion accompanied by the proposed brief in conformance with FRAP 29(b) and (c) and the corresponding circuit rules. The proposed amicus brief must not exceed 15 pages, exclusive of items that do not count towards page limitations as described in 11th Cir. R. 32-4. The cover must be green. An amicus curiae must file its proposed brief, accompanied by a motion for filing when necessary, no later than 10 days after the petition for panel rehearing being supported is filed.

## D.C. Circuit Local Rules

*Rule 29. Brief of an Amicus Curiae*

The rules stated below apply with respect to the brief for an amicus curiae not appointed by the court. A brief for an amicus curiae appointed by the court is governed by the provisions of Circuit Rule 28.

(a) Contents of Brief. The brief must avoid repetition of facts or legal arguments made in the principal (appellant/petitioner or appellee/respondent) brief and focus on points not made or adequately elaborated upon in the principal brief, although relevant to the issues before this court.

(b) Leave to File. Any individual or non-governmental entity intending to participate as amicus curiae must file either a written representation that all parties consent to such participation, or, in the absence of such consent, a motion for leave to participate as amicus curiae. (For this purpose, the term "governmental entity" includes the United States or an officer or agency thereof, the District of Columbia, or a State, Territory, or Commonwealth of the United States.) Any disclosure statement required by Circuit Rule 26.1 must accompany a written representation of consent to participate as amicus curiae or a motion for leave to participate as amicus. The time for filing is governed by FRAP 29(e); however, the court encourages individuals and non-governmental entities to file a written representation of consent or motion for leave to participate, and governmental entities to file a notice of intent to file an amicus brief, as promptly as practicable after the case is docketed in this court. Leave to participate as amicus will not be granted and an amicus brief will not be accepted if the participation of amicus would result in the recusal of a member of the panel that has been assigned to the case or a member of the en banc court when participation is sought with respect to a petition for rehearing en banc.

(c) Timely Filing. Generally, a brief for amicus curiae will be due as set by the briefing order in each case. In the absence of provision for such a brief in the order, the brief must be filed in accordance with the time limitations described in FRAP 29(e).

(d) Single Brief. Amici curiae on the same side must join in a single brief to the extent practicable. This requirement does not apply to a governmental entity. Any separate brief for an amicus curiae must contain a certificate of counsel plainly stating why the separate brief is necessary. Generally unacceptable grounds for the filing of separate briefs include representations that the issues presented require greater length than these rules allow (appropriately addressed by a motion to exceed length limits), that counsel cannot coordinate their efforts due to geographical dispersion, or that separate presentations were allowed in earlier proceedings. See Circuit Rule 28(d) (Briefs for Intervenors), and Circuit Rule 34(e) (Participation in Oral Argument by Amici Curiae).

*Rule 34*

(e) Participation in Oral Argument by Amici Curiae. An amicus curiae, other than one appointed by the court, will not be permitted to participate in the oral argument without leave of the court granted for extraordinary reasons on motion, except that counsel for the party supported by amicus curiae may consent to such participation subject to the provision as to number of counsel stated in paragraph (c) above. A motion by amicus curiae seeking leave to participate in oral argument must be filed at least 14 days prior to the date oral argument is scheduled.

*Rule 35*

(f) Brief of an Amicus Curiae. No amicus curiae brief in response to or in support of a petition for rehearing en banc will be received by the clerk except by invitation of the court.

**Federal Circuit Local Rules**

*Rule 29*

(a) Content; Form. In addition to the contents required by Federal Rule of Appellate Procedure 29, the brief of an amicus curiae must include a certificate of interest (see Federal Circuit Rule 47.4) in front of the table of contents.

(b) List of Amicus Curiae. The clerk will maintain a list of bar associations and other organizations to be invited to file amicus curiae briefs when the court directs. Bar associations and other organizations will be placed on the list if they request. The request must be renewed annually not later than October 1.

(c) Consent. If an amicus brief is filed on consent of all parties, then no motion for leave is required and the brief should state, pursuant to Federal Rule of Appellate Procedure 29(a), that all parties have consented to its filing.

*Rule 35*

(g) Amicus Curiae Brief. Except by the court's permission or direction, an amicus curiae brief submitted in connection with a petition for hearing en banc, a petition for rehearing en banc, or a combined petition for panel rehearing and rehearing en banc, must be accompanied by a motion for leave and must not exceed 10 pages. Except by the court's permission or direction, any brief amicus curiae or any motion for leave to file a brief amicus curiae must be filed within 14 days of the date of filing of the petition or response that the amicus curiae supports. If the amicus curiae does not support either party, then the brief or motion for leave to file the brief must be filed within 14 days of the date of filing of the petition.

*Rule 40*

(g) Amicus Curiae Brief. Except by the court's permission or direction, an amicus curiae brief submitted in connection with a petition for panel rehearing must be accompanied by a motion for leave to file and must not exceed 10 pages. Except by the court's permission or direction, any brief amicus curiae or any motion for leave to file a brief amicus curiae must be filed within 14 days of the date of filing of the petition or response that the amicus curiae supports. If the amicus curiae does not support either party, then the brief or motion for leave to file the brief must be filed within 14 days of the date of filing of the petition.

## *STATE RULES*

### Alabama Rule of Appellate Procedure 29

A brief of an amicus curiae may be filed only by leave of court granted on motion, or at the request of the court. The brief may be conditionally filed with the motion for leave. Unless otherwise provided by the court, the brief of an amicus curiae shall be filed within the time allowed the party whose position on the appeal the amicus brief will support. The brief shall follow the form prescribed for the brief of an appellee. A motion for leave shall identify the interest of the applicant, and shall state the reasons why the brief of an amicus curiae is desirable. An amicus curiae may participate in oral argument only upon motion and leave of court.

### Alaska Appellate Rule 212

(9) Brief of an Amicus Curiae. A brief of an amicus curiae maybe filed only if accompanied by written consent of all the parties, or by leave of the appellate court granted on motion, or at the request of the appellate court. The brief may be conditionally filed with the motion for leave. A motion for leave shall identify the interest of the applicant and shall state the reasons why a brief of an amicus curiae is desirable. Unless all parties otherwise consent, any amicus curiae shall file its brief within the time allowed to the party whose position as to affirmance or reversal the amicus brief will support, unless the court for cause shown shall grant

leave for later filing, in which event it shall specify within what period an opposing party may answer. The brief shall be in the form prescribed by this rule and shall be duplicated and served pursuant to the requirements of Rule 212(a)(2). A motion of an amicus curiae to participate in the oral argument will be granted only for extraordinary reasons.

## Arizona Rule of Civil Appellate Procedure 16

(a) Filing and Form of Brief; Participation in Oral Argument. A brief of an amicus curiae may be filed only if accompanied by written consent of all parties or by leave of court granted upon motion, except that leave or written consent shall not be required when the brief is presented by the State of Arizona or an officer or agency thereof, or by a county, city, or town. The brief shall be lodged with the motion, if any. The motion for leave shall identify the interest of the applicant, state that the applicant has read the relevant brief, petition or motion and shall state the reasons accepting applicant's amicus curiae brief would be desirable. A party desiring to respond to the amicus brief shall file the response within 20 days of service of a brief filed with consent or by a governmental entity or agency, or within 20 days of the Court's order granting a motion for leave to file an amicus brief. Rules 13 and 14 shall govern the form of an amicus brief, except that it shall not exceed 12,000 words in length if done in proportionately spaced typeface, or 35 pages if done in monospaced typeface, unless otherwise permitted by the court. An amicus curiae may participate in the oral argument only by leave of the appellate court.

(b) Time and Length Limits Applicable to Amicus Curiae Briefs in the Supreme Court. Parties desiring to file an amicus curiae brief shall file such briefs as provided by this rule, except that an amicus curiae brief relating to a special action petition shall be filed as expeditiously as possible after the special action petition is filed, as provided for in Rule 7(g), Rules of Procedure for Special Actions.

(1) Briefs Filed Prior to a Decision by the Court to Grant Review. Unless otherwise ordered by the Court, an amicus brief filed in

support of a petition for review or a response to a petition for review by the State, a county, city, or town, or an amicus brief accompanied by written consent of all parties, or a motion for leave to file the brief, shall be filed no later than 21 days after the filing of the response to the petition for review. Such briefs shall comply with the form and length requirements of Rules 6(c) and 23(c) exclusive of any appendix.

(2) Briefs Filed After the Court Has Granted Review. After the Court has granted review, and unless otherwise ordered, an amicus brief filed by the State, a county, city, or town, or an amicus brief accompanied by written consent of all parties or a motion for leave to file an amicus brief, shall be filed no later than 10 days after the date ordered by the Court at the time review was granted for filing supplemental briefing by the parties in the particular case. Such briefs shall comply with Rule 6(c) and shall not exceed the page limitation imposed for the parties' supplemental briefs.

(3) Responses to Amicus Curiae Briefs. A party wishing to respond to an amicus brief shall file the response within 20 days of service of a brief filed with consent or by a governmental entity or agency, or within 20 days of the Court's order granting a motion for leave to file an amicus brief. The response shall comply with the page and formatting requirements imposed on the particular amicus brief to which it relates.

(4) Late-Filed Briefs and Responses. Leave for filing a late amicus or response brief shall be granted only for good cause shown.

## Arkansas Rule of Supreme Court 4-6

(a) Briefs. Amici curiae attorneys may file briefs with the permission of the Court. The motion for permission should state the reasons why such a brief is thought to be necessary. If the amicus brief supports the appellant's position or is neutral, it is due at the same time as the appellant's brief; if it supports the appellee's position, it is due at the same time as the appellee's brief.

(b) Oral arguments. Amici curiae attorneys will not be permitted to participate in oral arguments.

(c) Petitions for rehearing. Amici Curiae attorneys will not be permitted to file a petition for rehearing in their own names and may participate only by first securing permission of the regular attorneys or of the Court to join in the motion or brief.

## California Rule of Court 8.200

(c) Amicus curiae briefs

(1) Within 14 days after the last appellant's reply brief is filed or could have been filed under rule 8.212, whichever is earlier, any person or entity may serve and file an application for permission of the presiding justice to file an amicus curiae brief. For good cause, the presiding justice may allow later filing.

(2) The application must state the applicant's interest and explain how the proposed amicus curiae brief will assist the court in deciding the matter.

(3) The application must also identify:

(A) Any party or any counsel for a party in the pending appeal who:

(i) Authored the proposed amicus brief in whole or in part; or

(ii) Made a monetary contribution intended to fund the preparation or submission of the brief; and

(B) Every person or entity who made a monetary contribution intended to fund the preparation or submission of the brief, other than the amicus curiae, its members, or its counsel in the pending appeal.

(4) The proposed brief must be served and must accompany the application, and may be combined with it.

(5) The covers of the application and proposed brief must identify the party the applicant supports, if any.

(6) If the court grants the application, any party may file an answer within the time the court specifies. The answer must be served on all parties and the amicus curiae.

(7) The Attorney General may file an amicus curiae brief without the presiding justice's permission, unless the brief is submitted on behalf of another state officer or agency. The Attorney General must serve and file the brief within 14 days after the last appellant's reply brief is filed or could have been filed under rule 8.212, whichever is earlier, and must provide the information required by (2) and comply with (5). Any party may serve and file an answer within 14 days after the brief is filed.

### Colorado Appellate Rule 29

Any amicus curiae shall file its brief within the time allowed the party whose position as to affirmance or reversal the amicus brief will support unless the court for cause shown shall grant leave for later filing, in which event it shall specify within what period an opposing party may answer.

A motion of an amicus curiae to participate in the oral argument will be granted only for extraordinary reasons.

### Connecticut Practice Book Section 67-7

A brief of an amicus curiae in cases before the court on the merits may be filed only with the permission of the court. An application for permission to appear as amicus curiae and to file a brief shall be filed within twenty days after the filing of the brief of the party, if any, whom the applicant intends to support, and if there is no such party, then the application shall be filed no later than twenty days after the filing of the appellee's brief. The application shall state concisely the nature of the applicant's interest and the reasons why a brief of an amicus curiae should be allowed. The length of the brief shall not exceed ten pages unless a specific request is made for a brief of more than that length. The application shall conform to the requirements set forth in Sections 66-2 and 66-3. The amicus application should specifically set forth reasons to justify the filing of a brief in excess of ten pages. A party served with an application may within ten days after the filing of the application file an objection concisely stating the reasons therefor. All briefs filed under this section shall comply with the applicable provisions of this chapter and shall set forth the interest of the amicus curiae. An amicus curiae may argue orally only when a specific request for such permission is granted by the court in which the appeal is pending. With the exception of briefs filed by the attorney general as provided by this rule, all briefs shall indicate whether counsel for a party wrote the brief in whole or in part and whether such counsel or a party contributed to the cost of the preparation or submission of the brief and shall identify those persons, other than the amicus curiae, its members or its counsel, who made such monetary contribution. The disclosure shall be made in the first footnote on the first page of text. Except for habeas corpus matters based on criminal convictions, if an appeal in a noncriminal matter involves an attack on the constitutionality of a state statute, the attorney general may appear and file a brief amicus curiae as of right. Notice of the attorney general's intention to appear and to file a brief shall be given to the appellate clerk and all parties no later than the date on which the brief of the party that the attorney general supports is filed, and the attorney general's brief will be due twenty days after the filing of the brief of the party that the attorney general supports.

### Delaware Supreme Court Rule 28

(a) When permitted. A brief of an amicus curiae may be filed only by leave of Court granted on motion or at the request of the Court.

(b) Motion for leave to file. The motion must be accompanied by the proposed brief and state:

- (1) The movant's interest;
- (2) The reason why an amicus brief is desirable and why the matters asserted are relevant to the disposition of the case; and
- (3) Whether the parties to the appeal consent to or oppose the motion for leave to file.

(c) Contents and form. An amicus brief must comply with Rule 13. The cover of the amicus brief must be green and must identify the party or parties supported and indicate whether the brief supports affirmance or reversal. An amicus brief must include:

(1) A table of contents, with page references;

(2) A table of authorities, including cases (alphabetically arranged), statutes, and other authorities, with page references;

(3) A concise statement of the identity of the amicus curiae, its interest in the case, and the source of its authority to file; and

(4) An argument, which may be preceded by a summary and which need not include a statement of the applicable standard of review.

(d) Length. Except by leave of the Court, an amicus brief may be no more than one-half the maximum length authorized by these rules for a party's principal brief. If the Court grants a party permission to file a longer brief, that extension does not affect the length of the amicus brief.

(e) Time for filing. An amicus curiae must file its brief, accompanied by a motion for filing, no later than 7 days after the principal brief of the party being supported is filed. An amicus curiae that does not support either party must file its brief no later than 7 days after the appellant's principal brief is filed.

(f) Reply brief. Except by leave of the Court, an amicus curiae may not file a reply brief.

(g) Oral argument. An amicus curiae may not participate in oral argument unless ordered by the Court.

## Florida Rule of Appellate Procedure 9.370

(a) When Permitted. An amicus curiae may file a brief only by leave of court. A motion for leave to file must state the movant's interest, the particular issue to be addressed, how the movant can assist the court in the disposition of the case, and whether all parties consent to the filing of the brief.

(b) Contents and Form. An amicus brief must comply with Rule 9.210(b) but shall omit a statement of the case and facts and may not exceed 20 pages. The cover must identify the party or parties supported. An amicus brief must include a concise statement of the identity of the amicus curiae and its interest in the case.

(c) Time for Service. An amicus curiae must serve its brief no later than 10 days after the first brief, petition, or response of the party being supported is filed. An amicus curiae that does not support either party must serve its brief no later than 10 days after the initial brief or petition is filed. A court may grant leave for later service, specifying the time within which an opposing party may respond. The service of an amicus curiae brief does not alter or extend the briefing deadlines for the parties. An amicus curiae may not file a reply brief.

(d) Notice of Intent to File Amicus Brief in Supreme Court. When a party has invoked the discretionary jurisdiction of the supreme court, an amicus curiae may file a notice with the court indicating its intent to seek leave to file an amicus brief on the merits should the court accept jurisdiction. The notice shall state briefly why the case is of interest to the amicus curiae, but shall not contain argument. The body of the notice shall not exceed one page.

### Georgia Supreme Court Rule 23

Amicus curiae briefs may be filed without prior permission and shall disclose the identity and interest of the persons on whose behalf the briefs are filed. Amici do not have standing to file motions for reconsideration, but may submit briefs in support of a motion made by a party.

### Georgia Court of Appeal Rule 26

Amicus curiae briefs may be filed without leave of Court, disclosing the identity and interest of the person or group on whose behalf the brief is filed and limited to issues properly raised by the parties. Only members of the Bar of this Court or attorneys appearing by courtesy may file amicus curiae briefs. Amicus curiae briefs shall conform to Rule 24(b)-(g).

### Hawaii Rule of Appellate Procedure 28

(g) Brief of amicus curiae. An amicus curiae brief may be filed only by leave of the appellate court. The order granting leave shall fix the time for filing the amicus curiae brief and any response thereto. The appellate court may allow or disallow the filing of such brief with or without a hearing. All amicus curiae briefs shall comply with the applicable provisions of subsection (b) of this rule. The attorney general may file an amicus curiae brief without order of the court in all cases where the constitutionality of any statute of the State of Hawaiʻi is drawn into question, provided that the attorney general shall file the brief within 30 days after the filing of the answering brief, or within 30 days after notice was received pursuant to Rule 44, whichever period last expires.

## Idaho Appellate Rule 8

An attorney, or person or entity through an attorney, may appear as amicus curiae in any proceeding by request of the Supreme Court; or by leave of the Supreme Court upon written application served upon all parties, setting forth the particular employment, if any, the interest of the applicant in the appeal or proceeding and the name of the party in whose support the amicus curiae would appear. The application shall also state whether leave is sought to file an amicus curiae brief or participate in oral argument, or both. Any objection to the appearance of an amicus curiae must be made by motion within 14 days of service of the application in the manner provided for motions under Rule 32. Leave to appear as amicus curiae shall be by written order of the Supreme Court which shall specify the manner of appearance by the amicus curiae attorney and state the time for filing of any amicus curiae brief.

## Illinois Supreme Court Rule 345

(a) Leave or Request of Court Necessary. A brief amicus curiae may be filed only by leave of the court or of a judge thereof, or at the request of the court. A motion for leave must be accompanied by the proposed brief and shall state the interest of the applicant and explain how an amicus brief will assist the court.

(b) Forms; Conditions; Time. A brief of an amicus curiae shall follow the form prescribed for the brief of an appellee, shall identify the amicus as such on the cover of the brief, and shall conform to any conditions imposed by the court. Unless the court or a judge thereof specifies otherwise, it shall be filed on or before the due date of the initial brief of the party whose position it supports. The color of the cover shall be the same as that of the party's brief whose position it supports.

(c) Oral Argument. Amicus curiae will not be allowed to argue orally.

## Indiana Appellate Rule 41

A. Content. A proposed amicus curiae shall file a motion to appear as an amicus curiae. The motion shall identify the interest of the proposed amicus curiae and the party with whom the proposed amicus curiae is substantively aligned, and it shall state the reasons why an amicus curiae brief would be helpful to the court.

B. Time for Filing. The proposed amicus curiae shall file its motion to appear within the time allowed the party with whom the proposed amicus curiae is substantively aligned to file its brief or Petition. If an entity has been granted leave to appear as an amicus curiae in a case before the Court of Appeals or the Tax Court, that entity need not again seek leave to appear as an amicus curiae in any continuation of that case before the Supreme Court.

C. Tender of Brief. The proposed amicus curiae shall tender or file its amicus curiae brief within the time allowed the party with whom the proposed amicus curiae is substantively aligned.

D. Belated Filing. The court may permit the belated filing of an amicus curiae brief on motion for good cause. If the court grants the motion, the court shall set a deadline for any opposing party to file a reply brief.

E. Amicus Curiae Appendix and Addendum to Brief. An entity granted amicus curiae status may not file an Appendix or Addendum to the Brief containing documents that are not within the Record on Appeal unless leave to do so has been first granted.

## Iowa Court Rule 6.906

(1) Appeal. An amicus curiae brief may be served and filed only by leave of the appropriate appellate court granted on motion served

on all parties, at the request of the appropriate appellate court, or when accompanied by the written consent of all parties. The brief may be conditionally served and filed with a motion for leave. A motion for leave shall identify the interest of the applicant and shall state the reasons an amicus curiae brief would assist the court in resolving issues preserved for appellate review in the case. An amicus curiae shall serve and file a brief within the time allowed the party whose position the brief will support. The appropriate appellate court for cause shown may extend the deadline for the brief, specifying the period within which an opposing party may respond. An amicus curiae's request to participate in oral argument will not be granted except for extraordinary reasons.

(2) Further review. Amicus curiae briefs shall not be filed in support of, or in resistance to, an application for further review of a decision of the court of appeals. If the supreme court grants further review, an amicus curiae brief may be filed upon leave of the supreme court granted on motion served on all parties, at the request of the supreme court, or when accompanied by the written consent of all parties. A motion for leave to file an amicus curiae brief must be filed within 14 days of the supreme court's order granting further review, and no response to the motion shall be received unless requested by the court. The motion shall identify the interest of the applicant, shall state the reasons an amicus curiae brief would assist the court in resolving issues preserved for appellate review in the case, and shall be accompanied by the amicus curiae brief. If the motion for leave to file an amicus curiae brief is granted, the parties may file a response to the amicus curiae brief within 15 days of the court's order granting the motion.

(3) Form of amicus curiae brief. An amicus curiae brief shall not exceed more than one-half of the length limitations for a required brief specified in rule 6.903(1)(g). An amicus curiae brief must comply with the format requirements of rule 6.903(1). An amicus curiae brief need not comply with rule 6.903(2) or (3) but must include all of the following:

a. A table of contents with page references.

b. A table of authorities containing cases (alphabetically arranged), statutes, and other authorities cited, with references to all pages of the brief where they are cited.
c. A concise statement of the identity of the amicus curiae and its interest in the case.
d. An argument.
e. A certificate of compliance, if required by rule 6.903(1)(g)(4).

(4) Criteria for allowing amicus curiae brief. An appellate court has broad discretion in determining whether an amicus curiae brief should be allowed. The court will base its decision on whether the brief will assist the court in resolving the issues preserved for appellate review in the case. In reaching its decision, the court will consider various factors, including those set forth below.

a. The court will ordinarily grant a motion for leave to file an amicus curiae brief if one of the following factors is present.
   (1) The party whose position the proposed amicus brief supports is unrepresented or has not received adequate representation.
   (2) The proposed amicus curiae has a direct interest in another case that may be materially affected by the outcome of the present case.
   (3) The proposed amicus curiae has a unique perspective or information that will assist the court in assessing the ramifications of any decision rendered in the present case.
b. The court will ordinarily deny a motion for leave to file an amicus curiae brief if one of the following factors is present.
   (1) The proposed amicus curiae brief will merely reiterate the arguments of the party whose position the brief supports.
   (2) The proposed amicus curiae brief appears to be an attempt to expand the number of briefing pages available to the party whose position the brief supports.

(3) The proposed amicus curiae brief attempts to raise issues that were not preserved for appellate review.

(4) The proposed amicus curiae brief will place an undue burden on the opposing party.

c. The court may also strike an amicus curiae brief filed with the consent of all parties if it appears the brief would not be allowed under the above criteria.

(5) Number of copies of amicus brief. Eighteen copies of an amicus brief shall be filed. In addition, one copy shall be served on each party.

## Kansas Appellate Procedure Rule 6.06

(a) When Permitted. A brief of an amicus curiae may be filed when:

(1) an application to file the brief is served on all parties and filed with the clerk of the appellate courts; and

(2) the appellate court enters an order granting the application.

(b) Filing and Service of Amicus Brief. A brief of an amicus curiae must be:

(1) filed not later than 30 days before oral argument; and

(2) served on all parties.

(c) Reply to Amicus Brief. Any party may respond to a brief of an amicus curiae not later than 21 days after the brief is filed.

(d) Oral Argument. An amicus curiae is not entitled to oral argument.

## Kentucky Rules of Civil Procedure, Court Rule 76.12

(7) Amicus curiae briefs.

A brief for an amicus curiae shall not be filed except on order of the appellate court pursuant to a motion specifying with particularity the nature of the movant's interest, the points to be presented, and their relevance to the disposition of the case. Payment of the filing fee specified in Rule 76.42(2)(a) shall be required with a motion for leave to file an amicus curiae brief and said motion shall be filed within fifteen (15) days of the filing of appellant's brief. An amicus curiae brief shall not exceed fifteen (15) pages, shall not contain appendices and shall be tendered with the motion.

**Louisiana Uniform Rules of the Courts of Appeals Rule 2-12.11**

Amicus curiae briefs may be filed only upon motion by the applicant and order of the court. The motion shall identify the interest of the applicant, state that the applicant has read the briefs of the parties, and state specific reasons why applicant's brief would be helpful to the court in deciding the cases. An amicus curiae may not request oral argument.

**Maine Rule of Appellate Procedure 9**

(e) Brief of an Amicus Curiae.

(1) General. Except as provided in paragraph (2) of this subdivision, a brief of an amicus curiae may be filed only if accompanied by written consent of all parties or by leave of the Law Court. A motion for leave shall identify the interest of the applicant and shall state the reasons why a brief of an amicus curiae is desirable. An amicus curiae brief shall be filed on the date on which the appellee's brief is filed, unless the Law Court for cause shown shall grant leave for later filing. Any party may file a reply brief replying to new matter raised by the amicus curiae within 14 days after service of the brief of an amicus curiae, or within such other time as the Law Court may specify in granting leave for later filing to the amicus curiae. The brief of an amicus curiae shall not exceed 50 pages, and any reply brief thereto may not exceed 20 pages, without prior approval of the Law Court, which shall be granted only upon a showing of good cause. The motion of an amicus curiae for leave to participate in the oral argument will be granted only for extraordinary reasons.

(2) Maine Tort Claims Act. In any action under the Maine Tort Claims Act, 14 M.R.S. §§ 1801 et seq., the Attorney General shall have the right to appear before the Law Court by brief and oral argument as an amicus curiae where the Attorney General is not appearing representing a party to

the action. Unless all parties otherwise consent, in any such action where the Attorney General has received notice of appeal as provided in Rule 2(a)(5), the Attorney General shall file an amicus brief within the time allowed the party whose position as to affirmance or reversal the brief will support, unless the Law Court for cause shown shall grant leave for later filing. In that event, the Law Court shall specify within what period an opposing party may reply to the Attorney General's brief.

## Maryland Rule 8-511

(a) Authorization to File Amicus Curiae Brief. An amicus curiae brief may be filed only:

- (1) upon written consent of all parties to the appeal;
- (2) by the Attorney General in any appeal in which the State of Maryland may have an interest;
- (3) upon request by the Court; or
- (4) upon the Court's grant of a motion filed under section (b) of this Rule.

(b) Motion and Brief.

- (1) Content of Motion. A motion requesting permission to file an amicus curiae brief shall:
  - (A) identify the interest of the movant;
  - (B) state the reasons why the amicus curiae brief is desirable;
  - (C) state whether the movant requested of the parties their consent to the filing of the amicus curiae brief and, if not, why not;
  - (D) state the issues that the movant intends to raise;
  - (E) identify every person, other than the movant, its members, or its attorneys, who made a monetary or other contribution to the preparation or submission of the brief, and identify the nature of the contribution; and

(F) if filed in the Court of Appeals to seek leave to file an amicus curiae brief supporting or opposing a petition for writ of certiorari or other extraordinary writ, state whether, if the writ is issued, the movant intends to seek consent of the parties or move for permission to file an amicus curiae brief on the issues before the Court.

(2) Attachment of Brief. Copies of the proposed amicus curiae brief shall be attached to two of the copies of the motion filed with the Court.

(3) Service. The movant shall serve a copy of the motion and proposed brief on each party.

(4) If Motion Granted. If the motion is granted, the brief shall be regarded as having been filed when the motion was filed. Within ten days after the order granting the motion is filed, the amicus curiae shall file the additional number of briefs required by Rule 8-502 (c).

(c) Time for Filing.

(1) Generally. Except as required by subsection (c)(2) of this Rule and unless the Court orders otherwise, an amicus curiae brief shall be filed at or before the time specified for the filing of the principal brief of the appellee.

(2) Time for Filing in Court of Appeals.

(A) An amicus curiae brief may be filed pursuant to section (a) of this Rule in the Court of Appeals on the question of whether the Court should issue a writ of certiorari or other extraordinary writ to hear the appeal as well as, if such a writ is issued, on the issues before the Court.

(B) An amicus curiae brief or a motion for leave to file an amicus curiae brief supporting or opposing a petition for writ of certiorari or other extraordinary writ shall be filed at or before the time any answer to the petition is due.

(C) Unless the Court orders otherwise, an amicus curiae brief on the issues before the Court if the writ is granted shall be filed at the applicable time specified in subsection (c)(1) of this Rule.

(d) Compliance with Rules 8-503 and 8-504. An amicus curiae brief shall comply with the applicable provisions of Rules 8-503 and 8-504.

(e) Reply brief; Oral argument; Brief supporting or opposing motion for reconsideration. Without permission of the Court, an amicus curiae may not (1) file a reply brief, (2) participate in oral argument, or (3) file a brief in support of, or in opposition to, a motion for reconsideration. Permission may be granted only for extraordinary reasons.

(f) Appellee's reply brief. Within ten days after the filing of an amicus curiae brief that is not substantially in support of the position of the appellee, the appellee may file a reply brief limited to the issues in the amicus curiae brief that are not substantially in support of the appellee's position and are not fairly covered in the appellant's principal brief. Any such reply brief shall not exceed 15 pages.

**Massachusetts Rule of Appellate Procedure 17**

A brief of an amicus curiae may be filed only (1) by leave of the appellate court or a single justice granted on motion or (2) at the request of the appellate court, except that consent or leave shall not be required when the brief is presented by the Commonwealth. The brief may be conditionally filed with the motion for leave. A motion for leave shall identify the interest of the applicant and shall state the reasons why a brief of an amicus curiae is desirable. Any amicus curiae shall file its brief within the time allowed the party whose position as to affirmance or reversal the amicus brief will support unless the appellate court or a single justice for cause shown shall grant leave for later filing, and shall specify within what period an opposing party may answer. A motion of an amicus curiae to participate in the oral argument will be granted only for extraordinary reasons. The same number of copies of the brief of an amicus curiae shall be filed with the clerk and served on counsel for each party separately represented as required by Rule 19(b).

## Michigan Court Rules

### *Rule 7.212*

(H) Amicus Curiae.

(1) An amicus curiae brief may be filed only on motion granted by the Court of Appeals. The motion must be filed within 21 days after the appellee's brief is filed. If the motion is granted, the order will state the date by which the brief must be filed.

(2) The brief is limited to the issues raised by the parties. An amicus curiae may not participate in oral argument except by court order.

### *Rule 7.306*

(C) Amicus Curiae Briefs. An amicus curiae brief may be filed only on motion granted by the Court and must conform to subrules (A) and (B) and MCR 7.309. The time for filing the brief corresponds with the time for filing the brief of the party whose position the amicus curiae supports. An amicus curiae may not participate in oral argument except by Court order.

## Minnesota Rule of Civil Appellate Procedure 129.01

Upon prior notice to the parties, a brief of an amicus curiae may be filed with leave of the appellate court. The applicant shall serve and file a request for leave no later than 15 days after the filing of the notice of appeal, the petition which initiates the appeal, the appellate petition for declaratory judgment, or the appellate court order granting review. A request for leave shall identify whether the applicant's interest is public or private in nature, identify the party supported or indicate whether the amicus brief will suggest affirmance or reversal, and shall state the reason why a brief of an amicus curiae is desirable.

**Mississippi Rule 29**

(a) Grounds for Filing. A brief of an amicus curiae may be filed only by leave of the appropriate appellate court, except that leave shall not be required when the brief is presented by the state and sponsored by the Attorney General or by a guardian ad litem who is not otherwise a party to the appeal. A motion for leave shall demonstrate that (1) amicus has an interest in some other case involving a similar question; or (2) counsel for a party is inadequate or the brief insufficient; or (3) there are matters of fact or law that may otherwise escape the court's attention; or (4) the amicus has substantial legitimate interests that will likely be affected by the outcome of the case and which interests will not be adequately protected by those already parties to the case.

(b) How and When Filed. A motion for leave to file an amicus brief shall be filed no later than seven (7) days after filing of the initial brief of the party whose position the amicus brief will support. The motion must be accompanied by the proposed brief of amicus curiae which shall be a concise statement not to exceed 15 pages. The party filing the motion shall also file with the motion a brief stating why the motion satisfies the requirements of Rule 29(a).

(c) Response to Motion. An opposing party who does not object to the motion for leave may respond to the amicus brief in the opposing party's response or reply brief pursuant to Rule 28(c) or 28(d). An opposing party who objects to the motion for leave shall file a response in opposition within seven (7) days pursuant to Rule 27 stating why the requirements of Rule 29(a) have not been met. For the purpose of Rule 31(a), the time for filing the next brief will run from the date the appropriate court enters an order on the motion for leave.

(d) Oral Argument. A motion of amicus curiae to participate in oral argument will be granted only for extraordinary reasons.

**Missouri Supreme Court Rule 84.05**

(f) Briefs and Suggestions of Amicus Curiae in This Court.

(1) Suggestions may be filed in this Court by amicus curiae in support or in opposition to the granting of applications for transfer. Such suggestions are not favored. The suggestions shall only be filed with the consent of all parties or upon order of this Court. The suggestions shall not exceed five pages and shall be filed only if submitted a reasonable time prior to consideration by this Court of the application. Consideration of the application by this Court shall not be delayed pending receipt of the suggestions.

(2) A brief may be filed by amicus curiae in cases before this Court on the merits. The brief shall only be filed with the consent of all parties or upon order of this Court. The brief shall only be filed if presented for filing within the time allowed for the filing of the brief of the party supported.

(3) If consent to the filing of suggestions or a brief by amicus curiae is refused by a party to the case, a motion for leave to file may be filed with this Court. The motion for leave to file shall identify the parties refusing consent, concisely state the nature of the applicant's interest, and set forth facts or questions of law that have not been, or reasons for believing that they will not adequately be, presented by the parties and their relevancy to the disposition of the case. The motion shall not exceed five pages. The brief shall be conditionally filed with the motion for leave. A party may file an objection to the filing of a brief of an amicus curiae concisely stating the reasons for withholding consent.

(4) Consent to the filing of suggestions or a brief of an amicus curiae need not be had when the suggestions or brief are presented by the attorney general or by a state entity authorized by law to appear on its own behalf.

(5) All suggestions and briefs filed by amicus curiae shall conform with Rule 81.18 and Rule 84.06, respectively, and shall be accompanied by proof of service.

## Missouri Western District Local Rules

*Rule V*

A brief may be filed by amicus curiae in cases before the court on the merits. The brief shall be filed only with the consent of all parties or upon order of the court. The procedure is set out in Western District Special Rule XXVI.

*Rule VIII-A*

A. DUE DATES:

. . . .

Amicus Curiae or Intervener's Brief—consent of all parties or by order of the court. Western District Special Rule XXVI.

*Rule XXVI*

(1) A brief may be filed by amicus curiae in cases before the Court on the merits. The brief shall be filed only with the consent of all parties or upon order of the Court. The brief shall only be filed if presented for filing within the time allowed for the filing of the brief of the party supported, or if filed upon order of the court within such time as the court may allow.

(2) If consent to the filing of a brief by amicus curiae is refused by a party to the case, a motion for leave to file may be filed with the Court. The motion for leave to file shall concisely state the nature of the applicant's interest, set forth facts or questions of law that have not been, or reasons for believing that they will not adequately be, presented by the parties, and their relevancy to the disposition of the case. The motion shall not exceed five pages. The brief shall be conditionally filed with the motion for leave. A party may file an objection to the filing of a brief of an amicus curiae concisely stating the reasons for withholding consent.

(3) Consent to the filing of a brief of an amicus curiae need not be had when the brief is presented by the attorney general or by a state entity authorized by law to appear on its own behalf.

(4) All briefs filed by amicus curiae shall conform to Rules 84.04 and 84.06 and shall be accompanied by proof of service.

(5) Amicus suggestions on motions for rehearing or transfer shall not be filed.

(6) Amicus curiae shall not be permitted oral argument unless leave is granted by the Court.

### Missouri Eastern District Local Rule 375

a) A brief may be filed by amicus curiae. Amicus curiae may also file suggestions in support or in opposition to the granting of a motion for rehearing and/or transfer to the Supreme Court, or suggestions in support or opposition to the issuance of an extraordinary writ.

b) The brief or suggestions may be filed only with leave of court. The motion for leave shall concisely state the nature of the applicant's interest, set forth facts or questions of law that have not been, or reasons for believing that they will not adequately be, presented by the parties, and their relevancy to the disposition of the case. The motion shall not exceed five pages. The brief or suggestions shall be conditionally filed with the motion for leave. The brief or suggestions shall only be filed if presented for filing within the time allowed for the filing of the brief or suggestions of the party supported, unless extended by the court.

c) Any party may file objections to the filing of a brief or suggestions of an amicus curiae no later than five days after the filing of the motion for leave.

d) Leave for the filing of an amicus curiae brief shall not be necessary when the brief is presented by the Attorney General or a State entity authorized by law to appear on its own behalf.

e) Amicus curiae shall not be permitted oral argument unless leave is granted by the court.

### Missouri Southern District Local Rule 15

(a) A brief may be filed by amicus curiae in cases before the Court on the merits. The brief may be filed only with leave of Court and only if presented for filing within the time allowed for the filing of the brief of the party supported, unless extended by the Court.

(b) The motion for leave shall concisely state the nature of the applicant's interest, set forth facts or questions of law that have not been, or reasons for believing that they will not adequately be, presented by the parties, and their relevancy to the disposition of the case. The motion shall not exceed five pages.

(c) Leave for the filing of an amicus curiae brief shall not be necessary when the brief is presented by the attorney general or by a state entity authorized by law to appear on its own behalf.

(d) All briefs filed by amicus curiae shall conform to Rules 84.04 and 84.06 and shall be accompanied by proof of service.

## Montana Rules of Appellate Procedure

### *Rule 2*

(2) Amicus curiae. One who is not a party, but who, upon invitation or leave of the supreme court granted on motion, files a brief in a pending proceeding because of a strong interest in the subject matter.

### *Rule 12*

(7) Brief of amicus curiae. A brief of an amicus curiae may be filed only upon invitation or leave of the supreme court granted on motion. A motion for leave shall identify the interest of the applicant, state the reasons why a brief of an amicus curiae is desirable, identify the party whose position amicus supports, provide the date upon which the brief can be filed, and indicate whether the other party consents to the request.

## Nebraska Court Rule § 2-109

(A) Time for Filing

  (4) Briefs of amicus curiae may not be filed without leave of court. (See § 2-106.) Leave to file amicus briefs shall not be considered within 20 days of oral argument.

## Nevada Rule of Appellate Procedure 29

(a) When Permitted. The United States, the State of Nevada, an officer or agency of either, a political subdivision thereof, or a state, territory or commonwealth may file an amicus curiae brief without the consent of the parties or leave of court. Any other amicus curiae may file a brief only by leave of court granted on motion or at the court's request or if accompanied by written consent of all parties.

(b) Foreign Counsel. If an amicus brief is prepared by an attorney who is not a member of the State Bar of Nevada, that attorney must move for permission to appear before the Supreme Court under SCR 42 and comply with Rule 46(a).

(c) Motion for Leave to File. A motion for leave to file an amicus brief shall be accompanied by the proposed brief and state:

- (1) the movant's interest; and
- (2) the reasons why an amicus brief is desirable.

(d) Contents and Form. An amicus brief must comply with Rule 32. In addition to the requirements of Rule 32, the cover must identify the party or parties supported and indicate whether the brief supports affirmance or reversal. An amicus brief need not comply with Rule 28, but must include the following:

- (1) A table of contents, with page references.
- (2) A table of cases (alphabetically arranged), statutes and other authorities cited, with references to the pages of the brief where they are cited.
- (3) A concise statement of the identity of the amicus curiae, its interest in the case, and the source of its authority to file.
- (4) An argument, which may be preceded by a summary.
- (5) An attorney's certificate that complies with the requirements contained in Rule 28.2.

(e) Length. Except by the court's permission, an amicus brief may be no more than one-half the maximum length authorized by these Rules for a party's brief. If the court grants a party permission to file a longer brief, that extension does not affect the length of an amicus brief.

(f) Time for Filing. An amicus curiae must file its brief, accompanied by a motion for filing when necessary, no later than 7 days after the brief of the party being supported is filed. An amicus curiae that does not support either party must file its brief no later than 7 days after the appellant's opening brief is filed. The court may grant leave for later filing, specifying the time within which an opposing party may answer.

(g) Reply Brief. An amicus may not file a reply brief.

(h) Oral Argument. An amicus may file a motion to participate in oral argument, but the court will grant such motions only for extraordinary reasons.

## New Hampshire Supreme Court Rule 30

(1) A brief of an amicus curiae may be filed only after leave is granted by order of the supreme court on motion or when accompanied by written consent of all parties to the case. An amicus curiae shall file a brief within the time allowed to the party whose position the amicus will support, unless the court for good cause shown shall grant leave for a later filing.

(2) When consent to the filing of an amicus curiae is refused by a party to the case, an original and 7 copies of a motion for leave to file may be presented to the court within the time allowed for the filing of the brief of the party to be supported. The motion shall concisely state the nature of the movant's interest, the facts or questions of law that have not been, or reasons for believing that they will not adequately be, presented by the parties, and their relevancy to the disposition of the case. A brief may be conditionally filed with the motion for leave. A party served with such motion may seasonably file an original and 7 copies of an objection concisely stating the reasons for withholding consent.

(3) Consent to the filing of a brief of an amicus curiae is unnecessary when the brief is presented for the State of New Hampshire by the attorney general (as amicus and not as a party); for any State agency authorized by law to appear on its own behalf by

its appropriate legal counsel; or for any political subdivision of the State by its authorized law officer.

(4) The court may on motion, in its discretion, permit an amicus curiae to be heard orally.

**New Jersey Rule 1:13-9**

(a) An application for leave to appear as amicus curiae in any court shall be made by motion in the cause stating with specificity the identity of the applicant, the issue intended to be addressed, the nature of the public interest therein and the nature of the applicant's special interest, involvement or expertise in respect thereof. The court shall grant the motion if it is satisfied under all the circumstances that the motion is timely, the applicant's participation will assist in the resolution of an issue of public importance, and no party to the litigation will be unduly prejudiced thereby. The order granting the motion shall define with specificity the permitted extent of participation by the amicus and shall, where appropriate, fix a briefing schedule.

(b) Briefs filed by an amicus curiae in any court shall comply with all applicable rules.

(c) Except as provided in subsection (f), motions for leave to appear as an amicus curiae in the Appellate Division shall be accompanied by the proposed amicus curiae brief and shall be filed on or before the day when the last brief is due from any party.

(d) An amicus curiae who has been granted leave to appear in a cause may, without seeking further leave:

(1) file a brief in an appeal taken to any court from a final judgment or appealable interlocutory order, provided that the brief is filed on or before the day on which the last brief is due from any party;

(2) file a brief in support of or in opposition to a motion for leave to appeal, provided that the brief is filed on or before the day on which the last brief is due from any party;

(3) file a brief in the Supreme Court in support of or in opposition to a petition for certification, provided that the brief is

filed on or before the day on which the last brief is due from any party; and

(4) file a brief on the merits after the Supreme Court has granted a petition for certification or a motion for leave to appeal, or after a notice of appeal has been filed, provided that the brief is filed in compliance with the time frames fixed in subsection (e) of this Rule.

(e) An amicus curiae who has not been granted leave to appear in a cause may file a motion for leave to appear in the Supreme Court in connection with a petition for certification, a motion for leave to appeal, or an appeal, provided that the motion is accompanied by the proposed amicus curiae brief. Except as provided in Subsection (f) of this Rule, motions for leave to appear as an amicus curiae in the Supreme Court in connection with a petition for certification or a motion for leave to appeal shall be filed on or before the day on which the last brief is due from any party. Motions for leave to appear as an amicus curiae in connection with an appeal shall be filed within seventy-five (75) days of the date when the Supreme Court posts on its public website a notice of:

(1) an order granting certification;

(2) an order granting leave to appeal; or

(3) the filing of a notice of appeal.

Untimely motions may be granted by the Supreme Court only on a showing of good cause demonstrated to the satisfaction of the Court.

(f) In the event that the Supreme Court, or the Appellate Division, has directed the parties to submit briefs in accordance with an accelerated schedule, an amicus curiae shall file its motion for leave to appear, accompanied with its brief, on or before the date fixed for the last brief due from any party.

### New Mexico Rule Annotated 12-215

A. Leave to file. A brief of an amicus curiae may be filed only upon order of the appellate court. A motion for leave to file an amicus brief shall identify the interest of the amicus curiae and shall state the reasons why a brief of an amicus curiae would assist the Court. The brief may be conditionally filed with the motion for leave. A motion for leave to file an amicus brief shall recite the position of all parties, as required by Rule 12-309(C) NMRA.

B. Notice. Counsel for amicus shall ensure that all parties receive notice of the intention to file an amicus brief at least fourteen (14) days prior to the due date of the amicus brief. The body of the brief of an amicus curiae shall indicate that all parties received timely notice of the intent to file the brief.

C. Time. An amicus curiae shall file its brief within seven (7) days after the due date of the principal brief of the party whose position it supports. An opposing party may file a brief in response to the amicus brief within forty-five (45) days after service of an amicus brief filed in support of the appellant or petitioner, or within twenty (20) days after service of an amicus brief filed in support of an appellee or respondent. If the Court, for good cause shown, grants leave for amicus to file a brief after the time allowed by this paragraph, the Court shall specify within what period an opposing party may file a brief in response to the amicus brief. Except by the Court's permission, an amicus curiae may not file a reply brief.

D. Form. A brief of an amicus curiae shall comply with the length limitations for a brief-in-chief and shall otherwise comply with the formatting requirements of Rules 12-213 and 12-305 NMRA. An amicus brief shall be filed and served in accordance with these rules.

E. Oral argument. The party whose position is supported by amicus curiae may share with an amicus the party's allotted time for oral argument. No additional time shall be granted except by leave of Court.

F. Disclosure. A brief filed under this rule shall indicate whether counsel for a party authored the brief in whole or in part and whether such counselor a party made a monetary contribution intended to fund the preparation or submission of the brief, and shall identify every person other than the amicus curiae, its members, or its counsel, who made such a monetary contribution. The disclosure shall be made in a footnote on the first page of the text.

## New York Code Rules and Regulations 500.23

Any nonparty other than the Attorney General seeking to file an amicus brief on an appeal, certified question or motion for leave to appeal must obtain permission by motion. Potential amici seeking information are encouraged to contact the Clerk's Office by telephone during business hours. Information on the calendar status of appeals and certified questions, Court session dates and appropriate return dates for amicus motions also is available on the Court's web site.

(a) Motions for amicus curiae relief.

  (1) Amicus curiae relief on normal course appeals and normal course certified questions.

    (i) Movant shall file an original and one copy of its motion papers, accompanied by an original amicus brief, with proof of service of one copy of the motion and one copy of the brief on each other party.

    (ii) If the motion is granted, in addition to the submission in digital format required by subsection 500.12(h) of this Part, nine copies of the brief shall be filed, with proof of service of three copies on each party, within the time set by the Court's order.

    (iii) The motion shall be noticed for a return date no later than the Court session preceding the session in which argument or submission of the appeal or certified question is scheduled. When an appeal or certified question is scheduled for argument or submission during the Court's January or September session, the motion shall be noticed for a return date no later than the first Monday in December or the first Monday in August, respectively.

(2) Amicus curiae relief on appeals and certified questions selected for review by the alternative procedure. Movant shall file an original and one copy of its papers, accompanied by an original and two copies of the proposed submission, with proof of service of one copy on each other party. The motion shall be noticed for a return date no later than the filing date set for respondent's submission on the appeal.

(3) Amicus curiae relief on motions for permission to appeal in civil cases. Movant shall file an original and one copy of its papers, accompanied by an original amicus brief, with proof of service of the motion and one copy of the brief on each other party. The motion shall be noticed for a return date as soon as practicable after the return date of the motion for permission to appeal to which it relates. The granting of a motion to appear amicus curiae on a motion for permission to appeal does not authorize the movant to appear amicus curiae on the subsequent appeal. A new motion for amicus curiae relief on the appeal must be brought pursuant to subsection (a)(1) or (2) of this section.

(4) Criteria. Movant shall not present issues not raised before the courts below. A motion for amicus curiae relief shall demonstrate that:

(i) the parties are not capable of a full and adequate presentation and that movant could remedy this deficiency;

(ii) movant could identify law or arguments that might otherwise escape the Court's consideration; or

(iii) the proposed amicus curiae brief otherwise would be of assistance to the Court.

(5) Opposing papers. Respondent may file an original and one copy of papers in opposition to the motion, with proof of service of one copy on each other party.

(b) Amicus curiae filings by the Attorney General.

(1) Amicus curiae relief on motions for permission to appeal in civil cases. The Attorney General shall file an original and one

copy of the submission with proof of service of one copy on each other party. The submission shall be filed without leave of the Court on or before the return date of the motion for permission to appeal.

(2) Amicus curiae relief on normal course appeals and normal course certified questions. See subsection 500.12(e) of this Part.

(3) Amicus curiae relief on appeals and certified questions selected for review by the alternative procedure. See subsection 500.11(j) of this Part.

## North Carolina Rule of Appellate Procedure 28

(i) Amicus Curiae Briefs. A brief of an amicus curiae may be filed only by leave of the appellate court wherein the appeal is docketed or in response to a request made by that court on its own initiative. A person desiring to file an amicus curiae brief shall present to the court a motion for leave to file, served upon all parties. The motion shall state concisely the nature of the applicant's interest, the reasons why an amicus curiae brief is believed desirable, the issues of law to be addressed in the amicus curiae brief, and the applicant's position on those issues. The proposed amicus curiae brief may be conditionally filed with the motion for leave. Unless otherwise ordered by the court, the application for leave will be determined solely upon the motion and without responses thereto or oral argument. The clerk of the appellate court will forthwith notify the applicant and all parties of the court's action upon the application. Unless other time limits are set out in the order of the court permitting the brief, the amicus curiae shall file the brief within the time allowed for the filing of the brief of the party supported or, if in support of neither party, within the time allowed for filing appellant's brief. Motions for leave to file an amicus curiae brief submitted to the court after the time within which the amicus curiae brief normally would be due are disfavored in the absence of good cause. Reply briefs of the parties to an amicus curiae brief will be limited to points or authorities presented in the amicus curiae brief which are not presented in the main briefs of the parties. No reply brief of an amicus curiae will be received. A motion of an amicus curiae to participate in oral argument will be allowed only for extraordinary reasons.

**North Dakota Rule of Appellate Procedure 29**

(a) When Permitted. An amicus curiae brief may be filed only with leave of court or at the court's request. An amicus brief must be limited to issues raised on appeal by the parties.

(b) Motion for Leave to File. The motion may be accompanied by the proposed brief. The motion must state:

   (1) the moving party's interest; and

   (2) the reasons why an amicus brief is desirable and why the matters asserted are relevant to the disposition of the case.

(c) Contents and Form. An amicus brief must comply with Rule 25 and Rule 32. In addition to the requirements of Rule 25 and Rule 32, the cover must identify the party or parties supported, if any, and indicate whether the brief supports affirmance or reversal. An amicus brief need not comply with Rule 28, but must include the following:

   (1) a table of contents, with paragraph references;

   (2) a table of authorities—cases (alphabetically arranged) , statutes and other authorities—with references to the paragraphs in the brief where they are cited;

   (3) a concise statement of the identity of the amicus curiae, and its interest in the case;

   (4) a statement that indicates whether:

      (A) a party's counsel authored the brief in whole or in part;

      (B) a party or a party's counsel contributed money that was intended to fund preparing or submitting the brief; and

      (C) a person—other than the amicus curiae, its members, or its counsel—contributed money that was intended to fund preparing or submitting the brief and, if so, identifies each such person; and

(5) an argument, which may be preceded by a summary and which need not include a statement of the applicable standard of review.

(d) Length. Except by the court's permission, an amicus brief may be no more than one-half the maximum length authorized by these rules for a party's principal brief (see Rule 32(a)(7)). If the court grants a party permission to file a longer brief, that extension does not affect the length of an amicus brief.

(e) Time for Filing. An amicus curiae must file its brief within the time allowed for filing the principal brief of the party being supported. An amicus curiae that does not support either party must file its brief within the time allowed for filing the appellant's principal brief. The court may grant leave for later filing, specifying the time within which an opposing party may answer.

(f) Reply Brief. Except by the court's permission, an amicus curiae may not file a reply brief.

(g) Oral Argument. An amicus curiae may participate in oral argument only with the court's permission.

## Ohio Appellate Rule 17

A brief of an amicus curiae may be filed only if accompanied by written consent of all parties, or by leave of court granted on motion or at the request of the court. The brief may be conditionally filed with the motion for leave. A motion for leave shall identify the interest of the applicant and shall state the reasons why a brief of an amicus curiae is desirable. Unless all parties otherwise consent, any amicus curiae shall file its brief within the time allowed the party whose position as to affirmance or reversal the amicus brief will support unless the court for cause shown shall grant leave for later filing, in which event it shall specify within what period an opposing party may answer. A motion of an amicus curiae to participate in the oral argument will be granted only for extraordinary reasons.

## Oklahoma Supreme Court Rule 1.12

(a) Amicus Curiae Brief May Be Filed Either by the Consent of the Parties or by Leave of the Chief Justice of the Supreme Court.

(1) Appeal. A brief of an amicus curiae which is confined to the issues raised by the parties and which does not exceed twenty-five (25) pages may be filed during the briefing cycle of an appeal if it is accompanied by written consent of all the parties. If consent is denied by any of the parties, the procedure in subparagraph 1.12(b) shall be followed.

(2) Original Jurisdiction Proceedings. Amicus curiae may not appear in an original jurisdiction proceeding unless authorized by order of the Chief Justice. See Rule 1.191. The brief of the amicus curiae must comply with Rules 1.10, 1.11, and 1.191. Amicus curiae is not allowed to raise or put in issue any new fact in the original jurisdiction proceeding. A brief of an amicus curiae shall be confined to the issues raised by the parties. The brief of the amicus curiae may not have exhibits or an appendix.

(b) Application to File Amicus Curiae Brief Without Consent by Parties.

(1) During Briefing Cycle of Appeal. The amicus curiae shall file a statement not to exceed five (5) pages which concisely discloses the nature and extent of the applicant's interest, states any facts or questions of law which may not be presented adequately by the litigants, and the relevancy of these facts or questions of law to the disposition of the cause. The amicus curiae shall mail a copy of the statement to the parties. If an objection is not filed within ten (10) days, consent shall be deemed to have been granted. If an objection is filed, the Supreme Court shall review the statement and the objections to determine whether to allow the filing of the amicus brief.

(2) Original Jurisdiction Proceedings. The amicus curiae shall file a statement not to exceed five (5) pages which concisely discloses the nature and extent of the applicant's interest, and states questions of law which may not be presented

adequately by the litigants, and the relevancy of these questions of law to the disposition of the cause. The amicus curiae shall mail a copy of the statement to the parties. Parties shall have ten days to object, unless the Court orders otherwise. The Supreme Court shall review the statement and any objections to determine whether to allow the filing of the amicus brief.

(c) Avoidance of Unnecessary Repetition. Before completion of an amicus brief, counsel for an amicus curiae shall attempt to ascertain the arguments which will be made in the brief of any party whose positions the amicus is supporting in order to avoid any unnecessary repetition of argument.

(d) Assignment and Disposition of Cause Not to be Delayed by Filing Amicus Curiae Brief.

(1) Appeals. The assignment and disposition of a cause will not be delayed pending action on a motion for leave to file an amicus curiae brief or to await the filing of a brief amicus curiae. If the filing of an amicus curiae brief is allowed either by the consent of the parties or by the Supreme Court, it must be filed within the briefing cycle set for the party supported, and in conformance with the applicable provisions of Rules 1.10 and 1.11. Extraordinary cause must be shown before an amicus curiae will be permitted to file a brief at any time other than during the normal briefing cycle or as allowed by Rule 1.12(g). No reply brief of an amicus curiae may be filed.

(2) Original Jurisdiction Proceedings. The disposition of a cause will not be delayed pending action on a motion for leave to file an amicus curiae brief or to await the filing of a brief amicus curiae. The time to file an amicus brief shall be governed by order of the court in the proceeding. No reply brief of an amicus curiae will be received.

(e) Leave to File Response to Amicus Brief. Leave may be sought by any party in the case to file a response to the amicus curiae brief.

(f) Oral Argument by Amicus Curiae. Amicus curiae may be permitted to participate in the argument granted in the case by the Supreme Court upon motion showing extraordinary cause.

(g) Amicus Curiae on Certiorari and Rehearing. In a matter before the Supreme Court on certiorari to the Court of Civil Appeals, amicus curiae may file a statement in support of or opposing certiorari only by order of the Supreme Court granting leave to file the statement. Amicus curiae may file a statement in support of certiorari only when a party has petitioned for certiorari. Amicus curiae may file a statement opposing certiorari only when a party has responded opposing certiorari. In a matter before either the Supreme Court or Court of Civil Appeals on rehearing, an amicus curiae may file a brief only by order of the court granting leave to file the brief. Amicus curiae may file a brief in support of rehearing only when a party has petitioned for rehearing.

## Oregon Rules of Appellate Procedure

### *Rule 6.10*

(2) An amicus curiae may present oral argument only if permitted by the court on motion or on its own motion.

### *Rule 8.15*

(1) A person [including an organization] may appear as amicus curiae in any case pending before the appellate court only by permission of the appellate court on written application setting forth the interest of the person in the case. The application shall state whether the applicant intends to present a private interest of its own or to present a position as to the correct rule of law that does not affect a private interest of its own. The application shall not contain argument on the resolution of the case.

(2) The application shall be submitted by an active member of the Oregon State Bar. A filing fee is not required. The form of the application shall comply with ORAP 7.10(1) and (2) and the applicant shall file the original and one copy of the application.

A copy of the application shall be served on all parties to the proceeding.

(3) In the Court of Appeals, the application to appear amicus curiae may, but need not, be accompanied by the brief the applicant would file if permitted to appear. In the Supreme Court, the application shall be accompanied by the brief sought to be filed. The form of an amicus brief and the number of copies of the brief shall be subject to the same rules as those governing briefs of parties.

(4) In the Court of Appeals, unless the court grants leave otherwise for good cause shown, an amicus brief shall be due seven days after the date the brief is due of the party with whom amicus curiae is aligned or, if amicus curiae is not aligned with any party, seven days after the date the opening brief is due.

(5) With respect to cases in the Supreme Court on petition for review from the Court of Appeals:

- (a) A person wishing to appear amicus curiae may seek to appear in support of or in opposition to a petition for review, on the merits of the case on review, or both.
- (b) Unless the court grants leave otherwise for good cause shown, an application to appear amicus curiae in support of or in opposition to a petition for review shall be filed within 14 days after the filing of a petition for review.
- (c) Unless the court grants leave otherwise for good cause shown, an application to appear amicus curiae on the merits of a case on review shall be filed:
  - (i) On the date the brief is due of the party on review with whom amicus curiae is aligned,
  - (ii) On the date the petitioner's brief on the merits on review is due, if amicus curiae is not aligned with any party on review, or
  - (iii) Within 28 days after review is allowed, if petitioner on review has filed a notice that petitioner does not intend to file a brief on the merits or has filed no notice, regardless of the alignment of amicus curiae.

(d) If a person filing an application to appear amicus curiae wishes to file one brief in support of or in opposition to a petition for review and on the merits of the case, the application and brief shall be filed within the same time that an application to appear in support of or in opposition to a petition for review would be filed. If a person has been granted permission to appear amicus curiae in support of or in opposition to a petition for review and the Supreme Court allows review, the person may file an amicus curiae brief on the merits without further leave of the court.

(e) If a party obtains an extension of time to file a petition for review, a response to a petition for review or a brief on the merits and if an amicus curiae brief was due on the same date as the petition, response or brief on the merits, the time for filing the amicus curiae brief is automatically extended to the same date.

(6) Except as provided in ORAP 11.30(7), with respect to cases in the Supreme Court on direct review or direct appeal, or other proceedings not subject to subsection (5), amicus curiae briefs shall be due as provided in subsection (4) of this rule.

(7) Amicus curiae may file a memorandum of additional authorities under the same circumstances that a party could file a memorandum of additional authorities under ORAP 5.85.

(8) Amicus curiae shall not be allowed to orally argue the case, unless the court specifically authorizes or directs oral argument.

(9) The State of Oregon may appear as amicus curiae in any case in the Supreme Court and Court of Appeals without permission of the court. The state shall comply with all the requirements for appearing amicus curiae, including the time within which to appear under subsections (4), (5), and (6) of this rule. If the state is not aligned with any party, the state's amicus curiae brief shall be due on the same date as the respondent's brief.

### Pennsylvania Rule of Appellate Procedure 531

(a) Briefs.—Anyone interested in the questions involved in any matter pending in an appellate court, excluding Petitions for Allowance of Appeal, although not a party, may, without applying for leave to do so, file a brief amicus curiae in regard to those questions.

(1) Unless otherwise ordered by the court, any amicus curiae shall file and serve its brief in the manner and number required and within the time allowed by these rules with respect to the party whose position as to affirmance or reversal the amicus brief will support, or with respect to the appellant, if the amicus brief does not support the position of any party.

(2) In an appeal proceeding under Rules 2154(b), 2185(c) and 2187(b), any amicus curiae shall file and serve its brief within the time allowed by these rules for service of the advance text of the brief by the party whose position as to affirmance or reversal the amicus brief will support or, if the amicus brief does not support the position of any party, within the time allowed by these rules for service of the advance text by the appellant. Alternatively, the amicus curiae may, but is not required to, serve an advance text and then file and serve a definitive copy of its brief. If the amicus curiae chooses to serve an advance copy and then file and serve a definitive copy, its deadlines for each are the same as for the party whose position as to affirmance or reversal the amicus brief supports or, if the amicus brief does not support the position of any party, as for the appellant.

(b) Oral argument.—Oral argument may be presented by amicus curiae only as the appellate court may direct. Requests for leave to present oral argument shall be by application and will be granted only for extraordinary reasons.

### Rhode Island Rule of Appellate Procedure 16

(h) Brief of Amicus Curiae. A brief of an amicus curiae may be filed only if accompanied by written consent of all parties, or by leave of the Supreme Court granted on motion or at the request of the

Court, except that consent or leave shall not be required when the brief is presented by the United States or an officer or agency thereof, or by the State of Rhode Island or an officer or agency thereof. The brief may be conditionally filed with the motion for leave. A motion for leave shall identify the interest of the applicant and shall state the reasons why a brief of an amicus curiae is desirable. Unless all parties consent, an amicus curiae shall file its brief within the time allowed the party whose position as to affirmance or reversal the amicus brief will support unless the Supreme Court for cause shown shall grant leave for later filing, in which event it shall specify within what period an opposing party may answer. A motion of an amicus curiae to participate in the oral argument will be granted only for extraordinary reasons.

## South Carolina Appellate Court Rule 213

A brief of an amicus curiae may be filed only by leave of the appellate court granted on motion, or at the request of the appellate court. The brief may be conditionally filed with the motion for leave to file. A motion for leave shall identify the interest of the applicant and shall state the reasons why a brief of an amicus curiae is desirable. The brief shall be limited to argument of the issues on appeal as presented by the parties and shall comply with the requirements of Rules 208(b) and 211. If leave to file an amicus curiae brief is granted, the appellate court will specify the period in which a response to the brief may be filed.

## South Dakota Rule of Civil Appellate Procedure 15-26A-74

A brief of an amicus curiae may be filed only at the request of the court or by leave of the court granted upon motion and notice to the parties. A motion for leave shall identify the interest of the applicant and shall state the reasons why a brief of an amicus curiae is desirable. An amicus curiae shall file its brief within the time allowed the party whose position as to affirmance or reversal the amicus brief will support unless the court for cause shown shall grant leave for later filing, in which event it shall specify within what period an opposing party may answer. An amicus curiae brief shall not exceed the page limitation set in § 15-26A-66.

Amici curiae counsel will not be entitled to participate in oral argument unless counsel for either party agrees to share his time and the court allows the appearance of amici curiae counsel.

## Tennessee Rule of Appellate Procedure 31

(a) Leave or Request of Court Necessary. A brief of an amicus curiae may be filed only by leave of court granted on motion or at the request of the appellate court. A brief may be conditionally filed with the motion for leave. A motion for leave shall identify the interest of the applicant and shall state how a brief of an amicus curiae will assist the appellate court.

(b) Form; Time; Conditions. A brief of an amicus curiae shall follow the form prescribed for the brief of an appellee. The court shall fix the time and conditions for the filing of the amicus curiae brief.

(c) Oral Argument. An amicus curiae may participate in oral argument only by leave of court granted on motion or at the request of the appellate court.

(d) Costs of Amicus Curiae Filing. The court in its discretion may assess the costs of filing the motion for leave to file an amicus curiae brief and all related filings against the amicus curiae, to be paid to the Appellate Court Clerk at the time of entry of the order granting or denying the motion.

## Texas Rule of Appellate Procedure 11

An appellate clerk may receive, but not file, an amicus curiae brief. But the court for good cause may refuse to consider the brief and order that it be returned. An amicus curiae brief must:

(a) comply with the briefing rules for parties;

(b) identify the person or entity on whose behalf the brief is tendered;

(c) disclose the source of any fee paid or to be paid for preparing the brief; and

(d) certify that copies have been served on all parties.

### Utah Rule of Appellate Procedure 25

A brief of an amicus curiae or of a guardian ad litem representing a minor who is not a party to the appeal may be filed only by leave of court granted on motion or at the request of the court. The motion for leave may be accompanied by a proposed amicus brief, provided it complies with applicable rules and the number of copies specified by Rule 26(b) are submitted to the court. A motion for leave shall identify the interest of the applicant and shall state the reasons why a brief of an amicus curiae or the guardian ad litem is desirable. The motion for leave shall be filed at least twenty-one days prior to the date on which the brief of the party whose position as to affirmance or reversal the amicus curiae or guardian ad litem will support is due, unless the court for cause shown otherwise orders. Parties to the proceeding may indicate their support for, or opposition to, the motion. Any response of a party to a motion for leave shall be filed within seven days of service of the motion. If leave is granted, an amicus curiae or guardian ad litem shall file its brief within seven days of the time allowed the party whose position the amicus curiae or guardian ad litem will support, unless the order granting leave otherwise indicates. The time for responsive briefs under Rule 26(a) shall run from the timely service of the amicus or guardian ad litem brief or from the timely service of the brief of the party whose position the amicus curiae or guardian ad litem supports, whichever is later. A motion of an amicus curiae or guardian ad litem to participate in the oral argument will be granted when circumstances warrant in the court's discretion.

### Vermont Rule of Appellate Procedure 29

(a) When Permitted.—The State of Vermont or an officer or agency thereof may file an amicus curiae brief without the consent of the parties, and without leave of the Court. Any other amicus curiae may file a brief only at the Court's request, by leave of Court on motion, or with written consent of all parties.

(b) Motion for Leave to File.—The motion may accompany the proposed brief and must state the movant's interest and why an amicus curiae brief is desirable.

(c) Time for Filing and Format.—An amicus curiae must file its brief within the time allowed to the party whose position it supports, unless all parties consent to a different time or the Court, for cause, grants leave for later filing, specifying the time in which an opposing party may answer. An amicus curiae brief must follow the form and filing requirements of Rule 32, and must be served on the other parties consistent with Rule 31(b).

**Virginia Rule 5:30**

(a) Stage of Appellate Proceedings. Subject to the requirements outlined in this Rule, a brief amicus curiae may be filed during the petition, perfected appeal or rehearing stages of the appellate proceedings in this Court.

(b) Who May File a Brief Amicus Curiae Without Leave of Court.
   (1) The United States or the Commonwealth of Virginia; and
   (2) Any other person whose filing is accompanied by the written consent of all counsel; and
   (3) Any person requested by the Court to file a brief amicus curiae pursuant to paragraph (f) of this Rule.

(c) Who Needs Leave of Court to File a Brief Amicus Curiae. Any person or entity other than those described in paragraph (b) of this Rule.

(d) When a Brief Amicus Curiae Must Be Filed. A brief amicus curiae will be accepted only if filed on or before the date on which the brief of the party supported is required to be filed. A brief amicus curiae may be filed at the time of filing of the reply brief of the appellant only if an opening brief amicus curiae has been filed.

(e) What a Brief Amicus Curiae Must Contain. A brief amicus curiae shall comply with the rules applicable to the brief of the party supported.

(f) This Court's Authority to Request a Brief Amicus Curiae. Notwithstanding the provisions of this Rule, this Court may request that a brief amicus curiae be filed at any time.

## Washington Rule of Appellate Procedure 10.6

(a) When Allowed by Motion. The appellate court may, on motion, grant permission to file an amicus curiae brief only if all parties consent or if the filing of the brief would assist the appellate court. An amicus curiae brief may be filed only by an attorney authorized to practice law in this state, or by a member in good standing of the Bar of another state in association with an attorney authorized to practice law in this state.

(b) Motion. A motion to file an amicus curiae brief must include a statement of (1) applicants interest and the person or group applicant represents, (2) applicants familiarity with the issues involved in the review and with the scope of the argument presented or to be presented by the parties, (3) specific issues to which the amicus curiae brief will be directed, and (4) applicants reason for believing that additional argument is necessary on these specific issues. The brief of amicus curiae may be filed with the motion.

(c) On Request of the Appellate Court. The appellate court may ask for an amicus brief at any stage of review, and establish appropriate timelines for the filing of the amicus brief and answer thereto.

(d) Objection to Motion. An objection to a motion to file an amicus curiae brief must be received by the appellate court and counsel of record for the parties and the applicant not later than 5 business days after receipt of the motion.

(e) Disposition of Motions. The Supreme Court and each division of the Court of Appeals shall establish by general order the manner of disposition of a motion to file an amicus curiae brief, including whether such disposition is reviewable or subject to reconsideration by the particular court.

## West Virginia Rule of Appellate Procedure 30

(a) When permitted. The State of West Virginia or an officer or agency thereof, or a County or Municipality of the State, may file an amicus curiae brief without the consent of parties or leave of the Court. Any other amicus curiae may file a brief only by leave of

Court or if the brief states that all parties have consented to its filing.

(b) Notice to parties. An amicus curiae shall ensure that counsel of record for all parties receive notice of its intention to file an amicus curiae brief at least five days prior to the due date.

(c) Motion for leave to file. The motion for leave to file an amicus curiae brief must be accompanied by the proposed brief and appendix (if one is necessary), and must state: (1) the movant's interest; (2) the reason why an amicus curiae brief is desirable and why the matters asserted are relevant to the disposition of the case; and (3) if an appendix is provided, a statement of why the material provided in the appendix is not otherwise readily available and why the materials in the appendix are relevant and necessary to the disposition of the case. Any party opposed to the motion may respond within ten days.

(d) Time for filing. Unless otherwise provided by the Court, an amicus curiae brief must be filed within the time allowed the party whose position as to affirmance or reversal the brief will support unless the Court for cause shown shall grant leave for later filing, in which event the Court's order may specify a time period within which an opposing party may file a supplemental brief in response.

(e) Contents of brief and appendix. The amicus curiae brief need not strictly comply with Rule 10, but must include the following in the order listed:

  (1) a cover page with the caption of the case and further identifying the party supported and whether the amicus curiae supports affirmance or reversal;

  (2) a table of contents, with page references;

  (3) a table of authorities with references to the pages of the brief where they are cited;

  (4) a concise statement of the identity of the amicus curiae, its interest in the case, and the source of its authority to file;

  (5) except for briefs presented as a matter of right on behalf of an amicus curiae listed in subdivision (a) of this Rule, a brief filed under this Rule shall indicate whether counsel for a

party authored the brief in whole or in part and whether such counsel or a party made a monetary contribution specifically intended to fund the preparation or submission of the brief, and shall identify every person other than the amicus curiae, its members, or its counsel, who made such a monetary contribution. The disclosure shall be made in the first footnote on the first page of text.

(6) The argument, exhibiting clearly the points of fact and law presented and citing the authorities relied on, under suitable headings.

An appendix must comply with the format, page numbering and general requirements of Rule 7 insofar as applicable.

(f) Oral argument. A motion of an amicus curiae to participate in the oral argument of a case on the Rule 20 docket will be granted only for extraordinary reasons.

## Wisconsin Statute 809.19

(7) Nonparty Briefs.

(a) A person not a party may by motion request permission to file a brief. The motion shall identify the interest of the person and state why, a brief filed by that person is desirable.

(b) If the brief will support or oppose a petition under s[ection] 809.62 or 809.70, the brief shall accompany the motion and shall be filed within the time permitted for the opposing party to file a response to the petition.

(c) Except as provided in part (b), the motion shall be filed not later than 14 days after the respondent's brief is filed and the brief shall be filed within the time specified by the court. If an unpublished opinion is cited under s[ection] 809.23(3) (a) or (b), a copy of the opinion shall be provided in an appendix to the brief.

## Wyoming Rule of Appellate Procedure 7.12

(a) A brief of an amicus curiae may be filed only by leave of court granted on motion or the request of the appellate court.

(b) The motion must be accompanied by the proposed brief and state:
   (1) the movant's interest in the issues raised in the case;
   (2) the reasons an amicus brief is appropriate and desirable;
   (3) the view of the movant with respect to whether a party is not represented competently or is not represented at all;
   (4) the interest of the amicus in some other case that may be affected by the decision in the case before the court; and
   (5) any unique information or perspective the amicus has that can be of assistance to the court beyond that the lawyers for both parties can provide.

(c) The amicus brief shall comply with Rule 7.01 except that no statement of issues, statement of the case, or an appendix shall be required. In addition the cover page must identify the party or parties supported and indicate whether the brief supports affirmance or reversal.

(d) The amicus brief shall not exceed 35 pages, and shall otherwise conform to the requirements of W.R.A.P. 7.05.

(e) An amicus curiae must file its motion not later than 11 days after the principal brief of the party being supported is filed. An amicus curiae who does not support either party must file its brief not later than 11 days after the first brief of any party is filed.

(f) An amicus curiae is not permitted to file a reply brief.

(g) Participation in oral arguments by the amicus curiae shall be granted only with the court's permission and the consent of the party supported, and only for extraordinary reasons with the time used to be charged against the party whose contentions amicus curiae supports.